S0-BBO-331

Simon Dingerich
1422 Frances
Elkhart, Ind.

SOUTH CENTRAL FRONTIERS

Studies in
Anabaptist and Mennonite History

Edited by
J. C. Wenger, Ernst Correll, Cornelius J. Dyck, Melvin Gingerich,
Guy F. Hershberger, John S. Oyer, and John H. Yoder

°*Out of print.*

Studies in
Anabaptist and Mennonite History

No. 17

SOUTH CENTRAL FRONTIERS
A History of the
South Central Mennonite Conference

Paul Erb

Herald Press, Scottdale, Pennsylvania, in cooperation with Mennonite Historical Society, Goshen, Indiana, is publisher of the series "Studies in Anabaptist and Mennonite History." The Society is primarily responsible for the content of the studies, and Herald Press for their publication.

SOUTH CENTRAL
FRONTIERS

A History of the South Central Mennonite Conference

Paul Erb

HERALD PRESS

Scottdale, Pennsylvania
Kitchener, Ontario
1974

Library of Congress Cataloging in Publication Data

Erb, Paul, 1894-
  South central frontiers.
  (Studies in Anabaptist and Mennonite history, 17)
  1. Mennonite Church. South Central Conference —
History. I. Title. II. Series.
  BX8129.M5E7   289.7′75   74-12108
  ISBN 0-8361-1196-6

SOUTH CENTRAL FRONTIERS
Copyright © 1974 by Herald Press, Scottdale, Pa. 15683
Library of Congress Catalog Card Number: 74-12108
International Standard Book Number: 0-8361-1196-6
Printed in the United States of America
Designed by Jan Gleysteen

Dedicated to the
Memory of

Reuben J. Heatwole
1847-1921

Pioneer Mennonite Homesteader in Kansas
Outstanding Christian Layman
Administrator of an Evangelistic Ministry
on the Western Frontier
Organizer of Churches and Sunday Schools
Secretary and Moderator of the
Kansas-Nebraska Mennonite Conference
Singing-School Teacher
Progenitor of Active Church Workers
Promoter of Mission Interests

LIST OF ABBREVIATIONS
See Bibliography for Complete Reference to Books and Periodicals

CL	*Christian Living*
CM	*Conference Messenger*
CPS	Civilian Public Service
GH	*Gospel Herald*
HT	*Herald of Truth*
MC	*Mennonite Community*
MCC	Mennonite Central Committee
MCD	*Mennonite Cyclopedic Dictionary*
MCH	*Mennonite Church History*
MDS	Mennonite Disaster Service
ME	*The Mennonite Encyclopedia*
MHB	*Mennonite Historical Bulletin*
ML	*Mennonite Life*
MQR	*Mennonite Quarterly Review*
MWR	*Mennonite Weekly Review*
MY	*Mennonite Yearbook*
MYF	Mennonite Youth Fellowship
SAT	*Sword and Trumpet*
VS	Voluntary Service
WMSC	Women's Missionary and Service Commission

PREFACE

Most of the district conferences of the Mennonite Church have published a   history of the beginning and the development of the congregations in their area. Up to this time the South Central Mennonite Conference has not done so. Melvin Gingerich, of the Mennonite General Conference Historical Committee, urged the conference to consider the preparation of a conference history.

Donald E. King, then conference historian, asked me in 1965 whether I would be willing to write this history, and the conference, later in that year, confirmed this request. I accepted the assignment, but on condition that I would have help. I suggested that I be a compiler and writer, with much of the basic research being done by congregational historians. Time and strength and opportunity made it impossible for me to explore cemeteries and courthouse records and congregational files. Other commitments, also, made it necessary to postpone my work on this assignment, so that most of my writing was not done until 1972.

Most of the forty-some congregations took seriously their task of accumulating materials and getting them into my hands. Obviously, the quality of these materials was uneven. I had to do my own searching in the files of the *Herald of Truth*. I made much use of congregational histories already written, especially of G. G. Yoder's excellent unpublished thesis on the four oldest congregations of central Kansas. I acknowledge my indebtedness to the actual wording of many of these sources.

The history is documented in some detail, though not completely. The unpublished sources are filed, so far as possible, in the Archives of the Mennonite Church at Goshen, Indiana. Some materials, however, have been returned to the persons furnishing them. To save space, initials often indicate organizations.

With the thousands of facts involved, it will be a miracle if there are no mistakes. Every effort has been made to secure accuracy. The congregational historians were close to their sources, and the compiler sent copies of each unit to one or more persons for checking. Many corrections were made, and there was a good deal of rewriting. I am sorry for any errors of fact or judgment which have not been corrected, and I must be held personally responsible for them.

As a member of one of the pioneer families of Kansas, I could draw a good deal on my own memory and understanding of these happenings of the past. In my years of work in the conference, I visited most of the communities, except the ones begun in recent years, particularly in south Texas, which has become a growing edge of the conference.

The treatment had to be limited to the area which includes the present congregations of the South Central Conference. It does include extinct congregations in that general area. It does not include churches and institutions which became a part of the Rocky Mountain Conference. The decision on this had to be arbitrary at times, as when the extinct Sherman County group in western Kansas is included, but the living congregation in Scott County, which is farther east, is not, because it is in the Rocky Mountain Conference.

I want to thank those whose cooperation has made the writing of this history possible: the Conference Executive Committee for its invitations to the task, and for the subsidy which helped me to meet expenses; the conference historians — Donald E. King and Willard Conrad — and the conference minister — Millard Osborne — who have given me every possible assistance; the congregational historians and other persons who sent me material and answered my questions; the several typists who interpreted my much-corrected handwriting. And I am extremely grateful to J. C. Wenger, Melvin Gingerich, and Guy F. Hershberger, of the Mennonite Historical Society, for extensive editing help, including the preparation of the bibliography and the maps.

This task has been for me a labor of love — telling the story of the people, the places, the churches that I have been interested in throughout the years. My prayer is that this history may be both a memorial to the past and a guide and inspiration to the present and the future.

Scottdale, Pennsylvania   *Paul Erb*
April 27, 1973

INTRODUCTION

The South Central Mennonite Conference consists of a scant fifty congregations with a total of about 4,000 baptized members in the states of Kansas, Missouri, Oklahoma, Arkansas, Louisiana, and Texas — plus several emerging congregations in Mexico. Since the first settlements of Mennonites in this region were made soon after the Civil War era, it is appropriate that a century later a history of these congregations should be published.

The choice of Paul Erb as author was both a natural and a happy one. Born in the home of a pioneer Kansas bishop, T. M. Erb, and reared in the Sunflower State, Paul Erb was himself ordained as a Mennonite preacher in the Pennsylvania congregation near Hesston, Kansas, in 1919. He has become known as an effective minister of the gospel and as a promoter of missions. He also taught for many years in the Hesston (Kansas) and Goshen (Indiana) colleges of the Mennonites. For eighteen years he served as editor of the church organ, the *Gospel Herald*. For a number of terms he also served as executive secretary of the Mennonite General Conference. He was co-opted to help prepare a new Mennonite Confession of Faith, adopted in 1963. Later he prepared a commentary on its twenty articles, entitled *We Believe*. Perhaps his most influential book to date was his study of biblical eschatology, *The Alpha and the Omega*, the Conrad Grebel Lectures for 1955.

The strength of the present volume is its full and detailed congregational histories. The casual reader may feel that frequently too much detail is given. But to the sons, daughters, and grandchildren of the participants it will be both interesting and significant. So too will it be of immense value to church historians, social scientists, and sociologists of religion. Evident throughout the volume are the discerning mind and sound judgment of a mature church statesman. The editors who read the manuscript critically were Melvin Gingerich, Guy F. Hershberger, John H. Yoder, and myself. The final editing was done by Editors Gingerich and Hershberger. We have already published three district conference histories: Illinois (1931), Indiana-Michigan (1961), and Ohio and Eastern (1969). The editors are indeed happy to add a fourth volume to these three, *South Central Frontiers*. They also express their appreciation to the South Central Conference for a subsidy which made possible this publication.

June 8, 1973   *J. C. Wenger*

CONTENTS

MAPS

THE SOUTH CENTRAL FRONTIER

THE SOUTH CENTRAL FRONTIER

There are pioneer souls that blaze their paths
Where highways never ran.
— Sam Walter Foss

Henry G. Brunk, arriving in central Kansas sick with typhoid fever, lies down under boards set in wigwam fashion, for their sod house was not yet laid up. In eight days he is dead, and his wife courageously makes a home for her children on the inhospitable prairie.

Daniel D. Miller as a small boy crawls into his bed under the table of a log house in Hickory County, Missouri, and eats corn bread every day, while his parents struggle for three years before, succumbing to grasshoppers, drought, and poverty, they return to Indiana.

Five-year-old Paul stands wonderingly as his father, Tillman M. Erb, on the bank of the Salt Fork of the Arkansas River, halloos to the man whose home is on the other side. This man, hearing the call, brings his big horses to take across the carriage which is too heavy for Erb's ponies to pull through the sand and the water. Erb is on the way to a bishop appointment with the Jet, Oklahoma, congregation. The ponies are led behind the carriage as they cross the shallow river.

Here are three episodes of Mennonite happenings on the mid-American frontier in the second half of the nineteenth century. The Mennonite pioneers of this frontier came from the older Mennonite and Amish communities of Pennsylvania, Maryland, Virginia, Ontario, Ohio, Indiana, Illinois, and Iowa.

Why did they come? Chiefly, because of land hunger. Land prices were going so high in the older settlements of the Eastern states that young people who did not inherit a farm saw no chance of owning one. And so like many other young Americans of the time, they "went west."

The West in these post-Civil War decades was beyond the Mississippi. "West of the Mississippi lay a huge new world," said F. J. Turner in his *Rise of the New West.* And in this new world was a great body of land, which could be secured for nothing or for very little.

Missouri was the gateway to this new world, as the magnificent arch that dominates the riverfront in St. Louis now symbolizes. The Missouri River was a highway for settlers, traders, and explorers. In its basin was an abundance of good farmland. By 1860, before many Mennonites had come, the state was well settled, mostly by Southerners.

During the Civil War Missouri was a battlefield. The state had voted against secession, but the governor had armed the state militia to fight on the side of the pro-slavery forces. Towns were burned and farms were abandoned. So when the war was over, there were many opportunities for the Mennonite settlers to get cheap land.

In Kansas it was the Homestead Act of 1862 that opened up millions of acres in the western two thirds of the state. Under this law any citizen, head of a household or twenty-one years old, could file a claim, and if he lived on the land and cultivated it for five years, it was his.

In order to encourage the building of railroads across the plains the government gave to the railroads the land in alternate sections five miles deep on either side of the right-of-way. The railroads raised capital by selling this land to settlers for something like $6 per acre. They ran big advertising campaigns. The Santa Fe got three million acres along its route from Emporia to the Colorado line. Some of those acres got into Mennonite hands.

But the Mennonite pioneers were not interested only in getting a deed to a farm. When they picked their new home area, they hoped that enough other families would settle there to make possible the establishment of a congregation, and that ministerial leadership might become available. Sometimes these hopes were realized, and a permanent congregation developed. Sometimes they were realized only for a period, with a church developing and then dying. And in many cases a family or two waited in vain for others to join them in church life. It became almost a pattern for families to isolate themselves in a place that appealed to them, and then to beg to be visited by traveling ministers. Much missionary effort went into following up these lonely families.

For instance, the first mention of Missouri in the *Herald of Truth* (May 1865) tells of Henry and Michael Shenk, of Elida, Ohio, going to that state "to see the country, and, if the prospects were good, to purchase land there." The two men might conceivably have been impressed with the country at two different places, and so there would be two places for the itinerant evangelists to visit! That sort of thing did happen among the individualists who dared the frontiers.

Daniel Brundage, of whom we shall hear often in this history, came from Indiana in the fall of 1868 and visited church members in Shelby, Linn, Moniteau, Hickory, and Jasper counties. He wrote: "I found no place that I liked better than Dade [he wrote it Date!] County [where no Mennonites had settled]. Raw prairie can there still be purchased at four dollars an acre." But he continued: "I feel that when brethren move to Missouri or other states they should try to settle more together and not scatter themselves too much into different localities. . . . And as I also have a mind to move to Missouri, I think it would be pleasant for us if we could gather a small company together . . . and form a little settlement and a church."[1]

He followed his own advice, for early in 1869 he moved, not to Dade County, but to Tipton in Moniteau County to shepherd a flock of sixty members who had no minister.[2] When he moved on to Kansas a few years later, he again went to central Kansas, where there already were a number of settlers.

There were still other motives which took Mennonite settlers "west." Henry Brunk was refusing to serve in the Confederate army when he fled from Virginia to Maryland. He feared what might happen if he returned home. And so, after his wife joined him in Hagerstown, they set out for the frontiers, first to Illinois, and then to Kansas. His was a part of the long trek of the Mennonites of the world from compulsory military service.

Probably some of the settlers simply had the wanderlust in their blood, and sought adventure in the West. The advertising made it sound daring and exciting. The pioneer experience was a complex of travel by boat and train, horseback and wagon; of blooming prairies and droughty homesteads and black tornadoes and raging floods; of Indian neighbors and white border ruffians and bighearted fellow settlers; of wolves and coyotes and jackrabbits and buffalo and antelopes and deer; of long trips for supplies like the one made by a woman in Hickory County, Missouri, which Effie V. Almond wrote about (unpublished essay), [3] who drove an ox team fifty miles north to Sedalia each fall for the clothes and food she couldn't grow. In between were the long privation and the loneliness.

It took a combination of economic need and curiosity and daring and stubbornness and faith for a Mennonite to take a family to the wilderness of Missouri and Kansas and Oklahoma, and keep them there until the family or two became a church, and the raw, open country became a cultivated, beautiful rural community. Hats off to those who had such courage and ingenuity.

These frontiersmen were pioneers. They came west just at the time when Walt Whitman was singing,

"These are of us, they are with us,

All for primal needed work, while the followers there in embryo wait behind,

We today's procession heading, we the route for travel clearing,

Pioneers! O pioneers."

These pioneers saw the train of wagon traffic on the Santa Fe Trail, cutting deep ruts into the creek banks. Later they saw the railroad builders laying the iron path across Missouri, Kansas, and Oklahoma. They saw the Indians driven before the army of homesteaders, stopping only in occasional migratory encampments, which the Mennonites sometimes visited. They at times participated during the seventies in killing by the thousands the buffalo which had to go if there were to be farms. After the railroad came to Newton and Hutchinson and Dodge City, they saw great herds of long-horned cattle come in from Texas, on their way to Eastern markets.

These pioneer frontiersmen had to tame raw country, whether it was the wooded hills of Missouri and eastern Kansas, or the sod plains of western Kansas and Oklahoma. There was poverty and hardship. Sometimes there was trouble from unrecorded mortgages. There were poor crops, one after another, for the rains were uncertain. Grasshoppers cleaned them out, more than once. There were near escapes from prairie fires and forest fires. There was always fuel for the kitchen stove in the wooded country, but on the prairie the fuel was buffalo and cattle chips, cornstalks, corncobs gathered from the pigpens, and even corn itself when it was in abundance and cheaper than coal. Money was usually scarce. Doctors were far away. There had to be much long-distance driving across country where roads were only trails and streams were unbridged. Note in this volume many references to these long, hard trips.

As the years passed, the character of the frontier changed, and the pioneers met conditions even more difficult. Their language changed from German to English, for their children, learning only English in the schools, did not understand the High German of the church. Other changes came in church life, like new styles of clothing and new modes of worship and instruction. Young people began to go to high school and college, and communication gaps yawned. There grew a demand for educated preachers. New inventions caused tensions: could a nonconformed Christian own a car or a telephone? There was less question about accepting electricity, household conveniences such as indoor plumbing, and tractors and combines on the farm. Radio met some resistance, but by the time television came, most people had observed that resistance to such things was futile.

A changing economy and more education brought new vocations into the church. There were still many farmers, but also a host of teachers, doctors and nurses, bankers and realtors, merchants, mechanics, factory workers, social workers, builders, and government employees. Mennonites shared in the rising standard of living, and higher incomes made possible more affluent living. The frontier of Christian humility and simplicity bristles with problems as wealth accumulates.

Much of this history of the South Central Conference is the story of the various congregations. Readers will observe a variety of ways in which these congregations were started. The first churches were made up of homeseekers, hunting economic opportunity. Such were Sycamore Grove, Spring Valley, Mt. Pisgah, Stuttgart, Pleasant View, and Gulfhaven. Mission Sunday schools developed into churches, as at Wichita and Oak Grove. A summer Bible school became a church at Three Brothers. Schism resulted in new churches at Bethel, Pryor, Greensburg, and Yoder.

It is good to note that mission outreach produced a great flock

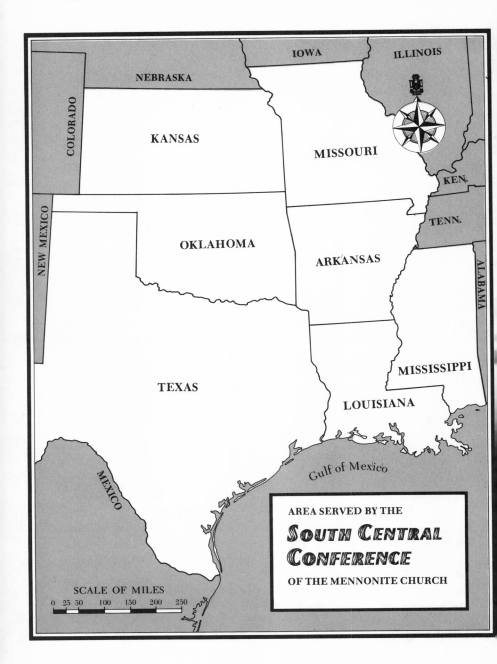

MEXICO

NEW MEXICO

COLORADO

KANSAS

NEBRASKA

IOWA

ILLINOIS

MISSOURI

KEN.

TENN.

ALABAMA

OKLAHOMA

ARKANSAS

TEXAS

MISSISSIPPI

LOUISIANA

Gulf of Mexico

SCALE OF MILES

0 25 50   100   150   200   250

AREA SERVED BY THE

SOUTH CENTRAL
CONFERENCE

OF THE MENNONITE CHURCH

of churches, especially in these later years; among them are Bethel Springs, Mt. Joy, Evening Shade, Argentine, Tenth Street, Buffalo, Des Allemands, South Hutchinson, and Lyon Street. Voluntary Service units grew into churches at Kansas City, Crossroads, Bethesda, and at a number of places in south Texas. The opening of a church school brought a church to Hesston. The swarming of a large congregation resulted in the birth of a new church at Harrisonville.

This history also tells about extinct congregations, and readers may well ponder on why they died. Some, like Cedar County, Missouri, the early settlements at Marion, Kansas, and the Milan Valley congregation in Oklahoma may have suffered from the scattering which prevented enough concentration of population to make a viable church. They died from mere discouragement.

Church troubles seem to have contributed to congregational disintegration. The story of Kill Creek, Catlin, Woodland (Wichita), White Hall, Hartford, Pleasant View (Missouri), and Walker points the moral that when dissension rears its ugly head, the brotherhood is sure to suffer. The Pennsylvania Church was affected for many years by its schisms, but ultimately other positive factors brought a happy conclusion.

Changing economic and population factors can also be hard on church life. White Hall died after the mines played out. West Liberty got smaller as the wheat farms got larger; Eureka Gardens became isolated by highway construction. The reader may be able to discern other conditions or situations that kill churches.

One may identify certain outstanding initiators on the South Central frontier. R. J. Heatwole was not only one of the first settlers, but he set up a plan of traveling evangelism to meet spiritual needs of scattered settlers. J. F. Brunk was by nature better fitted as a "starter" than for continued administration: he headed for a time a children's home at Hillsboro, was the first superintendent of the Kansas City mission, solicited funds for a sanitarium at La Junta (then in the Kansas-Nebraska district), and helped to start a mission at Hutchinson.

Lydia Heatwole, daughter of R. J. Heatwole, was the pioneer of nursing education in the Mennonite Church. Allen H. Erb set up a pattern for church administration of hospitals owned by communities, and introduced a new plan for building care facilities for the aged with capital furnished by those cared for. Florence Cooprider Friesen was the first Mennonite woman doctor in her denomination.

The conference produced many other men of accomplishment in the Mennonite Church. J. E. Hartzler was a college administrator and an outstanding speaker. J. M. Kreider, a bishop, served on church boards. Daniel Kauffman as a writer, and first moderator of Mennonite General Conference, was the most influential leader of the church for many years. T. M. Erb served many churches as a frontier bishop and was the chief founder of Hesston College. J. R. Shank made a career of rural missions and was for a long time a curriculum writer. J. W. Shank, his brother, was the first promoter of a mission in South America. Mahlon and George Lapp were effective in setting up the pattern of work in the India mission. J. D. Mininger became the dean of city mission workers of the church. His son Paul Mininger became the president of Goshen College and was the first to deliver the Conrad Grebel Lectures. Nelson E. Kauffman, after successfully building a city mission church, was the first Home Missions Secretary for the Mennonite Board of Missions. George R. Brunk pioneered in a new congregation, and then went east to become a major theological influence. H. A. Diener, a bishop and pastor, was a Mission Board and General Conference official. J. D. Charles set a precedent of academic excellence at Hesston College, and was, just before his early death, the chief writer of *Christian Fundamentals,* the doctrinal statement that served the church for forty years.

S. Paul Miller, in a long career as a missionary in India, played a leading part in the transition from mission to church there. Milton Vogt, a transfer from the General Conference Mennonites, gave his entire life to the India mission, including the beginning of the work in Bihar. Milo Kauffman, college president and an early Conrad Grebel lecturer, was a powerful builder of stewardship conviction. Daniel Kauffman, grandson of the first of that name and first secretary of stewardship under General Conference, developed a plan for implementing stewardship. G. G. Yoder, through his Conrad Grebel Lectures on Christian nurture, helped to turn the tide in the trend toward baptism in early childhood. Albert Buckwalter, a missionary in Argentina, was the first translator of the Scriptures into the Toba Indian language. His brother Ralph, as a pioneer missionary in Japan, helped to plant the Mennonite Church in Hokkaido.

There is a long list of items in which the Mennonites of this area have worked on frontiers. The idea of ten-cent merchandising, which has developed into the worldwide Woolworth chain, had its first expression in a Mennonite's store in Tipton, Missouri.

District church conferences, just developing in this era, got the backing of Daniel Brundage as he organized in turn the Missouri and the Kansas-Nebraska conferences. Lay participation came in early here. The office of bishop was changed into that of elected or appointed overseer by the South Central Conference in 1954. Daniel Kauffman, while still a member of the Missouri Conference, was the chief architect of the reorganization in the twenties which merged the Amish Mennonites and the Mennonites, and redrew the geographical lines of the conferences involved. Paul Erb and Paul Mininger, natives of this area, were members of the Study Commission which drew up the reorganization plan that brought the Mennonite General Assembly into being in 1971. And the South Texas Mennonite Church Council is one of the earliest functioning congregational clusters envisaged by the new organization plan.

Both the Missouri and the Kansas-Nebraska conferences were early advocates of a Mennonite General Conference, and Daniel Kauffman drew up the first plan of organization. When the Mennonite Evangelizing Board, the denomination's first general mission board, began its work, three of its fourteen members were from the South Central area. In 1881 the Missouri Conference passed a resolution favoring missions. Daniel Kauffman helped to organize Mennonite Publication Board, and was the first editor of the *Gospel Witness*, an official church organ. The services of a newly organized Board of Education were sought in the founding of a church school in the West (Hesston Academy and Bible School). When leaders on this Western frontier were promoting support of this school and the acceptance of higher education, there was still throughout the denomination a heavy apathy or outright opposition to high school and college education.

J. S. Coffman, pioneer Mennonite evangelist, came often to the churches of this area. Since he went to the places where he was welcome, this would argue that these Western communities were above average in their openness to this new means of evangelism. But even here caution was necessary. For Coffman's first meetings at Spring Valley, R. J. Heatwole announced the meetings only one evening at a time, lest opposition would be stirred up.

When there was severe loss to members at Mt. Zion through a tornado in the seventies, a question was sent to Indiana about a possible systematic plan for mutual aid, probably the first time this question was raised in the Mennonite Church. It was ahead of its day, however, for the Indiana Conference only counseled trust in the Lord.

The twentieth century saw the opening of institutions for the care of children (Argentine), the aged (Hannibal, Schowalter at Hesston), and the sick (La Junta and others in Colorado, Greensburg).

This was the era of city missions, and the South Central area looked with responsibility at the larger cities within its borders. City missions were established in Kansas City, Wichita, Hutchinson, and St. Louis. Each of these developed some specialty: child care, interracial cooperation, relief for the poor, and ghetto renewal, respectively.

Rural missions, too, found outstanding expression: among Ozark mountaineers in Missouri and Arkansas, and among Spanish-speaking migrants in south Texas.

In both city and rural fields the interest of the district was drawn to the minority groups, both the blacks and the browns, so that there have developed churches that are primarily black or Spanish. It is not surprising that in these churches questions of paternalism and minority autonomy have become a problem. The white workers and the conference officials may have been too slow in turning over responsibility, and the minorities may have irritated their white brethren by pressing their claims too hard. But the problem is being worked through; an outstanding example is the South Texas Council. When the Mennonite Mission Board moved into establishing a Minority Council, they found executive leadership in John Powell at Wichita and in Ruperto Guedea and Lupe De Leon at Mathis, Texas.

Around the turn of the century the churches of Kansas were influenced by a deeper-life movement, which gave a warmth to the experience of many, leaders and laymen alike. One result has been prayer meetings and much freedom in sharing by testimony. But at times this ran into the extremities of the holiness movement, as described in the histories of the Spring Valley and Pennsylvania churches. This has resulted in some losses. But no doubt the overall effect of the movement has been good, bringing values only now being realized in some other sections of the church.

The first wholly Mennonite summer Bible school was held at Hesston, promoted by Noah Oyer. Paul and Alta Erb wrote some of the first curriculum materials produced by the church. The most successful weekday Bible school was the one conducted for many years at Argentine.

In the earliest years of the Mennonite sewing circle movement, a circle began meeting in the Pennsylvania community. Young People's Meetings, then called Bible Readings, began there about 1900. There were no helps printed then, and the leaders had to provide their own programs. A Young People's Institute was held at Hesston in 1933, and Mennonite Youth Fellowship was first proposed to the Commission for Christian Education and Young People's Work by Paul Erb, secretary of Young People's Activities, in a meeting held at Argentine in the middle forties.

Mennonite Disaster Service was first activated at Hesston, under the name of Mennonite Service Organization.

In 1903 the Missouri Conference ruled that the lot need not be used in selecting men for ordinations. Its use has gradually declined, and now most ministers are chosen without the lot. However, in 1973 its use is still an option. Seminary students have served internships in recent years at Hannibal and Hesston.

As citizens of two worlds Mennonites have contributed to the economic order in which they lived. In an agricultural economy this might be in the improvement of the farming process. Around the turn of the century T. M. Erb and others were promoting dairying through the sale of hand-operated cream separators, and buying the cream at cream stations, from which it was taken to creameries to be made into butter.

In the past twenty-five years several companies at Hesston, headed by Mennonites, have invented, manufactured, and distributed internationally various machines for farm use. Some of these have radically affected methods of harvesting and haymaking. Recent diversification includes lawn-care machinery and office furniture. Now waste-disposal equipment is being added, which shows that the frontiersmanship is thoroughly up-to-date.

One frontier of Mennonitism is in the cooperation and/or merging of the various Mennonite branches. This process has been at work practically from the beginning in the South Central area. At the Pennsylvania Church, Amish Mennonite and Mennonite groups, after alternating services for a while, but always worshiping and sometimes communing together, actually merged membership by 1892, anticipating by many years the churchwide merger.

While the current branches of Mennonitism have no plans for organic union, relations are increasingly close. They always have been good, for in this part of the country there is no history of split or schism to create prejudices. The different branches are simply different waves of migration from Europe, so far as the (Old) Mennonites are concerned.

Hesston College and its leaders played a significant role in building understanding and cooperation between the (Old) Mennonites and those Mennonites who emigrated to the prairie states from Russia since the 1870s. For many years representatives from the latter group have been serving on the Hesston faculty. The children and grandchildren of these immigrants have attended Hesston. The graduates of both groups in their home churches continued to build understanding for each other's culture. For example, the former editor and the present editor of the *Mennonite Weekly Review* are both graduates of Hesston. In the military camps of World War I the conscientious objectors of both groups became close friends. Later their sons were in the same Civilian Public Service camps during World War II. From the very beginning of Mennonite Central Committee in 1920 members of both groups have worked together in Voluntary Service projects in many places both at home and abroad. D. H. Bender as president of Hesston College had many contacts with the leaders of the Kansas Mennonites from Russia and was a key figure in the union of Mennonite relief committees into one structure, the Mennonite Central Committee. Hesston began the inter-Mennonite Ministers' Week, held annually and bringing together the area ministers of the General Conference Mennonites, the Mennonite Brethren, and the (Old) Mennonites. The three Mennonite colleges of central Kansas cooperate in a program of outlining objectives and areas of cooperation. In Kansas the three major Mennonite groups have cooperated in bringing a Christian witness annually at the Mennonite pavilion at the State Fair.

A current method of merger among the Mennonites is congregational membership in two conferences at the same time. This practice began in Ohio. But by 1973 there were three congregations of the South Central Conference which had dual membership. United Mennonite at Premont, Texas, belongs also to the Mennonite Brethren; Rainbow Boulevard at Kansas City and Inter-Mennonite at Hesston belong also to the General Conference Mennonites. These three branches have been cooperating for several years in a ministers' conference.

In 1974 the larger Mennonite groups cooperated in celebrating the coming of the Mennonites to Kansas in the early 1870s: the

General Conference Mennonites and the Mennonite Brethren from Russia and the (Old) Mennonites from several Eastern states. The publication of *South Central Frontiers* is a part of this celebration.

Thus, as the frontiers shift, but persist, so God is providing the pioneers who are needed. The rest of this book tells the story of this frontier action.

> *For those the first with patient toil*
> *To break the clod and till the soil;*
> *For all such men since men began,*
> *We thank the God who made the man.*
> — Anonymous

SCATTERED MEMBERS IN MISSOURI

CHAPTER

SCATTERED MEMBERS IN MISSOURI

In this section on scattered members we tell of those prospectors for homes who settled where they liked it, hoping that others would come to make it a new Mennonite community. Perhaps this was as far as they could get — the wagon broke down or the money ran out.

1. Dallas County

The first communication to the *Herald of Truth* from Missouri was from H. E. Rexrode. In March 1866 he wrote from Long Lane, which is seventy-five miles southwest of Jefferson City, in the Osage River watershed. He was the only subscriber to the paper in the state. He seemed recently to have moved there, and he encouraged others "of small means"[1] to secure homes there. In January of 1868 he wrote that there were five families there. But the next month Benjamin Shantz said there were three.[2] Had two families left already? Or — do you count a bachelor explorer a family?

In May J. M. Brenneman, Elida, Ohio, one of the first to feel a pastoral responsibility for the frontiersmen, visited seven brethren here; he mentioned the Shantz and Shallenberger families.[3] He baptized one person and held communion, J. B. McConnell wrote in June.[4]

The next year John S. Good, from Page County, Iowa, traveled from Carthage to Long Lane by team. He visited the Rexrodes, and preached in a schoolhouse. He found eight members there.[5]

But by September 1872 all members had despaired of forming a congregation, and planned to move to Kansas. Where did they go? That is the last we hear of Dallas County.

2. *Montgomery County*

Benjamin Schantz, probably the same person who was at Long Lane the next year, lived at Wellsville, eighty miles northwest of St. Louis, in February 1867.[6] He wrote that there was no Mennonite church there. "There is a number of small settlements of our people in different parts of Missouri, but I have heard of only one place yet where there is an organized church and a minister." The one place might have been Hickory County, only forty miles northwest of Long Lane.

3. *Henry County*

The first Missouri obituary in the *Herald of Truth* (January 1868) was of Elizabeth Schneider, who died in this county on December 11, 1867. She was nine years old. Were her parents living here, or just traveling through when their daughter got appendicitis? (She died of "inflammation of the bowels," as did many people in those days.)

In 1879 John Culp and Henry C. Brenneman lived near Calhoun, which is thirty miles east of the permanent Cass County community.[7]

4. *Linn County*

In 1868 Daniel Brundage, minister in Morgan County, visited John and Jacob Bechtel, who moved to Enterprise from Ontario. Brundage originally came from Ontario, and might have known them there. Linn County was nearly one hundred miles north of Morgan County.[8]

5. *Gentry County*

Jacob Aeby wrote in German to John F. Funk. His letter was published in the *Herold der Wahrheit* in September 1868. Jacob, his brother, and their wives were on their way to Kansas, but hearing some unfavorable reports about Kansas, stopped at Berlin in northwestern Missouri. He said they had church and Sunday school. The land was good, and cheap, and others were invited to settle there.[9]

6. *Belton, Cass County*

Belton was twenty miles from the Sycamore Grove community in Cass County. D. F. Driver reported in 1874 that there were three members at Belton.[10] A Brother Bear was the only Mennonite here

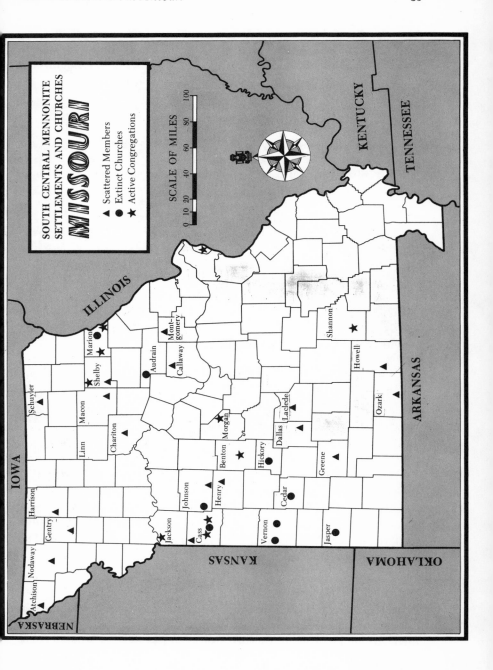

in 1881. Henry Harnish lived here in 1890. J. S. Coffman held meetings and attracted a household of people. J. B. Smith, while serving as pastor at Bethel, near Garden City, taught school at Belton and filled some Sunday appointments.[11]

7. *Harrison County*

John S. Good, of Iowa, visited a Funk family at New Hampton, in northwestern Missouri, in 1880. Mrs. Funk, seventy-eight, had not heard a Mennonite preach for sixteen years.[12] "The aged" Martin Funk, probably her husband, was received the next month into church fellowship on confession.[13]

8. *Macon County*

Dr. Jacob Blosser, forty years a Mennonite, died at Macon City in 1882, two years after moving from the Shenandoah Valley in Virginia. Macon City is twenty-five miles west of the Mt. Pisgah Church in Shelby County.

At La Plata, in the same county, some fifteen years later, Daniel Kauffman and John Brubaker held several meetings. Four persons from other denominations were received into the Mennonite fellowship. There is no record of later meetings here.

9. *Greene County*

J. W. Plank wrote in 1884 from Springfield in southern Missouri, asking for English-speaking preachers. There were no other Mennonites in Springfield, he said. [14]

10. *Callaway County*

A Sister Kettering, from this county, joined the church in Shelby County, sixty miles north, in 1884. She was the only Mennonite in her area of the state.[15] John Detweiler and John Brubaker visited her the next year and found a number of descendants of Mennonites there, "who hunger and thirst for the Word as we teach it."[16]

11. *Atchison County*

In 1884 Bishop Henry Yother (a variant spelling of Yoder), Gage County, Nebraska, whose name will emerge frequently in this history, visited brethren in this farthest northwestern county of Missouri; he held two meetings here.[17]

12. *Nodaway County*

In another northwestern Missouri county Mrs. Thomas J. Alexander died at Maryville in 1884. She was baptized in Illinois and maintained her relationship to the Mennonite Church until her death. [18]

13. *Johnson County*

L. H. Shank, Virginia settler in Morgan County in 1883, moved to Larned, Kansas, in 1884 to get a better farm. But in 1886, after a tornado had moved their house off its foundation, he traded his farm for one at Leeton, Missouri. J. S. Coffman visited the family there and held a few meetings. In 1891 they moved to Bowling Green, Florida, in hopes of improving the health of Mrs. Shank, who had tuberculosis. Here Mollie, a daughter (later to become Mrs. Daniel Kauffman) and her brother John R. wanted to become Christians. The father wrote to J. S. Coffman, who came from Indiana to Florida to meet the need of this lonely family. He preached in an unused Baptist church, and baptized the two young people in a shallow brook near the church. Before Mrs. Shank died, she asked her husband to take the children back to Missouri, which he did, first to Versailles, and later to Palmyra. [19]

14. *Chariton County*

J. L. Kreider bought half-interest in a "good church house" in 1889. L. J. Heatwole visited this group at this time. There were a few members there: J. L. Kreider and wife; F. W. Brunk, wife, and daughter. [20] Two years later J. S. Coffman preached three times here. The meetings were well attended, and seven people confessed Christ. [21]

15. *Howell County*

Five families were at Cureall (for their health's sake?!), twenty miles west of Birch Tree in 1888. They seldom held meetings. [22]

16. *Ozark County*

In the 1890s J. Borntreger, Noah D. Troyer, and C. K. Miller, perhaps others, lived here on the Arkansas border, next county west of Howell. Isaac A. Miller, from Ohio, held four meetings here and served communion late in 1891. [23]

17. *Schuyler County*

Mary, wife of Christian Kropf, died here in 1891. They were former residents of Ontario, Ohio, and Iowa.[24]

18. *Laclede County*

David Fry reported from Lebanon that Daniel Kauffman and John C. Driver preached there in June 1895.[25]

o   o   o

Since we are dependent on the *Herald of Truth* for most of the information about a scattered Mennonite population in Missouri, it seems probable that there were others, perhaps many, who did not write to the *Herald,* and so we do not know about them.

Daniel Kauffman wrote that the first Mennonite minister in Missouri was Martin Lapp, who, he said, came from Illinois in 1855, "labored with a small group of Amish Mennonites for a few years, and then moved to Shelby County."[26] The only group of Amish Mennonites known to be in the state that early were in Hickory County. D. H. Bender in 1921[27] repeated this information about Martin Lapp. Neither Kauffman nor Bender gave a source. Kauffman was a Missourian, and must have known a dependable oral tradition.

It will be evident to the reader how extremely valuable to Mennonite history are the facts preserved by John F. Funk's *Herald of Truth* to which most of the above citations refer.

EXTINCT CHURCHES IN MISSOURI

CHAPTER

EXTINCT CHURCHES IN MISSOURI

We have looked at settlements of Mennonites in Missouri which aspired to become congregations, but failed to achieve that goal. Now we look at a lesser number which did succeed, some for many years, but which have not survived until today.

1. *Hickory County*

The first Mennonites in Missouri settled in Hickory County, 100 miles southwest of Jefferson City, in the Osage River watershed. Joseph Naffziger, the first settler, came in 1855 or earlier. In 1856 Daniel Raber moved in from Lee County, Iowa, to join other Amish Mennonite families there. Land was cheap and wood for fuel and building was plentiful. At this time it was open-range country, and as the Civil War disturbances came on, Daniel Raber had 600 branded cattle. At the end of the war he had none. Raber himself was for a time a prisoner of the Confederates.[1]

After the war, in 1867, there were fifteen families in the community, but they had no minister. In 1871 Charles (Karl) Kuntze was ordained bishop.[2] Other earlier ministers were Martin Lapp (possibly the first), Peter Lehman, John Klopfenstein, and Peter Christner. The last minister was Lemon J. Miller, who was still there in 1905.[3]

These are other family names found in this congregation in its half century of life: Kauffman, Stuckey, Gerber, Hostetler, Gilliam, Neuenschwander, Diener, Rufenacht, Roth, Schindler, Stoll, Aker, Oesch, Rich, Gerstner.

After meeting in homes and schoolhouses for many years, the congregation built a meetinghouse in 1894, five miles southwest of Wheatland, on land donated by Christian Gerber. It was called Gerber's Church. The best farming land was here on the "Wheatland Prairie." But members were scattered from Elkton on the south to Quincy on the north. Even as late as 1887 they preferred to have their preaching in German. The highest number of members was about one hundred. There were nine accessions after meetings in 1894 by D. D. Miller, who had lived here as a boy (see p. 21). [4]

Families began to move away about 1882, and most of them were gone by 1910, although Daniel Kauffman reported one member there in 1936. [5] Some who stayed joined other Mennonite groups: the General Conference or the Defenceless Mennonites. Most moved to Johnson County to make up the Pleasant View congregation near Holden (see pp. 55-57).

After the open range was taken away, the farms were fenced and more intensively cultivated. Fertility declined, and families could not recover from the impoverishment of the Civil War raids. At times there was no ministerial leadership.

For whatever reasons, there is no Mennonite Church in Hickory County now. In 1936 one who grew up there visited his old community and tried to see his father's grave. He could hardly get to it. The graves of the Naffzigers and the Riches and the Kuntzes and the Oesches and the Gerstners were overgrown with weeds and brush. The church building was sold by the Missouri Conference; it was moved into Wheatland and remodeled as a residence.

2. *Bethel, Cass County*

The strongest Mennonite community in Missouri developed in Cass County, thirty miles southeast of Kansas City. The first congregation there was called Clearfork. Out of this one, two others were formed: Sycamore Grove and Bethel. Sycamore Grove is there today, and its history will be given in the next chapter. The story of Bethel belongs among the extinct churches. But this is not the story of a church that gradually died. It had its beginning in a schism, and it came to a happy end in the healing of that schism, after a coexistence of more than sixty years that was increasingly brotherly.

The beginnings in the development at Clearfork are the same for both Sycamore Grove and Bethel, and must be given here, so the reader can understand how Bethel came to be.

In 1860, before the Civil War broke out, Solomon Yoder, from the vicinity of West Liberty, Ohio, bought a farm near Harrisonville, right in the area of the border fight over the slavery issue. The Union government gave the historic Order Number Eleven, which called for all family heads in Cass and Jackson counties to move to designated areas, so that the Confederate-connected guerrilla gangs could be cleaned out. If Solomon had disobeyed, he would have been shot. He consented to what amounted to Union Army enlistment.[6]

This left his family alone, unprotected, in a strange country. Their home was raided for food. Once when Mrs. Yoder had cooked a piece of meat for the soldiers, she told them they might as well go on, for there was nothing more. A daughter became ill and died.[7] Her place of burial never was known to her parents.

A brother in Ohio, C. P. Yoder, hearing of these circumstances, came by train to Independence, Missouri, forty miles from Harrisonville. But martial law kept him from going further. Through the help of an army captain and a rebel prisoner, the Yoder family, leaving everything behind, was brought to Independence. Kind neighbors protected the furniture, but the buildings were burned. C. P. Yoder took the family back to Ohio.[8]

When the war was over, Solomon returned to Ohio. But very soon, in 1865, the family came back to Missouri, and the C. P. Yoders with them. The next two years other settlers joined them, from Pennsylvania, Ohio, Michigan, Indiana, and Illinois. One of the early settlers was Jacob C. Kenagy, a bishop and a schoolteacher, who was to be an effective leader until his death in 1894. In 1868 he organized the congregation in his log house with the following names among the first members: Yoder, Sharp, Kenagy (sometimes spelled Kenaga), Troyer, King, Zook, Kauffman, and Hartzler. Services began in the log home of C. P. Yoder, later moving to the McBride and the Smith schools.

Mrs. C. P. Yoder died in 1869, and a part of their farm was designated as a cemetery, and a cemetery association was organized in 1870. The Clearfork Cemetery is today one of the oldest and largest cemeteries in the county. It took its name from the nearby Clearfork Creek.

In 1870 it was decided to build a church. The site was donated by C. P. Yoder. The cost was $1700. At this time there were already 150 members. In 1872 Moses Yoder was ordained to the ministry. John J. Hartzler, a minister, came from Michigan in 1880.

The members at Clearfork came from about twenty different places. Most were Amish Mennonites, but they were used to different disciplines and church life. For instance, some saw the value of the Sunday school; others were sure it would bring "pride" into the church. Bishop Kenagy had helped David Plank in Ohio to start the first permanent Mennonite or Amish Mennonite Sunday school. There was Sunday school at Clearfork, probably as early as 1870. But, to avoid contention, the bishop had to stay away from the meeting until Sunday school was over. The wearing of buttons was an issue, as well as the use of English.

About 1875 the break came. A group of about fifty called in Benjamin Eicher from Iowa to be their leader. They became known as the Eicher Church, while the larger group was the Kenagy or Amish Church, named the Sycamore Grove Church in 1883. The two groups used the Clearfork building on alternate Sundays. One Sunday the Amish group found the building locked. They took steps to build a new church — Sycamore Grove. We come back to their story on p. 77.

A few years later the Eicher group was divided. One group organized the Mount Zion Church two miles southwest of Clearfork, which eventually disbanded.[9] Those who remained at Clearfork became known as the Yoder Church.[10]

By invitation J. S. Coffman held meetings for the Yoder group. He gave help in organizing in 1886 the Bethel Church, of which they were a nucleus. This church was more progressive, oriented toward the Missouri Mennonite Conference rather than the Amish. It used English. Members who were dissatisfied in the other Mennonite churches joined Bethel. For instance, one family came to Bethel so that their family could enjoy the Sunday school lesson helps which Sycamore Grove at this time was not using.

A new building was erected in 1887 2 1/2 miles south of Sycamore Grove. The building had a seating capacity of 350, and cost $1,900. In 1888 the Missouri Conference met here.

Bishop David D. Kauffman, of Versailles, had supervision of the new church until his death in 1896. In that year his son Daniel was ordained bishop and served Bethel until J. C. Driver was chosen in 1912 as pastor and bishop.

Daniel Kauffman and Daniel F. Driver of Versailles supplied the pulpit in the first years. For a few of those years Kauffman was resident as a schoolteacher. Then L. J. Heatwole, well known as an almanac calculator, came in 1890 from Virginia; but he returned to Virginia in 1893 for health reasons. In the next two decades a succession of ministers served: D. F. Yoder, D. Y. Hooley, A. D. Wenger, J. B. Smith, C. S. Hauder, J. E. Hartzler, and W. E. Helmuth.

Then J. C. Driver came from Larned, Kansas, in 1912, and gave a long period of faithful leadership, until the merger with Sycamore Grove in 1947. D. S. King assisted in the ministry from 1917 to 1930.

The first trustees were Christian Kauffman, S. L. Byler, and I. B. King. Deacons were Eli Kauffman, I. B. King, E. W. Byler, and J. B. Yoder.

Bethel was active in many ways: monthly appointments at Olathe, Kansas, and Belton, Missouri; services at Wallace School and the County Home; an evergreen Sunday school; youth fellowship and institutes; sewing circle; support for one of the members, Nellie Zook King, serving seventeen years as a missionary in India.

On November 8, 1936, the congregation celebrated the fiftieth anniversary of its founding. Four hundred persons, including many former members, made it a joyful and thankful homecoming. The membership at this time was 108, near the high point of the sixty-year history.

The deep feelings that had accompanied the original schism at Clearfork had largely subsided by the time of Bethel's founding. Relations were excellent between these two Mennonite churches just two miles apart. At first there were still some significant differences. For instance, at Sycamore Grove German was used even in the children's classes until 1895. Only German was sung until 1896; books used were the *Allegemeine Liedersammlung* and *Hosianna Pilger Lieder*. Bethel represented the Mennonite presence in the community and Sycamore Grove the Amish, in those days before the Mennonites and Amish came as near each other in culture as they were in faith.

But through the years the differences became less significant. The two congregations found many things they could do together: Sunday evening Young People's Meetings, alternating at the two places; evangelistic meetings and Bible conferences; literary society and young people's institutes; various special meetings; free pulpit exchange. It became less easy to see why a person belonged to one church rather than the other, or why they could not become one fellowship.

Early in the twenties there was a realignment of conferences, with the line between Mennonites and Amish breaking down completely. Then the two congregations found themselves belonging to the same conference — Missouri-Kansas.

Some Mennonites were moving away from both congregations, to find new homes in other states, and the membership in both churches was down. They saw they could get along with one building, possibly with one pastor. That would reduce operating expenses.

No one pushed uniting prematurely. But by 1940 they were ready to talk. A conference committee proposed some terms for a possible merger, but the congregations were not yet ready to accept them. A second try was made a few years later. The committee consisted of Alva Swartzendruber, Gideon G. Yoder, and J. G. Hartzler. They proposed a similar plan. This time it was accepted, and the merger became effective in August 1947.

The Bethel members brought letters, which were accepted as a group. One family joined a church in Harrisonville, and Bishop Driver and his wife moved to Colorado to be nearer their family. All the rest, more than fifty, became members of Sycamore Grove. The church building was dismantled, and the lumber was used in a remodeling program at Sycamore Grove in 1950, and in the building of a much-functioning church cabin just north of the church.

Thus ended the Bethel and Sycamore Grove detour in Cass County. They found unity and peace, not only in the Clearfork Cemetery, which both groups used through the years, but in the ongoing Sycamore Grove congregation (see p. 77).

3. *White Hall, Jasper County*

Eighty miles southwest of Hickory County is another frontier area that the Mennonites found early. Joplin, Carthage, and between them Oronogo, were located in a lead and zinc-mining area.

The early Mennonites came to Jasper County from Virginia and Iowa. During the Civil War a band of forty persons traveled by wagon from Allen County, Ohio, to Page County, in southwestern Iowa. They were thirty days on the road, and crossed the Mississippi River on ferry boats. Some of these people soon came down to Jasper County.

Joseph Blosser must have told them about the country here. He was a Virginian who may have come to Missouri as early as 1855. In 1867 he wrote from Carthage, "We have no Mennonite congregation here now, but I think the prospects are good."[11] That same year Samuel Brenneman came from Rockingham County, Virginia, and bought a farm four miles north of Oronogo. The next year his parents, Jacob Brennemans, and their five daughters came. Samuel met them at Sedalia, 120 miles north, which was the end of the railroad then. All the roads were just trails across the prairie, and travelers saw wild game like deer and prairie chickens.

J. S. Good was the minister in Page County, Iowa. By 1872 three of his children lived in Jasper County. He visited them and held eight meetings in various schoolhouses. He reported eight members there. He hoped to move there himself.[12]

Joseph Blosser married Margaret Stevenson at Carthage in 1869. He was not a minister, but when Ann Maria Good died in 1870, since there was no minister there, Blosser gave the "funeral discourse."[13]

Daniel Brundage visited the group, driving a span of mules from Morgan County by way of Hickory County.

Deacon Henry Hoffman from Iowa lived here a while during these years and held meetings in various schools. The Mennonites met together in their homes for many years. But they cooperated with people of other denominations in a union Sunday school held in a log building called the Backdoor School. The school had been built before the road was put through, and faced east. When the road was surveyed, it was on the west of the school. And so it was the back door that faced the road.

A need was felt for a resident minister. Bishop Daniel Driver was called from Morgan County in 1880 to ordain one. Joseph Weaver was chosen by lot and was the congregation's first minister. Among visiting ministers was Henry Yother, who at one time stayed here for six weeks.[14]

In 1882 John Blosser and John M. Shenk conducted meetings. At this time Joseph Good, youngest son of J. S. Good, was ordained deacon. It is noteworthy that at the same time his wife was ordained as a deaconess.

About this time D. D. Kauffman, father of Daniel Kauffman, great leader of our century, came from Morgan County to preach. He had always preached in German. But a number of the members understood only English. And so Kauffman, here in the home of Joseph Weaver, preached his first English sermon. One who heard it remembered years later that he spoke very well on the Passover. But when he prayed, he used his more familiar German.

The last decade of the century was a time of growth and prosperity for the congregation. The membership increased from about twenty to more than fifty, many of them relatives of Mrs. Andrew Shenk. Shenk, an able preacher, moved from Elida, Ohio, to Oronogo in 1895, and was the leader of the congregation until his death in 1937. He was ordained as bishop at the Missouri Conference held at Versailles in 1896. J. F. Funk officiated, and Daniel Kauffman was ordained bishop at the same time. Shenk traveled a great deal as an evangelist and in other denominational responsibilities.

Following one series of meetings a class of eleven was baptized. The highest membership reached was about eighty-five.

The congregation became very active in evangelistic outreach. D. S. Weaver, who donated the original capital for the children's Quarter Fund, came from this congregation. Tent meetings were held, resulting in a congregation of 17 at Oakland. Ministers from White Hall, the name of the public school in which the congregation met, filled appointments at many places in the area cornering near Joplin: fifteen in Missouri, five in Kansas, four in Oklahoma, and one in Arkansas. There were six branch Sunday schools. At one time it took five ministers to fill all the appointments.

For a number of years a union Sunday school met in the White Hall schoolhouse. With the increase of Mennonite members, the Mennonites took full charge. Then it was decided to build a church. Sarah Miller, a widowed nonmember, donated the land, the money was raised in the community and from other Mennonite churches, and the building was constructed in 1897. All bills were paid when the church was opened for use. It was called White Hall, from the White Hall school. Deacon Good wrote, "We have now a commodious house to worship in."[15] The Sunday school began to be "evergreen" (year-round), and the Missouri Conference met at White Hall in 1897. J. S. Coffman is thought to have preached the conference sermon.

Ann Maria Good, wife of Andrew Good, one of the pioneer members, was the first to be buried in the church cemetery, in 1870. Joseph Weaver gave the land for the cemetery, which was called the Weaver Cemetery.

The discipline in this church was always somewhat strict. Bishop Shenk required immersed people to be rebaptized, and the wearing of neckties was forbidden. But a number of people from non-Mennonite background became members. In the early years there was some objection to the preacher using notes in the pulpit.

Whitehall Church

Among those who held evangelistic meetings at Oronogo in these earlier years are the following: J. S. Coffman, A. D. Wenger, Peter Unzicker, John McCulloh, Noah Metzler, S. E. Allgyer, L. J. Miller, D. D. Miller, D. D. Zook, J. M. R. Weaver. One person remembers Coffman saying in a sermon on justification that his mother justified him by taking him across her knee and proceeding with the laying on of hands; evidently there was no objection to a little humor in the pulpit.

Ministers serving here, in addition to those already mentioned, were the following: Noah Shenk (Bishop Shenk's oldest son, ordained in 1898 by George R. Brunk for service at Neutral, Kansas; see p. 193); J. P. Berkey (ordained 1905; a one-armed man widely used as an evangelist); Perry Shenk (ordained 1905; another son of Bishop Shenk, and a successful evangelist; died in 1937, shortly after his father); Amos Kilmer; Harve Woolsey, ordained in 1911 (later preached in another denomination); J. T. Hamilton (ordained for Birch

Tree, where he served for a while); William Tweedy (ordained in 1914 for Oakland; died in 1950); E. J. Berkey (ordained before coming to Oronogo; a well-known evangelist); Kenneth Smoker (the last pastor, 1950-53). In 1928 Frank Buerge was ordained deacon; he later moved to Cass County. G. D. Shenk, another son of Andrew, was ordained after he moved west. Two members, Jesse Weaver and Levi Kilmer, later became preachers in other denominations.

Some additional family names in the congregation were Shupe, Gunning, Grimm, Ault, Downs, Bare, Cummins, Fuller, Gerig, Hall, Hostetler, Kutz, Lamar, Magers, Pound, Smith, Sills, Jantz, Ross, Bickel, Pletcher, Marner, Rider. Jasper County is not primarily a farming area. Vocations among the members included farmers, carpenters, threshers, lumbermen, meat cutters, barbers, miners, and teachers.

Various causes entered into the decline of the White Hall Church. One was economic. The mines of the area played out, and jobs were hard to get. Strict discipline may have alienated some members. A chief cause was no doubt in the disputes and factionalism which developed after 1900. There were critical attitudes and a lack of love and cooperation. In 1904 a committee was called in: Daniel Kauffman, George R. Brunk, L. J. Miller, D. G. Lapp, and John W. McCulloh. The committee identified causes of the factionalism, both from the outside and from within the brotherhood. The members signed acceptance of their report and recommendations, but confidence and brotherhood were not completely restored.

Members began moving away; they are now found in many parts of the country. Some went to other denominations. Some former members do not now hold membership elsewhere. With all this, there naturally came to be problems in financing the church.

The Sunday school ceased to operate in August 1953, when the regular attendance came from only one family, the Mark Goods. The building was given to the new Mennonite congregation at Walker, fifty miles to the north. In May 1954, a farewell service was held. For many former attendants it was a homecoming; for others, an expression of goodwill. Myrtle Shenk, widow of Perry Shenk, wrote for this occasion:

"For more than fifty years this place has been a retreat from the trials and cares of this world. . . . A number of ministers have gone from here to their last resting place. . . . If it had not been for them I would not likely have known the Lord. . . . White Hall will never be dead while we live. I am so thankful that this building will continue to be used in the service of the Lord. . . . We prayed that this building should not fall into secular uses."[16]

The White Hall building was torn down, hauled to Walker, and used in part to serve that congregation, which had lately moved into Missouri from Kansas (see p. 65). The church site, according to the terms of the deed, reverted to the Sarah Miller estate.

4. *Johnson County*

The peace following the Civil War permitted adventurous Amish and Mennonites to come into Missouri. Joseph Gerber, with a family of seven children, picked Johnson County as a good place to buy land. He came from Ligonier, Indiana, in 1867. He was the first Amish settler here.

At first the Gerbers drove fifteen miles west to worship with the small group in Cass County. Their daughter Susanna married Levi N. Yoder from Indiana, who, after a few years at Cherryvale, Kansas, returned to Johnson County to be near his wife's parents. George, the youngest son of the Gerbers, went to Indiana and brought back a bride, Anna Morrell. Soon her parents came, and her father, David, who had been ordained in Indiana, became the first minister of the congregation, which was organized in 1870.

Pleasant View Church

They met at first in the Pleasant View school five miles south of Holden, which is fifty miles southeast of Kansas City. The congregation came to be known as the Pleasant View church. Andrew Miller from Kansas and John Klopfenstein from Hickory County, together with other families from Hickory, moved in. A church building was erected in 1889, at a cost of less than $1300. "A. M. Church" was on a board above the door. This church was fifteen miles from the Sycamore Grove Church in Cass County. The membership reached sixty at the highest. Many people of the community attended.

J. S. Coffman visited here and wrote, "I visited Bro. David Morrell and his little flock at Holden."[17] Morrell and Klopfenstein visited Hickory County in 1887, and preached in the schoolhouse there.

After the elderly Morrell and Miller moved to Cass County in the nineties, Henry Rychener was ordained to the ministry. Under him the language of the services changed from German to English. But in 1899 he moved to Fulton County, Ohio, and the congregation had no pastor. So in May 1900, D. B. Raber was chosen by lot and ordained by J. J. Hartzler.[18] Raber had gone to Archbold, Ohio, in 1882, to be married to Mary Nafziger. But because he did not wear hooks and eyes, they could not be married there. So they went back to Missouri for their ceremony. Dan Raber's sermons sparkled with a backwoodsy dialect all his own, and he became well known throughout the church. When he moved to Portage County, Ohio, in 1911, the Pleasant View Church was again without a minister, and never secured another one. Raber's later years were devoted to mission work among the hill people who understood and loved him so well: bootleggers in the Ozarks, mountaineers of Colorado, blacks of Georgia, and miners of southern Ohio.

Pleasant View was among the many churches served in the evangelistic ministry of D. D. Miller, dynamic Amish Mennonite leader of northern Indiana. He was there in 1893 and 1897.[19] When J. E. Hartzler, later evangelist and college president at Goshen and Bethel, was ordained to the ministry to serve as pastor at Bethel, Garden City, Missouri, in 1904, he preached his first sermon in Johnson County.

Some family names here, in addition to those already mentioned, were Kennel, Gingerich, Slabach, Rushley, and King.

The demise of the congregation was partly from economic

causes and partly spiritual. D. B. Raber said they raised wheat and corn until the soil was robbed. But he also said the breakdown came from disagreement over the location of the cemetery.[20]

In the last years preaching was by ministers from Cass County. Families moved away, one after another, and by the 1920s no services were held. The last service was the funeral of L. N. Yoder, on January 16, 1924. I. G. Hartzler preached the funeral sermon — both for the man, who had been active as Sunday school superintendent and song leader, and for the congregation.[21]

The building was sold by the Western District Amish Mennonite Conference and moved away. The church benches were taken to Cass County for use there. The cemetery was taken over by the Medford Community Cemetery Association as a neighborhood burial ground. An endowment provides upkeep.

5. *Cedar County*

Jonathan Krichbaum, earlier from Snyder County, Pennsylvania, moved from Indiana to Cedar County. He wrote to John F. Funk in July 1870: "The Omish [sic] Mennonites are making a settlement here and they have a preacher with them and will soon commence to hold meetings."[22] The preacher may have been Samuel Yoder, for in that year a couple from Hickory County, which corners to the northeast from Cedar County, came to him to be married.[23]

A church was organized here in 1870, as Krichbaum had hoped.[24] When J. S. Good stopped here in 1872 on the way home to Iowa from Jasper County, he stayed at Krichbaums. A meeting was held in the home of Jacob Yoder, and there were twenty-two families there. The preachers were Bishop Samuel Yoder, John Snyder, and Joseph Kauffman. It was a goodly congregation indeed — mostly Amish, but Amish and Mennonites cooperating. They asked for help in building a church.[25]

But something must have happened — drought, grasshoppers, the financial panic of 1873? For J. S. Coffman stopped to visit them in 1883, and reported, "No organized church here."[26] Krichbaums went to Osborne County, Kansas, to visit their daughters, stayed there, and Anna Krichbaum died there in 1878.[27] Benjamin Troyer, an Amishman, died in Cedar County in 1884, and the men who conducted his funeral were not Mennonites; there was probably no minister with the congregation then.[28] Isaac Miller, of Ohio, visited

there and eight members communed in 1891.[29] Jacob Kauffman lived
here in 1894 and reported nine Amish members.[30]

But about 1890 some members joined the Defenceless Mennonites, and nothing is heard of the church in Cedar County after
1900.[31]

Not many records are left about this church. Few wrote to
the *Herald of Truth.* Since this settlement was only twenty-five
miles from the one in Hickory County, it seems this might be an
instance of failure to consult and find agreement on just which spots
on the frontier the Mennonites and Amish should pick for their
communities. If they had all chosen Cedar County or Hickory County,
just one of them, there might be a strong church there yet.

6. *Vernon County (Stotesbury Settlement)*

The first Mennonite settlement in Vernon County was an Amish
group which may have come about 1890.

In October 1902, the Western District Amish Mennonite Conference listed the Stotesbury congregation as among its member churches,
with Christian Schrock, of Stotesbury, as deacon. Stotesbury is in northwest Vernon County, approximately eighty miles due south of Kansas
City. The congregation was under the bishop oversight of J. J.
Hartzler, of Garden City.[32]

Mennonite Church History, by J. S. Hartzler and Daniel
Kauffman (1905), misspelled the address as "Statesburg" (p. 311),
and *The Mennonite Encyclopedia* repeats this misspelling. These
sources name C. C. Schrock as a first settler as well as the deacon.
The date of the first meetinghouse is given as 1894. The membership
in 1905 was eighteen.

The *Mennonite Yearbook and Directory*[33] for 1906 lists a congregation of fifteen members, with C. C. Schrock as deacon, but with
an address of Katy, Missouri. This post office, appearing in old
atlases, was situated about twelve miles due south of Stotesbury,
and two miles south of Eve. The listing is exactly the same in the
1907 *Yearbook.* But by 1908 it had disappeared, and so that is
probably about the time when the congregation ceased to function.
Because they never shared with the whole church through the
Herald of Truth, little is now known about Stotesbury.[34] The second
attempt to colonize in Vernon County came many years later, at
Walker (see p. 65 below).

Palmyra Church

7. *Marion County (Palmyra)*

Isaac K. Rohrer was a part of the migration wave that went west following the Civil War. He left Lancaster County, Pennsylvania, some time before 1869 with an older brother who was looking for a climate that would benefit his health. First he went to Alabama, where he married; after the birth of four children, his wife died. Then he moved to Texas and married again. Five children were born to this union.

When Rohrer saw a newspaper ad of a farm for sale near Palmyra, Missouri, he came north in 1883, purchased the farm, and spent the rest of his life there. Palmyra is near the Mississippi River, one hundred miles south of the Iowa border.

The Rohrers brought with them Aunt Jane, who had been a slave of the second Mrs. Rohrer. In the social system which followed the freeing of the slaves, she was a maid, and was called Mamma by all the little Rohrers, whom she loved and cared for as her own.

Isaac Rohrer was reared in a Mennonite home, and he was a Mennonite in his sympathies. But he had not been baptized, and it was not until 1898 that he and his son Isaac H. were baptized in the Sites schoolhouse, where the congregation was worshiping. He was always a wise counselor of the church officials. Except for his oldest son, who married a Pennsylvania girl and moved to that state, none of his children joined the Mennonite Church.

The Jacob L. Rohrer family came to Palmyra from Pennsylvania in 1884, and bought an old plantation farm, with its reminders of the slavery days. J. S. Coffman visited the Rohrers in 1886 and held three services.[35] He reported that there was no organized church there. In 1888 Rohrer wrote that they were the only Mennonites in Marion County, but that they looked for more from Lancaster County soon.[36]

In the early nineties the Jacob H. Hershey and Ezra Buck-walter families came. They were young people with small children. The group held monthly services at the Sites schoolhouse. Different Mennonite ministers visited and preached for them: D. D. Kauffman, Andrew Shenk, Daniel Kauffman, D. F. Driver. But Hershey once wrote late in May that he had not heard a Mennonite minister preach since March 6.[37] A union Sunday school soon fell apart.

The group held Bible study and Sunday school, but felt the great need for a resident pastor. Daniel Kauffman was the bishop of the flock, which had grown to seventeen members. He drove the 165 miles from Versailles to Palmyra twice a year.

In 1897 Jacob Hershey visited relatives in Pennsylvania. He carried an assignment from the congregation to find a preacher. After inquiries, he asked 28-year-old John M. Kreider whether he would consider a call to preach for them at Palmyra. On his return home, the congregation agreed that their bishop should extend this call. Hershey also wrote two letters, urging Kreider to accept the call of the Lord and the church. "We are just at the stage of our existence here as a church that we need help very bad, and I believe you are the one to help us," he wrote.

At the age of twenty, John Kreider had told the preachers at the Paradise Church that he wanted to be a Christian. They thought that one so young would hardly be capable of comprehending the meaning of salvation, but finally agreed to baptize him. Soon he was conducting a Sunday school in Ronks. He had only a grade-school education, but his grandmother Mellinger, who lived with his parents, had taught him much from the Bible when he was a child.[38]

In February 1898 at Paradise Bishop Isaac Eby ordained him, apparently not by lot, for service at Palmyra. Accompanying him to

Missouri was the John M. Hershey family. Mrs. Hershey was a sister of Mrs. Kreider.

The Kreiders settled on a rented farm with a twelve-room house. They went into dairy farming. Jacob Rohrer had developed dairying in the area. He had a creamery and a milk route in Palmyra and later opened a creamery in Hannibal. The Sunday product was a problem; Kreider would not sell milk that the cows gave on Sunday.

The coming of a pastor brought growth to the congregation. Other people moved in: Amos Landis from Oregon, Lee Naffziger from Johnson County, Ira Buckwalter and Martin Allison from Pennsylvania, Lewis Shank from Versailles (the one who had moved from Leeton to Florida in 1891, and now returned a widower). The membership grew to forty by 1906. Homes and schools were not large enough for meeting places. The Hardshell Baptist building in Palmyra, almost deserted, was rented. Here the Missouri Conference met in 1901. Young people drove from Versailles with "a real driver — Neal Driver." Andrew Shenk preached on "I also will show mine opinion" (Job 32:10), shaking his beard with conviction.

The organization of the congregation really dates from the arrival of Kreider. Ezra Buckwalter was soon ordained as deacon, but did not serve with mutual satisfaction and was relieved of his assignment. Later John H. Hershey was ordained in his place. Daniel Kauffman continued to serve as bishop until Kreider was ordained to that office in 1912. Kreider served as bishop also at Pea Ridge, Cherry Box, Linn, Hannibal, South English (Iowa), and Alpha (Minn.).

Jacob Rohrer had bought what was left of an old plantation farm. He sold this place to the Kreiders in 1906. John donated a corner of this farm for the building of a church in 1907. This was 2 1/2 miles east of Palmyra.

The church had a spirit of outreach. Meetings were held for a while on the Mississippi bottoms at Bay Island. There were services the first Sunday of each month at the County Infirmary for over fifty years. A number of the residents were converted. But the most permanent result was achieved at Pea Ridge, a community fifteen miles northwest of Palmyra. After several monthly appointments there the people asked for a series of nightly meetings. There were over twenty confessions, the nucleus of a congregation which grew up there (see p. 110).

There were many opportunities for preaching in the community: at funerals and various special occasions. One summer Kreider preached on the banks of North River. People sat on logs, in their buggies, or just stood during the service. One mother of a family nearby was converted. Monthly evening preaching services at the Sites schoolhouse were well attended. J. E. Hartzler and J. B. Smith held revival meetings there.

Children were taught to sing. There were singing schools by J. D. Brunk and Noah Showalter. J. H. Hershey liked to sing. Once he and his wife attended a singing in a Catholic home. But when the young people cleared the floor and began to dance, Hersheys thought they had better leave.

The church at Hannibal grew out of interest from Palmyra and Pea Ridge. Bishop Kreider cooperated closely with Nelson Kauffman in that work.

The congregation shared their pastor for much church work. He held many evangelistic meetings and Bible conferences. He was present in the historic meeting in Elkhart which appointed the denomination's first foreign missionaries, on February 12, 1899. He promoted education, sending all his children to Hesston College, and asking the family to go without a floor covering so they could give $25 to Goshen College. He served many years on the Mennonite Board of Education.

In the later years of the congregation John F. Kreider, Bishop Kreider's son, was deacon, and Harry Buckwalter, a brother of Mrs. Kreider, was pastor.

The congregation furnished the Mennonite Church a great many workers. J. R. Shank left school at Goshen and went to pastor at Pea Ridge and then to the Ozark mission field. He was single, and his sister Emma kept house for him. Mollie Shank became the wife of *Gospel Herald* editor and leading church statesman Daniel Kauffman (their marriage was the first performed by J. M. Kreider). Ira E. Buckwalter became pastor at Pea Ridge. Ruth Buckwalter was a city missionary at Chicago and Hannibal. J. W. Shank was influential in starting a mission in Argentina, and gave a lifetime of service there. Emma Hershey, as the wife of J. W. Shank, died in Argentina. J. M. Hershey was superintendent of the Mennonite Sanitarium at La Junta, Colorado, for many years. Charles Shank gave a term of service as a missionary in India. Emma Rohrer was a member of the first nurses' training class at La Junta, and was head nurse there for many years. Anna Kreider, wife of D. H. Bender, and later of H. A. Diener, was matron at Goshen College and at the Children's Home in Kansas City. Philip Kreider, before his early death from a brain tumor, was at the Kansas City Mission for two years. Paul Hershey and Elmer Hershey were bishop and deacon, respectively, at Gulfport, Mississippi. Kathryn Kreider was long a secretary at Mennonite Publishing House. John T. Kreider, son of John F., became a pastor in Kansas City and Orange, California. Harold, another son of John F., was superintendent of the Hannibal Mission, and then pastor at Osceola, Indiana.

Through the moving away of families and the employment of young people in other areas, the membership of the congregation, never large, was reduced to fifteen in 1955. And so in February 1956, it was disbanded. Six members were received at Pea Ridge, and six at Hannibal, both within easy driving distance in this day of automobiles and good roads. The church building was dismantled and the material taken to Pea Ridge for building needs there. Really, the congregation did not die; it just shifted its place of operation.

8. *Audrain County*

The last colonizing of the nineteenth century into Missouri was from Johnson County, Iowa, into east central Missouri. After a half century in eastern Iowa, some members were looking for cheaper land. While some went farther west, others looked to the south.

In the fall of 1897 three men drove with horse and buggy, about seventy miles a day, to the region to the east of Centralia. This is about fifty miles north of Jefferson City. They found pleasing farming country here, with land prices from $20 to $40 per acre. Crops did not look too good, but these Amish farmers felt the farming methods were poor, and that they could change that.

So in the spring of 1898 three families — J. C. Gingerichs, Elmer J. Guengerichs, and V. V. Swartzendrubers — moved down and bought or rented in the vicinity of Rowena, in Audrain County. Their address was Centralia, across the line in Boone County. In 1900 other families came, among them Preacher John Zimmerman from McPherson County, Kansas. The group met in homes for church services, but did not follow the Amish practice of eating the noon meal together. Sunday school was organized in 1900. All services were in German.

Other families moved in. Additional family names were Yoder

(Preacher Noah Yoder in 1902), Beachy (Emanuel, ordained minister in 1904),[39] Miller, Shetler, Nafziger, Overholt, Esch, and Hershberger. Some did not stay long. The highest number of families at one time was thirteen. They came mostly from Iowa, but also from Illinois, Michigan, and Texas.[40]

The community prospered. Farms ranged from 100 to 160 acres. They put up good houses and barns. Soil was built up and crops improved. Threshing in the neighborhood had been a long-drawn-out affair; at one place it took almost half a day to get the separator and the engine lined up. Thresherman Shem Swartzendruber could show them a better way.

But the Amish too had some things to learn. The hardpan subsoil was new to them. When the weather was dry, moisture could not get up through; and when it was wet, it could not go down through. Ponds and cisterns held water like jugs. Farming had to adapt to this. There were some crop failures.

Oversight of the congregation came from Iowa bishops. To keep up the German, the children had German Bible school for six weeks in the summer. The group supported the mission work of Rose Lambert in Turkey, and orphan work in India. They had visiting preachers: J. M. Kreider, A. C. Good, Fred Gingerich, C. D. Esch, Menno Esch, W. K. Miller. A plot of ground was leased from David Yoder, and seven persons were buried there; one, however, the wife of J. D. Guengerich, was later exhumed and buried beside her husband in Iowa. A church building was never constructed. The Strother schoolhouse was for some years the center of the settlement.

But gradually it became apparent that the colony would not last. In 1913 families began to move away: to Michigan, Iowa, Oklahoma, Kansas, Ohio, and Virginia. In 1917 the last two families left.

Community relations had been good. The people were from the South — Kentucky and Virginia. Confederate sympathies remained. There were blacks in the area, and when it seemed strange to the Amish that the whites did not eat with them, they were told, "Well, you eat with them and you will be counted one of them, that's all." These Amish with their beards and hooks and eyes and big black bonnets must have appeared very strange to their neighbors, but they were respected.

Several weeks before the last families — the Emanuel Beachys and the D. C. Esches — left, their neighbors came to see them. They said they would have been glad to attend their services if they had

been in English. They had learned to bake light bread, and the Mennonite women had learned to bake biscuits and real "co'nbread."
These neighbors were sorry to see the colony move away. They
helped to put their belongings on railroad cars. And they gave
them farewell with tears.

What forces caused this nineteen-year-old community to dissolve? One was controversy — over the telephone, for instance. Some
members got this new contraption into their homes; others felt that
it was too worldly. The argument broke fellowship. But there were
other causes too: crop failures, stormy weather — some building
cyclone shelters, blood ties in other places, poor hospital and medical
facilities, and some deaths. [41]

In 1867 J. M. Brenneman, of Elida, Ohio, after driving down
through Missouri, wrote: "A long time may elapse yet, till this
beautiful section of country shall all be inhabited." In Audrain
County there are six graves, once surrounded by a cement fence,
which testify to how much vision, consecration, hard work, and real
brotherhood it takes to invade a wilderness and build a successful
Christian community. It is too bad this one did not succeed; it had
so much of what it takes.

9. *Vernon County (Walker Settlement)*

This was a second attempt to colonize in this county (see
Stotesbury, p. 58). The first had been in the northwest corner of the
county. Walker is fifteen miles east of Stotesbury and nine miles
northeast of Nevada, the county seat.

Most of the people who went to Walker were from Yoder and
Hutchinson, Kansas. They had small farms and could not rent more
land. In May 1953 a group of five went land-hunting in Missouri and
Arkansas. Irvin Nussbaum, who was in school at Hesston College,
went with them as a potential member of the colony. The illness of
one of the men made them stop at Nevada overnight. They dropped
into a real-estate office, and the next morning looked at some farms,
which they liked.

While they wanted farms, they also wanted to stay together as
a group so that they could be a congregation and give a Christian
witness. All six of the men bought farms at $90 to $100 an acre.
One agent handled the whole deal, and all contracts were to be void
if six farms were not available. A community was assured, as all
the farms purchased were within a fifteen-mile radius.

The Mennonite church at Walker, Missouri, now owned and used by the Church of God in Christ, Mennonite

The families moved in July, August, and September of 1953. The congregation was organized on February 7, 1954, with bishops Harry A. Diener and J. G. Hartzler officiating. The following persons signed up as charter members: Eli, Opal, and Ivan Bontrager; Glen and Mary Kauffman; Irvin and Arlene Nussbaum; Russell and Blanch Showalter; Perry, Ruth, and Donnie Troyer; Melvin and Vicky Yoder; and George Holderman.

Holderman, a Mennonite minister who was teaching school at El Dorado Springs, eighteen miles east of Walker, preached for the group. But on March 14, according to the plan of the members, Nussbaum was ordained to serve as pastor. The ordination was by H. A. Diener, who was to serve as bishop of the congregation. There were fifty persons present, twenty-one of them visitors. The first communion was on March 21.

It was very dry in 1954, and the colony had to ship in two carloads of hay from Idaho. It was a difficult year, as the men had put everything into their purchases. The pastor especially, who was just beginning farming, was hard hit, but the others gave him some help. This mutual action no doubt strengthened the ties of brotherhood.

Others joined the group: Roy and Wilmer Millers from McPherson, Kansas, Richard Yoders from Hutchinson, Kansas, Lyle Wittricks from Nebraska, and Cecil Browns from Adair, Oklahoma. There were three brothers-in-law in the fellowship.

The congregation met first in the homes, then in an old school building. The community bought this for a community building, but services continued here. Quite a few community people were interested.

There came word that the White Hall church building at Oronogo, sixty miles to the south, was no longer being used. The remaining members there were willing to donate this building to the new congregation at Walker.

The building could not be moved intact because of steel bridges. In spite of objections from a few people who hated to lose a landmark, the building was dismantled in one day. The lumber was cleaned and stacked at Walker on a property which had been purchased. Buildings on this property were also torn down. So there was a big pile of clean lumber, and a building fund.

Building programs have often severely tested the unity of churches. So it happened here. The first plan had been to use the lumber to build a church like the one at Hutchinson, which used lumber from the Milan Valley church at Jet, Oklahoma. But some wanted a cinder-block building — nicer, but costing more. The block plan prevailed, which used some of the lumber, but not all of it. There was disagreement, too, about the type of furnace. The church was in use by March 1956, and by the end of the year the average attendance was forty.

Money had to be borrowed to pay for the blocks, and repayment became difficult, for some found it hard to pay their cash pledges. The lumber not used was auctioned off to members to build dairy barns. But still there was debt. Relations became tense, and members began to talk of moving away.

There were differences of opinion, also, about the use of television in the homes and an organ in the church.

The situation was further complicated by a change from bishop districts to state overseers. An overseer had been appointed by the conference for the Missouri churches. But some, including the pastor, wanted Bishop Diener to continue functioning at Walker. Diener lived in Kansas, and the older Kansas bishops did not feel free to function in Missouri churches. The South Central Conference failed to get this adjusted, and Pastor Nussbaum felt led to accept a pastoral assignment in Indiana. Other members left too. Efforts to find another pastor came to nothing.

The Church of God in Christ, Mennonite (Holdemans), have a large congregation at Rich Hill, in the next county to the north, and they were looking for room to expand. The building was sold to them, and most of the farms too. They took over the indebtedness on the church, and paid additional cash. The cash surplus was given to the South Central Mission Board.

Some members liked their homes and would have been glad to stay. They considered joining the Holdemans. But this would have required repudiating any earlier conversion and submitting to re-baptism, which they could not do.

So in 1962 this project, so well begun, failed after only nine years. Financially, the farmers were doing well. The soil was good and responded to good farming. They got out without financial loss, even with gain, for the land had doubled in cash value. The failure came from wrong congregational procedures, lack of brother-hood, and failure of leadership.

The members moved away. George Holderman had died suddenly in 1959, and was buried at Garden City.

At Walker, the Holdeman Mennonites, twenty-two families of them, fill the meetinghouse every Sunday.[42]

CHURCHES IN MISSOURI

CHAPTER

CHURCHES IN MISSOURI

1. *Mt. Pisgah, Shelby County*

The oldest Mennonite congregation in Missouri today is Mt. Pisgah, at Cherry Box, Shelby County. This is about forty-five miles west of Palmyra.

One of the early settlers in this area was Martin Lapp. But there are some problems as to where he lived in Missouri, and at what date. He was born in Clarence Center, New York, and later lived in Ontario. In 1840 he and his brother Samuel moved to Freeport, Stephenson County, Illinois, where he was ordained to the ministry, the first minister in the church there.[1]

From Freeport Lapp moved to Missouri. Weber in his history of the Illinois Mennonites says it was "early in the sixties." But Hartzler and Kauffman in their church history say it was about 1855.[2] However, in his *Mennonite Cyclopedic Dictionary*, Kauffman, the same author, says he came to Missouri "in the early sixties."[3] So it could have been during the Civil War (1861-1864), although that would have been a stormy time to come to Missouri. This may argue for an earlier date.

Where Lapp first moved to is also uncertain. *MCH* says that he labored with a small body of Amish Mennonites for a few years. The largest settlement of Amish Mennonites in those years, the only one for certain, was in Hickory County (see p. 45). Weber says Lapp was "the pioneer bishop of Missouri."[4] *MCD* repeats this, but neither author gives a source for this information nor tells us where he was ordained bishop. Would the Amish Mennonites have ordained a Mennonite (Lapp was not Amish) as their bishop? Perhaps the pressures of the frontier made it necessary.

From his first location, wherever it was, Lapp moved to Shelby County.[5] There he joined or was joined by other settlers from the several Mennonite settlements in northern Illinois. In 1865, quickly joining the tide of western migration after the Civil War, Benjamin Hershey bought 160 acres of prairie land from the Hannibal and St. Joseph Railroad for $2048. It was located fourteen miles north of Clarence, in the area of the present Mt. Pisgah Mennonite Church at Cherry Box. He bought additional farms for his sons and sons-in-law.

But Hershey did not move until 1871. Another Illinois buyer of Shelby County land in 1865 was Deacon Christian Lapp. Two of his brothers, Benjamin and Abraham, soon joined him.[6] Benjamin had been ordained to the ministry in Illinois, and Abraham was an "exhorter." In September 1866 the *Herald of Truth* listed among its subscribers Mrs. Leah Gsell at Shelbyville, fifteen miles to the southeast. Gsell was one of the family names at Morrison, Illinois.[7]

Benjamin Lapp was instrumental in organizing, probably before 1868, a congregation with twenty charter members. Although no records were kept, Deacon John G. Detwiler and Minister L. J. Johnston thought these were the charter members: Benjamin Lapp, Mariah Lapp, Abraham Lapp, Christian Lapp, Anna Lapp, Levi Mishler, Nancy Mishler, Jacob Cell, Mrs. Cell, Abraham Shellenberger, Lizzie Shellenberger, ————— Potter, Barbara Potter, John Brubaker, Maggie Brubaker, David Hershey, Lizzie Hershey, Jacob W. Johnston, Lydia Johnston.

Daniel Brundage, the bishop in Morgan County, visited the settlement in Shelby County in October 1868. He had to walk the fourteen miles from Clarence to Cherry Box. He visited the Christian Lapps and reported "some ten members under pastoral care of Benjamin and ————— Lapp." The pastor whose name he could not remember was probably Abraham Lapp.[8]

Deacon Abraham Shellenberger wrote from Cherry Box, whither he had moved from Elkhart, Indiana, that there were eighteen members, with three ministers: Benjamin Hershey, Benjamin Lapp, and Abraham Lapp.[9] Hershey had been ordained bishop at Sterling, Illinois, in 1870, and he moved to Cherry Box in 1871. Here he served as bishop until 1888. For a few years he was in feeble health.[10]

Martin Lapp is never mentioned in the contemporary documents which we have, nor does he have a place in the oral traditions of the congregation. Perhaps he left Cherry Box before the congregation was organized. If he did indeed live in Shelby County, perhaps he lived so far from Cherry Box that he was not counted as one of the flock there. Or perhaps he was too old or incapacitated to serve in the ministry, as he died "at a ripe old age." We do know that he returned to Freeport, where he died in 1875.

Worship services were first conducted in the homes of the members and later at the Oak Hill schoolhouse one fourth of a mile north of Cherry Box. The first church house was built in 1872 about 1 1/2 miles south of Cherry Box.[11] Services were held every two weeks, with the Church of the Brethren using the building on alternate Sundays. In 1899 this building was sold to the Brethren, and the Mt. Pisgah Church built another building one fourth of a mile south of Cherry Box. This second building, remodeled in 1950, is still in use. The remodeling included a full basement, a heating plant, and an addition at each end. A new oak floor was laid in 1952, and new pews were installed in 1962. Cloakrooms and rest rooms were added in 1971, with the water piped in from the neighboring farm of Joe Yoder.

In the early days Ben Lapp took a disabled old man named George Boiler into his home. Boiler was baptized into the Brethren Church. In connection with this matter, there were what *MCH* calls "imprudent" actions of Ben Lapp. His ministry was taken from him. When Lapp left the community, Boiler went to stay with Chris Lapp. Later both Chris and Abe Lapp joined the Brethren. This whole matter caused much difficulty, and of course was hard on the life of the church.[12]

Henry Yother, of Nebraska, held evangelistic meetings here in 1884, probably the first at Mt. Pisgah. The Evangelizing Committee of the Missouri Conference helped with his traveling expenses. J. S. Coffman, pioneer Mennonite evangelist who gave much time to the churches in Missouri and Kansas, was there in February 1886. The church was too small for the crowds, and the services were moved to the Methodist Church. Coffman wrote:

"The church here has passed through many trials, and many of the members connected with us have moved away, as is usually the case in new settlements. But they seem at present to be enjoying a fair degree of prosperity."[13]

Coffman was at Mt. Pisgah again in 1890, and there were nine confessions.

The Sunday school was organized in 1885.[14] The German Sunday school which Abraham Shellenberger reported in 1871 may have been only a school for teaching the children to read German. The Sunday school was not "evergreen" until 1900. Teachers were changed every quarter. The following report describes the school in 1892:

"Largest attendance for year, 54; smallest, 29; average, 40. We conducted our Sunday school in the following order: Introduction read and commented on by our superintendent, hearing of general questions, singing, repeating text verses, prayer by superintendent, reading of lessons, etc."[15]

Quarterly Sunday school conferences were held at Palmyra in 1907 and at Mt. Pisgah in 1908. These have continued among the northeastern Missouri churches to the present time. The first Bible conference was held in 1905. Young People's Meetings were begun as early as 1906.

The second conference of all the Missouri churches was held at Mt. Pisgah in 1874. For years this conference alternated each fall between Mt. Pisgah and Mt. Zion, at Versailles. In 1899 the conference met in the new church building.

The membership at Mt. Pisgah has never been large. The fluctuations in growth are shown in these figures: 1871, 18; 1880, 13; 1887, 16; 1893, 25; 1897, 35; 1908, 28; 1921, 42; 1931, 35; 1946, 31; 1951, 49 (the peak); 1971, 44. In 1896, when a young man convert joined the church, it was reported that he was the only young person in the church.[16] One reason for the church's failure to grow was that most of the members were more or less closely related. In 1946 all of the eight families in the church were related except one. Many of the young people found their marriage partners outside the church, and some were lost to the brotherhood.

But in 1946 Bishop Nelson Kauffman began working to get new blood into the church. It started when Daniel Kauffman moved in from Yoder, Kansas, to become pastor. Since then other families have moved in from Kansas, Oklahoma, Illinois, Pennsylvania, and California. The bloodstream of the congregation was almost completely changed. In 1968, of the 44 members, only four had been born in Shelby County. A survey by Nelson Kauffman showed that Mt. Pisgah is unusually receptive to "outsiders" coming into the church. People are getting better acquainted with the Mennonites. Members are active in the CROP program. Each year a Golden Age Banquet for all the elderly in the community helps to build bridges. Union services are held on Good Friday and Thanksgiving Day with local Church of the Brethren and Christian churches.

In 1876 John L. Brubaker, one of the charter members, was ordained to the ministry. He served at Mt. Pisgah until 1895, when he moved to Shannon County in a mission colonizing project of the congregation. In his later years at Mt. Pisgah he carried a pretty heavy part of the ministerial load. His struggle to make a living was recognized by the Missouri Conference in 1892 in the following brotherly resolution: "Since J. L. Brubaker is financially embarrassed, we recommend that he should be helped, either by loans at low interest, or by gifts."[17] His move to Shannon County was made possible by the help he received from brethren in several states.

There were two ordinations in 1894: John G. Detwiler as deacon, and Lafayette J. Johnston as minister. Wallace J. Kauffman, who had moved from Cass County in 1894, was ordained as minister in 1897. He has been described as an earnest worker with a good delivery. But his ministry was brief. He stepped on a nail, and after much agonizing pain died of lockjaw in 1899. George Bissey was ordained to the ministry in 1902, and was married to Hannah, daughter of J. L. Brubaker, in 1906. He preached until his death in 1942. Preacher John M. Yoder moved from Michigan in 1920, and served until he retired, and he and his wife, Nancy, moved to Parnell, Iowa, in 1951. L. J. Johnston died in 1940.

Daniel Kauffman, from Kansas, ordained as minister in 1946 and bishop in 1951, has served as pastor since 1948, except for the period from September 1959 to June 1961 when he was interim pastor at Hannibal, Missouri. During this interim John Otto, who had been living in Florida, was called by the congregation and licensed for the ministry. He served as pastor 1960-1962. He enrolled at Hesston College in September 1962. From 1956 to 1970 (fifteen years) Daniel Kauffman served as overseer of all the churches of Missouri in the South Central Conference.

The Mt. Pisgah Church has had six bishops in its history of over one hundred years. Benjamin Hershey was the first and only resident bishop until the Daniel Kauffman now serving was ordained to that office. After Hershey's death in 1888, David Kauffman of Versailles succeeded him as bishop. He was followed by his son, the

Daniel Kauffman, 1916-

first Daniel Kauffman. In 1912, several years after Kauffman moved to Scottdale, Pennsylvania, to edit the *Gospel Herald*, J. M. Kreider of Palmyra was ordained at Mt. Pisgah to be bishop of all the churches of northeast Missouri. At his death in 1946 he was followed by Nelson E. Kauffman. The second Bishop Daniel Kauffman is now pastor-bishop-overseer of Mt. Pisgah. He receives part-time support for his pastoral work in the congregation, and is permitted to give one third of his time and effort to his conference work. Since 1964 the congregation does the pastor's farm work for him, as a part of his support.

The congregation has had six deacons also. Christian Lapp and Abraham Shellenberger served terms of unknown length in the unrecorded early years. John G. Detwiler was ordained in 1892; he died in 1930. Noah Detwiler was ordained in 1922 and moved to Hesston in 1964. Reuben Harder was ordained at Versailles and moved to Mt. Pisgah in 1940; he died in 1968. Ben Detwiler, the incumbent deacon, was given that office in 1955.

Up to June 1948 the giving at Mt. Pisgah was done only by heads of families, who once a month filled out a form something like this:

India Orphans	*$2.00*
General Missions	*1.00*
District Conference	*1.00*
Home Support	*1.00*

The giving totaled less than $750 per year.

But in June 1948 a plan went into effect which literally revolutionized the giving program. The offering became a part of the Sunday morning service. For the first time offering plates were passed, and every member was given an opportunity to contribute. The offerings were not given to specified causes Sunday by Sunday, but to the Lord for the work of the church. The money given was prorated on a percentage basis to all the causes named in the budget which was adopted in the annual business meeting of the church.

The amount of the offerings went up immediately, and has continued to rise every year. From 1948 to 1968 giving increased from $750 to $8,370.

The church giving in 1967-68 went by the following percentages:

Home Support	*50%*
WMSA	*6 1/2*
Board of Missions	*20*
District Conference	*8*
Goshen Seminary	*2*
Area Overseer	*3*
Christian Civic Foundation	*1/2*

The total giving for that year averaged $191.23 per member, which was above the denominational average. Counting only the resident members who did the giving, that figure was $274.12 per member. The total given in the 1970-71 fiscal year was $11,944.54, which averages $271.44 for each member.

The list of evangelists who have labored at Mt. Pisgah through the years in the annual efforts to gather in the lost reads almost like a roll call of active Mennonite evangelists. Here are some of them: E. J. Berkey, S. S. Hershberger, L. J. Miller, J. D. Mininger, J. F. Bressler, Perry Shenk, B. B. King, James Bucher, E. F. Hartzler, Allen H. Erb, William Jennings, H. J. King, Nelson E. Kauffman, J. W. Hess, Wilbur Yoder, George R. Brunk, Elam Hollinger, Leonard Garber, Richard Birky, Hubert Schwartzentruber, James Detweiler, J. J. Hostetler, Ivan Headings, Harold Zehr, Leamon Sowell.[18]

2. *Sycamore Grove, Cass County*

The beginnings of the Sycamore Grove congregation in the Clearfork Church have been told in the story of the Bethel congregation (see p. 46).

Sycamore Grove Church before the remodeling of 1950

When it became clear that it was not workable for the Eicher and Kenagy groups to alternate in their services at Clearfork, Bishop J. C. Kenagy cited the example of Isaac in not contending for the wells he had dug. So they should build another church.[19] On November 8, 1882, the group met and decided to build a new house of worship. J. K. Zook was the chairman of the meeting, with D. J. Schrock as secretary. The building committee chosen was Isaac M. Yoder, Jonas Kurtz, and J. K. Zook.[20]

The site chosen was a scenic spot just north of the forks of Clearfork Creek, in a grove of sycamore trees. It is four miles northwest of Garden City, and less than a mile northeast of the old Clearfork Church. From this time the congregation took the name of Sycamore Grove.

The first trustees were Joe Miller, Michael Kurtz, and Stephen Kauffman. The church building, planned by J. K. Zook, was completed in the spring of 1883, and dedicated that autumn. The cost was about $2,500. The building was thirty-eight by sixty feet. As later remodeled, this structure still serves the congregation.

In front of the church there was a stile, or platform, near the doors, along the drive. Buggies and surreys were driven along the stile, and the occupants, particularly the women and children, could step out on it and then descend by steps to the ground level. There were two entrances, one for men and one for women, on either side of the pulpit, which was located on one of the longer sides of the room. There was no entrance on the side opposite the pulpit. The people going in faced the ones already there. This arrangement made it possible to see who was coming in without any turning of heads and stretching of necks. Coming to church late in that building had its automatic penalty of being stared at.

The men sat to the left, the women to the right. The main block of seats, in the center, had, until about 1910, a solid partition in the middle. One could not walk from one side to the other except through the back seat, next to the wall. This opening was used at funerals when the congregation walked in front of the pulpit to view the corpse, and then returned to their seats.

The first remodeling was in 1924. The entire building was raised two feet, a basement put in, the roof raised three feet to improve the acoustics, new flooring laid, walls plastered, new benches provided, extra windows added, and an addition built back of the pulpit. A Delco light plant was installed. (Since 1940 electric power has come from Rural Electric Administration.)

The second main remodeling was in 1949-50, after the merger with Bethel. The basement was enlarged and a new oil furnace was installed. A rear entrance was provided, with two cloakrooms and a vestibule. The church drive was relocated. As compared with the total building cost of $2,500 in 1883, this remodeling cost about $4,000.

At this time, also, the remaining lumber from the dismantled Bethel Church was used to build the church cottage. Located in the churchyard, it provides facilities for supplementary audiences, meetings of men or women separately, youth meetings, Sunday school classes, and family reunions.

At the time of the Eicher schism the membership at Clearfork was about 150. A third of those left, to form, after a decade, the Bethel congregation. And so Sycamore Grove, at its beginning, had about 100 members. This number grew to a peak of about 350 by 1894 and remained there until 1910. Part of this was from biological increase. Amish families were large. At one time, in 1908, thirty new members were baptized at one time; in 1910 thirty-three were baptized. But part of the increase was by continued migration from other Amish and Mennonite communities.

In 1911, however, more than sixty members withdrew to form a new congregation at Pryor, Oklahoma. Some of these, a few years later, moved on to Shelbyville, Illinois. This was not exactly a schism, although some who moved felt that Sycamore Grove was getting too worldly.

But a major factor in this division was the influence of the "sleeping preacher," John D. Kauffman. The "sleeping preacher" phenomenon first appeared in Amish communities in the 1880s. Four different persons in Mennonite circles were reported to have the power to preach complete sermons while in a state somewhat like a trance.[21]

The most influential of these was John D. Kauffman. He was born in Ohio, and exercised his unusual ministry in northern Indiana, in central Illinois, and in various Amish communities to which he was invited. He preached as a layman until his last few years, when he was ordained as bishop by his followers at Shelbyville, Illinois.

By some who heard him, Kauffman's preaching was regarded as directly inspired from heaven. "Spirit-preaching," they called it. Pius Hostetler would refer to what Kauffman said with such phrases as "the Spirit told us."[22] Kauffman's message was primarily a warning against those who disobey God's commandments. He encouraged many of the traditional practices, such as shunning, or the ban, and the use of German. He said Jesus was coming very soon.

This strange ministry came to Cass County four different times: 1882, 1892, 1896, and 1910. The community was divided concerning him. The ministers could not accept him, and he was not permitted to speak in the church. So he preached in Dave Hostetler's big house or in Ben Hartzler's new barn. It was just after his last visit that the migration to Pryor took place, and those who left were Kauffman's supporters.

As the congregation went on through the twentieth century, the membership figures have trended downward:

1908 - 350	*1948 - 258*
1918 - 290	*1958 - 225*
1925 - 272	*1966 - 200*
1932 - 285	*1972 - 145*
1942 - 206	

The loss was not great before the 1930s, except for the Pryor migration. But in the decade of the Depression economic pressures scattered the people of this agricultural community. The merger with Bethel in 1947 brought the roll up again, but the loss rate continued. In 1968 the start of the Harrisonville congregation (see p. 151) once more reduced the Sycamore Grove membership by more than fifty.

Jacob C. Kenagy was an outstanding leader. Born in Union County, Pennsylvania, in 1821, he moved to Mifflin County and then to Logan County, Ohio. He taught school in both Pennsylvania and Ohio. When he started to farm, he lived in a log house, and almost froze to death. He was progressive, being the first person in Logan County to own a sewing machine. He helped to organize the first permanent Mennonite Sunday school at South Union.[23] In 1850 he was ordained to the ministry, and a few years later as a bishop. He moved to Missouri in 1866, and organized in Cass County the Clearfork congregation of eight members, the story of which is told on p. 47 above. He saw it grow to almost 400.

He was on the side of broad-minded church rule, but always worked for peace. He did much visiting in homes, and was loved by his people. He held firmly to his principles. In 1862 at an Amish conference he defended baptism in a stream rather than a church. In his time he baptized hundreds, but everyone in a stream. He never preached at the Bethel Church, which represented a schism from his own bishop rule.

He always wore hooks and eyes on a frock-tail coat, and had a red chin beard. He helped to organize the Western District Amish Mennonite Conference in 1883. At the first session, held at Sycamore Grove, one of the questions was, "Is it permissible, in view of Bible teachings on nonconformity, to allow brethren to wear buttons on their clothes instead of hooks and eyes?" The next year the conference decided against making this a test of membership. All his life he had to struggle with questions like this. He never owned a buggy, but drove a good team hitched to a spring wagon.

A story that has come down through the years shows how resourceful Kenagy was in his church administration. A delegation from another community wished to consult with him about moving to Cass County. Already the bishop's work was difficult because he had members who wanted the church rules they had where they came from. Kenagy must have known what kind of clothing legalism this delegation represented and did not want them to come to Cass County. On the day they were to come, Kenagy dressed in an outfit belonging to one of his sons — suit, stiff-bosomed shirt, stand-up collar, and tie. He met the delegation and discussed their proposed move. They did not discuss clothing regulation. But the men decided not to come to this community, which was all right with Kenagy.[24]

Kenagy was well read, and a good Bible teacher. He was especially interested in prophecy. He died in March 1894 at the age of seventy-three. He had a heart attack while preaching on a Sunday morning and died a few weeks later. In 1893 he had lost his house by fire, and the early records of the church were lost with the house.

John J. Hartzler, Sycamore Grove's second bishop, was born in Mifflin County, Pennsylvania, in 1845, but moved with his parents to Michigan. There he was ordained to the ministry at the age of 29. He moved to Missouri in 1880. On the death of Kenagy, he was ordained bishop by Bishop Joseph Schlegel, of Milford, Nebraska. During his bishopric the church came to its maximum size, the language of the services was changed to English, and the Sunday school became a vital part of church life. He succeeded in keeping such cultural changes as the coming of the telephone and the automobile from becoming church issues. Naturally a reserved man, he was a lovable person and an effective leader. He officiated at eighty-two marriages and baptized over three hundred persons at Sycamore Grove. He had oversight of churches in Johnson County, Hickory County, Vernon County, Oklahoma, Arkansas, and North Dakota. Because he knew the young people did not understand German, he turned to English preaching in the last part of his life, and did it well, although his Scripture memorization was in German.

In 1914, at the age of sixty-nine, he had the wisdom unusual for his times to ordain a younger bishop, and to turn responsibilities over to him. He died in 1937 at the age of ninety-one.

Isaac G. Hartzler, another native of Mifflin County, Pennsylvania, came to Cass County in 1880 at the age of eighteen, and lived here the rest of his life. He was ordained deacon in 1904 and bishop in 1914. He had an outgoing personality, and was called to preach the funerals of many non-Mennonites. He wore a beard, and was a dignified-appearing person. Like other Amish Mennonite preachers of his time, he wore a lapel coat, without a tie. When the conferences merged in the 1920s there was pressure on him to wear a "plain" coat, which he yielded to with reluctance. His service to the church at large included the moderatorship of the Missouri-Kansas Conference. Five years before his passing in 1946, at the age of eighty-one, he turned bishop and pastoral responsibilities at Sycamore Grove over to his successor, W. Raymond Hershberger.

Hershberger lived his entire life in Cass County, and served Sycamore Grove as Sunday school teacher, superintendent, minister (ordained in 1939), and bishop (1941). He also served as bishop for five other congregations in Missouri and Kansas City. He served two years as moderator of the South Central Conference. He was an exemplary, faithful leader, and envisioned changes which he did not live to bring about. His heavy responsibilities were beyond his physical strength, and he died suddenly in January 1954. His death marked the end of an era in Sycamore Grove history.

In 1954 the South Central Conference replaced bishops with regional overseers in most of its congregations. So a new bishop was not ordained. Daniel Kauffman, as overseer for Missouri, gave general guidance. At the suggestion of the conference, Earl Buckwalter came from Hesston to serve for a year as temporary pastor. A church council was appointed to work with the pastor, to help make decisions regarding the standards and policies of the church, and to present recommendations to the congregation for approval or veto. The new era would put more responsibility on the lay members.

In July 1955 James D. Yoder, a son of the congregation, was ordained to serve as pastor. He was the first seminary-trained minister of the church and the first to be given financial support. The church bought a parsonage, with twenty acres of land. For three years the support was partial, and Yoder continued teaching school. In his fourth year, for the first time, the congregation gave its pastor full support. But in the summer of 1959 he resigned to further his education and to enter the field of educational counseling. The parsonage was sold, and property was purchased nearer to the church.

In September 1959 Leonard Garber became pastor. He had served an earlier pastorate at Winton, California, and came to Sycamore Grove after further schooling at Hesston College. He was given full support. He took some seminary and college work while here. He was a good teacher and an aggressive leader, cooperated well with ministers of other denominations, and won the respect of the community. But in May 1964 he resigned and moved to Indiana — to a new pastorate, to schoolwork at Goshen, and to the service program of the Mission Board at Elkhart.

Again an older man, Harry A. Diener, served on an interim basis — from August 1964 to September 1965. At that time Earl Eberly came from a four-year pastorate at Lyon Street, Hannibal, Missouri, to Sycamore Grove. He was born in Ohio. He attended school at Hesston. He led Sycamore Grove in the development of a new congregation at Harrisonville (see p. 151).

Other ministers and deacons, not designated as bishops or pastors, served the congregation under its system of multiple ministry. Moses Yoder, ordained in 1872, moved to Oregon in 1888. Joseph H. Byler moved here from Mifflin County, Pennsylvania, in 1889, but returned there in 1891. Peter Zimmerman moved in from Larned, Kansas, in 1889, and then to Peach Orchard, Arkansas, in 1896. David Morrell, from Johnson County, lived here one year 1897-1898. Andrew Miller, also from Johnson County, came in 1900 and moved to California in 1908. B. F. Hartzler was ordained in 1897 and moved to Pryor, Oklahoma, in 1911. Christian Reesor came from Illinois in 1907, and returned there in 1910. He lived to the age of 103.[25]

Levi J. Miller had a long and significant ministry at Sycamore Grove. He was ordained in 1894, at the age of twenty-seven, by the unanimous call of the church. He knew he needed to know the Bible much better, and so he made it a rule, every day just after dinner, to systematically read and study the Word. He was a very effective preacher. Once after a rather dramatic sermon, Jonathan Zook, an older member, told him he had preached a very good sermon, but warned him that the devil could also be very well pleased and would seek to make him proud. L. J. later testified that it was the best thing that ever happened to him. Miller held evangelistic meetings in twenty-two states and three provinces of Canada. He was president of the Missouri-Kansas Mission Board for seventeen years. The last fifteen years of his life were spent in Idaho and Kansas with his children. At the age of eighty-five he preached his last sermon at Upland, California. He died in 1952.

Another minister who preached some years at Sycamore Grove was S. S. Hershberger. Born in Indiana in 1883, he was ordained in 1913 to preach at Sycamore Grove. He served as field evangelist of the South Central Conference and conducted 125 series of evangelistic meetings. In his last years he lost his voice, and spent much time writing poetry.

Chauncey A. Hartzler, one of the sons of Bishop J. J. Hartzler, was ordained for mission work in Kansas City in 1906. He moved to Tiskilwa, Illinois, in 1913 for a long pastorate there. He was ordained bishop in 1914. His death came in 1947, although he had retired some years earlier. Another missionary ordination was that of S. Paul Miller. He was appointed by the Mennonite Board of Missions for service, and sailed for India in July 1941, after having been ordained by I. G. Hartzler. On arrival in India he was married to Vesta Nafziger, who had taught two years in India before his arrival. Together they have given more than thirty years to educational, medical, pastoral, and administrative work in India. In 1973 he brought to a conclusion the difficult task of transferring all mission property to the Indian church. Then he became development director at Yeotmal Seminary, and in 1974 was directing the move of that school to Nagpur.

Glen Yoder was ordained in 1945 to serve in the pastorate at Protection, Kansas. He taught in the mission school at Culp, Arkansas, and later became superintendent of the Mennonite Children's Home at Argentine, Kansas. His next assignment was as administrator at the Sunshine Children's Home, at Maumee, Ohio, 1964-1971. He is now director of an Ohio district office for the Division of Mental Retardation; his office is in Toledo.

George Hostetler was a deacon in the early years, but he moved to Oregon. The next deacon was I. G. Hartzler, ordained in 1904. John L. Zook moved here from Pennsylvania about 1910 and assisted with the deacon's work for several years before returning to Pennsylvania. In 1916, two years after I. G. Hartzler was ordained bishop, Frank P. Kauffman and Emery E. Yoder were elected, not ordained, as visiting brethren. They served thus until Frank Kauffman's death in 1930. Then in 1931 John A. Kauffman was ordained deacon.

In 1942 another retired missionary came to Cass County: Ezra Bowman, who had worked in Kansas City and the Osage River rural field. He passed to his reward in 1961.

Replacing Pastor Earl Eberly in 1969 was Elmer Yoder, another veteran bishop who had served at Allensville, Pennsylvania, and North Lawrence, Ohio. Although his was an interim appointment, he served until July 1972 when Kenneth Steckley, a Nebraskan who studied at Hesston College, became the new pastor.

Born in the Mennonite (Bethel and Sycamore Grove) community were many church leaders who have served in other areas. Among them are Joe D. Hartzler, bishop at Flanagan, Illinois; Henry J. King, bishop at Arthur, Illinois; Owen Hershberger, minister at Hesston, Kansas; Elmer D. Hershberger, bishop at Detroit Lakes, Minnesota; Nelson E. Kauffman, bishop at Hannibal, Missouri; Carl A. Kauffman, deacon at Creston, Montana; Jonathan Zook, bishop at Canby, Oregon; Milo Kauffman, bishop at Hesston, Kansas; J. E. Hartzler, president of Goshen College; J. G. Hartzler, bishop at Windom, Kansas; Oliver Hostetler, deacon at West Liberty (Kansas); John Harnish, minister at Eureka, Illinois; Lawrence Greaser, missionary in Puerto Rico; Allen Zook, minister at Versailles, Missouri.

The Sunday school organized at the Clearfork schoolhouse in the spring of 1868[26] was one of the early ones in the Mennonite Church. But it was twenty-five years before the Sunday school was fully accepted as a part of the Sunday service of the church. At first, those interested brought basket lunches and the Sunday school was held in the afternoon. The lessons were simply chapters read from the New Testament. The children were taught to read German, with secular material at first. "Tickets," small cards with a Bible verse and a picture, were given to children who memorized Bible verses. For a certain number of tickets the child received a larger card. For many years, after the class period there was a "review," with the children gathered on the front benches. The attendance record was secured by the secretary standing on the platform and counting the people. In 1896 the Sunday school became evergreen.

English was first used for the children's classes about 1895, and gradually for the whole group. Christopher Hostetler, father of Pius Hostetler, was one of the strong opponents of the use of English. One night he dreamed he saw a number of thirsty people standing around a well where cool water was being pumped. The people did not drink. He asked them in German why they did not drink. No one moved. Then someone told him these people understood only English. So he asked them in English, and immediately they began to drink. The dream convinced Hostetler of the need for adopting the English language.

Teachers were chosen by the pupils themselves. About 1915 teachers for children's classes were appointed, and ten years later, all teachers. Lesson quarterlies were first purchased in 1909. Muddy roads sometimes kept the Sunday school from meeting. Attendance improved when the road past the church was graveled. Branch schools developed with the growth of the missionary spirit: at the Zion School in 1907, and at Hadsel and Mount Zenia in 1921. For many years support was given in workers and funds to Sunday schools in the Osage River area.

The first Young People's Meeting was organized in 1893. Denominational helps for the Sunday evening meeting have been used in planning these meetings.

Mennonite Youth Fellowship, from about 1950, has been very active, taking the place of the earlier literary society. The youth have visited jails and nursing homes, maintained tract racks, given Christmas treats for the elderly, raised funds for mission projects, bought new hymnbooks, carpeted the church aisles, attended area and churchwide conventions.

The Sewing Circle met in the I. G. Hartzler home for the first time in June 1914. It has been an active group for many years, adopting the name of Women's Missionary and Service Auxiliary, and then changing Auxiliary to Commission. It now meets monthly in the church cottage. Another women's organization, formed in 1938, is the Mothers' Club, which has now become Homemakers. Each fall this group sponsors a Golden Age Banquet for members seventy and above. A Junior Sewing Circle (GMSA) was organized in 1940. Later this group became the Busy Bees and Wayfarers.

A Men's Fellowship functioned for a few years (1956-1963). There is now active participation in Mennonite Disaster Service. For a few years Pastor Leonard Garber had a "Boys' Shop" in a converted chicken house.

Singing has held a very large place in the life of this community. I. G. Hartzler once said it was the singing that kept him in Cass County. Until the 1920s instrumental music in the homes was frowned upon, and of course in the church there was nothing more than a tuning fork to give the song leaders their pitch.

For sixty years singing schools were held, in which all the young people learned to read music by syllables and so to sing hymns and gospel songs without the help of instrument or another person. Some of the singing-school teachers were Menno Detweiler, David Kauffman, Niles Slabaugh, Frank Blough, Simon Hartzler, Mose Hostetler, Emery Yoder, and Jess D. Hartzler. Simon Hartzler taught in Cass County for fifteen years or more. He was trained in the "music normals" of the singing-school movement, and knew such evangelistic singers as D. B. Towner, E. O. Excell, and P. P. Billhorn. The singing schools at first were held in schoolhouses, but later in the church.

Emery Yoder made a great contribution to Sycamore Grove singing as teacher, song leader, and chorus director. He took leadership in the social singings, which were held on Saturday evenings. These were social events which everybody attended. The songs were chiefly of the gospel hymn type so popular in that period. The song leading was passed around, so that many became competent. A few of the leaders were Levi Miller, Lee Zook, Sam Hershberger, Henry King, Amandus Hartzler, Clarence Hartzler, Will Kropf, Owen Hershberger, and Elmer Hershberger. When the Young People's Meeting committee selected song leaders, they had a list of more than fifty from which to choose, including many girls.

Another person much interested in Sycamore Grove music was Jess D. Hartzler. Visiting singing-school teachers recognized his talent and encouraged him to begin on his own. He was an accomplished song leader. He collected music books, and became perhaps the best-informed hymnologist in the Mennonite Church. His books are now a special collection in the Goshen College library.

The Sunday evening meeting at Sycamore Grove Church was often a song practice period, sometimes as often as once a month. Emery Yoder had charge of most of these. They learned new songs and corrected mistakes in the songs they knew. Many people became able to detect musical inaccuracies. In any meeting which was to feature singing there was usually a larger attendance.

"Special singing," in Mennonite parlance, is the singing of a small group — a quartet, octet, or chorus — to which the rest of the congregation listens, as they would to a spoken message. Such special music was slow in coming to Sycamore Church. Leaders felt it would foster pride and crowd out congregational singing. The Bethel Church had no rule against special singing, and so Sycamore Grove people first became involved in it in the Young People's Meetings held conjointly at Bethel on alternate Sundays. About 1904 a small group sang a song one evening. But there may have been critical talk about it, for no one tried it again until 1914. Dan Driver, Trusie Zook, and Lucy Yoder were home from Hesston, and there was a social singing at Trusie's home. These three and Ethel Yohn, Cora Schrock, Clarence Hartzler, Fred Plank, and J. D. Hartzler sang a number which had been used at Hesston. They later sang it at Bethel, to the delight of the congregation. The men's quartet of this group continued singing together, and sang at funerals. Later there was a quartet of Sycamore Grove men: Clarence, Amandus, and J. D. Hartzler, and Emery Yoder. There was a request for them to sing at a funeral, then in a regular meeting. The ministers consented (about 1914) and special music was on its way. There were other quartets and Emery Yoder organized men's and mixed choruses.

One thing that helped to bring the change was the fact that L. J. Miller, a well-liked leader, while holding meetings away from home, frequently participated in special singing. In discussions of the question he would simply admit this but would not argue against the prejudices of other ministers. At last the bishop no longer objected or simply acquiesced. But the special singing never crowded out the excellent congregational singing.

During World War I the position of the church against war brought misunderstanding and mistreatment from county and government officials. Community resentment increased, as people buried their sons killed in battle, and as the government practically used compulsion to get the required funds. Jacob Stehman was taken on the road near Garden City and tarred and feathered. S. S. Hersh-

berger was put in jail, though not convicted by any court. The
county judge told the sheriff to pick up J. C. Driver on the pre-
text of protecting him from the mob. The church expected her drafted
men to refuse military participation. According to the plan agreed
upon by a General Conference committee, the draftee was to go to
camp, but there refuse to wear the uniform or do any work beyond
caring for his own needs. Members of the church were to refuse to
buy war bonds.

Ora Hartzler was the first man drafted from Sycamore Grove. He
took in camp the stand of a conscientious objector, and was treated
severely. At least four other men were drafted. The experience of J.
D. Hartzler was typical. He arrived at Camp McArthur, Waco, Texas,
on September 7, 1918. The officers told him either to accept work
or get down and pray. He knelt and prayed for his persecutors. In
the stockade the prisoners held a mock trial and sentenced him to
a hundred lashes. They carried this out, for the last sixty-five
lashes using the buckle-end of the belt. That same evening in
another mock trial he was sentenced to five hundred more lashes
to be given the next evening. While carrying out this sentence they
would stop occasionally and ask whether he would work now. Receiving a negative answer each time, they began again until the whole
sentence was carried out. After a period in the hospital with the flu,
he was placed into solitary confinement on a bread-and-water diet.
His cell was damp and cold.[27]

J. D. Hartzler was court-martialed on November 26. The officer
assigned to his defense pointed out that he had showed no defiance
or sullenness. "To suspect this meek and mild-mannered young
man of being guilty of German propaganda or suspicious acts, is
impossible," he told the court. But Hartzler was declared guilty
and sentenced to five years' imprisonment at Fort Leavenworth, Kansas. As he left, a lieutenant said, "I'll bet you fight the next time."

He was released January 7, 1919. He left the fort in shirt
sleeves and overalls, though the temperature was below zero. While
awaiting his release papers, he slept on two bales of hay in a supply
building. To get his release he had to accept pay for his time spent
in the army camp. He spent some of this for an overcoat and to get
home. But as soon as he could earn it, he returned the money to the
government, and has a receipt showing that it was accepted.

It was because neither the church nor the government wanted to
repeat such experiences that later draft laws have provided a more

humane way to meet the conscientious-objector problem. In World War I the church expected its young men to bear the brunt of persecution in the army camps, where they did not belong. It was not the intent of the War Department that they should be abused there. But human nature being what it is, and channels of communication being so clogged under the stress of war, what might have been expected did happen. Circumstances were not pleasant in the home community, but the young men thrust into the maw of the war monster were the victims of what one of them called "a horrible arrangement." Perhaps on the whole they were more nonresistant than the folks back home who expected so much of them.

A few more details of Sycamore Grove history are of interest. For six months in 1960 a weekly program supplied by the congregation and entitled "The Way of Hope" was released over KDKD. Following that the Mennonite Broadcast "Way to Life" was used and paid by gifts from the church. The *Gospel Herald* Every Home Plan was adopted in May 1962. In the fall of 1965 the congregation accepted a recommendation of the church council "to observe open communion for all those who are of evangelical faith, in good standing with their home church, and whose lives testify that God has worked an act of grace in them."

The Western District Amish Mennonite Conference[28] first met, at the call of Bishop Kenagy, at Sycamore Grove in 1890. Later meetings here were in 1895, 1900, 1905, 1913, and, the meeting that approved the merger with the Missouri-Iowa and Kansas-Nebraska Mennonite conferences, in 1919. The Missouri-Kansas Conference met here in 1931 and 1945; the district's Church Extension and Evangelism Conference was held here in 1961.

Mennonite General Conference met at Sycamore Grove in 1921 in a tent north of the church; meals were prepared and served in the church sheds. This conference session is notable for its adoption of "Christian Fundamentals," which served, as the so-called Garden City Confession, for forty years as a statement of Mennonite theology.

The first of many Bible conferences was held in October 1908. A. P. Troyer was moderator and D. D. Miller and E. L. Frey were the instructors.

Young People's Institutes were held annually 1935-1950, also in 1956.

The tax method (e.g., two cents per acre for those owning fifty acres or less) was used to finance church expenses in the earlier years. Money for missions and charities was placed in slotted boxes fastened on benches near the doors. Sunday school offerings were for supplies, except once a month for missions. Offerings on communion Sunday were for the alms fund. In 1955 taxes were discontinued and a schedule of offerings was set up. After a self-study in 1959, planned giving was adopted with an annual budget. The giving of the congregation to all causes in 1972 was $22,000, which is $166 per member. The budget for 1973 was $23,000, for about 140 members.

The Sycamore Grove Centennial was observed in 1966, celebrating the hundredth anniversary, not of the organization of the church, which was two years later, but of the arrival of the founding families after the Civil War. Registered for this event were 354 visitors from 19 states and two provinces. Audiences numbered up to 600, and the meetings were held in a large tent. The theme was "O God, Our Help in Ages Past, Our Hope for Years to Come." Frank Troyer, at 96 the oldest member of the congregation, drove to this meeting from Garden City in his own car. Twenty-four former members, including H. J. King, J. D. Hartzler, Floyd Kauffman, and Milo Kauffman, spoke on the program.

In the centennial booklet, produced by Mrs. Earl Roth, Mrs. John G. McCarthy, and Trusie Zook, are quoted the words of Pastor Earl Eberly concerning the future: "This centennial celebration is a reproach to Almighty God if we receive nothing that will move us to cry,'O God, our hope for years to come.'"[29]

3. *Mt. Zion, Morgan County*

In April 1866 five families of Swiss Mennonites moved from Wayne County, Ohio, to Moniteau County, Missouri, near the Morgan County line in the central part of the state. These people were only one generation removed from their European Mennonite background.

They were joined in 1867 and the·years following by older American Mennonite families from Indiana, Ohio, Pennsylvania, and Virginia, who settled close by in Morgan County. "They brought with them different ideas, customs, opinions, and views on some points of doctrine; yet they granted each one the liberty of serving God according to his custom and conscience. This became the subject of a formal resolution adopted by the church May 9, 1869. The tendency was manifested on all sides to be united in *one* church. . . .

"They lived, worshiped, and took communion together on the principle: 'In the essentials, unity; in the non-essentials, liberty; in all, charity.' "[30]

In June 1867 J. M. Brenneman, Elida, Ohio, visited this area and found a flock of twenty members.[31] A year later he was here again, and gave communion to the congregation. Samuel Blough (Blauch) of Somerset County, Pennsylvania, served communion to 76 persons in 1870, at which time also he ordained as bishop Daniel Brundage, a minister who had moved from Indiana in 1869. The group in 1869 built a church in the heart of the Swiss settlement, which was given the name of Bethel. Prospects were bright for this new congregation.

But in the spring of 1871 difficulties arose. The Swiss had never practiced foot washing as an ordinance symbolizing humble service in brotherhood. The American Mennonites could not admit that this was a nonessential in which there could be liberty. Moreover, there were some cultural differences, such as language. They all understood German. But the Swiss had a Swiss dialect and the others spoke Pennsylvania Dutch. The American Mennonites, the fourth generation in America, were about ready to conduct church services in English; the Swiss would hold on to their German for forty years more.

The negotiations on these matters were never bitter, but they did result in a peaceful separation. Fifty-one members retained their membership at Bethel, assuming all responsibilities and debts on the church property. Later these joined the General Conference Mennonites.

The others organized a separate congregation under Bishop Brundage, and worshiped in the Fisher School, later known as Prairie Valley. They built their first meetinghouse in 1876, to which they gave the name of Mt. Zion. It is four miles southwest of Bethel, and in Morgan County, seven miles northeast of Versailles. It is three quarters of a mile from Prairie Valley.

But the harmony of the community was not broken. The two ethnic groups simply saw that it would be better to have two churches, Bethel and Mt. Zion. They have cooperated in many ways: an annual humn-sing, relief projects, dismissing services for each other's special meetings. When Bishop Brundage called the first meeting of the Missouri Conference (later called Missouri-Iowa) in 1873, his congregation did not as yet have a building, and so the conference

was held at Bethel, and no doubt the Bethel people helped
with the hosting.

There were at least thirty-six charter members in the Mt.
Zion congregation. Family names were Blosser, Brundage, Dettwiler,
Driver, Good, Horschheimer, Kauffman, Ramer, Shank, Weaver,
Wenger. As they had come into the area, they were helped in find-
ing homes by their Swiss brethren: the Lehmans, Weltys, Loganbills,
Basingers, Gerbers, Baumgartners, and others.

It is interesting to note that the Woolworth chain of stores
had its beginning among these pioneers. A son of Deacon Martin
Good opened a store in Tipton, limiting his stock to ten-cent items.
The business prospered. Later he moved to Michigan, and the business continued to grow. He sold it to Fred Woolworth, on condition
that he should receive a percentage of the profits as long as he
lived. He became wealthy, but gave first a tenth, then a third to
the Lord.

A tornado brought great loss to the community in May 1872.
Persons killed numbered twenty-six, including Jacob Blosser and
an infant daughter, who were buried in the first grave of the new
congregation's cemetery. Homes of other members were badly
damaged. Daniel Brundage suffered great loss: his buildings, furniture,
bedding, clothes, and the carpenter tools with which he earned his
living. Shortly afterward Brundage moved to McPherson County,
Kansas.

In 1875 the Missouri Conference inquired of other conferences
about a better plan to make good the property loss of members.
The Indiana Conference replied that the very best security is an
unshaken trust in God. This must be one of the first Mennonite
moves toward a plan for mutual aid. Daniel Brundage was the
preacher at this conference.

The first church building was erected on a two-acre plot, in
1876. It was a frame building, 24 x 40, with no basement. A Church
of the Brethren congregation in the community held their services
at Mt. Zion on alternate Sundays until they built in 1881.

This first building was torn down in 1905 and replaced by a new
structure, 36 x 54, with a small basement for the furnace. J. E.
Hartzler held the first revival meetings in the new church in 1906.

The present building is the result of remodeling in 1953-54 and
1959-60. Classrooms, a library, cloakrooms, and rest rooms have
been provided.

The first building had a pulpit modeled on Eastern patterns: a long desk across the rostrum served also as a cabinet for the Sunday school library and as a place for Sunday school records and literature. This pulpit was used more than seventy-five years, until the remodeling.

Sheds for the horses were built about 1910. But they were obsolete when cars came in, and were removed about 1950. These sheds were a long row of stalls, roofed over and boarded up on one side. The other side, away from the prevailing wind, was left open so that the horses could be driven in and tied without being unhitched from the vehicles. The sheds were a mercy to the horses who had to stand in the storm or cold for two hours.

The Prairie Valley School was purchased in 1957, and now serves as a fellowship hall and meeting place for the Women's Missionary and Service Commission. In 1961 Pastor Allen Zook moved into a new parsonage built on six acres of land just south of the churchyard.

Early membership records are not available. J. F. Funk found 17 or 18 families there in 1875. In 1893 there were 35 members.[32] The high point may have been in 1910, about 100 members. The

Mt. Zion Church

Mennonite Yearbook lists the membership as 71 in 1933, 49 in 1946, and 53 in 1972.

Many who moved here from the East later moved still farther west. In 1948 Pastor Leroy Gingerich observed that the first immigrants brought with them the farming methods of Ohio, Pennsylvania, and Virginia. With grain farming the topsoil washed away, exposing the yellow clay below. Only through a shift to stock farming could the fertility of the soil be maintained, and the farmers continue to make a living. There were many failures during the Depression years, and many families moved away.[33]

Sunday school in the early years was held only during the summer. The curriculum was chapters from the Bible. By the early 90s there were "lesson helps," and the Sunday school was "evergreen," around the calendar. The Sunday school library was begun before 1910, and now has almost 400 books.

A Youth Fellowship was organized in 1948, and the Girls' Missionary and Service Auxiliary in 1956.

The Sewing Circle was organized in 1912 with Maggie Driver as president. Now as the Women's Missionary and Service Commission the group rarely misses a monthly meeting.

The men of the congregation, as the Mt. Zion Fellowship, for fifteen years have put out a crop, the proceeds of which go for mission or church purposes. The crops were usually corn, soybeans, and hay. Labor and the use of machinery were donated. Gifts to missions were $200 or $300 each year. One project was the purchase of the Prairie Valley School for a community center.

Public prayer has been audible, in the kneeling posture, but standing for the benediction. Since 1940 the congregation stands for more prayers; since 1961 it remains seated for one prayer.

German was used in the early years, but never exclusively. David D. Kauffman was ordained for German preaching, but he changed to English before long. A few members used German lesson helps.

Prayer meetings were held before 1887, but not continuously. They were started again to pray for the men drafted during World War I. During gas-rationing days of World War II prayer meetings were held Sunday evening before the regular service. Sometimes prayer meetings have been in the homes — "cottage meetings" — with the territory divided into four sections. Winter meetings have been held in the homes, to save fuel.

The Virginia influence has been strong in the congregation

because so many members came from Virginia. Therefore, early tunes were from *Harmonia Sacra*. *Gospel Hymns* found a use, and later *Psalms, Hymns, and Spiritual Songs*. *The Church and Sunday School Hymnal* became the songbook when it became available in 1903, and its *Supplement* in 1911. *Life Songs*, both I and II, added their variety when they were published. The *Church Hymnal* was not used until 1950, twenty-three years after publication. Part singing was always acceptable. Numbers by smaller groups, called "special music," were used by 1911. Singing schools — seven of them between 1907 and 1940 — helped to keep music reading alive. Teachers were J. B. Smith, Claude Brunk, Edwin Swartzendruber, Noah Showalter, M. T. Brackbill, I. Mark Ross, and Paul M. Yoder.

For a time in the nineteenth century the place of baptism was a sensitive issue in the American Mennonite church. For some, because Jesus was baptized in the Jordan River, baptism should be performed only in an outdoor stream. And so at Mt. Zion baptism in the church building or in a creek was optional. But since 1910 all baptisms have been in the church.

Foot washing was formerly observed by all members in the church auditorium. But since 1961 the women go to the Sunday school room. The holy kiss is less observed than formerly, but always in connection with the foot washing service. Anointing for healing has been used occasionally, but always in a private service. Ordinations have been both by lot and by vote.

Marriages were solemnized in homes until in the 1940s. Since then weddings are held in the church, but this has never been made an issue. Singing may be by a quartet or by the congregation.

It is remembered that at the turn of the century men mourners at funerals kept their hats on. Bible conference teaching seems to have stopped that. Women mourners once wore veils over their faces. The wake has not been practiced since 1920. Viewing has been after the sermon until recently; the practice depends on the choice of the family. Singing was by the congregation until about 1911; now it is by a small group. Now discontinued is the use of singing during the viewing. The use of flowers is optional.

Sunday evening services have been usual since the early 90s. These have been Young People's Bible Meetings based on outlines in church publications. Business meetings were organized in the 1890s, when Daniel Kauffman headed the congregation. At first these were quarterly, later semiannual.

In the early years parents were expected to teach their children and bring them to commitment for church membership. But an atheistic schoolteacher had a strong influence in the community, and there were few young people in the church. Parents and leaders became concerned. Early in 1883 John S. Coffman, pioneer Mennonite evangelist, came to Mt. Zion. There were five confessions. Later in that year Coffman came again. Non-Christians and community people came to hear this unusual preacher. Through several years Coffman came often. J. C. Driver and Daniel Kauffman were converted in 1890.

Among other evangelists who have preached here are M. S. Steiner, C. Z. Yoder, Perry J. Shenk, Daniel Kauffman, C. F. Derstine, L. J. Miller, E. J. Berkey, Wilbert Nafziger, O. H. Hooley, William R. Miller, Richard Birky, M. A. Yoder, Wayne Yoder, Manasseh Bontreger, H. J. Zehr, Joe Esh, and Chester Slagell.

The Bible Conference, sometimes called Bible Normal, was a popular form of Bible teaching in the Mennonite Church at the turn of the century and until the twenties. Two visiting ministers would direct a Bible study on various doctrinal, ethical, and practical subjects. The meetings would be held two or three sessions a day for a week, more or less. Members of the audience would read assigned Scripture references, and the speaker would discuss their meaning. Interest ran high, and these conferences were a powerful means in the indoctrination of the laity.[34]

Bible Conferences were often held at Mt. Zion during the years 1899-1930. One of the last occurred in November 1927, with J. R. Shank and J. D. Mininger as instructors. Subjects were as follows: Practical Christian Living, Shank; Purpose of Prayer, Mininger, Christian Graces, Shank; Work of the Holy Spirit, Shank; Relation of Church and State, Mininger; Personal Work, Shank; Self-Denial, Shank; Relation of Minister and Laity, Shank; Relation of Laity to Ministry, Mininger; Modern Idolatry, Shank; Life Insurance, Mininger. Each evening, after the study of one topic, there was an evangelistic sermon by Mininger. Thus evangelism and Bible study were united.

One of the earliest Bible Conferences had both a Mennonite and a Church of the Brethren instructor, since it was the practice for the people of the two denominations to attend each other's meetings.

Communion has been held twice a year. The common cup was used until 1969, when individual cups were donated to the church. Daniel Kauffman, as he started to pass the cup, would always sing,

"Alas, and did my Saviour bleed?" Formerly all partook of the em-
blems as they received them; now they all partake at the same time.

Examination meetings, always held before communion, were
usually private in the counsel room. Members recall that some people
who needed discipline or admonition stayed in the counsel room quite
a while. Since 1954 the counsel meeting has been in the way of open
testimony. Since 1956 the church has had a council made up of pastor, deacon, and four laymen.

Money for church expenses was raised by assessments until about
1912. Offerings for special funds were given privately; sometimes a
bill was slipped into the deacon's hip pocket, and he was not supposed to look around to see whose "left hand" was giving it. (The
deacon was long the church treasurer.) Monthly offerings during
the service came in the first decade of the century. Offering plates
are passed every Sunday since 1959. Support of church causes is
through a budget since 1959, rather than by solicitation or special
appeals.

Church bulletins were used first in 1953. There has been a
Christian Living club since 1954, and the *Gospel Herald* is in every
home since 1963.

Summer Bible school began in 1937. Enrollment has been largely
from non-Mennonite homes. In 1964 the attendance was increased
50 percent as more black children from Versailles came to the school.
Since 1966 the local public school has had summer classes, and this
has decreased attendance somewhat.

Special Sunday school and missionary meetings have been held
occasionally, sometimes with the Providence and Lick Creek congregations from the Ozarks. One meeting about twenty-five years ago
was a combined Sunday school meeting and picnic. This is interesting,
because in 1881 the Missouri Conference had resolved "against attending circuses, fairs, and picnics."

An annual Brotherhood Sale for relief has been conducted in
cooperation with the Bethel congregation.

Members of this congregation have served on school boards and
as election judges. They participate in community projects and attend farm or business association meetings.

However, during World War I community relations were strained.
Abe Wenger refused to serve on the Council of Defense. Members
would not help the community to make up its quotas of Liberty
Bonds and Thrift Stamps. A federal officer came to investigate. Abe

Wenger, J. R. Driver, and Amos Gingerich were called to appear before him. These men explained why Mennonites could not support war measures. It was agreed that for three months the church would give $500 a month to the Red Cross. This was to demonstrate that the Mennonites were not clinging to their money selfishly. When the three months were up, the church was told they could contribute their money where they wished.

Mt. Zion has long had a strong mission spirit. The same Missouri Conference which in 1881 resolved against picnics and moustaches resolved "for doing mission work, at home before abroad; for regular contributions for missions."[35]

Only twenty-five miles south of them in the Ozarks lay a needy mission field. Preaching appointments began there in 1901. Preachers traveled sixty miles round trip on horseback or in buggies. In 1907 George R. Brunk held meetings in the area, and the next year J. R. Shank moved from Pea Ridge to the hills for a career as a rural missionary. In 1938 he had regular appointments at six places, extending into Arkansas. He did not retire from his strenuous program until 1956.

Another mission point was the Coffee Schoolhouse, ten miles from Mt. Zion. Meetings were held there from 1950 to 1958, when the schoolhouse burned down.

In recent years various organizations of the church have given three programs a year at the State Women's Prison at Tipton, fifteen miles north of the church.

Other missionaries from Mt. Zion include C. B. Driver and wife to Shannon County, Missouri; Eva Harder Brunk, Charles Shank, Minnie Swartzendruber Graber, and Mary Holsopple to India; J. W. Shank to Argentina; Bertha Wenger Swarr to Israel; and Caroline Nebel to Puerto Rico, and to Araguacema, Brazil, and Zaire.

A centennial celebration of the organization of the church was held July 17, 18, 1971. Out-of-state speakers were H. A. Diener, J. D. Graber, and Fred Gingerich. Many former members were present. Biographical sketches of all ordained men who have served the congregation were read, and there was recognition of all foreign missionaries from Mt. Zion. A history of the congregation was written for this occasion. Moderating the meeting were Pastor Allen Zook and Deacon Norman Wenger.

In historical perspective perhaps the most crucial moment in Mt. Zion history was one evening in October 1890. J. S. Coffman had been praying and visiting and preaching in the community for three weeks. One person for whose salvation he labored was a young widower named Daniel Kauffman.

Daniel was the son of Bishop David D. Kauffman. Born in Juniata County, Pennsylvania, in 1865, he came to Missouri as a boy of four. He was subjected to the influences of the pioneer neighborhood and was attracted to politics. He was a schoolteacher, had served three years as county commissioner (superintendent), and in 1890 was a candidate for the clerkship of the district court. His talents would probably have taken him far in public life.

Daniel attended Coffman's meetings at Mt. Zion, when he could get away from his campaigning. Doubtless he was attracted to this dynamic and spiritual preacher. One day the ex-teacher-evangelist visited Kauffman's schoolroom. The young teacher sensed that his visitor's main interest was in winning him to Christ.

Daniel was present in the last meeting of the series. He held Jimmie, his motherless son, in his arms. But he had given no sign of yielding to the convictions that he clearly felt. Coffman preached his sermon and gave his last invitation. As the last verse of the invitation song was being sung, Daniel Kauffman stood to indicate he had committed his life to Christ. The next month he was one of seven to be baptized.[36]

For the Mennonite Church it was a crucial decision. Daniel Kauffman was a man of great potential, and the direction of his life was radically changed. His gifts as speaker, teacher, writer, and organizer were now given to the work of the Mennonite Church, and for the next forty years he was the outstanding leader of that denomination.

He became a minister at Mt. Zion in 1892, and four years later was ordained as bishop to succeed his father. In 1894 he argued for a General Conference, which was being promoted by J. F. Funk: "If a General Conference would strengthen the whole church, why not have it?"[37] In that same year the Missouri Conference, of which he was elected secretary in 1893, submitted a plan "for the beginning of General Conference, the first plan submitted."[38] Thus he led in setting up the pattern of denominational structure which was destined to serve until 1971.

He was the first moderator of Mennonite General Conference at the age of thirty-three; he is the only man to have been moderator four times. Three times he preached the conference sermon, seven

Daniel Kauffman, 1865-1944, outstanding Mennonite leader

times he was chairman of the Resolutions Committee, and at some time served as chairman of most of the other important committees. He was at one time a member of twenty-two church committees and boards.

Kauffman encouraged the establishment of church colleges, and served as president of Goshen College at a critical time (1922-1923). He was a prolific writer at a time when not many Mennonites were writing. He wrote about twenty books; the most influential of these was *Bible Doctrine*,[39] which is still in demand. He was editor of the *Gospel Witness* (1905-1908) and the *Gospel Herald* (1908-1943). As preacher, organization man, and writer he was for decades the chief spokesman of the Mennonite Church.[40]

It is hard to imagine how much the Mennonite Church would have lost if Daniel Kauffman had decided that October evening in 1890 at the Mt. Zion Church to push on to high political office, instead of giving his life to the Lord and the church. Mt. Zion can always rejoice in this, a major contribution to the Mennonite witness in the world.[41]

Ordained leadership has been given to the congregation by the following:

Ministers and Bishops

Daniel Brundage	1868-1873
David Kauffman	1871-1896
Daniel Kauffman	1892-1924
J. C. Driver	1896-1905, 1912-1947

Ministers

Henry Harder	1906-1920
Amos Gingerich	1909-1934
D. F. Driver	1916-1920
C. B. Driver	1920-1955
A. Leroy Gingerich	1936-1962, 1966-1971
Allen Zook	1961-

Deacons

Melchior Brenneman	Early years
Jacob Huber	Early years

Martin Good	Early years
John C. Driver	1891-1912
Elias Swartzendruber	1910-1924
John S. Dettwiler	1920-1937
Reuben Harder	1937-1940
Jesse Wenger	1941-
Norman Wenger	1962-

Amos Gingerich, minister at Mt. Zion, 1909-1934

Ordained men at Mt. Zion in 1969 (l. to r.): Norman Wenger, deacon; Leroy Gingerich, retired minister; Jesse Wenger, retired deacon; Allen Zook, pastor

4. *Berea, Shannon County*

The Berea Church is near Birch Tree, a small town in the Ozarks, in Shannon County, of southern Missouri. It is halfway across the state, and thirty miles from the Arkansas border. It is a land of timbered mountains and scenic riverways and big springs. Not far away a river flows full-born from Blue Spring.

Late in 1894 two men from Milford, Nebraska, and two from Illinois joined John L. Brubaker, of Shelby County, Missouri, on a six-day land prospecting tour in the Missouri Ozarks. They were looking for a place where they could own their own homes. Near Birch Tree the land had been cleared of its valuable timber, and was selling for a few dollars an acre. Brubaker and the Illinois men liked it here well enough to purchase land.[42]

It may be questioned whether this was a good place for a Mennonite colony. One of the problems of the Berea congregation proved to be its mobility: families would stay only a few years and then move away. Some families did stay, but there was evidently no good economic base for a growing church.

Caleb Winey, a Kansas Mennonite minister fleeing from the "horrors of Kansas" in 1895, visited Birch Tree and was kindly entertained by the few Mennonites who by that time had moved in. He was not well impressed with the country, and he was disgusted with the misrepresentations of the land agents who lured people to financial ruin in this area. He said there was only a little soil between the stones of all sizes. The land was hard to clear of its stumps. Farming was primitive, with one-horse cultivators, and cradles for harvesting. He called the people who lived here "involuntary exiles, too poor to leave." "This is hardly the country for a prosperous Mennonite settlement," he wrote. He said the houses were log cabins, and the towns were shabby. "I would rather be a renter in Kansas than go there and try to hew out a home," he concluded.[43]

Winey went back to the dry, windy plains of Kansas, but John Brubaker saw an opportunity on the Faulkner place at Birch Tree. "It is through the aid of the brethren in Illinois, Pennsylvania, and Ohio that I am able to get a start, and our heavenly Father only knows how thankful I am."[44]

The Brubakers, Henry Neuschwangers, and Mace Headricks moved to Birch Tree in covered wagons. Their church services, every two weeks, were first held under a brush arbor at Brubakers, but later in the home which they built. Bishop Andrew Shenk came and organized them as a congregation in the fall of 1895. The E. B. Shupes from Neutral, Kansas, had joined them. There were six families, and the attendance was from 25 to 30. John Brubaker, who had been a minister at Mt. Pisgah since 1876, was in charge of the congregation. Every four weeks, also, he preached at Summersville, twenty miles to the northwest, where two Mennonite families lived.

A school was built in 1897, and it was used for a church until a meetinghouse was erected. Clara Brubaker, John's oldest daughter, donated the land for the school and was its first teacher.

By 1898 the membership was twenty-three. The next year the Benj. Detwilers moved from Shelby County, and it was decided to move ahead with a church building. Land for the church and cemetery was donated by Henry Neuschwanger. Ben Unruh, who later moved to Harper, Kansas, was the carpenter. All labor was donated, and the cost of the building was $160. The opening service was held in the spring of 1900 by George R. Brunk, of Kansas. The name, Berea, was suggested by Clara Brubaker.

The first person buried in the cemetery was 16-year-old Nelson Neuschwanger. He was fatally injured when his team hitched to a cultivator was frightened by lightning.

Fires seem to have been an unusual hazard in the little community. In 1905 the Faulkner home and its contents were destroyed. In 1907 three families — the Fred and Henry Neuschwangers and Mace Headricks — had stored their goods in Birch Tree while waiting for a car to move it to La Junta, Colorado. Almost all was destroyed in a fire. In 1910, on Easter Sunday, a forest fire burned the barn of the Benj. Detwilers and threatened their house and the church.

The Missouri Conference held its sessions at Berea in 1900 and again in 1906. A Bible Conference was held in 1923, with I. G. Hartzler and E. J. Berkey as instructors, and again in 1952, with J. R. Shank and Frank Horst. Ezra Stauffer once conducted a prophecy conference. There were programs by Hesston College gospel teams, by a chorus from Culp, Arkansas, and by workers from Garden City and Culp.

Evangelistic efforts were almost an annual feature, and reached many people of the community. As many as twelve persons were baptized at one time. Some of the best-known evangelists of the church served here. The list includes Andrew Shenk, Daniel Kauffman, George R. Brunk, J. M. Kreider, B. F. Hartzler, J. T. Hamilton, Peter Unzicker, J. E. Hartzler, Perry Shenk, J. M. Brunk, E. J. Berkey, J. W. Hess, Frank Horst, J. C. Driver, H. J. King, H. A. Diener, E. E. Showalter, D. D. Miller, S. S. Hershberger, Protus Brubaker, Leroy Gingerich, I. Mark Ross, Sanford E. King, W. R. Hershberger, John E. Wenger, and Ivan Headings. (It was a community sensation when Ivan Headings came in his airplane, and landed in the pastor's field.)

Family names in the congregation through the years include the following: Brubaker, Neuschwanger, Headrick, Shupe, Miller, Unruh, Lapp, Detwiler, Ebersole, Cowan, Johnson, Driver, Dester, Gindlesperger, Faulkner, Larrew, Reeves, Carr, Depriest, Altop, Cox, Hines, Allen, Hathaway, Templeton, Rosenberg, Lietner, Rutledge, Plank, Switzer. Some of these were people of the neighborhood who were won to Christ.

J. L. Brubaker moved away from Birch Tree because of his health in 1912. He died at the home of his youngest son, Protus, in 1924, and was buried at Versailles. Abraham Unruh was ordained in 1898, and ministered at Berea for a few years. J. T. Hamilton was ordained at Oronogo for Berea in 1906. He began his ministry there in April 1906, but went back to Oronogo in January 1907.

There was no resident minister 1912-1916. Ministers from Oronogo filled appointments twice a month. Members moved away, only a few remaining. Courage to continue was at low ebb. In 1914 the church building was sold to the Methodists. Berean members continued their work in cooperation with the Methodists. When the Benj. Detwilers, who had moved to Carver to help with the work along the Osage River, moved back to Birch Tree in 1915, the church building was bought back again. For a time the Sunday school continued as a union effort.

In March 1916, the *Gospel Herald* Field Notes reported a revival of interest at Berea: "For a time the work at Birch Tree was practically abandoned, and it was thought that it would be only a question of time when there would be no more Mennonites in Shannon County, but the Lord looked at it otherwise. Of late the work has revived, and C. B. Driver of Versailles, Missouri, was ordained at the Mt. Zion Church January 1, 1916, to shepherd the flock at Berea."[45] A survey at that time revealed that within 2 1/2 miles of the church there were 35 families, with 122 persons, thirteen and above. Of these, 73 made no religious profession and 49 professed to be Christians but had no church home. So the Berea Church had a real field for work.

C. B. Driver returned to Versailles in 1920. Once a month an Oronogo preacher came and preached three sermons — a sort of "feast, then fast."

In 1927 Leroy Cowan, a member of the congregation, was ordained, and served until 1939, when he moved to Oregon. Andrew Shenk, the first bishop, continued his supervision until his death in 1937. In 1936 there was an attempt to enforce the wearing of the plain coat and the cape, to which some members objected.

Alva Swartzendruber succeeded Shenk as bishop. He served until W. R. Hershberger took over this responsibility in 1945. On his death in 1954, Daniel Kauffman, the overseer of the Missouri churches, assumed bishop functions at Berea.

Hayden Depriest was ordained deacon at Berea in 1935. He

was the only deacon in the history of the church.

After Leroy Cowan moved away, the congregation again had no pastor until the already aged Noah Ebersole moved there in 1946. In 1949 he was given the help of Oney Hathaway, who was ordained at Pea Ridge to serve as pastor at Birch Tree. Hathaway was here for ten years — to 1959. Arlin Yoder came from Iowa in 1960 and was the pastor for three years — one year licensed and two years ordained. Since 1963 there has been no resident pastor.

Schoolteachers in the community have been a great help to the church, among them J. P. Berkey, Clara Brubaker, Esther Detwiler, and Roman Hershberger.

The Sunday school, evergreen from 1898, has always been the heart of the church program, continuing Sunday after Sunday and year after year, whether there was a pastor or not. A Sewing Circle was organized in 1917. The women unite with their Culp sisters in an annual fellowship, and with the community in a Day of Prayer. In recent years community women have actively participated in the Women's Missionary and Service Commission work. There has been a Young People's Meeting, a literary society, a junior sewing circle, and a mission study class. The first summer Bible school was held in 1940. This teaching feature has been successfully carried on with the help of many visiting teachers. A church-owned bus has been used since 1949 for the transportation of pupils of the summer Bible school and the Sunday school.

Outreach from Berea as a center has included preaching and other services at Summersville, Essex (four members once lived there), and the following schools: Innwood, Turkey Oak, Black Pond, Barlett, and Shady Grove.

The first wedding conducted in the church was that of Frank Larrew and May Detwiler in 1917.

During World War I the front of the church was painted yellow. John Detwiler was drafted, and went to camp as a conscientious objector to war. He was given a farm furlough in Iowa. After the war he volunteered for relief work in the Near East. In 1922 he transported ninety-nine children, two to five years of age, in carts, a distance of 500 miles, from Anatolia to Aleppo.

Other members of the congregation who participated in the church program away from Birch Tree may be mentioned. Mina Brubaker, as the wife of Dr. C. D. Esch, one of the first Mennonite medical missionaries, was a missionary in India for four terms, and later, as a widow, was a matron at the La Junta Hospital. Clara Brubaker was the wife of John R. Shank, longtime rural missionary in central Missouri. Protus Brubaker served a lifetime as a rural mission pastor in central Missouri. Esther Detwiler was a teacher at Iowa Mennonite School.

The church has had a strong interest in missions, hearing reports from the Kansas City Mission; from India through the Esches, Milton Vogts, and Mary Wenger (who became the wife of John Detwiler); from Argentina through Park Lantzes. They sent canned fruit to the Kansas City Children's Home. They also contributed money for mission work as they could. In 1916 a mission board treasurer's report had this item: "A little child from Birch Tree, Mo. — Child's welfare fifty-five cents, India Mission fifty cents."

A new church building, using native fieldstones, was erected in 1955.

The membership fluctuated a great deal through the years. The highest figure was 42, in 1936. The membership in 1972 was 10.

A member writes: "The congregation has witnessed families moving to other places, withdrawal from fellowship, loss by death, and many discouragements. We feel that God is able to supply all our need, as He has promised, and want to be faithful in service for Him until He comes."[46]

Berea Church

5. *Pea Ridge, Marion County*

Pea Ridge is the name of a rural community thirteen miles west of Palmyra, and seven miles southwest of Philadelphia, Missouri. These two post offices serve the seventeen family units now in the membership of the Pea Ridge Mennonite Church.

It was in 1903 that an old lady, Grandmother Maddox, who frequently visited in the home of J. M. Kreider, pastor of the church at Palmyra, told him one day about Pea Ridge. She had a daughter living in that community, and wished that a minister would go there to preach, as religious services were seldom held there.

Kreider was not the man to pass up an opportunity for preaching the gospel. An appointment was made for Sunday afternoon in the schoolhouse at Four-Corners, near an old country store. The people requested another service, and so Kreider promised to come back a month later. This was the beginning of monthly appointments at Pea Ridge.

The people were hungry for more preaching, and so in early autumn a series of meetings was held. Attendance and interest were very good. The field was ripe for harvest, and about six months later, in another series of meetings, a large number of people confessed Christ. Bishop Daniel Kauffman was called from Versailles, and after instructing them, he baptized twenty-three people of the community.

The next year, in 1905, a congregation was organized. John R. Shank, a young man from Palmyra who was attending Goshen College, was called to serve as pastor. He was ordained to the ministry on March 1, 1905, by Bishop David Burkholder.[47] At the end of the school year he settled at Pea Ridge, living with two of his sisters.

One of the new members, Joe Duff, and his family offered an acre of land as a site for a church building. It was near the Four-Corners schoolhouse. Before the end of 1905 a little white church building was dedicated. It was a frame building, 28 by 40 feet, with a seating capacity of about 150.

In 1907 Ira E. Buckwalter, of the Palmyra congregation, was ordained to participate in the ministry at Pea Ridge.[48]

In 1908 J. R. Shank moved to the Osage River country south of Versailles to begin his lifetime service there. To fill his place at Pea Ridge came John W. Hess, a young married man from Lancaster

County, Pennsylvania, who had given several years to the city mission work in Kansas City. He was ordained at Pea Ridge and served as pastor here until he moved to Manson, Iowa, in 1919.

Hess bought the farm adjoining the church and made his living by farming, by cobbling shoes, and by evangelistic work in other churches. He soled shoes while customers waited, he said, because it gave him a good chance to talk to them about salvation; they couldn't run away.[49] John Hess was a gifted evangelist, and he was away from home a good deal preaching to the many congregations who called him. It was good he had a faithful assistant in Ira E. Buckwalter to preach when he was absent.

The congregation did not depend for its growth on the migration of families from older Mennonite communities. Family names included the following: Ellis, White, Oppy, Philips, Fenton, Gibbons, Bremmer, Carlton, Duff, Golden, Edley, Crane, Tuttle, Bagley, and Hathaway. Through the years, as at most places, some members turned back, death claimed some, and others moved away. About 1930 there were only four families to carry on the work.

Midweek prayer meetings have been a part of the church program at Pea Ridge from its early days until now. Lizzie Hess tells how one evening she and Mrs. Buckwalter and the two older children of each came to prayer meeting at the church, but no one else came. As they went on with their prayer meeting together, mischief-makers locked them in with the key Mrs. Buckwalter had left in the keyhole. They also smeared with axle grease the sill of the only window the mothers could use as an exit. But the ladies were undaunted. They wiped off the grease and Mrs. Buckwalter took it home to use on her screeching baby buggy.[50]

When the Hesses left the community, they deeded their farm to the Mennonite Board of Missions. Some years later, in 1951, it was deeded to the congregation itself.

About 1915 a cemetery was started in the churchyard.

On Christmas Day, 1932, the church building caught fire and burned to the ground. Only the pulpit, benches, and a few books were saved. The congregation then met in the Hathaway home. In July 1933 the quarterly Sunday school meeting with Mt. Pisgah and Palmyra assembled in the loft of the big bank barn on the mission property. Services then continued in this barn until a new church building was erected.

By August 1933, although this was in the bottom of the De-

Pea Ridge Church built in 1957

pression, enough help came from other congregations to enable a beginning of another meetinghouse. With most of the labor donated by the neighborhood, the building was ready for dedication by October 8. Again it was of frame construction, but a little smaller — 26 by 30 feet, with a seating capacity of 100. J. M. Kreider preached the dedication sermon, and the following evening H. J. King, Harper, Kansas, began evangelistic meetings.

On September 22, 1940, Nelson E. Kauffman, pastor at Hannibal, Missouri, was ordained bishop to assist J. M. Kreider, who had been supervising the churches in northeastern Missouri since 1912. In the same service David A. Hathaway was ordained as deacon for the Pea Ridge congregation. In July 1944, at a special meeting, votes were taken for a new minister at Pea Ridge. David A. Hathaway was chosen. So on July 30 he was ordained to help Ira E. Buckwalter with the work at this place. A few months later, on October 22, David's brother Oney was ordained to replace David as deacon.

Bishop J. M. Kreider passed away at his home near Palmyra in February 1946. That left Nelson E. Kauffman with the bishop

Dedication service at Pea Ridge in 1957

responsibility in the northeastern area of Missouri. By 1947 Ira E. Buckwalter asked to be relieved of the work of pastor, and David Hathaway became pastor of the congregation. Deacon Oney Hathaway was ordained minister on February 20, 1949, to become pastor at Berea, Birch Tree, Missouri. After service there for ten years, he returned to Pea Ridge. In the meantime, in 1950, Oliver, another brother of David's, became deacon of Pea Ridge, a responsibility which he still carries.

In 1951 Daniel Kauffman, of Mt. Pisgah, was ordained as bishop to supervise the northeast Missouri congregations.

In November 1947 a Voluntary Service unit came to Pea Ridge. They were Percy and John Yoder, Jesse and Merle Zook — all from Pennsylvania. They painted the church ceiling and benches, and did other work on the church property. Percy Yoder conducted a singing school.

The first summer Bible school was held in 1948, with J. S. Neuhouser of Indiana in charge. Bible school continues each summer.

The fiftieth anniversary of the church at this place was celebrated on September 11, 1955. At this time negotiations were in process for closing the church at Palmyra and transferring some of the members to Pea Ridge. On February 5, 1956, the following persons were received by letter: Minister Harry Buckwalter and his wife, Harriet, M. Lena Kreider, Anna Bender, Daniel Bender and his wife, Amy. This brought the total membership to 32.

A larger church with additional facilities was needed, and the following building committee was appointed: Leslie Hathaway (chairman), Oliver Hathaway, Daniel Bender, and John Kreider. On July 27, 1956, the old building, the one erected in 1933, was torn down.

The new building has a full basement and a frame of 34 by 56 feet. It has a mothers' room, a prayer room, a library room, rest rooms, a fully equipped kitchen, and a gas furnace. David Hathaway preached the first sermon in the new church basement on March 10, 1957. The building was dedicated on June 23, 1957, with J. P. Brubaker, Edwards, Missouri, preaching the dedicatory sermon.

The program of the congregation has included the weekend entertainment of overseas students attending the state college at Kirksville, fifty miles to the northwest. In 1964, for instance, eight students came; they were from Japan, China, Germany, and Kenya. They were lodged in homes, attended church services, and fellowshiped at a dinner in the church basement. And in 1969 a group of twenty Chinese students worshiped at Pea Ridge, ate dinner with the members in the church, and gave an afternoon program of music and pictures of China.

The congregation uses the Every Home Plan for the *Gospel Herald,* with the official denominational paper thus going to every family unit.

Revival meetings are held each fall at this church. In 1956 Virgil Brenneman, Iowa City, Iowa, was the evangelist. Since the new church was not yet ready, the meetings were held in the Philadelphia Christian Church. They were well attended.

Joint Thanksgiving services are held annually with four other congregations of the area — Baptist and Christian. Services rotate from church to church, with the host church always having a guest speaker.

Pea Ridge observes the World Day of Prayer jointly with Mt. Pisgah and Hannibal. The Dorcas Sewing Circle was organized in 1942, and still meets monthly. There is a range of activity, in line with the program of the denomination's Women's Missionary and Service

The David Hathaways and their new sofa

Commission. One year they sent 94 quarts of fruit and vegetables to the VS unit in Kansas City.

In February 1961 Pastor David Hathaway and his wife were honored on their twenty-first wedding anniversary by a surprise fellowship dinner in the church basement. They were given a new davenport for their home.

In August 1961 Oney Hathaway and family moved to Anderson, Indiana, to serve in the pastorate there. In 1963 he returned to Pea Ridge, where he assists in the preaching. Both David and Oney have helped Overseer Daniel Kauffman in preaching appointments at Birch Tree. In 1972 David Hathaway tendered his resignation as pastor, and in 1973 he and his wife began a two-year VS term at Champaign-Urbana, Illinois.[51]

The congregation has never felt able to entertain the annual meeting of the South Central Conference, to which they belong. But when in 1962 the conference met in Hannibal on a college campus, Pea Ridge members helped to service the meeting.

Pea Ridge has, however, entertained smaller meetings of the state and the conference. Ten congregations met here in a doctrinal conference in 1963. The Missouri Mennonite Youth Fellowship annual meeting and banquet was held here in 1969, with Robert Hartzler of Iowa as speaker. The attendance was 120. And in January 1971 seven ministers from Oklahoma, Arkansas, and Missouri came for a ministers' workshop, with Russell Krabill and Millard Osborne as guest leaders.

Beginning in 1964 several of the congregation's young men have done Voluntary Service at Maumee, Ohio; Colorado Springs, Colorado; Sturgis, Michigan; and Berwyn, Pennsylvania. A farewell dinner has been given to each before his leaving; in this way the church expresses its oneness with the young men in their conscientious objection to war.

In 1965 the South Central Conference, in accordance with its constitutional provision, gratefully acknowledged the past services in the ministry of Harry and Ira Buckwalter, and gave them the status of retired minister, "with no specific responsibilities other than to preach at the request of the pastor . . . and such minor services as might be requested. . . ." The congregation accepted this action. Since that time, on April 21, 1969, Harry Buckwalter passed to his heavenly reward.

The congregation held services on July 3, 1971, at Maple Lawn Rest Home in Palmyra, in recognition of the ninetieth birthday of Ira Buckwalter. He and Lena Kreider are now guests at this home. Members of the Pea Ridge congregation hold two services a month at this home.

Men of the congregation have been active in Mennonite Disaster Service. On March 16, 1971, five men went to Inverness, Mississippi, where a tornado had done much damage a few days before. They gave five days to this service. In 1973 the congregation rented a booth at the Marion County Fair and sold 280 religious books.[52]

Pea Ridge has experienced growth in recent years. In October 1969 eight young people were baptized. The pattern of growth is seen in the fact that most of the young people who have been away in Civilian Public Service (CPS) and Voluntary Service (VS) have returned and established homes in the community. Some of them have brought wives into the fellowship by transfer of membership. The members in 1972 totaled fifty-two.[53]

6. *Lyon Street, Marion County*

Mark Twain made a tradition of Hannibal, Missouri, a town of twenty thousand fronting on the Mississippi. The fictitious characters of Tom Sawyer and Huck Finn are the best-known citizens, and tourists seek out the fence that Tom got his friends to whitewash for him.

Hannibal is in Marion County, only twelve miles from Palmyra. Here lived Ruth E. Buckwalter, who first began a Mennonite witness in Hannibal. About 1927 she would come to the city by bus to visit in the homes of the more needy people in Ricky Hollow. She moved to Hannibal in 1931 and held Bible classes in the homes. People were interested, and Bishop J. M. Kreider, her brother-in-law, held a series of meetings in an old schoolhouse. There were a few confessions. The next year Ira Johns came from Indiana and preached in an upstairs hall.

Miss Buckwalter asked for help in this work, and J. M. Kreider brought the need to the Mission Board of the Missouri-Kansas Conference. Nelson E. Kauffman, a graduate of the Bible course at Hesston College, was teaching school near Halstead, Kansas. He and his wife, Christmas Carol, who later became a well-known author, accepted the call to Hannibal, and came there in May 1934 with their only child. This was the bottom of the Depression, and it was a real step of faith on the part of both the Kauffmans and the Mission Board to start this new work.

The first meetinghouse was a storefront wedge-shaped brick building on Market Street, with a meeting room about 20 by 50 feet, and a seating capacity of 50. The Kauffmans lived on the second floor. Ruth Buckwalter introduced them to the people she had been working with. Many of them were unemployed and on relief. Some homes were made of store boxes and had dirt floors, with old oil barrels for stoves. The workers themselves had difficulties in making the available financing reach. One day Mrs. Kauffman suggested that Nelson should try to sell one of their quilts. He failed to find a buyer, but one man loaned him a dollar.

The men folks of the mission group would go to H. R. Buckwalter's farm near Palmyra to cut wood for the stoves at the church and the mission home. They would also grow potatoes, beans, and tomatoes for the mission family.

Thus began the Hannibal Gospel Mission. From the start there was a strong evangelistic emphasis. The first evangelistic services

*The work at Hannibal began
here on Market Street*

were held by J. D. Mininger in October 1934. There were forty-one who accepted Christ, and twenty-seven of these were baptized. Names among the twelve charter members of the church were Bagby, Lain, Smith, Vedenhauft, McDonald, Crane, and Snyder. They were all in the lower-income brackets of the laboring class. Many of them scarcely knew what Christianity was.

In 1935 Mrs. Kauffman's father paid for the site of a church building. That summer a tabernacle, 25 by 62 feet, that could seat 150, was built for the evangelistic meetings by J. S. Neuhouser.

The new church was built here on Lyon Street in 1936. Many men from the Iowa and Missouri churches donated labor, and the serviceable brick church cost only $7,600. The building was dedicated on December 13, 1936. The name was still Mennonite Gospel Mission; not until 1960 was the name of the congregation changed to Lyon Street Mennonite Church. Affiliation with the Missouri-Kansas Conference dates from 1935. The first trustees of the church were Nelson Kauffman, Leroy Zook, and Emery King.

A constitution was adopted in 1952, and has been revised several times since then. The first annual business meeting was held in September 1953. As a mission, regular financial reports were given to the Conference Mission Board until 1949, when Board sponsorship ceased. However, there was a Church Council from August 1948. The first members were Clyde Stutzman, Leroy Zook, Emery King, Arland Miller, George Gingerich, and Nelson Kauffman.

The congregation has no cemetery of its own, as various

cemeteries of the city are available. It is evident that the traditional cemetery near the typical country Mennonite church merely shows that a frontier church had to provide a burial place for its members; there is no feeling that Mennonite separation from the world is extended even to their burial. (In some areas of Europe in earlier centuries Mennonites were not permitted to bury their dead in the city cemeteries.)

From 1934 to 1942 baptisms in this church totaled 32. Sixteen were received by certificate of membership; 12 were transferred from other churches; 10 were received by confession. Seventy-five transferred to other congregations, a few to other denominations; 54 withdrew; 31 were excommunicated; 49 members passed away. The membership in 1972 was 52. Two factional disturbances at different times have had their deterrent effect.

Evangelistic meetings have been held every year, sometimes twice a year. From 1949 to 1955 this took the form of a tent campaign, with some of the denomination's best-known evangelists in charge: B. Charles Hostetter, Kenneth Good, Howard Hammer, John R. Mumaw, Myron S. Augsburger, and George R. Brunk. Publicity was given through the use of doorknob announcements, newspaper ads, blotters, placards, street signs. Evangelists preaching in the church included Maurice O'Connell, James Bucher, Jesse Short, Milton Brackbill, Hubert Schwartzentruber, and Roy S. Koch.

As a part of the "Hannibal for Christ" tent campaign in 1949, Kauffman spoke each weekday for five weeks over KHMO, a local radio station. As a follow-up of the campaign, "Christ for Today," a weekly Sunday morning broadcast was begun and continued until 1954. This radio program was supported by contributions of friends, listeners, and congregations. Few appeals for money were made on the air. Live music was provided by the Christ for Today Ladies' Quintet (Ruth King, Fern Stutzman, Madonna Eberly, Anna Margaret Kreider, and Carol Kauffman), and the Christ for Today Men's Quartet (Ben Eberly, Harold Kreider, Stanlee Kauffman, and Robert Hartzler). Recordings were also used. A sponsoring board was made up of various churchmen in Missouri and Iowa. The listening area included all of northeastern Missouri and a considerable portion of southeastern Iowa and western Illinois.

An effective form of evangelism has been the prison ministry. Prisons in Hannibal, Palmyra, and Jefferson City have been visited regularly. A dramatic conversion was that of Johnnie Allison, in jail

Bible school at the new church in 1939 — the older man (front center) is J. M. Kreider

at Palmyra for the murder of his father-in-law. Sentenced to a prison term in the State Penitentiary at Jefferson City, he gave a good witness to his fellow prisoners, several of whom constituted a congregation of believers visited every two weeks for a time by the Hannibal workers. Johnnie Allison's story was told by Carol Kauffman in the booklet, *Life with Life*, of which Herald Press printed 10,000 copies.

Thelma Johnson, also converted at the Palmyra jail, was baptized in 1963.

The Good Samaritan Hall furnished meals for poor men throughout two winters, 1939 and 1940. The city furnished the soup meat for these meals. This gave a good opportunity for Christian witness.

Between 1949 and 1953 three different buses were used to bring people to church.

At Lyon Street evangelism and service blend imperceptibly. From the early years young people from various congregations were brought in to help with summer Bible school, tent meetings, and other special features. Some came to help with the regular church program while they supported themselves through employment in the city, for a period up to four years. From 1961 to 1969 the Mennonite Board of Missions at Elkhart has maintained Voluntary Service units at Hannibal. They have worked at the Levering Hospital, the Beth-Haven Nursing Home, and at the Sheltered Workshop. The following men with their wives served as houseparents: Earl Eberly, Lee Miller, Russel Grove, Frank Keller, Emanuel Gingerich, and Stanley Ross. Workers at Beth-Haven have been very active in the total program of the congregation.

Beth-Haven Nursing Home was established in 1957 by the Mennonite Home Association, which administers the Home for the Mennonite Board of Missions. Peter Hartman has served as the administrator. Operations were begun in a century-old building. The full purchase price, $33,000, was recovered from operations in a period of six years.

Beth-Haven is the only professionally accredited nursing home within a 28-mile radius of Hannibal, and a new and larger plant was needed. Allen H. Erb, longtime leader in health care in the Mennonite Church, had made a study in 1957 on the need for a nursing home in the Hannibal area. Now a decade later he advised the planners in such matters as securing land, funds, and community support and cooperation.

A new site was purchased in September 1967 for a new nursing home. A Hill-Burton federal grant of $467,000 was secured; the remainder of the total cost of over $1,000,000 was borrowed from thirteen financial institutions in Hannibal, to be repaid out of operations over a period of years. In September 1970 construction began on the 29,000-square-foot building. In March 1972 it was ready for the first of its sixty residents.

The dedication on March 19 was attended by 1,400 people. Speakers were J. P. Russell, director of hospital and technical services of the Missouri Division of Health, and Luke Birky, secretary for health and welfare, Mennonite Board of Missions. The prayer of dedication was by 83-year-old Allen H. Erb.

Women's groups in forty-three Mennonite churches in ten states donated more than 650 pieces of linens and quilts. About thirty people staff the new home. In the old building twelve persons operate a shelter-care facility for twenty-eight ambulatory guests. There is a registered nurse at each location.[54]

At the time of the opening of the new facility the following directors constituted the Mennonite Home Association: Daniel H. Bender, president; Leslie F. Hathaway, vice-president; Willard B. Burkholder, secretary; Wendell D. Kreider, treasurer; Mrs. Donald W. Greene, John F. Kreider, Bayard C. Plowman, Dr. Merrill J. Roller, and Orland O. Yates.

In December 1968 the congregation wrapped 80 Christmas gifts for the children at the Diagnostic Clinic.

One of the by-products of the mingling of young people on the working force at Hannibal is a number of marriages. Nineteen couples who met at Hannibal were later married. The first couple who were married by Nelson Kauffman at the old Market Street Mission in 1936 were Leroy Zook and Naomi Detweiler.

An aid to the social life of the congregation is the church kitchen completed in 1966.

Several efforts have been made to promote interracial understanding. In 1961 and 1962 international students from Columbia and Kirksville, Missouri, were entertained. In 1969 a morning service was provided by the choir of the Bethesda Mennonite Church at St. Louis. The visitors ate with the congregation at a carry-in dinner. The evening speaker was Chauncey Lathem, assistant pastor at Bethesda. Just a month later the Mighty Men of Song, a black ensemble, gave a program.

Clothing drives, mother's classes, distribution of literature, counseling, helping couples arrange adoptions, working with broken homes: in these ways also the Hannibal Church ministers to its world.

The first youth organization was the True Blue Literary, organized in 1938. It gave way in 1956 to a more strictly youth program as a Mennonite Youth Fellowship, which engages in visitation work and raises money by various means.

The women organized a Dorcas Sewing Circle in 1946. Earlier in the mission program there had been sewing classes. In 1950 the name was changed to Women's Missionary and Service Auxiliary (WMSA), and in 1971 the Auxiliary became the Commission. They meet in the evening when the husbands of young mothers can take care of the children in late spring and summer; all day in fall and winter.

In the regular Sunday services the worship service has in recent years preceded the Sunday school. Time is given for testimonies and confessions, followed by prayer, sometimes silent.

Singing was at first from the *Church and Sunday School Hymnal* and *Life Songs No. 2*. In 1962 the MYF presented to the congregation the *Church Hymnal*. Singing is unaccompanied. Marvin Miller taught a singing class in 1955. There was a men's choir in 1962.

Bible Conferences were held from 1956 to 1964, with such speakers as G. G. Yoder, H. A. Diener, Allen Erb, and Richard Birky. Special speakers have been frequent: J. C. Wenger, "God's Word Written"; Clayton Beyler, "The Call to Preach"; Jacob Peltz, "To the Jew First"; Orval Shoemaker, to parents and young people.

The first church bulletins were used in March 1953. Up to that time pastoral letters were used to communicate to the congregation. In June 1958 the congregation first adopted the Every Home Plan for *Gospel Herald* subscriptions.

MYF and WMSC raise money by sale of cookbooks, car washes, moth cakes, and food. The church has used the budget plan of financing since 1961.

Since 1940, all weddings are in the church. Long wedding gowns and the wedding veil are now permitted. The holy kiss, used frequently before 1960, is now practiced only in connection with foot washing. The prayer veiling is still worn by the older members, but the younger generation is getting away from it. All women wore bonnets at first, made by Mrs. Kauffman. After she left (1956) there was no one to make them. Younger women now wear hats. Communion and foot washing are combined in one service, usually on a Sunday or Wednesday evening — this since 1963, to accommodate those working in hospitals and nursing homes. For years flowers were not allowed at funerals, but now are permitted.

The three northeast Missouri congregations cooperate in many ways: Sunday school, mission, doctrinal meetings; world day of prayer; Mennonite Disaster Service; hymn-sings; the three congregations hosted the South Central Conference on the Hannibal-Lagrange College Campus in 1962.

The Lyon Street Church participates in community activities. Ronald McKengie, a local officer, spoke at the church in 1966 on the prevention of juvenile crime. The church unites with others in a Thanksgiving service. They were invited by the Mennonite Brethren to a "singspirational" program and by the Pilgrim Holiness to a New Year's program. They use non-Mennonites in the pulpit, including a Lagrange College Bible teacher to teach a course on "How to Study the Bible." They accept the services of a women's auxiliary for Beth-Haven. The pastor and his wife attended an ecumenical prayer seminar at Springfield. The pastor's wife serves on the Board of Directors of the Day Care Center.

And yet there is a strong Mennonite orientation. Delegates attend conference and report to the congregation. They used *Glimpses of Mennonite History* for a Sunday evening text. The pastor teaches the *Confession of Faith*. Representatives attended Missions 69 and 71 and Probe 72. They study the *Mennonite Hour* course on witnessing. Representatives attended the Sunday school workshop at Kalona, Iowa. They welcome choruses and gospel teams from Mennonite schools and visits by Mennonite missionaries from many fields. They were willing to release Pastor Nelson Kauffman for a staff assignment on the Mennonite Mission Board.

In 1968 the library committee encouraged the reading of books by putting on a contest between "The Book Worms" and "The Book Barons." The losing group entertained the winners with homemade ice cream.

Mattie Kreider, as historian of the congregation, keeps a careful record of all events, including programs of special meetings.

Who were the leaders in the uninhibited and spiritual program at Lyon Street? First, the bishops and ministers. J. M. Kreider, veteran pastor and bishop at Palmyra, gave excellent cooperation to the young missionary he called to a difficult field at a difficult time. He served for six years, until he ordained Kauffman to the office of bishop in 1940. He died in 1946.

Nelson Kauffman, radio pastor

Nelson E. Kauffman, born in 1904 in Cass County, Missouri, was ordained to the ministry on August 26, 1934, and as bishop on September 22, 1940. With evangelistic zeal he applied his preaching and administrative abilities to the establishment of a mission and the building of a congregation. In addition to local responsibilities he carried denominational assignments: bishop of Missouri churches after 1946, extensive evangelistic work, and a long term as the president of the Mennonite Board of Education. At the call of the Mennonite Board of Missions to become Secretary of Home Missions, he terminated his work at Hannibal in the fall of 1956. In April 1973, after a short pastorate at Albany, Oregon, he came to Hannibal for a series of meetings just before the big Mississippi flood, and stayed through May to direct relief work.

However, he had shared his bishop responsibilities with Daniel Kauffman, pastor at Mt. Pisgah, who was ordained as bishop in 1951. Daniel Kauffman was elected to the office of overseer in August 1955 by the ministers and lay delegates of the Missouri churches in accordance with the new plan for supervision set up by the South Central Conference. Daniel Kauffman also served as interim pastor at Hannibal from September 1959 to June 1961.

Nelson Kauffman's immediate successor at Hannibal was Harold

Kreider, who had become associate pastor in 1953. After 1956 he
served as pastor until July 1959, when he resigned and moved to
Goshen, Indiana, to complete his college and seminary education.

One of Nelson Kauffman's real accomplishments at Hannibal was
the discovery and the training of pastoral talent. A total of twenty-
two men who came to Hannibal to help with the work there were
later ordained to the ministry and three as deacons. It was an education in Christian witness to go with Nelson on a visit to prisoners
in a jail and hear him talk to them.

When Daniel Kauffman returned to his church at Cherry Box, he
licensed Earl Eberly to take over at Hannibal in June 1961. A year
later Eberly was ordained. In 1966 he resigned to accept the pastorate
at Sycamore Grove in Cass County, Missouri.

Frank and Sue Keller came to Hannibal to serve as VS unit
leaders in 1964. Natives of eastern Pennsylvania, they had watched
with interest as some of their friends moved to northern Minnesota to do mission work. They too became self-supporting missionaries in that north country. Returning to Pennsylvania, they joined
a group of people who moved to a mountainous region in the northern
part of the state in the interests of evangelism. As a unit leader
at Hannibal, Frank's enthusiastic witness was contagious. In his
second year the church was without a pastor. He filled the pulpit
whenever called upon. In November 1966 he was licensed to preach.
After a year of service they returned to Forksville, Pennsylvania, because of Mrs. Keller's health. But in April 1967 they were back, and
Keller was again licensed to preach, and he served as pastor until
1968.

Peter Hartman, administrator at Beth-Haven, served as lay pastor during the winter's absence of Keller in 1966-1967. In 1974 he
is serving as the Conference treasurer.

Oliver Yutzy was licensed and installed as pastor in June 1968.
He was ordained to the ministry in 1969, and was still the pastor in
1973.

Two students of Goshen Biblical Seminary served as interns at
Hannibal under the supervision of Nelson Kauffman. David Mann
served his apprenticeship September 1954 to August 1955. He was
licensed in October 1954. He assisted in preaching, visitation, and
community outreach. He did some of the radio preaching. He organized and carried out the first children's and youth camp at Florida,
Missouri. He later became pastor at Albany, Oregon. When in 1970

he wished for a leave of absence, it is not strange that Nelson Kauffman should go to Albany as interim pastor.

Richard Miller was the second intern at Hannibal — from September to September 1955-1956. He was licensed in September 1955. The pastorate to which he moved was at Fort Dodge, Iowa.

Lyon Street has had two deacons. A. LeRoy Zook was ordained in November 1944, and has made a continuing contribution to the work from its very beginning.

John F. Kreider, son of Bishop J. M. Kreider and husband of the congregation's historian, was ordained for the Palmyra congregation in 1928. When the Palmyra congregation was dissolved in 1956, the Kreiders joined the Hannibal Mission Church. John has been a valued member of the church council.[55]

LeRoy and Naomi Zook

7. *Evening Shade (Osage River Churches)*

The westward flow of population after the Civil War brought many people from Kentucky, Tennessee, Indiana, and Ohio to the hills of Missouri. Traveling by covered wagon and on horseback, armed with rifles and axes, they established homes in a country that was similar to the hills from which they had come. Perhaps the hill land was cheaper than the more level land to the north. At any rate, when the Mennonites of Morgan County first made contact with the settlers along the winding Osage River, the Wilsons, Coffmans, Summers, Letts, Colliers, Carvers, and Kings were well established. They were not rich, but some of them farmed the rich bottomland and raised good crops. They knew that "where the redbird built its nest low," the water would not rise high enough to wash out the crops. Some built their log cabins on the ridges and hoed their corn on the slopes, hoping that erosion would not wash all the soil away. To get money to buy flour, salt, sugar, and their simple clothing, the men cut railroad ties out of the woods, and floated them down the river or hauled them to such railroad towns as Versailles, twenty miles away. Garden truck and sorghum for molasses they could raise, and there were berries and nuts in the woods.

Most of these people had church privileges in the East. But on this Western frontier they were beyond the reach of circuit riders, class leaders, elders, and camp meetings. Preachers were few. Sometimes a community could secure the promise of a preacher in some distant town to ride out once or twice a month. But the road was up and down hill, doubling its length as it wound down the valleys. A new man could easily make the wrong turn and lose his way. The hill folk had learned that even though a "meetin'" had been promised, they could not be sure of a preacher.

One particular community in these hills was called Wilson Bend, as one of the loops of the Osage formed the boundary of the Wilson farm. Carver was the name of the country store where people could bring their eggs and hides and trade them for groceries or cloth. Here was the post office, distributing the mail brought on the mail hack from Versailles. Nearby was a schoolhouse — at first a log building with a wood-burning stove in the center, homemade benches, and a scanty blackboard. Later there was a frame building with factory-made seats.

Preachers sometimes held meetings in the Carver Schoolhouse. But when so often the preacher did not arrive, the people became discouraged. Young people gathered along the river for dancing and drinking. This often led to fights and feuds.

One outstanding citizen, Charles Foster, although not a Christian himself, knew what the community needed. He had lived formerly in the Mt. Zion community, a neighbor of D. F. Driver. He told his neighbors at Carver that he knew some preachers who would come when they promised. And so the Mennonites were invited.

Daniel Kauffman, a young minister at the time, conducted the first service in May 1901, on Saturday evening, Sunday morning, and Sunday evening. The people liked what they heard, and invited the preacher to come back. From that time on there were regular monthly appointments. Usually it was D. F. Driver who went, and so this was really missionary outreach from Mt. Zion, one of the early examples of rural mission work. It was a three-day trip, 30 miles each way. Early Saturday morning the preacher was on his way in a buggy. At Gravois Mills he halted for rest, and for food and water for himself and his horse. By evening he drove into the gate of some participating family for a supper of cornbread, meat, and gravy. There would be two or three services, and Monday he would drive home again. He expected no remuneration, either for his services or to furnish the horse and buggy for a strenuous trip on a rocky road. In seven years D. F. Driver wore out two buggies.

In 1904 a Sunday school was organized so there could be services even when there was no preacher. Mrs. Desta Wilson was the superintendent. Occasionally there was a series of evangelistic meetings with such evangelists as D. D. Miller of Indiana, J. E. Hartzler of Cass County, George R. Brunk of Kansas, J. M. Kreider of Marion County, and J. R. Shank, recently ordained for mission work at Pea Ridge. In 1908 there was a class of converts who had never before made a profession. A total membership of 20 was in prospect for the organization of a church. J. L. Collier, a former Baptist, was ordained deacon in August 1908 by Daniel Kauffman, and J. R. Shank came to serve as pastor. The first trustees were S. M. Carver, J. L. Collier, and John Calfee. So Wilson Bend was now a regular organized church in the Missouri-Iowa Mennonite Conference. They met in the Carver Schoolhouse.

For Shank this was the beginning of a lifetime of service with and for his beloved hill people. The typical farm home of the community consisted of a log or frame house, a log barn to shelter a few horses and cows, a pigsty in some fence corner, and perhaps a shed for a small flock of chickens. Water was obtained either from a nearby spring or drawn from a well with a bucket and a rope over a pulley. The first year Shank lived in a two-room log house a mile from the school. His sisters Emma and Rose kept house for him for two years. After that he was a boarder for many years.

The new congregation immediately began to plan for a church building. Construction got under way in August 1909 and by Septem-

This church building served at Carver
until the lake waters came to its doors
in 1931

John R. and Clara Brubaker
Shank, who loved and
served the hill people

ber of the next year the cement-block building, looking out over the
Osage River bottoms, was ready for dedication. A. D. Wenger
preached the dedicatory sermon, and in the week following held
evangelistic meetings. A few members were added, including one
woman from another denomination who requested to be baptized
again by pouring.

The new church had homemade benches and was heated with
wood stoves. Men of the congregation would spend a day in the
woods occasionally to cut fuel. Kerosine lamps were used for lighting.
There was a low rostrum for the pulpit at one end. Later this was
moved to one side and the seats rearranged so that the rowdies of
the community could not so easily slip in to make disturbances.

In 1911 Shank bought a small farm and erected a modest new
house. He farmed the tillable acres and raised chickens, despite the
raids of egg-sucking snakes and blood-sucking weasels. For many
years he supplemented his income by writing educational materials
for Mennonite Publishing House. By this time his pastoral services had
made him known and respected on both sides of the river.

J. C. Gingerich and family came in 1913 and for three years
gave their help in the work at Carver. The work was growing and
there were calls for preaching at other places. The Proctor work
opened when a woman converted at Wilson Bend moved to that section northwest up the river. The Jenkins appointment came through
those who were often at Wilson Bend meetings. The Purvis work
started because a member at Wilson Bend, Andy Purvis, had formerly

lived there and wanted his old neighbors to hear this teaching. At Proctor a man told of teenagers at Little Buffalo who had never been in a religious service. At Little Buffalo people were present from across the river at Lick Creek and Sagrada who said there were no services of any kind in their community. This touched the heart of Shank, and he could not rest. On a Monday morning he and H. A. Diener forded the Osage and rode horseback through a sandstorm twelve miles up the river to Sagrada. At the store and post office they left word of a meeting that night at the school. Taking turns, they preached each night, Monday to Friday.

So this was the pattern of expansion: the word spread of the availability of preachers; the requests came for appointments; a new center of preaching was established.

In 1916 eight members were received at Purvis, a hamlet down the river. H. A. Diener and family located at Proctor and stayed for five years. In 1917 E. C. Bowman and wife came from Kansas City. They lived in Shank's house. He came back to live with them and the house was enlarged. In 1918 Bowman was ordained and took his turn in preaching. In 1923 Mrs. Bowman died. Bowman went to Canada, and Herman Swartzendruber and family came from Hesston College with his family to help in the work. After three years Bowman returned and the Swartzendrubers moved to Iowa.

In 1925 J. R. Shank was married to Clara Brubaker, a schoolteacher from Birch Tree, Missouri. She understood well the ways of the hill people, and her coming was a blessing both to her bachelor husband and to the church.

In 1921 J. P. Brubaker and his wife, Ida, came to this field, locating near Holst Schoolhouse, not far from Proctor. He was ordained to the ministry by Bishop J. C. Driver. Brubaker was the brother of Clara Brubaker, and like J. R. Shank, he was destined to give a lifetime of service in this mission field.

Two circumstances that could not have been anticipated greatly affected the work in the Osage River area. The first was the coming of World War I, and opposition to the position of the Mennonite Church against war. Even before the war some opposition was voiced on account of Mennonite teaching against the use of tobacco, the remarriage of divorced people, fashionable dress, and worldly amusements. Some Mennonite members became unsettled and joined other groups who had come in to destroy what had been accomplished. Others returned completely to a life of sin.

When war broke out, the opposers used the excuse of patriotism to fight the Mennonite Church. They accused the Mennonites of being traitorous sympathizers with the Germans. Many who had been sympathetic listeners before now heartily turned against the Mennonite doctrine and would have nothing to do with its message-bearers. Stones and rotten eggs were fitting expressions of the hatred in the hearts of many. At Purvis Mr. Dunaway, with whom Shank was boarding, was threatened with trouble if he did not get rid of the "yellow" preacher. Shank returned to his home at Wilson Bend and closed the services at Purvis, keeping in touch with the members personally. At Proctor E. C. Bowman was egged while he was preaching, which he accepted without rancor.

Although many members became afraid and withdrew from the church fellowship, the workers could not be frightened away. Some appointments were dropped for a time, but as best they could the workers tried to keep in contact with members and with anyone who needed and would accept their help. During the flu epidemic of 1918 Shank went into homes where no one else would go and cared for the sick. It was hard to see that he was an enemy of the country. The Mennonites were on the alert to again open services as opportunity afforded.

With the return of peace the whole field, including Purvis and Proctor, was opened again to Mennonite preaching. The opposers were probably ashamed, and kept silent. However, the damage done to the weak in faith could seldom be undone.

And yet the church was not knocked out. There were twenty members when Shank arrived in 1908. In twenty years 120 persons were received into the church. The membership in 1928 was fifty-six; distributed as follows: seven at Sagrada, across the river; fourteen at Holst; three at Proctor; twenty-five at Wilson Bend. Given normal conditions, the church might have grown as the gospel was preached, and lived, at places new and old up and down the Osage.

But the second hindering circumstance was the building of the Bagnell Dam, which revolutionized the life of the area. As early as 1911 surveys were being made to discover the possibilities of this region for recreation and vacationing. With good roads it would be within easy weekend driving distance from big cities. The dam could make the electricity needed to turn this whole region from yesterday into today. The water backed up from the dam would form one of the largest artificial lakes in the country, with hundreds of miles of beautiful shoreline. But of course everyone would have to move out of the bottoms, and a new kind of people would serve the affluence and pleasure of vacationers.

In 1930 the Wilson Bend congregation yielded to the inevitable and voted to sell the church site to the Union Electric and Development Company. The actual building of the dam had begun in 1929. From February to September, 1931, the lake filled and the water came within 100 feet of the front step of the church. Its position was impracticable, and so the church which had been so carefully built in the early days of the work in this region was taken down and sold. The money from the sale was kept for use in building another preaching center somewhere. From the former church site one now looks down on the beautiful Lake of the Ozarks, which reaches as far as Warsaw, forty-five miles west of Bagnell.

Now the old river crossings are only a memory. Like the time Shank and J. M. Kreider were fording the river in a buggy to get to Lick Creek. It had rained and the water was rising. As the water came into the box of the buggy, they moved their baggage up into the seat. Then they themselves got on to the seat. Kreider prayed, and they got across safely. Or the time when Brubaker was needing to cross when the river was ice-covered. Rather than go an extra eight miles on horseback, he stabled his horse with neighbors, cut a stout stick, and crossed on the ice, testing it all the way across with his stick.

Already in 1925, after J. R. Shank's marriage, E. C. Bowman had moved to Linn, seventy miles to the northeast, to shepherd a family group who had moved there from Pea Ridge to engage in lumbering on a tract of timberland they had purchased. These people kept their membership at Palmyra, and J. M. Kreider was much interested to see that they had spiritual care. The people at Linn were the same kind of folk Bowman had labored with around Carver — "proud" to be called hillbillies. It was not hard to interest the children of the community in summer Bible school. This was held in a school at Freedom for a number of years, with an attendance of thirty-five to forty-five. Teachers came from Hannibal and Palmyra. Alice Hershberger came from Cass County to teach the children, and after a time she became Mrs. Bowman.

Once William Jennings held meetings, and there were nineteen converts. All of these had been Bible school pupils. Some, however, joined the Methodist Church.

Church services were held first in the Philips home, later in a union church in Freedom. A Snyder family moved in from Hannibal. The highest membership was twenty-nine, with thirty to forty attending. For a time there were Sunday schools.

Because of hard times and unemployment during the Depression, families moved away. By 1940 Bowman was in ill health, and once a month called on Leroy Gingerich at Versailles for help. In 1942 the last two families moved to Peoria, Illinois, where they became active in the church. After about twenty years of Mennonite witness in this community, the work was closed.

At Carver, only one family, that of S. M. Carver, was left of the old community. The schoolhouse had been moved, and appointments were made there. At Purvis also the school was moved, and appointments continued. At Jenkins war prejudice had turned the people against the Mennonites and the schoolhouse was still closed to them. But in 1933, after the old school was lost in a fire, and a new one replaced it, some of the families began to wish for services again. They were not refused.

The Shanks moved to a place near Bond, toward Bagnell Dam, and operated from there for a time. Then they moved to the Mt. Zion community in order to be able to serve some of the Holst families who had moved to Florence, fifteen miles north of Versailles. Late in the thirties Shank moved back to the hills. During these years the developing work at Culp, Arkansas, was added to his responsibility, and he went down there frequently.

Leroy Gingerich and wife, of the Mt. Zion congregation, conducted a Sunday school at Rocky Ridge, a schoolhouse. Shank needed Gingerich's help in meeting preaching appointments, and so in 1936 he was ordained to the ministry for service in the Ozarks, as well as at Mt. Zion. Shank and Gingerich each gave part of one Sunday a month to Mt. Zion. One Sunday they were at Rocky Ridge and Florence, and another at Bond, Jenkins, Purvis, and Carver. Thus did these indefatigable workers do all in their power to see that all who wanted to hear the gospel should have the opportunity.

This was also the era of the rising use of the summer Bible school. In 1936 M. M. Troyer, the field worker of the Missouri-Kansas Conference, came to the district to hold Bible schools — one at Lick Creek south of the Lake and the other at Jenkins, north of the Lake. Three young women from other areas came to help. Cars of the preachers brought pupils from a distance. The enrollment was

50. At Lick Creek the workers stayed in the Brubaker home nearby; at Jenkins they cooked their meals in the school and slept in homes of the community. Neighbors showed their appreciation by giving food — here where for fifteen years Mennonites were not welcome in the community.

In the forties it seemed best to erect another church building in the Carver area, and to coordinate the witness from there. And so the Providence Church was erected, and dedicated in February 1948. For a number of years there was good attendance there. Bible school was held each year until 1954. At that time the health of both John Shank and his wife was failing. Attendance had not kept up as they had hoped. Some of those who had formerly been attendants were now busy looking after needs of weekenders at motels, restaurants, and filling stations. The Shanks moved to Versailles, where they could be cared for by relatives. They both died in 1958, bringing to an end a devoted and sacrificial ministry in which they met many needs of their area in that time. There was no longer an organized church on the north side of the Lake. Needs of scattered members are being looked after by the Mt. Zion ministers.

When the plan for the big Lake made necessary the reorganization of the entire work in the Osage country, it was decided that the J. P. Brubakers should move across the river, first to Cable Ridge, and then to Lick Creek. In 1930, the year before the Lake filled in, they loaded all their belongings in a wagon and forded the Osage to their new field. They moved first into an old log house with loose floor boards and plenty of chink holes for ventilation. Five years later they were able to move into a new house built of concrete and stone. They were thirty miles from town, from a doctor, or an undertaker. So the people of this area often needed their help. Not until 1947 were undertakers used regularly. When death came to a home, the minister and his wife often went to the home and prepared the body for burial. A neighbor would make a coffin, which would be hauled by team and wagon to the graveyard for the burial. The missionaries also spent many nights sitting up with the sick.

In this area Brubaker filled appointments in schools at Cable Ridge, Post Oak, and Lick Creek. There was good interest.

Lick Creek is located in the northwest corner of Camden County. The address was first Sagrada, later Edwards, which is fifteen miles distant. When the Lake formed, it enclosed the community so that it could be entered only from the south.

Lick Creek Church

First services were held here in 1917. In 1919, after a revival effort, three women were received as the first members. In 1930, when the Brubakers moved in, the membership was five. By 1938 there were some twenty members. A congregation was organized in 1939 by Bishop J. C. Driver. A constitution was adopted. The highest membership at any time was twenty-seven. More than forty persons have had membership here at some time.

After the consolidation of schools the Lick Creek Schoolhouse, with a plot of ground, was sold to the Lick Creek congregation for a sum of $50 on April 9, 1953, and trustees were elected.

Attendance at Sunday school ran as high as fifty. Bible school was held for twenty years, 1936-1955, with enrollment as high as forty-five. A sewing circle was organized in 1943. At first circles in Iowa paid for the cut garments to be made for relief, but after 1964 the circle paid for its own materials. Meeting monthly, they made garments, quilts, and comforters. From 1930 there were Sunday night meetings, but none after 1950.

Esther Detwiler and Lydia Driver each taught school for several years at Lick Creek and helped in church activities. In 1941 the V. D. Miller family moved here from Kansas City and stayed until 1949. They were a help to the church.

But economic conditions were against the church. People moved away for better opportunities. Young people moved away to get jobs. Electricity came in 1950 and the telephone a little later. This helped the standard of living, but it also made bills that had to be paid. One old widow lady said that it used to be if she could raise ten bushels of corn, with her fruit and vegetables, she had her living. But not now. Few can make a living on their hilly acres. The timber on the hills furnishes fuel, but little else.

And so the attendance went down. At one time in 1966 there were no families with children in the community. In July 1967 the Brubakers moved to Versailles, but continued services until November 4, 1967, when there were nineteen in attendance. Two weeks before they moved there was a homecoming day at the church, with one hundred there for dinner. Two of the remaining members transferred to Evening Shade, and others are attending nearby churches. The Brubakers continue to visit in the community.

Evening Shade is the only congregation of the Osage field now affiliated with the South Central Mennonite Conference. It had its beginning after the scattering which came with the Lake development. The E. E. Estes family moved to the Post Oak community, on the south side of the Lake, farther west toward Warsaw, and requested services. Beginning in 1933, Brubaker preached here once a month. In 1938 the Brubakers held the first summer Bible school. A few years later the V. D. Millers started a Sunday school. This was discontinued for a short time in 1946 and then started up again under the sponsorship of the Sycamore Grove congregation, where W. R. Hershberger was bishop.

The Post Oak building was in such bad repair that the services were moved to the Evening Shade school building, which was later purchased.

When the Millers left the community in 1949, other workers from Sycamore Grove carried on. Alfred Yoder and wife lived in the area for a time. The Maynard Yoder family took leadership responsibilities in 1953. In 1956 Yoder was licensed and later ordained to the ministry.

In May 1959 the building was completely remodeled inside and a dedication service was held on June 28, 1959. In 1972 there were twenty-three members. Services are held Sunday morning and evening and Wednesday evening. A carload of workers comes from Cass County to help with the Sunday school.

Thus runs the story of seventy years of rural mission work in mid-America. Work was done in many communities we have not mentioned. Nor have all the people been named who were a part of this effort. One cannot describe the work as a glowing success.

There were mighty adversaries, and no doubt mistakes were made
But the gospel was presented where there was hunger for it, Bible
truth was presented without apology, and many lives were redeemed
Said one lady, "If no one else was helped, it was worthwhile because
I was saved."[56]

8. *Kansas City Mennonite Fellowship*

The Kansas City Mennonite Fellowship is a Mennonite Church
in the hospital area of downtown Kansas City, Missouri. It is a direct
development from a Voluntary Service program.

In 1948 the Mennonite Relief and Service Committee (Elkhart
set up its first long-term Voluntary Service unit. Its three members
worked at the Kansas City General Hospital. They were housed
at the Mennonite Gospel Center, many blocks away. In October of
that same year these volunteers moved into a unit home at 2515
Holmes, within easy walking distance of the hospital. However, these
nurse aides and orderlies continued to help with the church work a
the Gospel Center and at another mission Sunday school.

The house on Holmes was adequate for unit living until the
number increased to sixteen, and the VSers felt the call to serve the
neighborhood. There was a growing conviction for weekly Bible and
craft classes, with different age-groups meeting each afternoon afte
school and work hours.

To get more room the unit in 1954 moved across the street to
2512 to a larger building that had once been a funeral parlor and
later a cosmetics supply house. Unit members spent hours of plus
service in sanding floors and building in shelves before they car
ried their possessions to their new quarters. Carrying the freeze
across the street made good publicity. The community could hardly
ignore the unit after that!

Almost from the beginning, the VSers had been concerned fo
community youngsters that swarmed on the streets around them. The
new quarters gave them space to put their convictions into action
The first clubs were organized in 1954. These not only kept the chil
dren off the streets, but also opened doors into community homes
Summer Bible school (beginning in June 1956) helped in this, so tha
parents eventually began to ask, "Why can't we have Bible schoc
all summer long?" The young people decided they could; at least, o
Sunday morning. Sunday school began in July 1956, and a real effor
was made to reach whole families for God and His church. Evening

Winifred Mumaw with a Bible school class at Kansas City

Pastoral call by Roman Stutzman at the apartment of Melvin and Edith Yoder

and midweek classes were added to the program, and a worship committee was appointed.

The group was organized into a congregation on December 8, 1957; the community requested the name Kansas City Mennonite Fellowship. Edwin I. Weaver, a former overseas missionary, was the first pastor. He and his wife, Irene, commuted from their home at Hesston. Most of the VSers and nurses wanted to be associate members, but the following were the nine charter members: Roman and Marianna Stutzman (unit leaders), Ronald Stutzman, Sue Farmwald, Vera May Miller, Henry Collins, Bernice Collins, Harold Burnett, Gerald Burnett. Five of these brought letters of transfer, two were received on confession of faith, and two were baptized.

In March of 1958 Roman Stutzman was licensed as pastor. At this time the average attendance was sixty. The meeting place was the big living room of the VS Center. Sunday school classes were scattered all over the place. In August 1958 the congregation was received into the South Central Conference.

A Bible class for mothers met weekly to discuss household hints, child training, and other practical subjects, as well as to meditate on the teachings of the Bible. Some of the women were Christians from other denominations who were concerned about their own spiritual welfare and about community outreach. Others admitted they were not Christians. Their presence indicated a hunger for the Lord and for association with the church.

In the summer of 1958 the church began to feel burdened because two bars were operating on the corner a few doors above the Center. They prayed about that matter. One evening eleven-year-old Billy Golden prayed that the Lord would remove them "because they make men drunk." He continued with: "This job is a little job for You, God." Not long after that one tavern closed and the building, 2500 Holmes, was rented by the church. It was redecorated and dedicated for worship instead of dissipation in September 1958. In the spring of 1959 the apartment upstairs was redecorated to be used by the Stutzmans as a parsonage. Both floors needed a lot of work, but the unit members and community friends pitched in to help. One woman said, "And just to think — you let us help to fix up the new church." Some of the men who once met in the tavern worked toward its transformation into a sanctuary of the Lord.

The congregation saw the ordination of Stutzman to the ministry in 1960. Through the years since then student nurses, young couples

The building that was converted from a tavern to a church

from the community and from Mennonite background, young people working in the city, and neighborhood people have kept the average attendance around sixty. Because of its mobile character the church has ministered to a procession rather than to a static group. People who have lived and served in the Holmes Street area continue to move out and find avenues of service in their new communities. This "witness-to-those-around-you" has been stressed through the years.

The Youth Center has made possible a ministry to unchurched "city kids" off the concrete jungle. The program was recreation, table and indoor games, clubs, hobbies, Christian counseling.

There have been baptismal services, weddings, memorial services, Mennonite inner-city meetings, pastoral and home church facilities for VSers and student nurses, Bible school for children and adults, services of thanksgiving and praise, with petitions for God's continued blessing and guidance.

The Voluntary Service program was terminated in the summer of 1963. Since 1948, 205 young people have served here. The former unit building was now an adequate church facility: the basement and garage for classes, the first floor for a worship center and a kitchen, the second floor a fellowship room for student nurses in the Hesston College program, and an apartment. Ron Hargett and wife, a working couple, occupied this; Ron was appointed assistant to the pastor.

The formal dedication of the new Center was on June 9, 1963.

Stutzman was installed for another term as pastor. Milo Kauffman, South Central overseer, conducted the service and announced a small subsidy by the conference for the fellowship. Over one hundred people attended this service.

Ray Horst, secretary for relief and service for the Board of Missions, noted that this marked the close of a fifteen-year working relationship. "This is a significant milestone in the life of the Kansas City Mennonite Fellowship," he said. "It is also the fulfillment of the VS unit begun in Kansas City. The Board hopes to see a similar pattern of church development in other locations."

A year later the parsonage was moved to the apartment in the church center, since the Hargetts had terminated services. In the fall of that year, 1964, there was announcement that the General Hospital would expand and that the people in the target area of the church would be evacuated in this urban-renewal project. The church council discussed the task of the church in this changing inner-city community. The congregation decided unanimously that the church should stay, that she should allow her witness to "take new shapes."

A vision for teenage work became a priority in the summer of 1965. The church should reach the dozens of young people near her door — teenagers who would not come to church. A neighbor couple pointed out that groups were already congregating daily on a corner three blocks south from the Fellowship Center. Dialogue took place on the street, and a building at 2805 Holmes Street was rented. With the help of the conference and the Elkhart VS Office a I-W man, Art Zehr, was brought to the city to lead recreational activities at the Mennonite Teen Center, thus launching another VS program.

Art was replaced in September 1966 by David and Audrey Thompson who, along with another VSer, Warren Ehrisman, occupied the apartment above the Center. A year and a half later this VS team reported enthusiastically about their program. About seventy-five inner-city young persons were using the facilities. The Girls' Club was learning to cook, sew, and knit. There were various boys' clubs, and a Bible study club for those of MYF age. A fair number of community youth were willing to participate in church-and-MYF-sponsored activities. There was good hope that community people would begin attending church as a result of Center contacts.

This program was sponsored jointly by Voluntary Service, Elkhart, and the Kansas City Fellowship. The WMSA of the conference had been helpful in many ways. The entire church at this location was communicating with the youth of the community — listening to them and in a small way meeting one of their basic needs: providing a place, a "pad" as they called it, where they can trust and be trusted. The emerging program developed slowly under the guidance of the Holy Spirit. The construction program had by Christmas, 1971, claimed properties to within a half block of the church.

The Stutzmans, after twenty years of service at Kansas City, moved in September 1972 to a position as hosts and tour guides at the Mennonite Information Center, a half block south of the Germantown Church in Philadelphia, the oldest Mennonite church in America. On September 17 they were given a final farewell by representatives of the more than 300 Voluntary Service workers to whom they were "Pop and Mom" through the years. On September 21 the mayor of Kansas City gave them the key to the city. He cited the Stutzmans for "outstanding service to the people of Kansas City," and added, "Your dedication to your church and your community have earned you the admiration and respect of all the people of Kansas City." John Heyerly succeeded Stutzman as pastor.

The membership of the Kansas City Fellowship in 1972 was thirty-seven. Many, in the procession to which she has ministered, will not be found on her membership roll, but nevertheless they feel a oneness in mission and a thankfulness for the visible church at the Kansas City Mennonite Fellowship. But changed circumstances called for the end of the congregation in 1974. [57]

9. *Bethesda, St. Louis*

Bethesda was the name of the pool in Jerusalem in Jesus' day where there was a great concentration of human need — the blind, the lame, the withered, and the helpless. Here Jesus healed an invalid man. And so Bethesda is a fitting name for a church that has the kind of ministry that Bethesda Mennonite Church has had in the heart of the St. Louis slums.

The first exploration of this city as a possible location for Mennonite outreach was made in the spring of 1956 by James Lark and Victor Esch. The same summer an interested Voluntary Service unit was assigned there. The unit consisted of four women and two men, one each from Indiana, Ohio, Pennsylvania, Iowa, and two from Saginaw, Michigan. They lived in an apartment owned by the Zion Evangelical and Reformed Church on Twenty-fifth Street.

They assisted the congregation there with a crafts program and a Bible school. They also conducted two Bible classes in the Pruitt-Igoe Housing Project, where the two fellows spent much time working with the Evangelical and Reformed pastors in a survey of the project.

In November 1956 James and Rowena Lark moved to St. Louis. They lived at 2229 O'Fallon, Apt. 906. This is in a densely populated, blighted area of the city. The Pruitt-Igoe Housing Project covers a land area of approximately 60 acres and houses fifteen thousand people, and the Sheridan Area surrounding it houses another twelve thousand. The people here have to endure vandalism, unfair prices, housing in disrepair, rats in the houses, and alleys full of garbage. They stay here rather than braving discrimination and rejection in less crowded areas of the city.

The Larks organized the Pruitt Homes Sunday school in January 1957, with sixteen present the first Sunday. The order of service included opening exercises, memory work, a song period, a class period, a review period, and dismissal with the Lord's Prayer and the singing of "the three Amens."

After a six-month period, however, the Pruitt Sunday school was closed because of a law against holding religious services in government housing. In September, Sunday school and church services were resumed at 2600 Howard Street, two blocks from the housing project.

The Larks were aging and wished to retire. And so the Mennonite Board of Missions sent Hubert and June Schwartzentruber, Canadians, to St. Louis. In November 1957 they moved into the apartment where the Larks had lived, and took over the work which the veterans had begun. They faced tremendous problems as they purposed to present in this ghetto setting a concerned and loving Christ embodied in a concerned and loving brotherhood.

The congregation was officially organized in May 1958. Carol, Rosa, and Joszet Hudson were baptized, and Willa, Billy, and Harold Mitchell, Lucy Foster, and Anna Melton were received into the fellowship on confession of their faith. These eight charter members formed the nucleus of the Bethesda Mennonite Church. The first communion service was held in connection with the organization.

In June 1958 the congregation moved into its present housing at 2823 Dayton Street. The next year the Mennonite Board of Missions purchased this building for $4,500. In turn it was sold to the congregation, involving the members immediately in the responsibility

James and Rowena Lark

of the ongoing program. The last payment on the property was made in 1963 through a special morning offering of $289.36, given on June 16.

Of course this building, like practically all others in the area, required renovation before it could serve the purposes of the church. The first floor became the worship center. The cross-shaped pulpit symbolized discipleship. The communion table spoke of fellowship — with God first, and then with men.

The third floor was remodeled in December 1958 — an apartment. The second floor got its turn in March 1959, and became classrooms and a VS apartment. Finally in January 1960 the basement got a cement floor, as it was made into class and club rooms. At various times other renovations were made — tile on the basement floor, siding on the walls, carpeting in the church, paint or paper on some walls.

There was help from the wider brotherhood. A group of men from Iowa laid floors. Carloads from Illinois and Missouri papered the apartments. A couple from Indiana repaired window and door frames. An Ontario couple, on vacation, made repairs. St. Louis Mennonites worked shoulder to shoulder with folks from the country. This was the witness of brotherhood — a language the ghetto could understand.

The first summer service unit to serve the new congregation, and in the new location, came June 15, 1958. While they were there the first summer Bible school was held, with 75 pupils enrolled. In October of that year Hubert Schwartzentruber was ordained to the ministry.

The Bethesda Mennonite Church applied for membership in the South Central Conference and was accepted in August 1960. During the same month the congregation became a member of the Metropolitan Church Federation of St. Louis.

In August 1962, after much discussion in which the congregation faced what their needs were and how they could best be organized to meet these needs, a constitution for Bethesda was approved by membership.

While these organizational matters were being taken care of, at the same time the program of action was rapidly developing. At Bethesda social and spiritual needs have been seen as existing together. The congregation has recognized that they need Christ as a Redeemer from sin. But they also need freedom, jobs, education, homes, safety, security, health care. And the program has worked toward the meeting of all these needs together.[58]

The church was open every day for reading, counseling, preschool classes, clubs, youth activities, as a meeting place for community organizations. The Sunday worship often had overflowing crowds.

There were special evangelistic meetings: John F. Garber in the fall of 1958: Dale Schumm at Easter, 1959; Osiah Horst at the first anniversary in June 1959; Arthur Cash in July 1959; John Garber again in October 1960; Dale Schumm again in 1962; O. O. Wolfe for Passion Week in 1964.

There has been summer Bible school: 75 children in 1958; 239 in 1959; 250 in 1960; 326 in 1961 (a parade from the Project each morning with drums and flags); 414 in 1962; 300 in 1963; 250 in 1964. In 1965 there was a joint school with Northside Team Ministry with over 600 enrolled. But after that it was decided to use different media for teaching.

The Bible clubs have been successful. These classes for children met in homes in the Pruitt-Igoe Housing Project once a week. For several years flannelgraph materials from Child Evangelism were used; later, materials from the Bible Club movement. They began in 1958, with sixty children enrolled. By 1961 there were nine clubs, and a closing rally was held at Bethesda Church with all groups represented. In 1962 there were 14 clubs with over 400 children enrolled. These clubs have continued each year. In 1966 a quiz was held on the lessons taught during the year.

The first Women's Fellowship meeting was held in the second-floor apartment on April 24, 1959. The women have continued to meet monthly for a fellowship type of meeting, sometimes during the day, but often at night. Several winters they also met regularly during the winter months for sewing and knitting classes under the leadership of the pastor's wife.

Several Christmas seasons there was intensive Bible study for adults in the community. Daniel Kauffman, the regional overseer, taught these two years, and one year Peter Hartman of Hannibal, Missouri, taught a music class.

Each year, beginning in 1959, there has been a Watchnight Service which consists of candlelighting and a prayer period at the entrance of the new year, followed by a communion service. A choir was organized in May 1960. The choir has sung each Sunday morning during the worship service, as well as giving special programs in neighboring city churches and in Missouri and Illinois Mennonite churches. Mrs. Nettie Taylor has served as director. A doctrinal conference for the Missouri area Mennonite churches was held in May 1961.

Day-camping has been popular. In this children have been taken to the park each day for planned recreation, crafts, and Bible study. This was begun in 1962 with 84 children participating. In 1963 the camping lasted for six weeks. Of most interest in 1964 was the Family Day camping when parents were encouraged to bring their families to the outings. In 1965 an extensive day-camping program for children of the community was held for six weeks by the summer VS team. An effort was made in 1966 to combine the day-camping with the vacation Bible school conducted for eight weeks by the summer VSers and the Northside Team Ministry.

The first winter, 1957-58, saw Tuesday evening prayer services in homes in the Project, with five to eleven persons present. On Thursday evenings adult Bible studies were held in the pastor's home with an attendance of up to twelve. At various times adult Bible studies have been held in neighboring apartments.

Through the years many other ways of meeting needs have developed. There is "The Handle," a small coffee shop operated by the church near the school. St. Louis schools have no hot-lunch program and so there is need for hamburgers, chili, hotdogs, cold drinks, cookies, and candy at a price the children can pay. MYF on Friday nights provides bowling, volleyball, and table games. One of the problems is to keep those out who don't belong. It seems that the whole community would like to join MYF. There is a certain amount of free taxi work that can hardly be avoided if the church is a brotherhood: rides to the bus depot, the hospital, even to the market.

One important way to meet needs is to get some of these promising young people out of this environment into that of a church school. More than fifteen have had that privilege. A scholarship fund has been established in memory of Darlene Grays, who was killed by quarreling men at the housing project in 1968. She was a high school junior. The fund is administered by the Bethesda Church Council.

For such a varied program a great many people have been needed. Every summer a group of VS people — up to eleven in one year — have come to "where the action is." Then there have been long-term VS workers: the Ray Gehmans from Harleysville, Pennsylvania, the David Hershbergers from Kalona, Iowa, the John Gochnauers from Lancaster, Pennsylvania, the Duane Stutzmans from Hesston, Kansas, the Don Garbers from Michigan, and others.

Principles of Christian stewardship have been taught, and there has been a growing response. Total missions giving in 1959 was $185. By 1966 this had grown to $804.55. The giving total of the congregation in 1971 was $9,233.

The church is now in its second decade, which has brought some of the most exciting projects. One is the expansion of the church plant on Dayton Street. There were 95 members in 1972. The facilities were long outgrown. A new worship area was built behind the original building, with a seating capacity of 150. The basement floor includes a church kitchen and a meeting area. The original basement was re-modeled to contain classrooms and rest rooms, and the old church area has been turned into library, study rooms, and teaching areas. The congregation is now better equipped to serve its community. The remodeling cost $85,000 and was financed largely by the congre-gation. It speaks to the community of the church's intention to stay.

The other important development in which Bethesda is involved is Jeff-Vander-Lou (JVL), a community self-help corporation formed primarily to rehabilitate the run-down housing of Yeatman, the North St. Louis ghetto in which Bethesda is serving. JVL is not an organizational arm of Bethesda. Bethesda is a church, not a construction or realty corporation. But JVL first met at the church. Pastor Schwartzentruber was a vital part of it from the beginning, and the corporation operates on the ideal of service that the church teaches. Jeff-Vander-Lou (the name comes from three bounding streets of the area of its operation) is putting into social performance the faith of the Bethesda Church.

It all had its beginning in January 1966 when a city alderman asked a retired black schoolteacher to help organize a federal beautification project in Yeatman. Mrs. Spotts insisted that doing something about housing was more important than planting trees and shrubbery. She got a bit of encouragement on this, and so, looking for someone to give this a real push, she went to Hubert Schwartzentruber. He introduced her to Macler Shepard, a black leader with many skills. He was ready to take hold.

So here was the nucleus of workers that knew what Yeatman needed. It was not a church committee. But the white Mennonite pastor was on it, and the church was available for meetings.

The 19th Ward Beautification Committee incorporated itself as Jeff-Vander-Lou, and took the offensive. They gave the city a list of 200 buildings, asking for inspection. As JVL expected, most were declared "unfit for human occupancy." If they could be bought cheaply, JVL could begin rehabilitation.

But where was the capital for buying them? Schwartzentruber tried church agencies, but the idea was pretty new. He and Shepard tried Washington, but the government wanted them to demonstrate that they could build houses and get unions to train local blacks.

Money for the first house came from a local politician; a successful businessman financed six more and an office for JVL. He also persuaded a shoe company to build a factory in this area and to train local help. Here was the prospect of over 400 jobs. Shepard bought up for the factory a whole block lot by lot. Men were being trained both for the factory and for the construction crafts — the unions were giving in.

JVL homes were being sold at prices the people could afford. But to keep these prices down JVL needed contributed labor. Mennonite Disaster Service sent help to this area of perpetual disaster — carloads of men week after week.

Various Mennonite contributions came: a Mennonite Mutual Aid low-interest loan, Illinois gifts and loans, a gift from an Iowa Sunday school class, and a donation from a Hesston nonprofit foundation which also paid for the services of Jim Marner as a coordinator of labor, Cecil Miller as bookkeeper, and his wife, Judy, as a preschool teacher. Total Mennonite investment in three years was $134,000.

St. Louis capital was made available to JVL to develop a medical clinic where 17 specialists take time away from their regular practice to give these people, at prices they can pay, the medical care they need. There is also an Opportunity House, where families can live while their houses are being renovated, and to provide room for classes where people are taught budgeting, nutrition, and child care.

One hundred and twenty-six houses have been rehabilitated and almost as many more are on the way. Seventy-four new apartment units are under construction (June 1972). The plan is working because many people respect and trust each other. Better than almost any other Mennonite church, Bethesda has united a spiritual and a social ministry. All together it is a Christian ministry that makes sense and that many people are accepting.

"We still have regular Bible studies and the other things, but we have to show people we love them and God loves them through us," said Helen Robinson, a member of the congregation.

Since there is no Head Start program close to Bethesda, the church has been conducting a preschool program. In 1971 eighty-four different children were able to learn a few basics which a middle-class-oriented school system takes for granted a child knows when entering kindergarten. Preschool also gave training to some high school and adult aides.

In 1971 the staff of the church consisted of full-time pastor, crisis minister, secretary, and two directors of Preschool and Learning Center. In addition there were many volunteer and part-time workers, and five Mennonite persons serving full time in the community, but not responsible directly to Bethesda Church.

Bethesda's ministry to the total Mennonite brotherhood varied. Hesston College Interterm has sent students here for study and observation. Opportunity and experience have been provided for Voluntary Service and Disaster Service personnel. There has been exchange hosting as between the city church and the rural churches. Pastor Schwartzentruber's abilities and experience have had much churchwide use: Board of Overseers of Hesston College, Board of Congregational Ministries, Home Missions Committee of Board of Missions, Section Chairman in Probe 72 and Mennonite World Conference, many articles for periodicals, and speaking engagements in churches and conferences.

Hubert Schwartzentruber concluded his long ministry in St. Louis on November 1, 1972, when he moved to Goshen, Indiana, to serve as Secretary of the Commission on Peace and Social Concerns under the Board of Congregational Ministries of the Mennonite Church. At Bethesda a pastoral team of three laymen, two black and one white, are leading the congregation: Eugene Gentry, Helen Robinson, and William Helmuth.

10. *Harrisonville, Cass County*

The newest Mennonite congregation in Missouri is located in Harrisonville, the county seat of Cass County, which for one hundred years has been the chief shopping center of the Mennonite community which lies ten miles to the east. The congregation in Harrisonville is an extension from the Sycamore Grove congregation. Harrisonville is a growing city of 5,000 people, located along a new four-lane, north-and-south highway. It is forty miles south of metropolitan Kansas City.

Several forces furthered the movement which resulted in the organization of a congregation in Harrisonville. The Sycamore Grove congregation was influenced by the economic trends of the times, and the members were no longer all on farms. A number of families and some retired people were living in Harrisonville. For several decades there had been some discussion of the establishment of a church in this town, both for the sake of these families and to evangelize unchurched people there.

The centennial observance in August 1966 had urged the forward as well as the backward look, and some of the members were unwilling merely to repose on their history. A Sunday school class of young people discussed Harrisonville as a possible direction to move. Conference overseer for Missouri Daniel Kauffman planned to propose outreach in their county seat at his next meeting with the congregation.

Then in November 1966 a meeting for council members and conference delegates was held at Mt. Pisgah, and four persons from Sycamore Grove attended. Nelson E. Kauffman, home missions secretary of the Mennonite Mission Board, probed and challenged concerning congregational purposes. The report of the Sycamore Grove people the next Sunday stirred many in the congregation. The Sunday Evening Worship Committee agreed to bring Nelson Kauffman to their church to help them find God's will for their witness in the county. The Church Council approved and in December Kauffman came. He proposed a self-evaluation study, and suggested methods for the study.

In January the whole congregation voted in favor of this facing up to whatever might be God's will for Sycamore Grove. The following Sunday Daniel Kauffman was present and added his urging. A new work in Harrisonville was being frequently mentioned.

In the following weeks of 1967 six committees, involving thirty-seven persons, worked more than 500 hours to complete their assignments. The Church Council appointed four persons to give an unbiased interpretation of the findings: Overseer Daniel Kauffman, Mission Secretary Nelson Kauffman, Ivan Lind of the Conference Executive Committee and Harold Dyck of the Conference Ministerial Committee. This committee pointed out troubled spots and urged the congregation to be open to the changes indicated.

The Church Council took the challenge to heart. They visited every home, listening to all concerns and visions. A great deal of tension had been aroused by the study and the recommendations. The chief issue was the new congregation in Harrisonville. Some were sure this was the Spirit's will; others were just as sure that this was wrong. To some it looked like progress; to others, like decline. To some it was church extension; to others it was a church split. The council, endeavoring to conciliate and reconcile, sat often until midnight or past.

Finally, October 3, 1967, was set as the date for a congregational vote. Daniel Kauffman, overseer, and Allen H. Erb, another member of the Conference Executive Committee, were invited to supervise the vote. The results showed that two thirds favored starting a church in Harrisonville.

Twelve families felt led to be a part of the new congregation. The council helped them to get organized. Committees were appointed: worship, building, finance. The heads of these committees made up the steering committee to take care of the administration of the budding congregation. Prayer groups were started in the neighborhood that was selected for the church location. The group met on Sunday evenings from May 1968 in the parlors of the Methodist Church, and after July in the parsonage. Pastor Eberly decided that he would not remain in the area to pastor either church, and the search for a pastor was begun. Counsel was given by Daniel Kauffman and other conference leaders. James Christophel, pastor of the Fish Lake congregation in Indiana, agreed to become the pastor at Harrisonville, beginning in the fall of 1968.

One object of this outreach was to witness to the homes of the community. It was decided that a day care center or nursery would be an effective means to this end. And so on September 3, 1968, a nursery school called Kinder Kastle was opened in the basement of the Jay Hartzler home. The teacher was Trusie Zook, a retired first-grade teacher. The initial enrollment was eleven.

Three members of the group purchased a possible land site for a church building. Members of the group pledged a total of $70,000, to be paid over a period of four years. Paul Buerge was chairman of the finance committee.

October 6, 1968, was the official beginning of the new congregation. In the morning service at Sycamore Grove the entire group communed together, symbolizing that this was not a break of fellowship. Overseer Kauffman, who officiated in the day's services, read the names of the fifty-one members who were transferring from Sycamore Grove to become charter members of the Harrisonville Mennonite Church. Pastor and Mrs. Christophel and one other person joined the transfers from Sycamore Grove to make a total charter membership of fifty-four. Among names of charter families were Hartzler, Schrock, Buerge, Zook, Yoder, Hershberger, and McCarthy.

James Christophel was installed as pastor of the new church. The congregation met at first in basements of members' homes, and later in the basement of the parsonage, so that it was jokingly called the underground church.

Ground was broken for the new church building on June 15, 1969. By that time the membership was sixty-two. There was symbolism in the groundbreaking method. The pastor held the handles of a farmer's walking plow, and members with ropes pulled the plow through the sod. The pastor said, "Today as we put our hands to the plow, we proceed with the faith of a farmer who plows and plants in hope of a crop. It is fitting that we should use a plow because we have been a people of the land, but today we are planting a church in the city. . . . To make this plow go, we must all pull together as one. There are mighty machines that can move the soil faster than we can, but there are no machines that can take the place

Groundbreaking for the new Harrisonville Church

of individuals in the ministry of the church."[59]

The building is one story, 114 by 50 feet. Folding partitions make the interior flexible for multiple use. As building began, there was $13,000 cash on hand. Money to complete the project was borrowed from a local bank. The building was dedicated on June 28, 1970. It is located on Highway 2 near the city limits.

The Kinder Kastle was moved to the new church for its third year. The enrollment had climbed to sixty.

Christophel resigned the pastorate in January 1970 and returned to Indiana. In the absence of a regular pastor, students of the Nazarene Seminary in Kansas City served the congregation in Sunday services. One of these students, Danny Gales, agreed to be pastor for one year. He was commissioned by Overseer Kauffman, and received as an associate member of the congregation. The group was encouraged by Pastor Gales' leadership in a program of evangelization. Twenty-one new members were added to the congregation in April 1971, bringing the total membership to 85.

Conference suggested Merle Unruh of Atwater, California, as a permanent pastor. He and his family visited the congregation, after which he was unanimously invited to become pastor. He was installed in November 1971 by Daniel Kauffman and Conference Minister Millard Osborne.

The Harrisonville Church dedicated in 1970

Besides regular Sunday services and the nursery school, Harrisonville Mennonite Church has participated in Wednesday evening Bible studies, family retreats, MYF tours, Rural Bible Crusade, and women's and men's prayer groups. A choir has been organized and participates regularly in the Sunday morning service.

Twelve persons were received as new members on December 12, 1971, making the total membership almost one hundred.

Renewed interest in Sunday evening services was realized through Bible quizzes with Sunday school classes competing. Kids' Korner has the interest of children. Concluding the service is a sermonette by the pastor.

Discussion (D) groups meet for fellowship, Bible study, and prayer in the homes of members. Neighbors are invited to these groups, which meet on either Tuesday or Thursday of each week. Appreciation for these meetings is evidenced by good attendance and open discussion concerning the Scripture outlines being followed. They have proved an effective means to church growth.

A kindergarten teacher from Holland, sponsored by MCC, served Kinder Kastle in the 1971-72 school year. The enrollment in September 1972 was eighty.

An evangelism program followed a potluck dinner in October 1972. The membership was 110 in September 1972, with a significant number coming from non-Mennonite backgrounds.

A WMSC retreat sponsored by the Harrisonville and Sycamore Grove congregations was held October 27, 28, 1972.

Some may deplore the tensions which were created in the division of the Sycamore Grove congregation, and may still think the decision was a mistake. And the motives for the division may not all have been purely evangelistic. But the conference as a whole can profit from this example of a congregation which met a changing situation responsibly and took evangelistic outreach seriously.[60]

SCATTERED MEMBERS IN KANSAS

CHAPTER

SCATTERED MEMBERS IN KANSAS

The settlement of Mennonites in Kansas followed the pattern of, and was almost contemporary with, the settlement of Missouri. As settlers poured west at the close of the Civil War, it was easy to cross the border into Kansas. The wooded waterways and the hills of eastern Kansas were much like Missouri. Best homestead opportunities and cheap railroad land, however, were in the western two thirds of the state.

1. *Clark County*

The only Kansas subscriber to the *Herald of Truth* in March 1866 was A. H. Martin, whose address was "Meniola." If this is the place now spelled "Minneola," it is strange to have the first Kansas Mennonite of record living so far west. Minneola is 25 miles straight south of Dodge City. At that date there was no railroad in those parts. It was Indian and buffalo country, but there was a post office. It would be interesting to know more about this adventurer Martin.[1]

2. *Osage County*

Four families of Amish Mennonites lived at Burlingame in 1869. They had moved that spring from Lee County, Iowa. Jacob Kauffman was one.[2] Daniel Klopfenstein died there in 1873.[3] There were still Mennonites in Osage County, twenty miles south of Topeka, in 1890, when J. S. Coffman visited four families of cousins at Carbondale.[4]

Thousands of agents in the East promoted emigration to the Kansas plains

3. *Franklin County*

A "Bro. Hartman," at Ottawa, read Funk's Mennonite church paper in May 1870.[5]

4. *Montgomery County*

Levi N. Yoder came from Indiana to Holden, Missouri, and married a daughter of Joseph Gerber, the pioneer of the Johnson County community. The young couple first settled, about 1870, at Cherryvale, 20 miles from the Oklahoma border in eastern Kansas. But they soon returned to Holden (see p. 55).

5. *Gage County, Nebraska*

Because of his important ministry to the Mennonites of Missouri and Kansas, the settlement of Bishop Henry Yother (a variant spelling for Yoder) at Blue Springs, just across the Nebraska line near Beatrice, must be a part of our conference story.

Yother's father was from Bucks County, Pennsylvania, and moved to Westmoreland County, Pennsylvania. Henry, one of ten children, was born near Mount Pleasant, Pennsylvania, in 1810. He united with the Mennonite Church at the age of 21. His wife was Catherine Moyer, and they had 12 children. After his wife died, Yother moved to Livingston County, Illinois, and in 1871 to Gage County, Nebraska. Here he lived until his death in 1900. His grave is at Alverton, near Scottdale, Pennsylvania.

Henry Yother was ordained to the ministry in Westmoreland County, Pennsylvania, in 1845, and to the office of bishop in 1851. He preached in both English and German. After his move to Nebraska he was not officially connected with any one congregation. There was no one else of his branch of the church near Blue Springs.

But he was especially concerned about the Mennonite families on the frontiers. He traveled a great deal to minister to these scattered families and groups. Often he drove a horse, and rode in a two-wheeled rig. He traveled to Marion and McPherson counties, to northeastern Kansas and to western Missouri. His visits usually included a few sermons and communion, sometimes a few baptisms. In a few cases, he stayed a week or more. In 1892 he preached every three weeks in Nemaha County, which was fifty miles from his home. He paid much or all of his costs of travel. After 1894, however, he served under direction of the Evangelizing Committee at

Elkhart, Indiana, and received some financial help for expenses.

In 1884 he wrote: "I traveled in the name of Jesus in connection with the Old Mennonite Church of which I am a member over 53 years." He preached also for the Amish and the Russian Mennonites. He performed marriages and assisted in ordinations. His was a sacrificing and significant frontier service. Once when past eighty he missed a train and carried a heavy satchel over twenty miles in order to keep an appointment.[6]

7. *Doniphan County*

John S. Good, of Page County, Iowa, visited at White Cloud in June 1872. He stopped at the A. C. Hershey home. There were three members in Doniphan County. This is in the northeast corner of the state.

6. *Marion County*

The real beginning of permanent Mennonite settlement in Kansas was in Marion County, twenty-five miles northeast of Newton. This was in the Cottonwood River valley, the beginning of the rich, level prairie stretching endlessly toward the west. M. W. Keim, a Mennonite from Johnstown, Pennsylvania, helped to attract Mennonites to this area. He bought 5,000 acres of land in the winter of 1869-1870, and was selling it to home-seekers.

Daniel Brenneman, of Elkhart, Indiana, described thus the "Kansas enterprise":

"Brethren who have not the means to procure themselves in the East, prompted by a sense of duty to themselves and their children, have emigrated to the West, at the sacrifice of their church privileges, have taken up their abode as strangers in a strange land, in the hope that they would be followed by others of their brethren of like faith with them; that churches would be organized. . . . Many have been sadly disappointed and are today scattered abroad.

"We found no place more suitable for our purpose than Marion County, Kansas. . . . A number of our people have already purchased land there."[7]

In 1871 Daniel, Margaret, and Christian Kilmer, all unmarried, came from Elkhart County, Indiana, and took up homesteads in southeastern McPherson County, just across the county line from Marion. They were followed in 1872 by their father Michael.

The country was as yet largely uninhabited in that year. Michael

Kilmer, traveling across the prairie north from Newton, saw one sod house and one frame house in a distance of eleven miles.[8]

But the settlers were pouring in. Louisiana E. Abbott, a writer from Emporia, described it: "There were a few months since no sound was heard but the howl of the wolf, or the hiss of the rattlesnake, and interminable stretch of grass beneath and sky above . . . there is now a thriving farming community established, and though they are yet without preaching, they endeavor to consecrate the Sabbath by meeting to study the Bible. They have a Sabbath school organized with Father Kilmer, a Mennonite, as superintendent, and all orders of Christians unite in the work. . . .

"There are several Mennonite families settled in the vicinity, and a minister of this church will meet a hearty welcome."[9]

When Daniel Brenneman visited here, he said that where one year before scarcely a dwelling house was to be seen, he found an assembly of about one hundred. There were Mennonites, Methodists, Baptists, Lutherans, Quakers, and Roman Catholics.[10]

The first Mennonite to settle at Marion (then called Marion Center) was R. J. Heatwole, who became a major figure among Mennonites of the West (see Frontispiece and dedication). He was the youngest son of John S. Heatwole, and the grandson of David Heatwole, a pioneer in the Shenandoah Valley of Virginia.

His mother was a Swank, from an English-speaking family. She could not talk "Dutch" when she was married, but came to believe that it was worldly to talk English. Reuben — R. J., her youngest son — barely remembered his mother's death. But he did remember her last words to him: "Rubie, be a real good boy." Those words set the course for his life. He was slight and walked with a limp on a built-up shoe. But he was a persistent and devoted church worker. He took on himself the responsibility to see that ministers visited the scattered members on the frontier. His efforts in this type of evangelizing made it possible for him once to say, "But one brother and one sister in this state have not been visited by some of our ministers within a little over six months."[11]

R. J. was a singer and a promoter of Sunday schools and missions. He was never ordained, although he was in the lot eleven times. That means that in eleven instances of ordination, he was voted for, and accepted by the church, as a candidate for ordination. But the slip indicating the Lord's choice was never in the book he picked up. As a layman, however, he served as both secretary and moderator of the Kansas-Nebraska Conference. When the Mennonite Evangelizing Board of America was organized at Elkhart, Indiana, in January 1892, of the fourteen members elected, two — Levi Yoder of Cass County and J. C. Driver of Morgan County — were from Missouri and one — R. J. Heatwole — was from Kansas.

During the Civil War, R. J. was one of a company of more than a dozen Mennonite men who struck out through the mountains of West Virginia for the North and freedom from compulsory military service in the Confederate Army. In this company also was Henry G. Brunk, married to R. J.'s sister Susan. The men got through to Hagerstown, Maryland. Mrs. Brunk, a strong and courageous person, drove north through the army lines to find her husband. Walking the streets of Hagerstown, uncertain where to turn, she saw him through the window of a shoe shop where he was working.

Heatwole and the Brunks went to Henry County, Illinois, and farmed in partnership. But there was no Mennonite Church there and no prospect for one. And so the next chapter of their epic story takes them to Kansas, following the western star of empire.

Heatwole went to Kansas to investigate. He liked it and bought two neighboring quarters of railroad land six miles west of Marion, one for himself and one for Henry G. Brunk. R. J. moved to his place in June 1872. The Brunks were to come overland the next year in covered wagons.[12]

In July Heatwole visited the Kilmers in McPherson County, and he met Margaret, his future bride. This match was inevitable: for neither one was there much choice in the Mennonite community, and they were persons of a kind, having both deliberately taken up the rigors of frontier living.

Noah Good also moved to Marion County in 1872. He came from Page County, Iowa. He built a log cabin. Benjamin W. Bare, who came from Elkhart, Indiana, had married Noah Good's daughter Magdalena and also moved to Marion County, as did Emanuel Shupe, another son-in-law of Noah Good. Bare moved on a claim and cut stove wood for $1 a cord. The grasshopper invasion of 1874 devoured even a crop of peaches, leaving only the barkless branches and the peach pits. Bare said he would have left, but couldn't.

Shupe's house was a dugout, with the roof nearly at ground level. It was difficult for visitors to find on the open prairie, but it made a cheap and warm house.[13]

Isaac Weaver was another immigrant from Iowa. In December

Ho! For the New Kansas.

We invite the attention of all who are contemplating a change of location, or who want

A FARM OR HOME IN THE WEST

TO THE SPECIAL ADVANTAGES OF THE

LANDS

OF THE

ATCHISON, TOPEKA AND SANTA FE R. R.

SITUATED ALONG THE BEAUTIFUL

COTTONWOOD AND ARKANSAS VALLEYS, THROUGH SOUTH-WESTERN KANSAS.

FIRST.—It is a NEW COUNTRY, recently opened for settlement by the building of the Atchison, Topeka and Santa Fe Railroad.

SECOND.—For its CHOICE CLIMATE. In latitude 38 north, the latitude of Central Kentucky and Virginia, RICH SOIL, and abundance of PURE WATER.

THIRD.—The large proportion of VALLEY LAND.

FOURTH.—HEALTH. Its altitude 1,000 to 3,000 feet above the level of the sea, a porous subsoil and well drained surface, no stagnant water or overflowed lands, alone tell the story of its HEALTHFUL CLIMATE.

FIFTH.—Its rapid settlement, unprecedented in the history of the West, with the cream of Eastern immigration, has given it prosperous churches, schools, mills, and the conveniences of a well settled community.

SIXTH.—By the 1st of November, 1875, the A. T. & S. F. R. R. will be COMPLETED TO PUEBLO, COLORADO, there connecting with the Rocky Mountain system of railroads, and, as Kansas is the nearest Agricultural State, her products will find a ready and profitable market in the extensive mineral regions developed by the extension of this road.

SEVENTH.—With all other advantages we offer our lands at the LOWEST PRICES and on the MOST FAVORABLE TERMS of any Land Grant in the West.

The Cottonwood and Arkansas Valleys are destined to become densely settled—the homes of rich and prosperous communities.

STOCK RAISING.

The abundance of excellent water in SPRINGS and RUNNING STREAMS, combined with CHEAP LAND of superior quality, covered with nutritious grasses, and the finest climate in the world, makes it the finest stock country in the West.

In selecting a new HOME, cast your fortune with a GREAT ENTERPRISE like the **Atchison, Topeka and Santa Fe Railroad,** which is destined to be the favorite thoroughfare across the Continent.

Everyone seeking a NEW HOME should, by all means, visit our lands before locating.

TERMS OF SALE:

TERMS NO. 1—Is on eleven years' time, with seven per cent. interest. One-tenth of purchase money paid down at time of purchase, and one year's interest on the remainder. The next two years, only interest payments. Afterwards, one-tenth of the principal, and interest on the remainder annually, until the contract is paid out.

TERMS NO. 2—Is on eleven years' time, with only the interest, at seven per cent. for the first four years. After that time, one-eighth of the principal, and interest on the remainder annually until the expiration of the contract.

TERMS NO. 3—Are our Short Credit terms, where, in consideration of the purchaser paying one-third of the principal, and ten per cent. interest on the remainder, and the balance in one and two years, we make a discount of TWENTY per cent. from the price.

TERMS NO. 4—Is a cash sale, where we make a discount of TWENTY per cent. from the appraised value.

For full particulars, and any special information desired, address,

A. S. JOHNSON,
Acting Land Commissioner for the A. T. & S. F. R. R. Co.,
TOPEKA, KANSAS.

The earliest Mennonite churches were in the Cottonwood and Arkansas valleys

1872 at the request of the Indiana Conference, Henry Yother visited Marion and McPherson counties; he found fourteen members at the two places. He came again in February 1873 and performed the marriage ceremony for R. J. Heatwole and Margaret Kilmer.[14] He made both trips by buggy. What courage it took to drive across the roadless, bridgeless prairie in midwinter!

In 1873 came Peter Neuschwanger and Daniel Brundage from Missouri to McPherson; Henry Hornberger from Pennsylvania to Marion; John Evers from Virginia to Marion; Jacob Holdeman from Nebraska to McPherson. John Evers was an "earnest and zealous preacher,"[15] and served especially the Marion group. He preached the first sermon by the first (Old) Mennonite minister settling in Kansas in Good's loghouse in Marion County. Indians were not far away.[16] Daniel Brundage served the McPherson County group, but as a bishop carried responsibility for the entire settlement.

We go back to the Henry Brunks for the most tragic story of the migration to Marion County. As a plasterer, Brunk had made enough money in Illinois to get good teams and equipment for the trip to their waiting farm in Kansas. The couple now had six children. The youngest of these, George R., years later told the story in verse:

> *Then came the time of which they long had dreamed*
> *To seek a home and settled peace and rest;*
> *I can see the prairie schooners day by day,*
> *Slow winding to the dim and distant west.*[17]

Traveling was difficult across Missouri. People remembered the Mormons and were unfriendly to the wagon train. The Missourians, who had lost their contest with the Free Staters in the Civil War, were prejudiced against anyone going to Kansas. They refused even drinking water, and the Brunks had to drink from roadside ponds and streams. And so when they pulled off the Santa Fe Trail to reach their farm a few miles to the south, the whole family was ill — big, strong Henry desperately so.

> *Worn and haggard they reached the journey's end;*
> *He looked about upon the fertile plain,*
> *Then weak and sick he seeks the sheltering shed,*
> *But never rises from his couch again.*

Susan Heatwole Brunk Cooprider, pioneer Kansas Mennonite mother of extraordinary courage and accomplishment

They had no house in which to lay the sick man, and so set up some broad boards wigwam fashion. It was November, and sick people needed better protection. Eight days after their arrival Henry Brunk yielded his life to typhoid, and was buried in the southwest corner of their farm four miles east of present Hillsboro, along what is now Federal Highway 56. Just thirty days later Henry G., Jr. was born, and thirteen days after that five-year-old Fannie died, from typhoid also. Three more days, and on December 22, eleven-year-old Sarah succumbed to the dread disease. The next April Baby Henry G. died of lung fever. So instead of the beginning of a happy farmstead, this lonely widow had a row of four graves on her farm.

A neighbor offered to break her sod for $3 per acre. She had some money from the sale of a team, and hired him. He wanted the money in advance, to which she had to agree. He never plowed the sod, and though he ultimately became wealthy, he never paid back the money he took from this stricken woman.[18]

Trouble continued. Four years after the death of Henry Brunk, when Joseph, the older son, was twelve years old, and helping to earn the living, his hand was caught between the rollers of a cane mill and his arm had to be amputated below the elbow. Then the mother and her one-armed boy had to manage the farm operations.[19]

One fascinating detail of life on the Marion County frontier is the furrow that was plowed to guide travelers between the Marion and McPherson settlements. R. J. Heatwole, who helped to make this primitive road, explained the reason for it many years later: it was plowed, he said, "So we might find our course along this furrow back and forth to worship together without losing the way, along which there was nothing to break the monotony of the journey save the flocks of prairie chickens, and the small herds of antelopes cantering from us in the distance."[20]

The furrow extended from the County Line a mile east of the Spring Valley Church to a point just west of the cemetery on the Brunk farm. This was a distance of fourteen miles. (Reports that the furrow was twenty-three miles long came from the supposition that it reached from the Spring Valley Church to Marion Center.)

The furrow was made in 1875, probably on the suggestion of Daniel Brundage, to whom the country was still new, and who was filling regular appointments in the area where Heatwole and Mrs. Brunk were living.

Gideon Yoder[21] concluded that the men who plowed the furrow were "very likely" Daniel Brundage, R. J. Heatwole, and Billy Weaver. So that the road would stay on the section line, two men went ahead and drove stakes according to the corner stones placed by the surveyors. One man drove the team, thought to be Christian Kilmer's, and held the handles of the breaking plow.

The furrow road came to be known as the Marion Road, and it was used by settlers other than the Mennonites. Families traveling westward used it, as well as caravans going to Western harvests.

A delegation of Mennonites from Russia visited Kansas in 1872 and central Kansas was chosen as a chief center of their migration. Their first settlement in Kansas was in Marion County in 1873. By November of 1874 a total of 315 families of these brethren, about 1,575 persons, had settled in central Kansas, more than in any other state. Goessel and Hillsboro, which lay between the Marion and McPherson American Mennonite settlements, became chief center for the immigrants from Russia. The two groups which carried the same denominational name always lived as friendly neighbors, but historical and cultural differences prevented their merging into one group. Their separation was not schismatic; they merely came to America at different times and from different countries.

A major catastrophe of 1874 was the sudden invasion of grass-

Trains like this provided the cheap transportation which brought Mennonites to Kansas after 1880. Note the windmill which pumped water into the wooden tank from which the steam engines were supplied.

hoppers. On a Thursday afternoon in July the insects came like clouds in the sky and in a short time destroyed nearly everything that was green. Women attempted to save their gardens by throwing blankets and quilts over the vegetables. But the bedding was eaten full of holes, and all vegetables were devoured by the voracious creatures. Mrs. R. J. Heatwole placed an empty keg over her largest head of cabbage. But the family milk cow broke through the fence, upset the keg, and ate the cabbage.[22]

A request went to Eastern churches for financial aid, since crops had been destroyed by drought and grasshoppers. It was signed by Daniel Brundage, John Evers, Henry Hornberger, M. R. Smeltzer, Isaac Weaver, R. J. Heatwole, Daniel W. Kilmer, and H. B. Burkholder.[23]

In spite of the hardships, the migration to Kansas continued. Bishop Brundage ordained other leaders. In 1875 Jacob Holdeman was ordained to the ministry, and Henry Hornberger as deacon. In 1876 Hornberger was ordained minister, and Pete Neuschwanger as deacon. Emmanuel Weaver came from Missouri to Marion County, and was ordained as deacon in 1877. In that year Daniel Wismer, a minister, moved in from Waterloo, Ontario. But in January 1878 John Evers died. His wife had died in 1874. They left a family of five children.

In April 1878 there were eighteen members in the McPherson County group, including two ministers and a deacon. Preaching was in both German and English. In Marion County there were twenty-seven members, including two ministers and a deacon. After the death of Evers there was no one who could preach in English.

The McPherson County group developed into the Spring Valley congregation. The southern extension of the Marion County group, toward Peabody, became the Catlin congregation. No permanent congregation developed at Marion, either southeast of Marion Center where Noah Good and his children lived, or at Canada, six miles west of Marion Center.

There were only a few members at Marion when John S. Coffman visited there in 1886.[24] But monthly services continued at the Good Schoolhouse. As late as 1893 services were held here every two weeks by Caleb Winey and B. F. Hamilton, ministers at Catlin.[25] For a while there were services three Sundays at Catlin and the fourth Sunday at the Good Schoolhouse.

Since the Catlin congregation was dissolved in 1961, there is no congregation of the South Central Conference in Marion County.

8. *Jewell County*

John Snyder moved to this northern Kansas community in 1872.[26] He was a minister when he came to Kansas from Pennsylvania, for when he died in January 1886 it was stated that he had been a minister for forty-one years.[27] C. D. Beery moved in 1873 from Michigan, but stayed only a year. John Snyder wrote that there were four families in the group living near Jewell City, which is 100 miles north of McPherson. He reported having meetings every two weeks. "The aged brother, Pre. John Snyder and wife," went to nearby Osborne County at least once for communion.[28]

John H. Detweiler died in Jewell County in 1877,[29] and a Mrs. Rhodes, of Virginia, in October 1880, died at Beloit, in adjoining Mitchell County.

Snyder wrote that buffalo were to be found fifty to one hundred miles west of them. His three sons killed twenty-seven in a January hunting trip.[30] This was the decade in which the buffalo were practically exterminated from the plain country. Hunting them was great sport, and farming country could not continue to be buffalo range.

9. *Brown County*

Early members in Brown and the adjoining Nemaha in the northern tier of counties were from Bucks and Montgomery counties in Pennsylvania. J. B. Mensch and H. Wismer filled appointments here in September 1889.[31] When J. S. Good, of Iowa, drove on from Doniphan County to Brown, and preached for the three members there, they reported that it was the "first preaching they heard, of their own faith, since living in Kansas."[32] Henry Yother visited "the few brethren" near White Cloud in February 1876. In the early seventies Daniel Brenneman met at Sabetha two men, Kiper and Oberholtzer, who were moving to Kansas. Jost Yoder moved to Brown County from McLean County, Illinois, in 1883.[33] Three Amish families were at Robinson in the summer of 1885. Two of them were Jonathan Yoder and Jonathan Stoltzfus.[34]

In 1892 Henry Yother preached at Sabetha every three weeks. This was seventy miles from his Nebraska home. In 1894 the membership here was twenty-six.[35] In 1897 E. L. Yoder reported that J. M. Nunemaker held meetings at Hamlin.[36]

There must have been Mennonites in Brown County as late as 1904. For in that year (September) Peter L. Landis wrote that he had been a reader of the *Herald of Truth* from its first issue. (That would have been forty years.)

10. *Labette County*

Nothing is recorded of Mennonites in this southern-tier county except that Anna Carson, sister of Preacher Jacob Hildebrand, of Virginia, died in November 1879 at Parsons, Kansas.[37]

11. *Cowley County*

Abraham Means wrote from Arkansas City, just above the Oklahoma border southeast of Wichita: "Don't move west simply because you hear that someone has done well financially. Investigate thoroughly . . . it is by far the wisest to rent for a few years. If you have but limited means, then stay where you are. . . . When you move away from good friends, I can say from experience that you sacrifice much."[38] This warning is probably a commentary on his own choice of a home away from church fellowship.

Means was born in Bucks County, Pennsylvania, and died in Cowley County, Kansas, in 1897. In his migration west he had lived in Medina County, Ohio, where he married Mary Leatherman. In 1854 the couple moved to Elkhart, Indiana, and thirty years later, in 1884, to Arkansas City, Kansas.[39]

Mrs. Means wrote shortly after their move to Kansas, "I often get hungry for the bread of life."[40] Both had joined the Mennonite Church in Indiana. Since church fellowship meant so much to them, one does not know why they spent out their later lives in isolation. Abraham joined the Brethren in Christ Church, but Mary became a member of the Pennsylvania Mennonite Church at Newton. The author faintly remembers her coming there sometimes for communion.[41]

The Meanses were glad for visiting ministers. "As the people are English, we need preaching in that language at this place," wrote Mrs. Means in 1892. This was in appreciation for the ministry of John M. Shenk and John Blosser in a schoolhouse in 1891.[42]

Hettie, wife of Hiram T. Albert, died at Arkansas City in July 1885. She was from Lancaster, Pennsylvania, and since her obituary appeared in the *Herald of Truth,* she may have been a Mennonite.[43]

12. *Miami County*

Martha Bachman, widow of Benjamin Bachman, died in November 1887, at Paola, in eastern Kansas, forty miles south of Kansas City. Her obituary appeared in the *Herald of Truth.*[44]

13. *Saline County*

Henry Yother found six members in Saline County, but no organized church. He held communion with them.[45] Concerning two families living ten miles from Salina, J. S. Coffman wrote: "The families of the brethren who live isolated from the church drift away from the faith of their fathers."[46] It was this realization that motivated the strenuous efforts to keep in touch with those scattered across the frontiers.

Saline County is in north central Kansas, fifty miles northwest of Newton.

14. *Butler County*

A. H. Kauffman moved from Illinois to Burns, Kansas, in January 1885.[47] Burns is between El Dorado and Florence, on the edge of the blue-stem pastures of the Flint Hills. The next month eleven men met at Burns to look at the land. S. A. Lewis, Atkinson, Illinois, bought land east of Burns. David Hamilton, of McPherson County, and Henry Pletcher of Marion County, bought tracts west of town. Hamilton moved to Burns soon after. Lewis Shank, of Missouri, went farther and bought in Barton County, southwest of Great Bend, where Minister E. M. Hartman had decided to locate.[48]

A year later Kauffman wrote that he expected five families to move to Burns soon, and hoped that B. F. Hamilton, of Peabody, could preach for them.[49] These hopes were evidently not realized, for David Hamilton, after waiting and hoping for six years, moved from Burns, where he was "away from church privileges," to Oregon.[50]

15. Barton County

Lewis H. Shenk (see p. 41) moved from Morgan County, Missouri, to Pawnee Rock in February 1885. He reported that schoolhouses are used there for churches and that there are no other Mennonites there. Evidently E. M. Hartman did not move to the land he had purchased in Barton County.[51] Shank did not stay long in Kansas. Barton County is in central Kansas.

16. Chase County

J. P. King, for 27 years an Amish bishop, died in Chase County in January 1887. Joel Gnagy and three Holdemans — John, Levi, and Samuel — lived there late in 1887.[52] Amos Hess, one of the founders of Hesston, lived for a few years after 1900 along Cedar Creek near Wonsevu — also Titus Weaver, a son-in-law.

17. Edwards County

Several Mennonite families lived at Offerle in 1887.[53]

18. Finney County

Minister Michael Shank and a few others took homesteads in Finney County, north of Garden City, at Terryton.[54] There were ten members in 1893, with Shank serving as their preacher.[55] Nancy Ramer, his wife, died in 1896. There were still seven members here in 1904, and Shank was still their minister.[56]

19. Rice County

Rice County is just to the west of McPherson County. Andrew Shenk in 1892 visited a family here who had not been visited by any

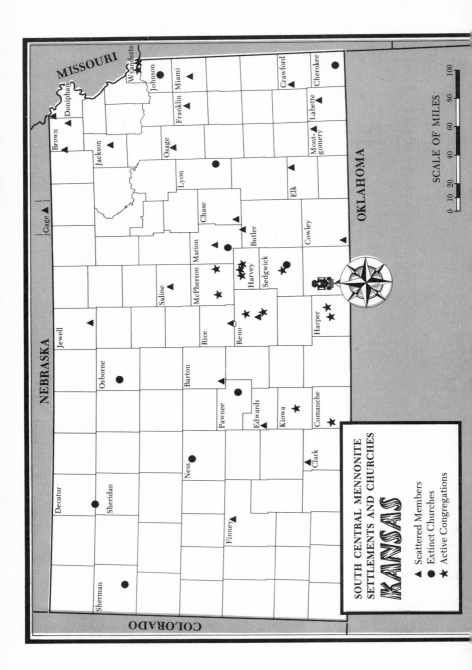

SOUTH CENTRAL MENNONITE
SETTLEMENTS AND CHURCHES

KANSAS

▲ Scattered Members
● Extinct Churches
★ Active Congregations

SCALE OF MILES

0 10 20   40   60   80   100

Mennonite minister for eight years. R. J. Heatwole told him at that time that there were at least twenty places under his care that ought to be visited regularly.[57] The next year there were nine members in Rice County, and monthly services were held by ministers from West Liberty, twenty miles to the east.[58] In 1903 a Sunday school was organized in Rice County, where George R. Brunk held services every two weeks in a schoolhouse for "a miscellaneous assembly of Catholics, Methodists, Campbellites, Adventists, etc."[59]

20. *Jackson County*

Late in 1893 R. J. Heatwole first learned that there were Pennsylvania Mennonites living in Jackson County, between Mayetta and Holton, twenty miles north of Topeka.[60] It must have been only the J. G. Longenecker family, for in 1894 it was reported that there were two members.[61] However, Barbara Nissley Garber (1843-1903) lived at Holton since 1880.[62] Early in 1895 T. M. Erb preached here for two weeks. His round-trip ticket from Newton cost $5. The interest was good, and thirteen persons confessed Christ. R. J. Heatwole wrote: "They desire our confession of faith and to know of our doctrine. . . . Some one ought to go soon and instruct them or some other denominations will. We can organize there if someone will move in and carry on the work."[63]

J. L. Winey, who had been ordained at the Catlin Church in 1887, was sent to Jackson. He stayed only a short time, however, and in 1902 he died. After his death other Peabody ministers — Caleb Winey and M. E. Horst — filled appointments every two weeks.[64] D. D. Zook was appreciated as an evangelist. Lizzie Longenecker, a daughter of J. G., wrote that the group there considered him their pastor.[65] A few years later the large Longenecker family moved to Harvey County and became neighbors of D. D. Zook and active members of the Pennsylvania congregation.

21. *Reno County*

In the years 1898 and 1899, three Mennonite families moved into Reno County at the west edge of a large Amish settlement southwest of Hutchinson. The Jerry Troyers, coming from McPherson County, and the N. E. Millers, from West Liberty, Ohio, each had a number of teenage children. Concerned about their children, these parents contacted Bishop S. C. Miller, of the West Liberty Church, who came and helped them organize a Sunday school in what was then known

as the Bussinger Schoolhouse, where these children attended school.
N. E. Miller was elected superintendent. Bishop Miller was much
interested in the work, and attended every fourth Sunday, preaching
a sermon after Sunday school. He often brought along some members
from West Liberty. A number of neighbors and young Amish folk
attended, and the building was often quite well filled.

Miller reported this activity to the Kansas-Nebraska Conference,
and it was decided to provide preaching every other Sunday, with
other ministers from Marion, McPherson, and Harvey counties helping
in the schedule. Matthias Cooprider and Charles Yoder helped from
West Liberty, J. M. R. Weaver and D. D. Zook from the Pennsylvania
Church, and Daniel Diener and C. W. Miller from Spring Valley,
and Michael Horst from Catlin. R. J. Heatwole often accompanied
the ministers, and was a favorite of the young folks.

In a short revival service by D. D. Zook there were a number
of confessions, and after a few instruction meetings seven young
people were baptized by Bishop Miller, assisted by Deacon R. C.
Yoder. As the applicants were kneeling in a creek of nice clear
water, Yoder led in singing "For You I Am Praying."

When several families moved away later, conference considered
whether to continue, or to advise the few remaining to move where
there was an established church. The latter counsel prevailed. Today
there is a large Conservative Mennonite church a few miles east, and
a Beachy Amish church five or six miles east from where the schoolhouse stood where these early services were held.

22. Elk County

The Frank G. Roupp family, natives of Harvey County who later
lived in Wichita and helped to start mission work there, bought a
stock ranch near Fall River in the 1930s, and lived there for a number of years. They attended the Pilgrim Holiness Church, but at
one time sponsored meetings in a school near their home conducted
by a Mennonite evangelist.

                                    o   o   o

This survey of scattered members in Kansas has been dependent
chiefly on reporting in the *Herald of Truth.* One can be sure there
were many others who followed various leads in homeseeking — land
agents, reports from friends and relatives, homeseekers' excursions,
and the mere chances of being at a certain place at a certain time

— but whose moves did not get into the record. Implicit in the story is an abundance of hope and disappointment, some successes and many failures. Some tried at various places to become a part of a viable fellowship. Many simply became, with their families, a part of the churches and the communities where they had settled, and were lost to the church of their fathers.

A bright feature of this segment of Mennonite history is the "mission work" of the time — the effort to shepherd all these scattered sheep. To R. J. Heatwole, Amos Hess, and others who felt this responsibility, a Mennonite family or group of families was an opportunity and call for visits by ministers as often as possible. A report to the church in 1894 said there were eight places without ministers which were getting regular services. There could have been forty, but there were then only nineteen Mennonite (MC) ministers in Kansas.[66] Tremendous was the time and energy spent in trying to keep the Mennonite family together, to evangelize new communities, and to build new churches. The ministers not only contributed their time, but usually they paid for their travel.

Since the days of the geographic frontier are past, Mennonites still scatter to locations where there are no other Mennonites. Now it is not to find new homes. A new nonagricultural economic order moves men about from one plant or office to another, and professional people go where there is need for their training. In the process many are lost to the church, as they were one hundred years ago. And some become the nuclei of new churches where they go. More than half of the Kansas churches in the South Central Conference today were established since 1900. And loyal young Mennonites of Kansas are giving the witness of their church around the world.

EXTINCT CHURCHES IN KANSAS

CHAPTER

EXTINCT CHURCHES IN KANSAS

1. *Kill Creek, Osborne County*

One of the earlier Mennonite settlements in Kansas was made on Kill Creek, fifteen miles southwest of Osborne, the county seat of Osborne County. This is about eighty miles northwest of Salina, in the north central part of the state. This country is rich, rolling land in the Solomon River valley. Kill Creek got its name from a massacre of early settlers at this place.

The first settlers came from Ontario about 1875, under the leadership of Bishop Henry Newschwanger. Abraham Shellenberger and family migrated from Cherry Box, Missouri, in 1876. Jonathan Krichbaums came from Cedar County, Missouri, in 1878. Caleb Winey migrated from Juniata County, Pennsylvania, in 1879. The Michael Graybills came from Richfield, Pennsylvania, in 1881. Names of other settlers were Lapp, Bickel, Near, and Schweitzer.

Newschwanger had been ordained to the ministry in Ontario in 1867 (MCD). He was ordained bishop in Osborne County, and the congregation was organized before 1880. Caleb Winey was ordained to the ministry in 1879. Abraham Shellenberger was a deacon, and his son, Jonathan L., was also ordained as deacon in 1896. Newschwanger, Winey, and Abraham Lapp have been named as the first ministers of the congregation.[1] Bishop Newschwanger became involved in dissension with other ministers and was ultimately estranged from the church (MCD).

The group first met in homes, and then seems to have shared

with other denominations in Sunday services. Howard Ruede, a Moravian, in 1877 and 1878 wrote letters from this community which were published in *Sod House Days*.[2] In one letter, September 1, 1878, he said, "We all went over to Hackerotts this morning, having heard that Mennonite services were to be held there. Word is always passed around the neighborhood several days in advance. On arriving in sight of the house it seemed . . . that Lutheran services were in progress. . . . About 11 o'clock the Lutherans vacated the room and the Mennonites took possession. Mr. Yoder [Yother], the Mennonite preacher, preached a very disconnected sermon in English, at the close of which Bishop Newschwanger made a few remarks in German. . . . About 2:30 . . . Yoder delivered his farewell sermon to the Kill Creekers, as he expected to start tomorrow morning for his home in Nebraska."[3] He says they sang Mennonite hymns indiscriminately, and got a good deal of music out of them.

The Kill Creek congregation built a meetinghouse in 1880, and laid out a cemetery alongside the church. The churches in Columbiana and Mahoning counties, Ohio, were among those who contributed to the cost of this building. By 1887, however, it was sold to the Presbyterians. As the Mennonites probably numbered less than twenty, maintenance may have been too much of a burden. Half of the cemetery was reserved for free burial grounds. It has remained unplotted.

After the sale of the church, services continued for some years in the school. After Caleb Winey left there was a sermon only when there were visiting preachers: S. C. Miller, Albrecht Schiffler, D. G. Lapp, G. J. Lapp, Daniel Diener, George R. Brunk, J. M. Nunemaker, among others. David Garber was once there for a series of meetings.

Two incidents come from the recollections of the J. L. Shellenberger family. One is the liking of J. M. Nunemaker for elderberry pie. When Mrs. Shellenberger knew he was coming, she'd bake his favorite pie, and Nunemaker would reward her by taking a second piece.

One time when George R. Brunk came to preach, he asked to be met at the Osborne railroad station. Jonathan Shellenberger, still a young man, drove in to meet him. He was dressed in a cowboy outfit and must have looked pretty fierce. At any rate, since neither man knew the other, and since Brunk felt it safer to ignore the cowboy, Shellenberger went home without the preacher, and Brunk had to find his own way to Kill Creek. The story is made funnier by the fact that Shellenberger was a small man and Brunk was six feet plus, and not often afraid of anybody.

The Kill Creek congregation entertained the "Conference in Kansas" in the following years: 1879, 1880, 1881, 1883, 1885. The congregation reported its membership to the Kansas-Nebraska Conference well into the first decade of the twentieth century. The largest membership reported was twenty-four in 1897.

By the turn of the century it was apparent that this congregation would not continue, even though there were still 16 members in 1905. Differences in the brotherhood and a number of successive years of crop failure in the nineties contributed to the failure.

Caleb Winey moved to Peabody, Kansas.[4] Some members joined other denominations. Milton Nears moved to Texas. Schweitzers moved to Protection, Kansas. As a final step Deacon J. L. Shellenberger moved away, first to Canton, and then to Hesston, Kansas. When Maud, a daughter of this family, was in her final illness, she requested that she should be buried in the cemetery at Kill Creek, where her grandparents on both sides are buried. Menno, son of the Shellenbergers, was one of the Near East Relief team in the 1920s, and died of smallpox on the banks of the Euphrates, and is buried there. A grandson, Dr. Wallace Shellenberger, in recent years did excellent service for the refugees during the civil war between Nigeria and Biafra.[5]

2. *Catlin, Marion County*

Although no permanent congregation developed close to Marion Center, the settlement to the south of this county seat became before 1880 the Catlin congregation. The first four families were the Noah Goods, their two daughters, married to Benjamin Bare (living in a dugout named "The Bare Den"), and Emanuel Shupe, and John Barnes, whose wife was a Lehman.

These first families who lived several miles southeast of Marion Center were joined in the spring of 1878 by the John Newcomer family from Cumberland County, Pennsylvania. From Florence, the end of the Santa Fe Railroad at that time, they drove a hired vehicle to the Noah Good dugout, which had board walls about three feet above the ground and a board roof, with wide cracks, to break the wind and shed most of the water. They received the hearty welcome characteristic of the frontier. They bought a farm three miles from Peabody, which was about twelve miles southwest of the Goods. Some other early settlers: Henry Hornberger, who came in 1873 from Pennsylvania; John Evers in 1874 from Virginia; E. C. Weaver, the

first deacon to serve the congregation, in 1875 from Missouri; the
Dohners from Franklin County, Pennsylvania, in 1876; Philip Doerr
and Ben Snyder in 1876 from Ontario.

By 1880 it was clear that the developing congregation would be
near Peabody, not Marion Center. The group near Marion held Sunday school — and preaching, when they had it — at Good's Schoolhouse, and the group near Peabody participated in a union Sunday
school at Weaver's School.

Migration to Peabody continued in the eighties. John Shelley
came from Juniata County, Pennsylvania, in 1884, and the next year
L. L. Beck, Harry Gish, and John Erb were welcomed from Lancaster
County of the same state. Joel Good moved in from Cass County,
Missouri, in 1885.

By 1886 the membership of the congregation was sixty-five. A
number of young people attended services who were not members.
The group needed a more adequate meetinghouse, and a special
meeting was called to consider building. Solicitation showed that funds
would be available. For $75 two acres were purchased on the north-
west corner of the Henry Hornberger farm as a building site and for a
cemetery. Hornberger had already begun this burial ground when one
of his children had died. Some graves were moved here from the
Brunk burial plot west of Marion and the Hershinger graveyard one
mile south of the Catlin cemetery. The deed was made to E. C.
Weaver, deacon of the congregation. There were no trustees until
1910, when I. B. Good, Sam Cockley, and L. L. Beck were elected
to be responsible for the property.

The church was one mile west and three and a half miles
north of Peabody. The first cost was $1,500. In addition to contribu-
tions made by the members, a number of community people gave
liberally. Donations also came from Pennsylvania and Ontario.[6] Much
of the labor was donated.

Laurence Horst has described the building: "The building was
made twenty-eight by forty-four feet, with the long side toward the
road. The pulpit was the old-fashioned style — high and long. Kerosine
lamps were set in brackets located periodically around the room, with
two back of the pulpit. The building was well constructed."[7]

The architecture was traditionally Mennonite. The style of the
building has been likened to a cracker box, intended for use rather
than beauty. Following Pennsylvania usage, all the ordained men,
called "the bench," sat on the platform, which had to be long enough

to accommodate all of them. The desk was as long as the platform. After the sermon by one of the preachers, all the others were expected to give their testimony to the message. For this reason it was good to have them already behind the pulpit. There may have been times when a short preacher's dozing was mercifully concealed.

The new church was named Catlin, from the name of the township in which it stood.

This Catlin building was turned halfway around in 1903. Formerly the pulpit was on the long, east side of the building. In the remodeled structure the pulpit, still to the east, was at the end. Pillars which had fallen during the moving were not replaced, and the pulpit was cut down both in height and length. A new furnace under the church replaced two potbellied stoves.

Baptisms in those early days were conducted in North Doyle Creek, two and a half miles south of the church. Candidates would kneel in the shallow stream as the water would be dipped up by the hands of the officiating bishop. Strong springs just up the creek from this place kept the water flowing here in dry seasons and in winter.

Although some of the members at Catlin had participated in the union Sunday school at Weaver's Schoolhouse, there were some who opposed the Sunday school as worldly. Not until 1888, two years after the church was built, was a Sunday school organized at Catlin. The first record book of the congregation tells about this: "The Peabody Church met for to organize a Sunday School at the Church House March 18, 1888. 1) Br. [B. F.] Hamilton was elected moderator of the day, 2) Bro. A. H. Kauffman was elected as superintendent of the school for the term of the summer, 3) Bro. J. Shelly, assistant, 4) Secretary and treasurer, Bro. H. A. Pletcher, 5) the name of the school was in order and the above name was adopted. 6) Bro. Sam Cockley as chorister, and Bro. Tom Pletcher as assistant."

The first session was held on April 15, 1888. There were five classes, with thirty-nine present. The highest attendance that summer was sixty-six.

The Sunday school at Catlin was not "evergreen" at first. It closed the last of September and opened again in March. This was because poor roads and conveyances not adapted to bad weather made it hard to attend in the wintertime.

Until 1891 the Sunday school was held at "half past two in the P.M." This new service in the church program was careful not to intrude upon the regular church service. When it was moved to the forenoon, it followed the church service. Those not wishing to participate did not need to stay. This symbolized keeping the church in first place. Later the order of the morning service was reversed.

One of the charges against the Sunday school was that it was "worldly." One aspect of this worldliness was the cooperation with people of other denominations, or even nonchurch members, in the union Sunday school. And so about the time of the beginning of the Catlin school a conviction was developing in central Kansas that the Mennonites should have their own Sunday schools. In answer to a question brought to the Kansas-Nebraska Conference in 1890, this answer was given:

"In order to keep ourselves as far as possible from the evil tendencies of society, such as we find in what we call worldly Sunday schools, those opposed to our faith, such as non-conformity to the world, etc., it was decided by the conference that our Sunday School be organized by the church alone."[8]

The study was entirely from the New Testament. At Catlin a small question book was used. It was a series of sixty-one lessons of religious instruction for the young, in questions and answers. It was compiled by a committee approved by the Mennonite bishops of the Lancaster Conference, and published by the Mennonite Publishing Company at Elkhart, Indiana, in 1887.

The first evangelistic meetings at Peabody were conducted by J. S. Coffman in the late eighties. Following this, meetings were held almost annually by some of the well-known evangelists of the church: J. M. Shenk, J. S. Shoemaker, A. C. Good, J. W. Hess, E. J. Berkey, J. M. Kreider, J. D. Mininger, J. F. Bressler, Allan Good, E. M. Yost, Allen Erb, and many others. There were many baptisms, and additional Mennonites moved into the community, like in 1911, when five couples presented letters: H. E. Massels, Sam Buckwalters, and E. E. Rissers from Harvey County, Harve Evers from Pennsylvania, and L. O. Kings from Oklahoma. Between 1897 and 1929, sixty-nine members were received. The membership was never large, but it was large enough to constitute a church home and provide a context for service.

A considerable number of ordained leaders have served the congregation. The first bishop was Daniel Brundage, who came from Morgan County, Missouri, in 1873, and moved to Indiana in 1889. He was a good organizer, and gave much to the four congregations he served in central Kansas: Catlin, Spring Valley, West Liberty, and Pennsylvania. At Catlin occurred an unfortunate clash with Joseph Dohner, one of the members. Brundage was a carpenter, and was building a house for Dohner. There was an argument about the roof. Dohner wanted a gable roof, and Brundage argued against it. Among other reasons, he felt the steeper gable roof a mark of pride. While Dohner went to town, Brundage cut the rafters according to his ideas. The matter became, about 1881, a church affair, and Brundage lost his bishop's office for a few years. Dohner got another carpenter to build the house as he wanted it, and his large family was lost to the church.

Gideon Yoder thought that Brundage was restored to his office in a second ordination by lot.

Daniel Wismer was the second bishop for the four churches. He was ordained by Albrecht Schiffler of Roseland, Nebraska, after the Brundage trouble. He lived in the Canada settlement west of Marion. After his wife died in 1885, he returned to his native Ontario, and Brundage was bishop again.

In 1889 B. F. Hamilton was ordained bishop. He was born in Philadelphia in 1825, the son of Franklin Hamilton, who was a nephew of Secretary of the Treasury Alexander Hamilton, and a personal friend of George Washington. The boy grew up in the German Reformed Church at Allentown, Pennsylvania. He moved with his parents to Ohio. After his marriage he went to Indiana, where his wife died. He then married Catharine Holley, and after his conversion was influenced by her to join the Mennonite Church. In 1867 he was ordained to the ministry, and in 1883 moved to Cherokee County, Kansas, where a small settlement was developing, and three years later to Peabody. He farmed the rest of his life five miles northwest of Peabody. While living here he was ordained bishop, to take the place of Daniel Wismer. On his way home from the ordination at Spring Valley, he stopped at a Mennonite home to warm up and was asked, "How did the lot fall?" He replied, "It fell heavy, very heavy." When Bishop Brundage retired to Indiana, Hamilton served some part of the four-congregation circuit until his death in 1898.

T. M. Erb, who had been ordained bishop for the Pennsylvania congregation, served as bishop at Catlin from 1898 to 1929. Part of this time D. H. Bender was associated with him in this oversight. Harry A. Diener became bishop on the death of T. M. Erb, and served until Milo Kauffman was ordained bishop in 1938. Kauffman, as bishop or overseer, served the congregation until the year of its dissolution, 1961. Of these bishops, only Hamilton was a resident member of Catlin.

Of the ministers, the first one, John Evers, could not read when he was ordained at the Pike Church in Virginia in 1859. His wife taught him to read, and he became a dearly loved pastor of the Kansas congregation when he came West. His early death at forty-four "was sincerely mourned."[9]

Henry Hornberger was the first man chosen from the Catlin congregation for ordination. He was called to the ministry in 1866, two years before the death of John Evers. Hornberger's ministry was marred by some instability. After an unfortunate incident involving the Hornberger and Doerr young people, both of those families about 1884 withdrew from the Catlin Church. This wound was hard to heal.

The second man ordained to the ministry was Jacob L. Winey, a native of Juniata County, Pennsylvania. He was ordained in 1887 while still single. He married a Pennsylvania girl and in 1895 was sent to Jackson County, Kansas, to pastor the small flock there. In a few years he returned to Peabody, where he died in 1902.

The ordination of J. L. Winey was the occasion of one of the unfortunate occurrences which counted against the success of the Catlin congregation. In the lot with Winey was A. H. Kauffman, who, coming to Peabody from Burns in 1877, had been an active worker in the church. He was certain that he was called to preach, and that the lot should have fallen on him. He left Catlin and began preaching for the Mennonite Brethren in Christ, who were now holding services at the Weaver School. This branch of Mennonites, founded by Daniel Brenneman when he was disowned by the Mennonites of northern Indiana in 1874, was more emotional and preached the two-stage experience advocated by other "holiness" groups of that time. Kauffman claimed to experience a special baptism of the Holy Ghost, and had a friend rebaptize him and ordain him to the ministry. He set up a tent a half mile north of the Catlin Church and held a series of meetings. This was all an implied repudiation of the Mennonite Church, in which he had once served as conference secretary. Kauffman later moved to Michigan, and started a group which he called the Apostolic Church.

In 1879 Caleb Winey had moved from Juniata County, Pennsylvania, to Osborne County, Kansas. In that same year he was ordained to the ministry by Bishop Henry Yother. From 1879 to 1888 there were seven crop failures, and the Wineys were destitute. He appealed to his brother-in-law, L. L. Beck, to move his family to Marion County. Beck, accompanied by John Newcomer and Harve Evers, took three teams and wagons the two hundred miles to Osborne County.

The return journey took five and a half days. The Wineys had five children, from thirteen to five, and also took along 83-year-old Michael Shirk. It was winter and Beck once said, "If a typical Kansas storm had come upon the prairie, we would have frozen to death."

Winey preached at Catlin until disabled by paralysis in 1926. He was a scholarly person, with a gift for effective phrases. In 1905 when most older people frowned on the new "devil's wagon," he once said in a sermon, "I will not be surprised if in five years from now some of the good Mennonite brethren will be riding in cars." He lived long enough to see none of them riding in anything else.

Michael E. Horst, born in Maryland, moved to Harvey County in 1888, and was ordained to the ministry in 1890. He moved to the Catlin community in 1899, where he ministered until he died in 1915. He and his wife died only five days apart.

Other ministers who served at Catlin were L. O. King (1910-1916), J. F. Brunk (1916-1930), the "one-armed preacher," oldest son of Henry G. Brunk, and Noah E. Ebersole (1923-1943).

The third ordination out of the congregation was that of Laurence Horst, a grandson of both M. E. Horst and L. L. Beck. He was twenty-one years old when he was ordained in 1936. He served in the ministry here until he moved to Chicago in 1954.

Laurence Horst gave his best to the ministry at Catlin. Much of the time he lived at Hesston, where he made his living by teaching at Hesston College. For a few years he was in Indiana and Texas continuing his education. He had hopes for a time that the congregation could be rebuilt.

After Horst left for a city mission pastorate in Chicago, a number of men served in the pulpit of the little church. Among them were Alvin Kauffman, Lowell Wolfer, Gideon G. Yoder, Edward Hershberger, Arnold Dietzel, and Paul Friesen.

The first minister ordained at Catlin for service elsewhere was Frank Horst, a brother of Laurence. In January 1941 he was ordained, with the consent of the congregation, for a mission pastorate in northern Arkansas. Later he preached in Idaho, and in 1972 was

CATLIN MENNONITE CHURCH

IN 1873 THE HENRY HORNBERGER AND JOHN EVERS FAMILIES WERE THE FIRST MENNONITES TO SETTLE IN THE CATLIN COMMUNITY. DURING THE YEARS FROM 1873 TO 1885 THEY WERE JOINED BY 12 MORE FAMILIES FROM THE EAST.

THEY ATTENDED UNION SERVICES AT THE WEAVER SCHOOL HOUSE ONE MILE NORTH OF THIS LOCATION AND AT CANADA AND MARION, KANSAS.

IN 1886 THE CATLIN MENNONITE CHURCH WAS BUILT AND DEDICATED.

THE CONGREGATION GREW FOR 75 YEARS AND THE CHURCH WAS A WORSHIP CENTER FOR THE COMMUNITY. WITH MANY MOVING ELSEWHERE IN 1961 THE MEMBERSHIP DISSOLVED AND MOVED THE CONGREGATION TO HESSTON.

Trustees of the Catlin congregation erected a monument near the entrance to the cemetery on the southwest corner of where the building stood. The top plaque pictures the church. One side plaque gives historical data about the church, and another about the cemetery.

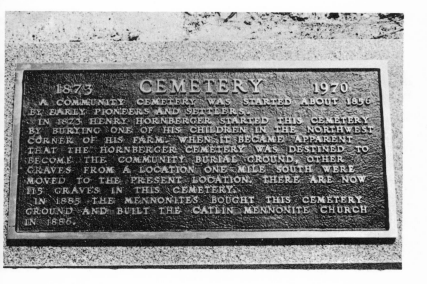

serving as the pastor of a Mennonite Church at Warden, Washington.

The only weddings solemnized in the Catlin Church were those of two daughters of Jacob Horst and Anna Beck, who are also the parents of Frank and Laurence. Edna Horst was married to Allen White in 1936, and Dorothy Horst was married to Paul Diener in 1950.

The congregation had only two deacons in its history. The first, E. C. Weaver, who was ordained in Morgan County, Missouri, before he moved to Marion County in 1875, served until he moved to North Dakota in 1895. In that same year L. L. Beck was ordained by lot, with Bishop B. F. Hamilton officiating. He is the only deacon called from the congregation to this office. He died in 1950 at the age of ninety-five, having lived all his mature years in Kansas on the land which he purchased in 1884.

L. L. Beck easily holds the record for years of faithful service in this congregation. And there can be no doubt that more than any other one man he held the congregation together during the stormy and trying experiences of its existence. During his later years it was a question whether a congregation so small could continue to exist. But L. L. Beck could not even consider such a question. Catlin must go on. Just before his death he asked his son to see to it that the doors were never closed, this in spite of the fact that when his wife died fourteen years before, fear in the family that the Catlin cemetery might not get good care influenced them to bury her in the Pennsylvania Cemetery in Harvey County. So L. L. Beck is not buried at Catlin, but beside his wife in Harvey County.

Perhaps one opportunity to build up the congregation was lost when the members were not willing to recognize the call of Harris Beck to the ministry. Harris, L. L. Beck's oldest son, was affected by the holiness fervor which ran through this and other Kansas churches at the turn of the century. Nevertheless, he still felt free to express his call to the ministry. In that time young Mennonites were not supposed to say such things until the church had called. Moreover, his father did not favor his getting an education to prepare for preaching. And so this promising young man joined the Methodist Church, where he became a prominent leader.

The Catlin Church was unfortunately located on a dirt road, and the mud could get deep and slippery. This was especially bad after the automobiles came. One Sunday the families rolled in to church over frozen roads. By the time of dismissal, however, the road had thawed into sticky mud that packed up against the fenders. The cars were stuck, one behind the other, in a row. Someone had to bring a farm wagon to take the people home. The next morning when the roads were again frozen, the men returned to take their cars home. Many times special meetings had to be postponed because of impassable roads.

After the venerable defender of Catlin was gone, again questions arose about its continuance. Moving the church to Peabody would get away from the bad roads. But there were objections to that. A survey showed that a number of members had moved to Hesston, where they were working. So finally in 1961 there was a majority feeling that the congregation should be dissolved. Many of the members joined the Whitestone Church at Hesston.

The church building was torn down, and the lumber sold at auction. The church had not been incorporated, and the last trustees — Lester Beck, Allen White, and Paul Diener — continue to hold the property. The cemetery is maintained in good condition. The county government gives $100 a year for cemetery upkeep. There are 116 graves, and burial will no doubt continue here.

The trustees took the initiative in soliciting money to erect a monument near the entrance to the cemetery. Money was given by former members and relatives of those buried in this community burial ground. The monument stands on the southwest corner of where the building stood. The top plaque pictures the design of the church building. One side plaque gives historical data about the church, and another about the cemetery.

The Catlin congregation has given freely in the support of missions and other phases of the church program. It has contributed workers. In 1941 Frank Horst was ordained for the rural mission field of Arkansas, and at this writing Laurence Horst is doing overseas mission work in Ghana. Many young people converted here were later in Christian service from ocean to ocean.[10]

The Catlin Church was host to the Kansas-Nebraska Conference in 1899 and 1908. L. L. Beck served as the first president of the conference mission board.

3. *Bethany, Cherokee County*

"I am the first Mennonite that ever preached in this county." Thus Samuel A. Mishler wrote to the *Herald of Truth* in 1881.[11] He had moved from Illinois, where he was likely ordained, to Brush

Creek, in the southeast corner of Kansas, only ten miles or so from
the borders of both Missouri and Oklahoma (Indian Territory then).
The next year he writes that twelve members had come there with
him, but one (Elizabeth Hulley) had died. He asks help for building a
church.[12]

That summer Mary Nice, widow of Joseph Nice, died and was
buried "in the new Mennonite graveyard." She had three sons in
Cherokee County.[13]

Mishler lived near the Stowell (later Golden Rule) School, six
miles southwest of Neutral. Another minister, Naffziger, lived north of
Columbus. Early in 1883 Deacon Abe Kuhns moved to Cherokee
County from Illinois, and wrote that they needed a church building.
Later in the same year Minister B. F. Hamilton came from Indiana,
and lived here three years before moving to Peabody, Kansas. Many
years later Minister James Hamilton, a son of his, preached occasionally at Neutral while he lived at Oronogo, Missouri.

The Kansas Conference met at Neutral in May 1884 and again
in May 1886. By 1884 the membership was thirty-three.[14] Henry
Yother of Nebraska held meetings for two weeks in schoolhouses.[15]

Mennonite names in Cherokee County included Miller, Mishler,
Schmidt, Kuhns, Hamilton, Mast, Hooley, Troyer, Walker, Naffziger,
Shupe, Imhoff, Nice, and Shenk. One group worshiped in the Neutral
School. Later the two groups worshiped together and in 1900 built
a church a mile southeast of Neutral. It seems the two groups which
thus merged may have been Amish and Mennonite.[16] The church
was named Bethany.

The Kansas-Nebraska Conference, meeting at Spring Valley in
1888, resolved that "in the case of bishop S. A. Mishler . . . this
conference [to which he has belonged] has decided that he shall be
no longer a member of the church until he bring forth 'fruits meet
for repentance.' " Since this left the congregation without a minister
Joseph Weaver of Jasper County, Missouri, was asked to hold ser
vices for them as often as possible. At that time there were about
twenty members.

S. A. Mishler moved back to Illinois in 1892. In 1893 Abe Kuhn
was a minister, and a younger Samuel Mishler served as deacon. There
is also a record of a Bishop Michael Mishler, who died in Cherokee
County in October 1890.[17]

Strawberry-growing became one of the industries of this com
munity. Singing classes were conducted by N. H. Shenk, who was

also a schoolteacher. A mission Sunday school was held one summer in a nearby schoolhouse. There were some conversions here.

One of the faithful members at Neutral was Anna Shupe, wife of E. B. Shupe. She was a dealer in religious literature, a person of conversational ability, and very conscientious. Her vocation created opportunity for talking about the gospel with many different classes of people. Living near the church, she entertained many visitors in her home.

The Bethany Church was transferred in 1896 to the Missouri-Iowa Conference, since it was near the White Hall Church at Oronogo.[18] In 1903 the Missouri-Iowa Conference convened with this congregation. This session ruled that ministers may be ordained by voice of the church without the use of the lot.

In 1899 Noah H. Shenk, a son of Bishop Andrew Shenk, was ordained for service at Neutral. Efforts were made to build up Bethany. J. M. Shenk held evangelistic meetings late in 1897, at which time he visited the Joseph Myers family, who had moved from Indiana in 1884 and had settled across the line in Oklahoma.[19] In 1901 Bert Shupe, son of E. B. and Anna Shupe, married Maud Bryant at Oronogo and became a teacher in Cherokee County. After Noah Shenk moved to Oregon, T. M. Erb in March 1907 ordained Amos Geigley, a young Pennsylvanian, for the work at Neutral. But most of the families were already relocating: Bert Shupes and Sam Schmidts (Alice Shupe) to Newton and Al Kuhns to Colorado. Geigley, after only a few months' effort at Bethany, went to Goshen College for further training. Before 1910 the church was closed, and the few remaining members joined other churches. The church building was sold and remodeled as a residence.[20]

4. *Olathe, Johnson County*

Johnson County is on the eastern edge of Kansas, just south of Kansas City. There was a Mennonite congregation at Olathe, the county seat, for about twenty-five years. It had its beginning in 1884, when Samuel Ernst and three of his married children came from Lancaster County, Pennsylvania.

Ernst had founded in 1871 a quarterly publication, *Der Waffenlose Waechter* (The Weaponless Watchman). It was published at Millwood, near Gap, Pennsylvania, from 1871 until 1884, when Ernst moved to Kansas. It continued publication at Olathe, probably until about 1890.[21]

Additional settlers came to Olathe from Pennsylvania, Nebraska, and Indiana. Among them were such names as Zimmerman, Hershey, Gehman, Wanner, Plank, Moyer, Martin, Evers, and Kauffman. Originally the group met to worship in the Bethel Schoolhouse a mile northwest of Olathe. The congregation was organized in 1887, but there was no resident minister. Several persons were baptized in that year, and the group hoped to "build up a strong church here in time." J. S. Coffman visited here in 1888, as did other traveling preachers from time to time.

The little congregation was visited regularly by ministers from Cass County, Missouri, just across the line. L. J. Heatwole, pastor at Bethel, arranged for monthly meetings in 1890, and in 1893 he ordained J. H. Hershey to the ministry. Hershey gave leadership until he moved to Roaring Spring, Pennsylvania, about 1902. J. M. R. Weaver and A. L. Hess, a layman, both from Hesston, Kansas, held a series of meetings at Olathe in January 1894.

In 1898 the congregation, which had been meeting at various places in and about the city, bought a Presbyterian church building near the Public Square. But the congregation never prospered, and shortly after Hershey left there were no more services. However, some members remained at Olathe. Samuel Ernst died in 1909. There were 11 members there in 1903.[22] Paul Erb conducted the funeral of an aged sister there in 1919, and found other members living there. Daniel Kauffman said that there was one surviving member in 1937.[23]

5. *Hartford, Lyon County*

Another ultimate failure in church-building in Kansas was at Hartford, along the Neosho River, fifteen miles southeast of Emporia and eighty-five miles east of Newton. All that remains today is a deserted but rather well populated cemetery, called the Borntreger graveyard, a few miles west of Hartford. It is no doubt named for Joseph J. Borntreger, Old Order Amish preacher. With another Amish family Borntreger had moved to this area about 1880.

But the main group who moved here were Amish Mennonites from Union County, Pennsylvania. In 1883 Isaac Stoltzfus came to Lyon County, and in 1884 cooperated with real-estate interests and the railroads in promoting a tour among his relatives and friends from Union County, and also from Champaign County, Ohio. They saw the Kansas prairies in June, when Kansas is usually at its best. They were eager to move to this land of promise.

The Union County group were looking for a place to go. Dissension over Sunday school and discipline had led to the silencing of Bishop Elias Riehl, who then united with the Mennonites of Juniata County. The dissolution of the Amish Mennonite congregation was hastened by the death in 1880 of Christian Stoltzfus. Each of his twenty children or their families had inherited $3,000, a large sum in those days. Most of these purchased land at Hartford.

Early in 1885 the group chartered what was called an immigrant car, and loaded on it their furniture, some of it made of cherry and walnut. There were special rates for such a carload of belongings being sent to a new frontier. They stopped in Ohio to allow Eli Stoltzfus to marry a bride to go with him to the new settlement in Kansas. In the group were also the widow of Christian Stoltzfus and the following sons, daughters, and grandchildren: Isaac and family, Jonathan and family, the widow of Simeon and her family, Nancy (Mrs. B. Frank Umble) and two sons, preacher David and family, Benjamin B. (unmarried); preacher Andrew Miller and family, his brother John O. Miller and family, and Rebecca and Jonas Riehl, both unmarried. There was also the Jonathan J. Warye family from Ohio.

Daniel Rich, whose wife was a Widmer, had moved from Iowa to Lyon County in 1870. He leaned toward the General Conference Mennonites, who conducted a Sunday school at the Fleming Schoolhouse south of Hartford, and occasionally had a preacher from central Kansas. Ben Stoltzfus married one of Rich's daughters. In his later years, when it was clear that a General Conference church would not develop here, Rich joined the Amish Mennonites.

Joseph Schlegel, of Milford, Nebraska, at first gave the group bishop oversight. But in 1886 John P. King, who had been minister and bishop at the South Union Church in Logan County, Ohio, for many years, moved to Lyon County in order to provide a farm for each of his sons. But there was an unrecorded mortgage on the tract which he bought. The family lost all its money, and within two years Bishop King died of typhoid fever. Bishop D. J. Zook of Newton came in 1889 to marry two couples. D. D. Kauffman became a preacher at Hartford. Joseph Schlegel, from a family who moved to Hartford from Thurman, Colorado, was a minister and was ordained as bishop in 1891.[24] He moved to Hydro, Oklahoma, in 1906.

There were troubles with the leadership. John Whitaker was ordained to the ministry, but never preached. When they organized a

Sunday school, the only person willing to be superintendent was Jonas Riehl, who was not a church member. A deacon, Joseph P. Stuckey, was the cause of much trouble because of his rash speech and alleged falsehoods and business irregularities. He was no longer a member of the church at the time of his death. His wife, Mattie, whose first husband had been Simeon Stoltzfus, moved to Herington, Kansas.

This settlement seemed doomed to ill fortune. There were four lean years just after the Eastern immigrants arrived, in which dry, hot winds burned up the corn which had looked so promising in early summer. The chinch bugs sucked the life out of the stalks so that even the fodder had no feeding value. There was no wood for fuel, and coal had to be worked for and hauled from strip mines ten miles to the north. The children gathered cow chips (the dried droppings of cattle) to cook the cornmeal mush which they ate week after week. Epidemics swept through the community — la grippe, diphtheria, and typhoid fever — so that when the Eastern families left about 1890, they left many of their loved ones in the Borntreger cemetery. The Frank Umbles, for example, buried three sons there.

For the picture of what life was like at Hartford in those years we are indebted to the memory and the literary ability of John S. Umble, one of the sons of Frank and Nancy Umble. He vividly described the starvation of a steer, the death of a bloodhound from heat prostration, the emotion induced by an ordination by lot, the five-cent bunch of firecrackers in which they indulged on the Fourth of July, the snowstorm in which his father, wrapped in a buffalo robe, drove off to the funeral of John King, his own terror when two wolves crossed his path as he was going to school, the neighborhood feast when one of the farmers had shot a wild goose, the piles of rabbits with which the men returned from a hunt, and the tubfuls of fish taken from the Neosho River.

Here is Umble's description of the church life centering at the Fairview School, for this group never built a church building.

"There was the church service every other Sunday with its singing; its worship service was always appreciated with great regularity. But since there were several ministers and church services were held only every other Sunday, there was a long enough interval between the sermons so that the congregation found something new and interesting in them when they heard them repeated once more. The congregation always looked forward to services conducted by visiting ministers. Especially beloved were Preacher David Zook, of Harvey County, and Bishop Joseph Schlegel, of Nebraska. Zook's sermons had a warm evangelistic note that appealed even to an eight-year-old boy. 'Joe' Schlegel had an interesting sermon and his kind jovial disposition endeared him to the hearts of the people.

"All the services were conducted in German with a considerable sprinkling of Pennsylvania 'Dutch.' The hymnbook was the 'Allegemeine Liedersammlung.' But to many of the members the singing was unsatisfactory, too slow, and the tunes too old or too difficult. The writer remembers hearing his parents discuss the singing. Finally Mother persuaded Father to lead a hymn sung to a popular secular tune. Father could not sing; Mother could. But women did not lead hymns in church. However, when Father started the hymn on the next Sunday Mother gave him such good support that the singing was a 'success.' The writer was too young to note anything odd about it at the time and for once joined in the hymn. But he has since wondered what the congregation thought when Father started the hymn to the tune, 'There'll be somebody waiting, waiting, There'll be somebody waiting for me.'

"Naturally, since he was under ten at the time and since the counsel meetings of the congregation were open only to its baptized members, the writer may not be in a position to speak authoritatively about church government and discipline. But, probably because the group came from a rather conservative Amish Mennonite background, little attention seems to have been given to such matters as dress. The western frontier settlements seem to have allowed for more freedom in such matters. To the church service the women wore a large plain stiff bonnet with an attached short cape at the neck, and under it the rather large neatly starched and ironed devotional covering. The writer does not recall that any of the women of the congregation except his grandmother wore this covering at any time except on Sunday. She may have worn it constantly because she had a bald spot at the top of the back of her head. Instead of a coat the women wore over their shoulders a large black shawl folded into a triangle.

"The men wore a regular business suit. The writer recalls that his father owned a hook-and-eye vest, probably brought from Pennsylvania, but he does not remember that it was used for any special purpose or occasion. Most of the clothing, not only for women and children but also for men, was homemade. Amish Mennonite mothers were neat seamstresses.

"Mother never removed the plain band gold wedding ring from her finger until it grew too small. Then she needed help in removing it but took it to a jeweler to have it enlarged. She continued to wear it for some years after the family moved to Ohio. Then, in consequence of Bible Conference teaching on the 'wearing of gold,' she removed it and never wore it again. She also owned and sometimes wore in Kansas heavy plain gold loop earrings suspended from holes in the lobe of the ear. It seems that piercing the lobe of the ear and wearing earrings was supposed to be a deterrent to attacks of headache!"[25]

In reading of the financial vicissitudes of this community, the author, a Kansan, can't help remembering that his own forebears during these very years were getting well established in Harvey County, where the winds were just as hot, the rains just as meager, and the chinch bugs probably just as voracious. Umble, in fact, remembers that there were good years, with bushel after bushel of peaches, an enormous yield of mulched potatoes, bushels of peanuts, and unbelievably large "Ironclad" watermelons, sweet and juicy. But the rough frontier life, the church troubles, and the heartbreaking losses by death, had robbed the Easterners of the will to endure and survive. They never did learn what hard winter wheat would do in this rich black soil and semiarid climate. Their memory of lush living in Ohio and Pennsylvania was too recent.

By 1891 all the Stoltzfus family had left except Ben, who waited till near the end of the century to return to Ohio, and a career as a Mennonite city missionary.

However, other people came to Hartford — the Kauffmans, the Steckleys, the Schlegels, the Suters, and the Whitakers. But there were factions, shown in the argument over the location of a church building. One faction wished it located on the cemetery plot, the other in the pasture field of one of the members. The vote on the matter was nearly a tie. Then suddenly, almost without warning, all the members of the one faction moved away. That was the beginning of the end for the Hartford congregation, though there were still twenty members there in 1903.

6. Sherman County

The first correspondence to the *Herald of Truth* from Sherman County, Kansas, reports the death of David H. Hartzler, who had lived there only a short time.[26] Two years later the brotherhood was informed that "a number of Amish Mennonite brethren live in Sherman

County." They were without a minister, but had an evergreen Sunday school and sixteen or eighteen members.[27]

By 1890 there were ten or twelve families there, mostly from Davis County, Iowa. They built a sod meetinghouse with a dirt floor at Topland and held the first service on January 12, 1890.

Sherman County is in the westernmost tier of Kansas counties, and the Mennonite families lived about twelve miles south of Goodland. Some of the headwaters of the Republican River flow from here. It is in the high plain country.

The settlement here did not last. But it was only seventy-five miles from Thurman, Colorado, and in the same kind of country. Thurman became a permanent church, Topland did not. This illustrates the uncertainties of frontiering.

7. *Decatur-Sheridan Counties*

Seventy miles east of the Sherman County settlement was another effort of the Amish Mennonites to plant a church in northwest Kansas.

The settlers bought farms between a point twelve miles south of Oberlin, in Decatur County, to near Selden in Sheridan County. This is a land of level prairies, but also of creeks in canyons between high bluffs. Marketing facilities were good on the Burlington at Oberlin or on the Rock Island at Selden.

There were eight families here as early as 1886. Shibboleth was the post office address of most of them in those days.[28] John Birky was ordained by Joseph Schlegel.[29] When Levi Zimmer died in 1889, his funeral was conducted by John, Joseph, and Joseph H. Berky. Half the people in the congregation were named Birky, with one or another of the four spellings.

Joseph Schlegel and Joseph Gascho held four meetings in December 1889. There were seven decisions. The church was growing. In that same month Eli Kauffman and Lena Steckley were married by David J. Zook of Newton, Kansas.

J. S. Coffman preached a few sermons here in 1890. He noted with interest that practically all the families lived in sod houses, and in writing about his visit to Selden he described how the sod houses are made: they are, he said, "built of a thick wall of sods, a board roof a little higher than you can reach, overlaid with sod. They find a kind of magnesia (native lime) along the banks of the creeks which they use to plaster the inside of these houses, which hardens and adheres well until it gets wet. When this is white washed, as most are, it looks well indeed. The houses are warmer in the winter and cooler in summer than houses of other materials."³ He noticed also that the meetinghouse was made of lumber There were twenty families in the church when Coffman was there

Ammon E. Stoltzfus was married to Lizzie Schrock by John C Birkey in October 1895, and was ordained to the ministry by Joseph Schlegel in June 1897. By 1899 the congregation's bishop was Joseph Schlegel, not of Milford, but of Hartford. In that year D. G Lapp of Roseland, Nebraska, held two weeks of evangelistic meet ings. J. M. Nunemaker was another visiting preacher in 1899, and he pleased the greater part of the congregation by preaching in German

In 1903 Ammon Stoltzfus was the only preacher here. The peo ple were moving away. But the end was not yet. M. E. Horst, o Peabody, held meetings in December 1905, and the five who accepted Christ were baptized by Bishop Schlegel.³¹

At the Western A. M. Conference held at Milford in 1908 A. E. Stoltzfus, with an address at Selden, was registered as attend ing, and the *Yearbook*³² listed the Decatur-Sheridan congregation a having twenty-two members. But by 1913 the congregation was n longer listed and Minister Ammon E. Stoltzfus had moved to Woo River, Nebraska.

8. *Pleasant View, Pawnee County*

In the summer of 1885 two mature family heads from centra Illinois came to Pawnee County, about where central Kansas takes o the characteristics of the high plains of western Kansas. They wer looking for a place where they and their children could own farm and make a living. One of them, John B. Zook, "was fifty years ol financially broke, and had ten children." The other homeseeker wa David H. King, who had eight children.

Near Larned these men were befriended by Charlie Wad worth, a well-to-do sheep rancher and land agent. He sold them lan on reasonable terms, promised employment to all the boys o enough to work, and offered the use of his ranch house until the could make other arrangements. Three families moved out in the fa of 1885. They were two sons and a daughter of David King. I December the first baby of the group was born to Sam B. Kings — daughter Emma, who many years later, as Emma Risser, was to writ the history of the Pennsylvania congregation.

The new settlers got a cold introduction to their new home, for the famous blizzard of 1886 struck Kansas in February. Just after that three more families moved from Illinois: the two older men who had scouted the land the summer before, and Peter Zimmerman, a minister. The party of twenty-seven persons came in two immigrant cars with three or four horses, a cow, their household goods, two wagons, and a few implements. These families all seemed to want to live as neighbors, and they all bought land from Wadsworth about ten miles southeast of Larned.

But building homes was not the only interest of these people. They were deeply religious. J. B. Zook was a descendant of Hans Zaug, an Anabaptist minister at Bern, Switzerland, who was imprisoned because he refused to baptize his children into the Reformed state church, and he lay in prison for a number of years to 1659. Then he was released on condition that he would leave Switzerland and never return. He went to Germany with his large family. His descendants migrated to Pennsylvania, then to Ohio, and to Illinois. The Kings probably had a similar history.

So now here in Kansas a first concern of these families was meeting for worship and teaching. They arrived on a Saturday, and on Sunday they had services in the Eureka Schoolhouse, which was the meeting place of the congregation until 1904. Peter Zimmerman preached, and J. B. Zook was elected Sunday school superintendent.

The interest in the Sunday school flourished from the beginning. People drove in wagons, but they didn't mind going considerable distances. There were a number of German people in the neighborhood and a few of the Sunday school classes were held in the German language. Even the children's class (called the ABC class) learned the German alphabet. It seemed important to get the children ready to read the German Bible. His grandson remembers that J. B. Zook used to say, "I'll see what my German Bible says; the German makes it so much plainer."

The last Sunday school meeting in 1886 was December 12. The school was not evergreen. D. H. King reported that there had been thirty-six sessions, with an average attendance of sixty-eight. There were only twenty members of the church. Many who attended belonged to other denominations, and so this was something of a union Sunday school.[33]

There was a Sunday evening meeting too, called a Bible reading. A committee would choose a subject for discussion, and also a leader, who would select pertinent Scriptures and write them on slips. These slips were handed to different ones to read and discuss. Emma King Risser remembered how glad she was when she was old enough to have a reference to read.

Revival meetings were held with some regularity. D. D. Miller (Indiana) was one of the first evangelists. He influenced some of the younger families to have regular prayer and Bible reading in the home. Daniel B. Zook, son of J. B. Zook, and his wife Mary (Mollie), became active members of the Mennonite Church under Miller's influence. D. D. Zook, T. M. Erb, and J. M. R. Weaver, of Harvey County, often came to preach, and were greatly appreciated. When one German man died, the family wanted a German funeral, and D. D. Zook was brought to preach the sermon.

The community had a happy social life. Literary society, spelling and ciphering matches, and singing school comprised the entertainment. These also were held in the Eureka Schoolhouse. Two of the King brothers, Joe and Ben, could teach singing, and their services were sought in surrounding districts. The songbooks used were *Pentecostal Hymns* and *Gospel Hymns*.

Peter Zimmerman moved to Cass County, Missouri, in 1889, and for a number of years the congregation had to depend on visiting preachers. One of the regular attendants of the service was D. S. Bowman, a member of the Church of the Brethren. A strong contender for his beliefs, he was interested in establishing a Brethren church, and he often brought in Brethren ministers. The Mennonites realized that if a Mennonite church was to develop, they needed a minister. In 1904 David S. King, son of D. H. King, was called to the ministry and ordained by Bishop S. C. Miller. This gave new life to the church, as there was preaching every Sunday.

But Bowman insisted that every other Sunday there should be a Brethren preacher, and he agreed to find one. For this and other reasons both groups decided to build a church house. The Brethren went three miles west of Eureka, and the Mennonites two miles south for their building sites. D. S. King helped to build the new church in 1904 and 1905.

But before this time there had been reverses. Three of the King families — S. B. King, E. J. King, and C. W. Neuhauser — moved to Harvey County in 1905 or 1906. Michael Zook, who had moved from Illinois, died within a year, and his wife a few years later. The wife of Preacher D. S. King died in childbirth in 1890, and several others of the church community died in the nineties. D. S. King married Barbara Kauffman of Garden City, Missouri, in 1897. But because of ill health the Kings moved to Tuleta, Texas, in 1906, along with J. W. Collins, who had married Rosa Zook. The loss of all these families was a severe blow.

So there was a new church building, but very few members. Even so, the small children who were not yet members looked forward to the Sunday services with eager anticipation. The older children of the original families had found partners in the community, and a number of these spouses later joined the Mennonite Church. Now a number of non-Mennonites moved into the community, and some of them quite regularly attended the church. The Meredith family was one of these. Their daughter Helen attended Hesston Academy and met Ira Raymer from Missouri. They were married in 1917, she joined the church, and they became one of the dependable families in the church.

In 1907 the Collins family returned from Texas. In 1908 two ministers from Colorado decided to move to Larned. They were Joe C. Driver and John M. Brunk, each of whom had a family. The John Hartzler family had moved in from Ohio. Such additions were the transfusion the church needed. People knew that Larned was on the map, and there were many visitors. Even if one minister was called away to preach, another was there to fill the pulpit.

In 1910 John Brunk moved to Hesston to get more education. He felt the need, as he was being called into evangelistic work. This was a setback for the Larned church, but there was still one minister, and services were held twice each Sunday and once in midweek. Sometimes during the fall or winter months there was a Bible Normal and evangelistic meetings.

In May 1910, during a severe thunderstorm, Pastor Driver, who lived near the church, aroused the community by telephone to say that the church had been struck by lightning. There was no fire-fighting equipment available, and the building was completely destroyed. The members decided to rebuild at once. This new building was to have a basement and a more modern gas-lighting system. There were only fifteen members, but friends and neighbors gave free labor. The building was dedicated in the fall of 1910, with D. H. Bender preaching the dedicatory sermon. The church was now named Pleasant View.

The pastor received no remuneration for his services except perhaps some free work in his fields. He sold his farm and in April

1911 moved to Garden City, Missouri, for a long term of service at the Bethel Church.

Pleasant View was again without a minister, but was determined to carry on. The conference mission board arranged monthly visits of ministers, many of them from Hesston, which after the opening of Hesston Academy and Bible School in 1909 was becoming a Mennonite center of population and church work. Walter and Abner Zook attended Hesston Academy, and often brought other Mennonite young people to the community for summer employment.

T. M. Erb was bishop at this time and was a pillar of sympathy and concern. Allen H. Erb, his son, preached his first sermon away from home at Larned. Paul Erb often preached here, as did L. O. King, an Erb son-in-law. Another son-in-law, Alvin R. Yordy, became a high school principal in the community, and he and his wife were active in the little church.

In July 1912 D. H. Bender was a visiting preacher. In an evening service, as the first song was announced, the carbide lights began to flicker. J. W. Collins went to the basement to investigate. When the congregation had sung the two words "Blessed Assurance," there was a terrific explosion. The pulpit and the heat register hit the ceiling. Floor boards were torn up the length of the building. One bench was thrown crossways over others where children were sitting. A small fire started, but Collins was able to put it out. There were thirty people in the room, half of them children. Some were bruised, but no one was seriously injured. The burns on the hands and face of J. W. Collins were the worst. Surely God's protecting hand was there.

Now the little flock had neither pastor nor meeting place. They went back to the Eureka School, but not for long. Several hundred dollars and some hard work made the church usable again.

On May 12, 1918, Bishop T. M. Erb, in the Spring Valley Church at Canton, Kansas, ordained Edward Diener to the ministry to serve at Pleasant View. The afternoon of the same day he united in marriage Ida White of Newton, Kansas, and Abner Zook, who planned to make their home at Larned. A few months later Diener was married to Mary Buckwalter. He served as pastor at Pleasant View until February 1927.

These were happy years of worship and service. In the latter part of 1918 Daniel B. Zook was ordained to the office of deacon. "Now you are a fully organized church," said the officiating bishop,

T. M. Erb. Meetings were held with regularity and dignity. The people felt they had a church home. There were speakers and quartets and choruses from Hesston. One Christian Workers' Conference had eighteen names on the program, such as J. D. Mininger, J. D. Charles, John Thut, S. M. Kanagy, J. D. Graber, D. D. Miller, D. G. Lapp, H. A. Diener, and R. M. Weaver.

After Diener moved to a church in Iowa in 1927, the course of Pleasant View was rather hazardous. There was less contact with people of similar belief. There was lack of full accord with some of the dress rules of the Mennonite Church. But eight children of the three or four families of the church had all been taken into the Mennonite Church by baptism and were ready for college. There were invitations to unite with either of the other churches of the community.

When Deacon Daniel B. Zook died in 1940, the remaining members decided to close the church and unite with the Methodist Church. But they continued to be appreciative of their Mennonite background. Abner Zook served on the Board of the Mennonite-operated Greensburg Hospital from 1949 to 1960. He and his wife continue to be faithful readers of the *Gospel Herald* and the *Mennonite Weekly Review*. They believe that the Pleasant View Church has touched many lives for good.[34]

The pews of the church were given to the Greensburg Mennonite Church, which was just being established fifty miles to the south. The church building was purchased by the Nazarenes for $300 and moved to Hoisington, Kansas, thirty miles to the north. Fifty dollars was given to the Mennonite Church in Tuleta, Texas, $100 to the Mennonite Board of Missions, and $75 to each of two local churches, the Brethren and the Methodists. The land on which the church stood went back, according to the terms of the deed, to the heirs of the donors, John B. and Katherine Zook.

About thirty-five members of the Mennonite families lie buried in the township cemetery. In 1969 a monument was erected in this cemetery with plaques to memorialize the four churches of the community: Mennonite, Brethren, Methodist, and Catholic. All these churches have now closed.

9. *Ness County*

Ness County is in the high, level plain of western Kansas, sixty miles west of Great Bend, and 120 miles east of the Colorado line.

There were Mennonites here by February 1881: C. Brundage, Jonas Mishler, and Thomas Pletcher. Brundage had moved from Marion County. In 1886 Minister S. C. Miller of the West Liberty Church invested in a farm in Ness County, and lived here a few years. Both Mennonites and Amish lived in this community. D. J. Zook, Amish bishop at Newton, held communion and baptismal services in April 1888. A Sunday school was organized in the summer of this year. There were fourteen members, with E. M. Shellenberger serving as their pastor. Family names in these years included Schrock, Eash, Williamson, Hostetler, Ummel, Kauffman, Troyer, Oesch, and Gerber.

In 1889 E. M. Shellenberger lived at Ransom, which is in the northern part of the county, and preached every two weeks.[35] By 1893 the attendance here was 100 or more.[36] In 1889 Jonas B. Stutzman and A. Ummel were ordained to the ministry and Jacob Aeby (Eby) to the office of bishop.[37] After the wedding of Alvin Mast and Laura Burkholder on August 3, 1890, as the guests were singing German hymns, a bolt of lightning killed Lucinda Oesch, and seriously burned her two sisters. Jacob Aeby performed the marriage ceremony and reported the tragedy.[38]

M. Z. Troyer wrote in 1892 that Isaac A. Miller was the first traveling minister that visited Ransom for over three years. The tendency of the Ness County Mennonites to live in scattered places is seen in the report that Michael Gerber, at Riverside, was the only Mennonite within ten miles.[39] A prairie fire devastated much of Ness County in March 1893, coming within three miles of Gerber's home. A church was organized in Ness County in 1893, after a visit of J. M. Shenk. E. M. Shellenberger was the minister.[40] This was in the Ransom area. However, southwest of Ness City, Jonathan Mishler ministered to thirteen members.[41] Two Oesch families in 1893 had a typhoid epidemic. The doctor was twenty miles away, and charged seventy-five cents a mile for making calls.[42]

The Evangelizing Board late in 1894 was sending a preacher to Ness County every two months.[43] T. M. Erb preached there August 11 and 12, 1894.[44] In June 1897 there were only six members in Ness County, according to J. B. Williamson.[45] S. C. Miller preached in June 1900 for a group including J. B. and L. M. Williamson. The next year J. B. Williamson died.[46] In May 1901 T. M. Erb spoke twice to the "few in numbers" at Ness City, of which L. M. Williamson was one.[47] Eli Hostetler, a minister moved from North

Dakota about January 1, 1903. A Sunday school was organized at Ness City in 1903, with Arthur Williamson as superintendent and Christian Ummel assistant.

But the congregation gradually died out, although as late as 1922 a widow Ummel, with three or four daughters, was much interested in keeping (Old) Mennonite affiliation, and the Kansas-Nebraska mission board was filling regular appointments there with services being held in the General Conference Mennonite church in Ransom.[48]

10. *Eureka Gardens, Wichita*

Wichita, a growing city of nearly 300,000, is the metropolis of central Kansas. It is close to the state's Mennonite centers, and by the twenties some Mennonite families had moved here. At this time any large city had come to be a challenge to Mennonite mission interest. At the annual meeting of the Kansas-Nebraska Mission Board in 1917 the question of starting work in Wichita was first raised. In 1919 the Kansas-Nebraska Conference appointed a committee — J. D. Charles, B. F. Buckwalter, and H. A. Diener — to work with the Mission Board in opening the work.

A location was found in a residential section on South Pattie Avenue, in the southeastern part of the city. The building was a new house which did not yet have inside partitions.

On April 17, 1921, the first service was held. Fifty people from the community attended. D. H. Bender preached the first sermon. The preaching for the first months was done by ministers of surrounding Mennonite churches, and it suited their schedules better to have the services on Sunday afternoon and evening. Paul Erb was the pastor in charge and his father, T. M. Erb, was the bishop. Teachers came down from Hesston College. Vernon and Grace Shellenberger were appointed as mission workers. Financial support came from surrounding congregations, but Shellenberger earned part of his own living in the plumbing business.[49]

In October John W. Hess held meetings at the mission. In November two young people were received into church fellowship in the first baptismal service. Twenty-four participated in the first communion service. At Christmastime a young mother accepted Christ, and in June 1922 Leroy Thayer was baptized. He had accepted Christ as he listened to a radio sermon, and he was looking for a church home.

For many years an important part of the congregation in Wichita consisted of the Mennonite girls who were working in the homes of the well-to-do people on the "Hill." They had a club, helped with the teaching and visitation work, and helped to give the Mennonites a good name in the city. As many as thirty-five were in the city at one time.

By the spring of 1923 it was clear that a church building was needed. It was decided that it should be on Woodland Avenue, in the northwest corner of town. F. G. Roupp and his family, who were active participants in the church in those early years, lived just across the street from the selected site. Roupp was a contractor, and he supervised the building of the new church. The building and the grounds cost only $4,300. Only $121 was paid out for labor.

The new building was dedicated in February 1924. T. M. Erb presided, and organized the congregation of about twenty-five members. D. H. Bender preached the dedication sermon. Earl Buckwalter presented the building to the community. The evening sermon was by H. J. King, who shortly after this moved to Wichita and was the congregation's first resident minister.

In October 1925 the group decided unanimously to ordain a deacon. Vernon Shellenberger was chosen by lot and ordained by T. M. Erb. A few months later Almond, the little son of the Shellenbergers, died of pneumonia. It was the first funeral for the group.

Henry King left Wichita in the fall of 1926, and in January 1927 a minister was ordained. Two were in the lot: Deacon Vernon Shellenberger and Leroy Thayer, one of the first to be baptized by the mission. Thayer was chosen and ordained by bishops H. A. Diener and T. M. Erb. The congregation now had a minister whose permanent home was in the city, and whose chief interest could be the church, although he was self-supporting.

By 1931 the membership had grown to more than forty. In 1933 it was decided that the official name of the congregation should be Woodland Mennonite Church. Almost all members attended the midweek prayer meeting, and during these Depression years the attendance was increasing. At the Christmas program in 1935 more parents of the children attended than ever before, and in meetings by Nelson Kauffman in January 1936 there were eight confessions.

But that year a theological question began to cause dissension. Pastor Thayer began preaching the second work of grace theory of holiness, which had caused division in the nearby Pennsylvania congregation near Hesston thirty years earlier. This was offensive to some of the members. H. A. Diener was now serving as bishop. He and Alva Swartzendruber spent a few days trying to effect a reconciliation. But Thayer resigned, and he and his family united with the Nazarene Church.

Again the church had to depend on visiting preachers and workers from Hesston College. The laity were faithful in carrying on, but the spirit of the church was damaged by the trouble. In the spring of 1939 the Shellenbergers also joined the Nazarenes.

I. Mark Ross, who had been among those coming down from Hesston, took up residence in the church basement in May 1939 to serve as pastor. He was ordained in 1940, but received only partial support from the district Mission Board. The labors of the Rosses increased the Sunday school enrollment and brought a Bible school enrollment of sixty. Ross started a church paper called *Woodland Echoes,* and his work with adolescent boys gave him the name of "Brother Ross" in the whole community. He left in 1945 to continue his studies.

Allen White and family moved from Peabody to Wichita in 1939, and he served Woodland as Sunday school superintendent. He became the connecting link between the Woodland and the Eureka Gardens phases of the Mennonite Church in Wichita.

In April 1948 Glen Whitaker and family came to Wichita to serve in the pastorate of Woodland. Whitaker started making wall plaques, which young people helped him to distribute in rest homes, tourist camps, and children's homes. Fern Whitaker opened neighborhood Bible classes in 1950. Many children attended the classes held in the church basement.

Another form of witness was a radio broadcast. Although the Sunday morning attendance at church services was small, the congregation had an active program and many people were getting a Christian testimony. But health problems threatened the Whitakers, and it seemed that some other part of the city might have greater needs.

The last service was held at Woodland on September 28, 1953. The building was sold to the Church of God, and thus a Christian witness continues in the neighborhood, but not through the Mennonites.

Pattie, Woodland, Eureka Gardens — these are three phases of a continuum of Mennonite witness in Wichita. Eureka Gardens had its beginning in the concern of Allen White for greater outreach in the city. In 1943, ten years before the closing of Woodland, he asked the Council of Churches to suggest a needy area. He was urged to consider Eureka Gardens, an area four by seven blocks. This was just outside the city limits on the southwest. White drove through the area after church and found many children who said they had not been in Sunday school.

White approached the mission board of the conference, but there was little interest. In 1947 he talked to Merle Bender, Y president at Hesston College, and Laurence Horst, the faculty sponsor. They were interested. A survey revealed that 200 children in the area did not go to Sunday school. A basement building was available. It took a lot of cleaning, and water seeped up through the floor. But the young people were not afraid of hard work. On December 6, 1947, the Sunday school was opened. Within a year the enrollment was sixty. Archie Janzen was the superintendent.

In the early part of 1949 the South Central Conference Mission Board took over the work and Merle Bender was asked to serve as the first pastor. Bender was ordained at his home church, East Fairview, Milford, Nebraska, in May 1949. The service was in charge of Joe E. Zimmerman, bishop at East Fairview; Earl Buckwalter, bishop at Eureka Gardens; and R. P. Horst, president of the South Central Mission Board.

In June the Benders moved to Wichita. At first they lived in the home of the Whitakers, who were resting in Colorado for the summer. Bender preached at Woodland on Sunday evenings, as it was hardly possible to have evening meetings in the basement at Eureka Gardens. In September they moved into an apartment. A corner lot was purchased and the building of a church began. Bender was carrying a full course as a senior at Friends University, and putting in forty hours a week on church construction besides pastoral duties.

Students from Hesston and working girls helped with the Sunday services, and volunteers from the congregations helped with the building. Among them was Fred Bitikofer, who came from Canton with supplies from his wife's canning, and stayed from several days to a week at a time. In January 1950 the Benders moved to a small house in the Eureka Gardens area.

The church was built outside the city limits, and had no plumbing. But by March it was ready for dedication to the spiritual needs of this community. M. A. Yoder preached the dedicatory sermon, and Jess Kauffman held a series of meetings the next week.

The Whitakers moved to the Woodland basement to be nearer

their work, and Allen White, who owned the house they had lived in, made it available for the Benders. They needed a larger house, for a summer service unit moved in with them. Four girls worked at a hospital, and helped with summer Bible school and Sunday school. In 1951, likewise, a service unit helped, as well as Margaret Horst, a veteran worker with young people who could contribute maturity to the team. The Bible school enrollment that summer was 286, which challenged the competent staff headed by Laurence and Marian Horst. In the winter of 1951 Samuel Janzen held meetings, and craft classes were begun.

In 1951 Merle Bender moved to Hesston to serve as public relations director. The Leo Millers, who had been among the students working at Eureka Gardens, were asked to take charge of the congregation. Miller was ordained to the ministry in September by Earl Buckwalter, with Milo Kauffman preaching the sermon.

During the next few years various improvements were made on the church building. An electric clock was purchased by one of the charter members. The concrete floor was covered with tile, most of the work contributed by a neighbor who attended church only occasionally. Window air coolers were installed, with the water being carried from the parsonage. Storage cabinets were built in the Sunday school rooms. A sign was placed outside the church.

The improvement most needed was the installation of rest rooms, nine years after the construction of the building. By this time the city's sewer lines had reached Eureka Gardens. A well was put down to get water. The cost of this improvement was $875, which was paid by the congregation, and much of the work of extending the building was donated.

The first seats for the auditorium were used theater seats, which were easily tilted backward. By 1964 better benches were secured from the Hesston and Greensburg churches. The street in front of the church was paved. A retainer wall along the sidewalk made some landscaping possible. The mother's room got a speaker system and a window into the auditorium to make the ladies a part of the congregation.

Between 1956 and 1963 Eureka Gardens did not use the services of Hesston students. But in October 1963 the Hesston Y made an effort to get some students into the surrounding churches on Sunday morning. And so through the year a carload of students came to Eureka Gardens each week. They participated as opportunity arose,

Eureka Gardens Church

*Early workers at Eureka Gardens (l. to r.): Irene
Springer, Ruth Landis, Laverne Vogt, Helen
Hostetler, Donna Lou Bender, Merle Bender, Leo
Miller*

and the fellowship with the congregation became very close. During
the next two years students came on Sunday evenings to meet with
the young people. In the fall of 1966 it was requested by the church
council that the students again come on Sunday mornings. This
they did until 1970.

The ladies began to meet in 1954 for monthly work and fellowship experiences. These meetings were in the evenings when the

husbands could care for the children. This fellowship was a means of bringing new people into the church. It was traditional for the women to clean the church each spring. At times some of the ladies had a morning prayer fellowship.

In 1956 the parsonage on Millwood Street was sold and another one purchased just three doors from the church. A recreation room was added to this house which could serve fellowship purposes, since the church had no basement for such uses. Sunday school classes could meet in the parsonage because it was close to the church. To supply the need for fellowship the practice developed of having a Sunday church dinner, often in a city park shelter house. On these bimonthly occasions there was no evening meeting. Sometimes the fellowship included other Mennonite churches of the city.

The young people occasionally went to Rocky Mountain Mennonite Camp. In 1963 twelve of them were able to go, accompanied by their pastor and his wife. For two years they had been working for the necessary funds. It was with a real sense of accomplishment that this group reached the top of Pikes Peak. The church ground was large enough for a ball diamond, and for some years the pastor spent two evenings of the summer weeks playing with the fellows of the community.

In 1964 there was conversation concerning a possible change of the type of head covering worn by the ladies in the church services. The church council invited Howard Zehr, area overseer, and Clayton Beyler, New Testament instructor at Hesston College, to come and discuss this with the members. The consensus of the discussion was written up into a statement. This statement encouraged some type of covering. As a result there was freedom to wear different types of covering. But a number continued to wear the traditional type.

Still earlier, in 1960, there was interest in securing an organ. Funds were contributed for the purchase of an old-fashioned reed organ. This was first used before the services and during intermissions and the receiving of the offering. Gradually, however, it was used to accompany the singing.

In 1963 the congregation joined the Every Home Plan for *Gospel Herald* subscriptions.

Sunday school superintendents who followed Archie Janzen were Delmar Byler, Leo Miller, Roman Hershberger, Stanley Kuhns, Argie McElmurry, Virgil Miller, Bill Miller, Clinton Detweiler, Menno Yoder, and Phillip Headings.

Evangelistic meetings were held once or twice a year. Among the evangelists were Elam Hollinger, Edward Miller, I. Mark Ross, Joe Esh, D. A. Raber, Alvin Kauffman, John Landis, Milo Kauffman, Sanford Oyer, Howard Zehr, and Wallace Jantz.

The membership grew, but only slowly. The following were the charter members in 1950: Marvin Bean, Darlene Born, Wayne Fields, Pat Marks, Melvina Roder, Deodie Smith, Pauline Wood, Winona Harris. By 1955 there were 28 members, and in 1960 there were 23. In 1968 the membership was 32. The members were mostly young people, but without the backing of their homes, many lost out. One of the improvements through the years was a trend toward family attendance and adult membership.

In August 1967 the sixteen-year ministry of Leo Miller at Eureka Gardens came to an end. He left to attend Goshen Biblical Seminary. Henry King filled in until the next year, when Keith Schrag came from Premont, Texas, where he had been pastor of the Chapel of the Lord for two and a half years. Schrag was licensed and installed by Milo Kauffman, overseer, on October 6, 1968.

A reappraisal of the Eureka Gardens situation was necessary. The census of the community had gone down, and there was a prospect for continued substandard housing. Limited-access roads had cut the church off except from the west, and it was difficult for some to locate it. It seemed best to relocate and get a more attractive and serviceable building. However, there were still needs to be met in the Eureka Gardens area.

Arrangements were made to hold worship services at the St. Paul United Presbyterian Church on West Street, not far from Eureka Gardens. A schedule permitted each denomination to hold its own separate services, although there were a few forms of cooperation. In this building there was plenty of room. The old building on Taft Street was used for various kinds of community service. Eureka Gardens also cooperated with the other Mennonite churches of the city in an urban council. These churches were Tenth Street (South Central Conference), Open Bible . . . First Mennonite (Mennonite Brethren), and mainly, Lorraine Avenue (General Conference Mennonite).

Early in 1970 several families transferred to Mennonite Brethren membership. Those who agreed with the direction the work was taking at Eureka Gardens continued to meet on Wednesday evenings for fellowship and decision-making concerning the community outreach.

The Leo Miller family in 1958

In May the services on West Street were discontinued.

On May 27 there was a fire in the Eureka Gardens building. The insurance and volunteer labor made it possible to repair the building and adapt it to the kind of community services which were being projected. The remaining members had neither personnel nor finances for a Sunday program, and so they attended other churches. The conference continued its pastoral subsidy until the end of the summer of 1970. There was support from individuals and the Wichita Cooperative Ministries.

Technically, the Eureka Gardens congregation as a member of the South Central Conference came to an end in 1970. But the summer program was carried through. A General Conference VS unit helped, with Schrag as their adviser. Melvin Schmidt came to Lorraine Avenue as pastor in June, and his congregation was interested in assuming sponsorship of the work in the Eureka Gardens community. They engaged Keith Schrag as community minister. In April 1971 he was ordained to the ministry, with representatives from both conferences participating. His ministry is official for both groups. Some consideration has been given to making Lorraine Avenue inter-Mennonite, with membership in both conferences. The work is being done cooperatively, but in 1973 the Eureka Gardens property was still owned by South Central. Schrag was a member of the South

Central Executive Committee. Some support came from the Elkhart Compassion Fund.

The program at Eureka Gardens Community Center includes preschool classes for three-and-four-year-olds, nutrition classes for area ladies and youth, a Senior Citizens Club, counseling, sewing and ceramics classes, playground activities for school-age children (directed by Hesston College students on Saturday mornings since 1968), camping, a food bank for needy families, and involvement in community organization on the west side through the West Side Involvement Corporation. This total program is carried on with an emphasis of Christian love and service. Part of the search at Eureka Gardens is how to keep proclamation and service in balance.

Although responsibility for directing the ministry rests with the Lorraine Avenue congregation, financial assistance and counsel are received from the Western District (GC) and South Central (MC) conferences. There are various occasions when students from Hesston and Bethel colleges make extensive use of the Eureka Gardens ministry to further their education. Congregations in the surrounding Mennonite communities frequently request the Eureka Gardens resources to help them grow in insight and provide for service opportunities. They have also contributed hundreds of dollars' worth of food for the food bank, in response to a short article which appeared in the *Gospel Herald* and *The Mennonite* in the summer of 1972. The entire program here is an exploration of how a believers' church can become a reconciling agent amid poverty, oppression, and hostility.[50]

CHURCHES IN KANSAS

CHAPTER

CHURCHES IN KANSAS

1. *Spring Valley, McPherson County*

The Spring Valley Church is the oldest congregation in the South Central Conference. It grew out of the settlement of the three Kilmer young people in southeastern McPherson County in 1871. The name of the church comes from the township in which it is located. Its address is Canton, a small town two miles west and three miles north of the church. It is three and a half miles south of where the Santa Fe Trail crossed the state in the early days.

For the early settlers the nearest railroad was at Florence, then Newton. The government land office, where they made their claim for homesteads, was at Salina, fifty miles to the north.

In addition to early settlers mentioned in the preceding chapter, in the first thirty years these names appear among those who migrated from Pennsylvania, Ohio, Indiana, Illinois, Missouri, and Miami County, Kansas: Brenneman, Weaver, Young, Loucks, Landis, Butler, Yoder, Selzer, Kornhaus, Hamilton, Bitikofer, Diener, Wenger, Miller, and Smeltzer.

Overlapping the Spring Valley territory were the farms occupied by the German-speaking Mennonites who arrived from Russia in the seventies. One living near Spring Valley was Henry Sommerfeld. There were eleven children, and they could not all ride in the carriage when they drove to church at Goessel. So the four oldest boys — Henry, John, Jake, and Lenhart — walked or rode horseback to Spring Valley. They joined the church there and married (Old) Mennonite girls. The parents were not opposed to this, although it was hard for the elder Mrs. Sommerfeld not to be able to talk to her English-speaking daughters-in-law.

The first settlers met in homes once a month for a church service. Bishop Henry Yother served them their first communion service in December 1872. The first services were in German. German was discontinued about 1889.

In 1875 the first meetinghouse was constructed. Bishop Daniel Brundage, who had homesteaded a farm in 1873, donated the site for the building on the southeast corner of his farm, and he probably did the construction. It was twenty-four by thirty-two feet, and it cost $400. Assisting the members in the building were a number of non-Mennonites. Gifts and loans came from friends in Pennsylvania.

The meetinghouse was used also for a time as a school. John Martin taught here, and Nelson Pool cut cornstalks to keep the building warm. At one time a family lived in this building until they could rent a farm.

The congregational cemetery is on the north side of the church. The first burial was for the senior member of the McNicol family, who had moved from El Dorado in 1871, and had built the first frame house in the township.

Another early grave was that of a migrating woman who died in a tragic accident. Her family was moving westward on the Marion Road. A revolver hung in the front of the covered wagon. The mother accidentally discharged the revolver and was killed. One of the Mennonites, Jacob Landis, and his daughter (later Mrs. Daniel Diener) assisted the family in arranging for the burial. A native rock marks the grave of this unknown woman.

The second meetinghouse at Spring Valley, built in 1892, had on it the name "Old Mennonite Church." No doubt the same name was on the first church. Since both migrations of Mennonites, from the East and from Russia, were settling the Spring Valley area at the same time, it is likely that those who had been in America longest thus distinguished themselves from their brethren from Russia. In this they were following the practice of congregations in the East who called themselves Old Mennonites to distinguish themselves from other branches, or "new" Mennonites. Even today, though "Mennonite Church" is the official name of the branch to which the South Central Conference belongs, other branches find "Old" Mennonite (abbreviated OM) a convenient distinguishing name.[1]

The first meetinghouse was used for seventeen years. By 1892 it was too small. On a certain communion Sunday there were visitors from the East. One of them, J. K. Brubaker, of Rohrerstown, Pennsylvania, saw how crowded the church was. He reported this at home, and the bishops approved offerings to help Spring Valley in building a new church. Groffdale, Martindale, Smoketown, and Churchtown responded and sent a total of $74.

The new building was thirty-six by fifty feet. After some years a furnace was installed. Just before the 1911 conference two anterooms were built on the west end to provide more room and facilities. At the entrance to the churchyard stood a platform about two and a half feet high. The wagons would be driven up to this platform. This made it easy for the occupants to step from the wagons to the platform, and then down a few steps to the ground.

In 1946 the church building was moved and remodeled. It was moved back from the road to the highest spot in the churchyard. A basement was put under the church, and an addition built to the east end. A propane heating system was also installed. The cash cost of this improvement was $3,752.37.

Four single young men came to Spring Valley in the early years. One we have already noted — R. J. Heatwole. His marriage to Margaret Kilmer in February 1873 was the first wedding in Kansas among the Old Mennonites.

The other three were C. W. Miller, Samuel Wenger, and Daniel A. Diener, who with their families were significant in Spring Valley history.

C. W. Miller came from Indiana in 1874. He married Kathryn Landes at Spring Valley and in 1890 was ordained to the ministry. He moved to Texas in 1907, and in 1909 to Protection, Kansas. Moving to Hesston, he discontinued his active ministry. His last years were spent at Adair, Oklahoma, where he died at the ripe age of 103.

Samuel Wenger drove a mule team from Morgan County, Missouri, in 1880. He married Elizabeth Landes, and was the father of Mary Wenger (now Detwiler), who served two terms in India as a missionary nurse.

Daniel A. Diener came from Amish background in Lancaster County. He came to Kansas in 1884 and after several years married another of Spring Valley's daughters, Lydia Landis. In meetings held by J. S. Coffman in 1889, Diener and his wife were converted

and became members of the congregation. Ordained the very next
year, he became the longtime leader of the flock.

Spring Valley leadership has been marked by faithfulness and
stability. The organizer of the congregation, Bishop Brundage, was
called "Old Faithful Bishop Brundage." The writer's grandmother used
to refer to him as "Old Father Brundage." He organized the three
other original congregations of central Kansas — Catlin, West Liberty,
and Pennsylvania. Practically every Sunday morning he preached at
one of the churches of his circuit — a circuit rider of the prairies.
But instead of riding a horse, he hitched his old gray Charlie
to a homemade two-wheeled cart, without springs, except for the wagon spring seat fastened to the axle. The horse pulled his load with a
collar and a chain harness. There was no need for a breeching for
the shafts were fastened to the hames. This kind of a vehicle was
a matter of conscience with Brundage. But the bishop was an old
man, and deserved more comfort. Some brethren wanted to provide
an easier-riding road wagon, but he declined — that would be too
worldly!

Brundage was an earnest speaker, and he stressed Christian experience. He spoke most naturally in German. He was in danger of
mistakes when he tried to speak in English, but he would attempt it.
Once at the Pennsylvania Church he was speaking on the permanent
effect of the Word of God. "Not one tit or jottle shall pass away," he
assured the congregation.

Another time he was going to the Pennsylvania Church. After
he had started he remembered that he had forgotten his *Minister's
Manual;* he probably needed it for a baptism or funeral service. He
drove back home, and didn't tie his horse. Old Charlie trotted
over to another farm. So the bishop was late, and drove his horse
pretty fast those fifteen miles. When he got to the church, his horse
was in a lather. Some of the people felt he didn't treat his horse
right, and they asked him to make a confession.

Bishop Brundage was a good organizer. While living in Missouri
he organized the Missouri-Iowa Conference. In Kansas too he saw
the need for the ministers and workers getting together. So the first
conference in Kansas was held in the new church at Spring Valley
on April 14, 1876. Perhaps R. J. Heatwole urged him on in this,
for he served as the first moderator. This was the beginning of the
Kansas-Nebraska Conference.

Before he retired to Indiana in 1889, the bishop ordained what he hoped would be adequate leadership for his four congregations. In spite of whatever faults he had, he was always a responsible churchman.

To succeed him as bishop, Brundage ordained B. F. Hamilton in 1887. He served as Spring Valley's bishop until his death in 1898.

S. C. Miller, whose home was with the West Liberty Church, was also ordained bishop by Brundage in 1887. He succeeded Hamilton as Spring Valley's bishop, and served until George R. Brunk, also of West Liberty, was ordained bishop in 1898 by Albrecht Schiffler. Brunk was Spring Valley's bishop until he moved to Protection, Kansas, in 1907.

T. M. Erb, of the Pennsylvania congregation, was the bishop at Spring Valley from 1907 until the ordination of D. H. Bender of Hesston in 1912. Bender had oversight of Spring Valley until 1925, when J. G. Hartzler of West Liberty was ordained bishop, and was assigned the responsibility at Spring Valley. Bishop Hartzler served twenty-seven years, longer than any previous bishop. When family health interfered, he was replaced in 1952 by Harry A. Diener, second of the Diener sons, who was now resident at Yoder, Kansas. He was bishop at Spring Valley until the overseer system of the conference was adopted in 1960.

It will be noted that, except for a few years under Bishop Daniel Wismer, Spring Valley has had only one resident bishop, Daniel Brundage.

A number of ministers have labored in the congregation. The first one ordained from the membership was Jacob Holdeman in 1874, one year after he moved to Kansas. He preached in English. In 1889 he moved to Harper, Kansas, and then to California, where he died in 1911.

Matthias Cooprider was the second husband of Susan Brunk, and the father of her three youngest children. He had migrated to Kansas from Indiana. He had not been a Mennonite, but accepted the faith and Mrs. Brunk accepted him. He was ordained to the ministry in 1885, and preached at Spring Valley for eight or ten years before he returned to West Liberty.

John Kornhaus moved to Kansas from Illinois in 1886 or 87. He was a minister when he came. He died in 1889.

The second man ordained from the laity at Spring Valley was Henry Loucks, chosen by lot in 1889. This ordination was an attempt on the part of Bishop Brundage to provide a minister for the congregation he was about to leave. Loucks was a good man and a good mechanic, being the neighborhood thresher. Brundage thought Loucks should be able to lead the congregation because he was a good "fix-it man." But Loucks never preached, although he did read the Scripture at least once. At his request he was relieved of the charge given him.

To take his place bishops S. C. Miller and B. F. Hamilton ordained C. W. Miller and D. A. Diener, two of the men who had come to Kansas single. Evidently the feeling was that two ministers were needed.

D. A. Diener served for a period of forty-four years, until his death in 1934. Much credit goes to him for the stability of the congregation. During World War I, when so-called patriots were trying to force the Mennonites to buy war bonds, a mob came one night and tarred and feathered both Daniel and his son Charles. At a later date the father again suffered indignities. He accepted these experiences with a spirit that won respect both for him and his church.

George Landis, who earlier served as deacon, moved back to Spring Valley and served in the ministry 1906-1912. He had been ordained at Jet, Oklahoma, in 1901.

Ministers who served briefly at Spring Valley in the early decades of this century were D. S. Brunk and J. L. Brubaker.

Charles Diener, son of D. A. Diener, was ordained to the ministry in 1917. Like his father, he had a long ministry, all in this congregation. In 1960, after preaching for forty-three years, he resigned on the theory, he said, that "it is better to do it five minutes too soon than ten minutes too late." But at this writing he still preaches on occasion and serves as sexton of the cemetery. The combined ministries of father and son, though overlapping nearly 20 years cover most of a century.

One other minister chosen from the congregation was Edward Selzer, ordained in 1935. He also resigned in 1960.

Edward Diener, another son of D. A., was ordained in his home church in 1918, but for service at Larned, Kansas. Harry A. Diener after brief service at Proctor, Missouri, and the Kansas City Mission, was ordained to the ministry in 1915 for the rural mission work in the Missouri Ozarks. In 1921 he moved to Yoder, Kansas and in 1923 was ordained bishop. After his retirement he served in interim pastorates at Cass County, Missouri, and Gulfport, Mississippi.

In 1960 Rollin Yoder, a grandson of R. J. Heatwole, was in

Charles Diener, minister at Spring Valley since 1917

stalled as pastor. After two years he resigned.

In 1964 James Hershberger of Hesston was ordained and installed as pastor by Milo Kauffman and Earl Buckwalter. Together with this pastorate he served as administrator of Schowalter Villa at Hesston. In 1972 he discontinued his pastorate in order to devote more time to the Villa and to conference duties. In 1973 he was elected as chairman of the Commission on Stewardship under the Board of Congregational Ministries of the General Assembly.

Peter Neuenschwander was the first deacon at Spring Valley. He died in 1889. George Landis was ordained deacon in 1890 and served till he moved to Oklahoma in 1902. The third deacon, Aaron Landes, was ordained by Bishop Brunk about 1907. He died in 1924. J. L. Shellenberger moved into the community and assisted in the work of deacon 1910-1915, when they moved to Hesston. In 1925 William S. Landis was chosen by lot, with D. H. Bender officiating. He died in 1946. The present deacon, Herman Sommerfeld, was ordained in 1948 by bishops Hartzler and Diener.

As at Catlin, some members at Spring Valley participated in a union Sunday school. This was held at the Bunker Hill Schoolhouse across the road from the church. For a while it was transferred to the Emma School, two miles south, where a United Brethren minister would preach a sermon after Sunday school. Later it was moved back to Bunker Hill. The early Sunday schools used both English and German. The Spring Valley Sunday school has always been evergreen.

Here too, about 1890, the Mennonites decided to have their own Sunday school. C. W. Miller was the first superintendent. Those who have followed him include Joe Schrock, G. B. Landis, Aaron Landes, Ira Yoder, Harvey Yoder, William Landis, Ammon Bitikofer, D. A. Wenger, Jonas Wenger, A. D. Diener, Edward Diener, Charles Diener, Harold Sommerfeld, Herman Sommerfeld, Edward Selzer, Allen Bitikofer, Leroy Bitikofer, John Wenger, Jesse Diener, and Elvin Selzer.

Among the teachers Fannie Landis was outstanding. When the church had no picture cards or rolls to help teach the lesson, she often walked over two miles to and from the church on Saturday afternoons to place a drawing on a blackboard to help her teach more effectively the next day.

Fannie worked at the Chicago Mission for a while about 1905. After her return, she helped to start Sunday evening Bible readings, as they were called. When the church made available Young People's Meeting topics, they were used at Spring Valley. Fannie Landis also taught mission study classes on Sunday afternoon.

Edward Diener for a few summers conducted a mission Sunday school at Contention Schoolhouse eight miles north of the church. Also for seven or eight years there was a mission Sunday school at Battle Hill School six miles north of Canton. Two series of evangelistic meetings were held there, by D. D. Miller and Jess Kauffman.

The women of the congregation began to meet regularly for sewing circle in 1918. There has been a midweek prayer meeting for many years. A Mennonite Youth Fellowship was organized in 1960, sponsored by Leroy and Doris Bitikofer.

Spring Valley claims the distinction of having the first evangelistic meetings in the Kansas-Nebraska Conference. This meeting was held in November 1889 by John S. Coffman, pioneer Mennonite evangelist. At this time the Mennonite Church was fearful of this kind of evangelism. And so, when Coffman was invited to Spring Valley, R. J. Heatwole announced the services only one evening a* time. He feared opposition if he would announce meetings a week in advance. However, the meetings did last a week. Only one invitation was given, and that was the last evening. Eight souls confessed Christ.

Two of these were D. A. Diener and wife. On his way East, Coffman stopped in Cass County, Missouri. He reported to D. Y. Hooley the conversion of D. A. Diener, stating that he was a very promising young man. "Of course," he observed, "he has a moustache, but I think he will lose that." The wearing of the moustache was condemned by Mennonites for many years, on the grounds that it had a military connotation. Diener did shave off his moustache, and grew a beard instead, which was acceptable. He wore a neatly trimmed beard the rest of his life.

Evangelistic meetings became an annual event at Spring Valley. Through the preaching of George R. Brunk the Sommerfeld brothers were brought into the church. The series by Jacob L. Winey in 1902 was especially successful. There were many unconverted young people attending, and many parents were burdened for their sons and daughters. The Holy Spirit deeply convicted. Several evenings before the close of the meetings, Winey gave an invitation, and about twenty young people accepted Christ. The total response in the meetings was thirty, and soon thirty-three were added to the church by baptism and confession, the largest ingathering at one time in the history of the congregation.

The promotion of experiential salvation in central Kansas around the turn of the century was the occasion for some extremes. A man by the name of Isenhower led a movement of holiness enthusiasm in Dickinson County. Some Mennonites were affected by this movement. From Spring Valley two young men, Ira and Harvey Yoder, had attended meetings in Abilene and claimed a new experience of cleansing and power, which, of course, they wanted others to have.

One Sunday, when J. M. R. Weaver of Harvey County preached, these young men planned with Harris Beck of Peabody to capitalize on the opportunity of testimony extended to ministers after the sermon. However, Bishop George R. Brunk had heard of this plan and warned the Yoder boys not to undertake such a move. At the conclusion of the sermon, Harris Beck ran to the front of the room, waving a Bible over his head and singing a song, the first verse of which ran:

I have a letter from my Father in my hand,
Written by an elder brother, it was grand.
It was written unto me by one beyond the sea,
I'm as happy as I can be in this land.

The Yoder boys heeded their bishop's warning and did not come to Beck's assistance and after he gave his testimony, the meeting closed.

On another occasion the Yoder brothers told D. A. Diener that "God doesn't wash you right away; He saves you and washes you later." Diener replied with a bit of reasoning by analogy, "Do you think I would wait until some time after my boys were born to wash them?"

The new movement held an extreme position on divine healing — that it was wrong to use medical help. Harvey and Ira, who were twenty-one and nineteen, contracted typhoid fever. Neither would take medicine; the Lord would heal them, they said. After Ira died, a Mr. Engle, who worked at an orphanage near Hillsboro, joined some friends in praying for Harvey. They told him to get up, for he was healed. He did get up, but died shortly afterward. Other brothers, who were sick also, got a doctor and recovered.

Other people of the congregation were also affected. The unity of family life was strained. How Bishop Brunk handled this situation was described by "one-armed Joe," George's older brother: "After a two-day trial every member of the congregation was asked by him to answer three questions, which all but six did satisfactorily, four of these returning later:

1. *Do you believe that the Mennonite Church is a church that God recognizes and blesses?*
2. *Are you willing to work for her defense, extension, and upbuilding?*
3. *Are you willing to submit yourself to her government and discipline?*

While George steadfastly opposed, among other things, the extreme 'divine healing' of the quack holiness cults, he strongly believed in Biblical divine healing, being himself several times healed of the Lord when the doctors had given him up."[2]

A number of Bible conferences, some of them in connection with evangelistic meetings, were held at Spring Valley. The first one was in 1908 with George R. Brunk and J. P. Berkey as instructors; and the last one in 1933 with John Thut and Alva Swartzendruber in charge.

After the first session of the Kansas-Nebraska Conference met at Spring Valley in 1876, this conference met here frequently, at least as long as Daniel Brundage was an active leader. Other years were 1877, 1879, 1880, 1881, 1883, 1885, 1888, 1894, 1902, 1911, 1920. The newly formed Missouri-Kansas Conference, now renamed the South Central Conference, met at Canton in 1934 and 1947.

The singing among the frontier Mennonites was one-part, and in German. The first songbooks were only those owned by the members, which they brought to church from their homes. Since there were not enough to go round, the minister would read one line of the hymn, then someone would "raise the tune" and the congregation would sing that line. At Spring Valley that may well have been R. J. Heatwole, for he was a good singer. There was no musical instrument.

After a while part-singing came in. The conference in 1890 was given this question: "Is not the church conforming to the world and doing wrong by singing more than one part in music?" The conference decided that four-part singing was in order. This kind of singing involves music reading. To teach this there was an occasional singing school. One winter R. M. Weaver had two sessions a week at Spring Valley, riding a bicycle or a horse the eighteen miles one way from his home in Harvey County. The music rudiments text used was *Ever New*.

Hymnbooks used in the services were the following: *Hymns and Tunes, Gospel Hymns* (Numbers 1-6), *Pentecostal Hymns, Church and Sunday School Hymnal* with *Supplement, Life Songs 1 and 2,* and *The Mennonite Hymnal*. They never used the *Church Hymnal*, which was widely used in the conference 1927-1969.

Another first about Spring Valley is the taking of a regular Sunday offering. In an annual business meeting on methods of Christian giving, a weekly offering was proposed by the Sunday school field worker. It was tried and has been found satisfactory. Up to that time offerings were taken whenever a need was presented. When the India Mission was begun at the turn of the century, support was slow in coming in. Orphans had to be turned away because there was no money to buy rice. J. F. Brunk, who was present on one occasion, got up and said the Lord needed $500 for India. Before the meeting closed, most of the amount was pledged. Giving has been liberal. Pastors, however, received little financial help. Since 1960 partial support is given.

In 1950 most of the members were farmers. Economic changes in Kansas are sharply indicated by the fact that in 1972 about 75 percent of the family heads are employed in factories in Hesston. Some of them commute to work, and some, with homes in Hesston, drive fifteen miles to church on Sundays. The morale and loyalty of the congregation are good. There is a large and active group of young people. However, there are few young couples and few small children.

The Spring Valley congregation observed the centennial of its founding June 2 and 3, 1973. The observance began with a music festival on Saturday evening. On Sunday morning there was a centennial worship service, followed by a meal served at the Canton High School. In the afternoon the congregation's history was narrated with the aid of slides. Wilma Diener, a granddaughter of Daniel Diener, was chairperson of the Centennial Committee. Messages were by Harry A. and Charles Diener.[3]

2. *Whitestone, Harvey County*

On December 20, 1964, an opening service was held in the Whitestone Mennonite Church, newly built in the northern part of Hesston, Kansas. On that day the congregation met for the last time in their old meetinghouse, the Pennsylvania Church, three miles southeast of Hesston. This farewell service, led by Earl Buckwalter, pastor for many years, heard historical talks by Emma Risser, Oliver Miller, and Elmer White. Then the congregation journeyed in a body to the new church for a worship service. That evening the Sunday school Christmas program was presented as the first full service at Whitestone.

This event was the end of one era for this group, and the beginning of another era, each with its own name. The Pennsylvania congregation, after seventy-nine years in its location near Trousdale (later Zimmerdale), became the Whitestone congregation in a new location in Country Acres, in the growing town of Hesston.

The Pennsylvania congregation was the third of the original Mennonite churches in the central Kansas circuit. First Mennonites in this Harvey County setting were the Joseph Shirk family from Indiana, who came in 1875, but finding no other Mennonites joined the Methodists. Samuel Fergusons came from Iowa in 1877

The Fergusons, the Kilmers, and R. J. Heatwole, married to Margaret Kilmer, though living in McPherson County, were nearer to what was to become the Pennsylvania community than they were to Spring Valley.

The church got its name, not by deliberate decision, but as a sort of nickname because most of its members were immigrants from Pennsylvania. The first family were the David Weavers — parents, six sons and three daughters — who came in 1880 from the Weaverland section of Lancaster County. They settled four miles northwest of Newton. Martin Zimmerman (for whom Zimmerdale was later named) came the same year. Solomon Martin came in 1883. Soon after came the Hess brothers — Daniel, Amos, and Abram, for whom Hesston was named. Other Pennsylvanians were Jacob B. Erb and Francis W. Horst (1885) and Amos Graybill (1888). In these years too came M. E. Horst, J. A. White, David Reiff, Jacob Z. Burkhart, Noah Eby, and Henry Horst from Maryland; Charles Rodgers, and John Shelley from Illinois; J. P. Brenneman from Ohio.

Another Pennsylvania strain was added to the Harvey County church in the five Amish Mennonite families who came from 1885 to 1889: David J. Zook, Chris Lantz, David Schertz, Eli and Joseph Byler. They were from Mifflin County, the "Big Valley" of central Pennsylvania. David J. Zook was their ordained minister when they came, and was soon ordained bishop.

Other settlers who came before 1900 were Samuel Nettrower, George Royer, John Evers, E. J. and S. B. King, C. W. Neuhauser, Christian Metzler, and Thomas Pletcher. Some of these pioneers were single men, but most of them had families with children, and so the growth of the congregation was rapid.

This group of Mennonite believers began to meet in the District 79 Schoolhouse, a half mile north of Trousdale, probably in 1883.[4] In the fall of 1885 David Weaver was ordained as minister and Jacob B. Erb as deacon, and the organization as a congregation probably dates from that time. Leah Erb, who lived until 1939, was the last of the charter members to pass away. Even before a meetinghouse was erected, the church got its name, for on June 6, 1886, T. M. Erb wrote in his diary, "To church at Pa."

Until about 1892 the Mennonites and Amish Mennonites had separate organizations, although they both worshiped in the same schoolhouse. Each group attended the other's services, and ministers

from each group preached for the other. Bishop David J. Zook
once asked J. S. Coffman, a Mennonite, to preach the sermon in an
Amish communion. The Amish and the Mennonites came to be one
except in name. A merger seems to have been effected by 1892,
for the last "Amish" communion of record was held in March
1892. This was thirty years before the merger of Mennonites and
Amish Mennonites was accomplished churchwide.

Although the schoolhouse served well as the place for the first
preaching service, the first communion, the first Sunday school, the
first ordinations, the first singing school, and the first evangelistic
meeting, by 1885 the group decided to build a church. The first site
selected was right at Trousdale, a half mile south of the schoolhouse. The first of the group to die, Mrs. Solomon Martin, was
buried here. But then came news of the location of the new Mis-
souri-Pacific right of way to this site. There were fears that passing
trains would frighten horses and disturb the services. And so a
three-acre plot was purchased from Solomon Martin a mile north
of Trousdale, and Mrs. Martin's body was moved to begin the
cemetery there. Fifteen persons subscribed the $100 needed to pur-
chase this land "to be used as a church and burying ground and
known as the property of the old Mennonite denomination." Here
too the term "old" was used to distinguish themselves from their
other Mennonite neighbors.

Building of the church began in 1886 and was completed
in 1887. The frame structure was thirty by forty feet. There was
no basement. Two anterooms, with a vestibule between, were at
the front end, facing the road. The building was heated by two
stoves. The benches were homemade, and the ceiling was low.
There were two "amen corners." The pulpit was long and
high, after the Pennsylvania pattern. The bench behind it was often
filled to capacity with five or six ordained men. There was a
water bucket just inside the door to the rear. And two collection
boxes on the jamb of the door into the vestibule received the giving
of the people for church expenses. Janitor Sol Martin was to receive fifteen cents each time he made a fire and swept the
room.

This building cost a little over $1,000. The money was con-
tributed by the members, both Mennonite and Amish, by business
firms in Newton, and by congregations and friends in Pennsylvania,
Maryland, and Ohio.

There was no dedication for a church in those days, but on August 13, 1887, T. M. Erb painted on the front of the church its name, "Pennsylvania Mennonite Church." A hedge fence marked the boundaries along the road, and yellow locust trees separated the lines of hitching racks.

D. D. Zook was ordained to the ministry by his father, Bishop D. J. Zook, in August 1890. The bishop returned to Pennsylvania, probably the next year. Before leaving he turned the eldership of the church over to his son, D. D. Zook. While "Davy" was not ordained bishop, the Amish group accepted him in this capacity. Soon after, the merger became a reality, and officially D. D. Zook was one of the ministers of the united congregation.

By the turn of the century Zook, converted under the preaching of J. S. Coffman, was an effective preacher, evangelist, and counselor. He had pulpit manners all his own. He never wore a "plain" coat, but a black shirt without a tie. He had a short red beard, and his black hair was unparted. He gestured constantly, and his earnest language was full of colloquialisms. He moved about constantly in the pulpit. When others preached, he expressed agreement with a frequent "Yes, sir; yes, sir."

He became leader of the schism of 1913, described on a later page. This division was basically on issues, not on leadership. But a member of one of the separating families used to explain to her children what happened as a redrawing of the line between the Mennonites and Amish, which the merger was supposed to have obliterated. It was obvious that the defection of some of the families was an expression, not of theological conviction, but of loyalty to D. D. Zook, a former elder whom they loved. When a bishop was ordained in 1912, when doctrinal controversy was at its height, they surely remembered that he once exercised bishop functions.

This congregation had grown in numbers. The attendance was sometimes as high as 240, and in July 1902 the congregation voted for a larger place of worship. While services were held in a temporary structure, the old church was dismantled and a new one built at a cost of $2,300, almost two thirds of which was subscribed beforehand. The new structure was forty by sixty, over a partial basement. It had comfortable seats for 250 people. The ceiling was higher, and the pulpit was smaller. The anterooms were placed at the east end, behind the pulpit. So people entered from both ends: the older people through the anterooms, and the young peo-

Young people of the Pennsylvania Church at the F. W. Horst home in November 1908. A few identifications, numbering from the left. Reclining: (2) Vernon Reiff, who became treasurer of the Mennonite Board of Missions. First row: (1) Silas Horst, pastor at South English, Iowa. Second row: (2) Anna Erb, wife of L. O. King, pastor at Hutchinson; (5) Tillie Horst, wife of Charles Diener, pastor at Spring Valley; (8) Mabel Erb, wife of James Kaufman and mother of Daniel Kaufman, first secretary of stewardship. Fourth row: (6) Mary Buckwalter, wife of Edward Diener, pastor at Larned. Top row: (1) Allen Erb, promoter of Mennonite hospitals; (3) Frank D. King, Sunday school superintendent at Chicago Home Mission.

ple and visitors from a front porch. The lights were still kerosine, but there was a coal furnace in the basement.

The new church was dedicated in January 1903, with George R. Brunk preaching the sermon.

In 1906 a long row of sheds was built along the north side of the church ground. These were for the protection of the horses, and were used until cars had replaced the horses, about 1925.

Another improvement came in 1909, when a gas lighting plant was installed, and Sunday school space was secured by completing the basement. In 1925 electricity replaced gas for lighting. In less than fifty years: candles, kerosine, gas, electricity!

The last changes in this building were made between 1947 and 1956. A 14 x 28 annex on the front provided entrance and cloakrooms for everybody at the same end — to the basement as well as the assembly room. A new automatic oil-burning furnace was installed. The pulpit was lowered, the floor sanded, the benches angled toward the pulpit, the walls redecorated. One person — a friend but not a member of the congregation — paid for many of these changes which totaled more than the cost of the first church building.

Early bishop leadership was given to the Pennsylvania congregation by the bishops of the other central Kansas churches: Daniel Brundage, Daniel Wismer, and B. F. Hamilton. The first resident bishop was T. M. Erb, except that the Amish group had the oversight of the Zooks, father and son. T. M. Erb and George R. Brunk became bishops in a double ordination in 1898 by bishops S. C. Miller and Albrecht Schiffler, of Nebraska. Brunk was ordained for primary responsibility at Spring Valley, and Erb at Pennsylvania. At the time of the bishop ordination Erb lived at Harper, Kansas, but he returned to Harvey County in 1900, and served as bishop until his death in 1929, receiving assistance from D. H. Bender during a period of serious illness.

Tillman M. Erb was nineteen when he came west with his father, Jacob B. Erb, in 1885. Two years later he married Lizzie Hess, a Pennsylvania girl who came west to visit her brothers in Harvey County. Although he farmed for a number of years, he was also active as a businessman, operating creameries at Hesston, Newton, and Harper, and doing much to develop dairying on the frontier farms. He was one of the founders of Hesston College, and was its business manager from its founding in 1908 to his death in 1929. As minister, bishop, and conference official, he served actively on the Mennonite frontier in the West.

Erb was converted in 1887 under the preaching of J. S. Coffman at the Pennsylvania Church. His call to the ministry was in a double ordination in June 1893. J. M. R. Weaver was the other person called; both were to serve the Pennsylvania Church. B. F. Hamilton and S. C. Miller officiated. New preachers were needed because David Weaver had suffered a throat affliction which kept him from preaching. And R. J. Heatwole had more places for services than he had preachers.

In 1912 a gaslight plant exploded in the Erb home near Hesston, severely burning the father and fatally burning a daughter. Although Erb lived seventeen years after this, and was able to perform his church functions in part, his injuries did lead to two amputations and to his death in 1929 at the age of sixty-four.

Shortly after Erb's death, bishop charge at Pennsylvania was given in 1930 to Bishop J. G. Hartzler, who served until 1947. At this date Pennsylvania again got a resident bishop when Earl Buckwalter was ordained to this office by voice of the congregation, Bishop Hartzler officiating.

Earl Buckwalter was ten years old when the B. F. Buckwalter family moved to Kansas from New Holland, Pennsylvania. Growing to manhood, he served a number of years at Pennsylvania

Bishop Tillman M. Erb; note the left ear, crippled in a burning accident

as Sunday school superintendent. He was ordained to the ministry in 1929, a few months after the death of T. M. Erb. He and Paul Erb served as co-ministers until 1941. Then he served as pastor — bishop-pastor after 1947 — until his retirement in 1961. His is the longest pastoral ministry in the history of the congregation. His pastorate was mostly self-supported. He made his living as an expert auto mechanic. By the time of his resignation as pastor the congregation had also accepted the conference plan of overseers instead of bishops, and so Bishop Buckwalter was no longer carrying that responsibility. Since his retirement, however, he has given valued interim pastoral service in south Texas, at Sycamore Grove in Missouri, and at the Crystal Springs Church near Harper, Kansas. In 1973 he was a resident in Schowalter Villa.

The first minister of the congregation was David Weaver, pioneer settler. He was ordained in September 1885, and lived until 1905. He and his descendants have had an important part in the life of this church. A son, J. M. R. Weaver, became one of the ministers; another son, Reuben, was Sunday school superintendent for a number of years before he was ordained and sent to Harper, Kansas. Grandchildren have been responsible members; one of them, Edwin I. Weaver, became a missionary to India. And a great-grandson, Jerry, son of Edwin, is the present pastor (1974).

The second ordination was of Jacob A. White in 1886, who continued his ministry for three years. M. E. Horst was chosen from among eight in the lot in 1890. He moved to Peabody in 1899. In a double ordination (with T. M. Erb) J. M. R. Weaver was ordained to the ministry in 1893.

John M. Weaver was born in Lancaster County, Pennsylvania, and came west with the rest of the pioneer Weaver family. (Because he had an uncle named John M., he inserted another initial into his name — J. M. R. Weaver.) He went far into a life of sin, including drunkenness. But he was converted under the preaching of John S. Coffman. An omnivorous reader, he was self-educated. He was a good Bible student and an eloquent speaker, and in his earlier evangelistic work preached to crowded churches. Soon after his ordination he and his family drove to Pennsylvania with a team and carriage, preaching on the way.

Weaver was impulsive and sometimes found teamwork difficult. There were periods when he would not preach, and would absent himself from the communion service. He lived a few years at

Tuleta, Texas, but was back in Kansas and participated in the schism of 1913. Nine years later he returned to the Pennsylvania Church, and was welcomed heartily. His faithfulness in these years redeemed earlier instability. But his most effective ministry was past, and he died in 1929, a few months after the death of his colaborer, T. M. Erb.

Erb, Zook, and Weaver were the ministerial team for a number of years. In 1919 Paul Erb, son of T. M. Erb, was ordained for missionary service. When the war interfered with his going for this service, by vote the congregation invited him to serve in the ministry at Pennsylvania. He was a teacher and official at Hesston College until 1941, when he moved to Goshen College, and on to a varied service in the Mennonite Church: editor, committee and board member, and secretary of General Conference. In his retirement he lives at Scottdale, Pennsylvania.

Ministers who served briefly at Pennsylvania included E. M. Shellenberger, in the eighties, and J. M. Brunk in the second decade of this century. Shellenberger moved to Ness County and Brunk to Gulfport, Mississippi. Some were ordained here to serve elsewhere. Amos Geigley, who had come to Kansas from Lancaster, Pennsylvania, was ordained in March 1907 for the small church at Neutral, Kansas. In September of that year three men were ordained on the same day: Chris Reiff for Newkirk, Oklahoma, R. M. Weaver for Harper, Kansas, and L. O. King for Manchester, Oklahoma. Reiff later returned to Harvey County and assisted in the preaching for four years until he moved to Indiana in 1922.

In later years there were other ministers. Owen Hershberger moved to Hesston in 1941 and was assistant to Earl Buckwalter until illness prevented. F. S. Brenneman, who practiced medicine in Hesston following 1947, placed his membership at Pennsylvania. He had been a missionary and preached as called upon. When Earl Buckwalter retired in 1961, Donald E. King, grandson of T. M. Erb, became pastor and served for five years. John Friesen, a missionary on furlough from India, then served as interim pastor until June 1967, when Jerry Weaver became pastor of the Whitestone Church. In October he was ordained to the ministry by his father, Edwin I. Weaver, and Milo Kauffman, overseer.

Other sons of the congregation who were ordained for service abroad were S. M. King, ordained for India by J. G. Hartzler in 1936, and Albert and Ralph Buckwalter, ordained by their father,

Earl Buckwalter, pastor at Pennsylvania Church, 1929-1961

Earl, in 1947 — Albert for the Argentine Chaco and Ralph for Japan. Delbert Erb, son of Paul Erb, went to Argentina in 1951 for a career as a lay missionary.

Only three deacons have served the Pennsylvania congregation: Jacob B. Erb, B. F. Buckwalter, and Gaius Horst.

Jacob Erb was a young Lancaster County farmer who caught the fever of western migration. He joined a prospecting company who came by train to Abilene and then overland to Marion and Harvey counties. Erb liked Harvey County best, and later bought a farm there, three miles northwest of Newton. The family moved in 1885, and became charter members of the new congregation. On the same day in 1885 that David Weaver was ordained as minister, Jacob Erb was ordained deacon, and he served in this office until his death in October 1908. He was most comfortable speaking in his native Pennsylvania Dutch. So he seldom spoke in church services, but the Mennonite use of deacons did not require that. He functioned quietly and efficiently. The Erb home was the stopping place through the years of a procession of visitors from Pennsylvania. He formed close friendships with some of the Mennonite immigrants from Russia.

B. F. Buckwalter moved to Kansas from Lancaster County, Pennsylvania, in 1905, only a few years before he was ordained deacon to succeed Jacob Erb in December 1908. When votes of the congregation were taken for this ordination, Buckwalter was unable to make up his mind as to whom he should vote for, and so did not vote. Every vote cast was for him, and so the lot was not used, the first such ordination in the congregation. Buckwalter was one of the last in the congregation to wear a beard. He was a deeply spiritual man, and he and his family made a real contribution. He served for about eighteen years, and then moved to Iowa, where he died in 1936.

The last deacon ordained was Gaius Horst, a son of the pioneer Francis Horst. He was ordained by lot in 1926 by Bishop T. M. Erb. Gaius served the congregation faithfully until 1946, when he moved to Sterling, Illinois, and later to Michigan, where he died. Since then the congregation, like some others of the conference, has given the deacon functions to trustees and other elected officials.

The greatest tragedy this congregation has known grew out of misunderstanding over the theological issue of sanctification. This resulted in two schisms: a smaller one in 1903, and a more serious one in 1913. This whole episode was studied carefully by G. G. Yoder, and his unpublished account is the best record of the issues and the events. These paragraphs are largely selected and summarized from his objective work and some from the history by Emma Risser.

It is clear from the Dordrecht Confession and other documents that the Mennonite Church believes in holiness — a new life which depends on a new birth. So the issue at Pennsylvania was not the necessity and possibility of holiness, but rather a definite "second" work of grace as a requirement in the plan of salvation. In the nineties Kansas Mennonites were greatly influenced both by the Great Awakening in the entire Mennonite Church and by the holiness revival which had swept the country with Wesleyan emphases.

A group of laymen met in weekly "teachers' meetings" following 1890, and found new richness in Christ. This was followed by prayer meetings. Many attended camp meetings of the Brethren in Christ, the Mennonite Brethren in Christ, and the Free Methodists, and had new experiences for which they learned a new vocabulary. Visiting Mennonite evangelists like J. S. Coffman, J. L. Winey, Noah Metzler, J. M. Shenk, and Andrew Shenk taught a deeper spiritual experience than many had known.

The Kansas-Nebraska Conference in 1899 adopted a position that "the baptism with the Holy Ghost is as necessary to be obtained as conversion and that it becomes the duty of every believer to seek and tarry until they have it definitely experienced." The next year the conference resolved that bishops should pray at baptisms that applicants who "have not yet received the Holy Ghost" might receive Him. Some leaders both in the conference and in other parts of the church were concerned about this language.

Influences from without the church began to produce some radical attitudes. Some members refused medical help, even to refusing to wear glasses. Others thought it was wrong to eat pork. Some made extreme claims of sexual purity. One went into a trance and foamed at the mouth. Several were sure they were called to preach. There were charges that the church was dead.

None of the ministers was involved in this wildfire, and most of the members suspected the claims of these extremists. In June 1903 bishops Albrecht Schiffler, S. C. Miller, and George R. Brunk came to correct the situation. They asked members to sign a promise of loyalty to the church. Eight couples and several single persons refused to sign and were excommunicated. Later two of these returned. The seceders started a "mission" in Newton. But this came to nothing when the men could not agree on who the preachers should be. Most of these people gradually found themselves in the Nazarene Church, which was just being formed at this time. A son of one family, who many years later became a prominent Nazarene official, said: "It didn't have to happen. They all believed in holiness, but called it different names."

Ten years later came the second break, this time dividing the ministerial team. Again the issue was not the sanctified life, but rather whether there is normally a twilight zone of sin and defeat between conversion and sanctification. Belief in the two-stage salvation was taught vigorously by D. D. Zook and J. M. R. Weaver. Bishop T. M. Erb increasingly saw reasons for rejecting the concept that one born again still had a heart full of sin. He gave his position on this in his last sermon before his serious accident in September 1912. Without doubt the coming of several Eastern men to Kansas at this time to found and teach in Hesston Academy and Bible School contributed to the crisis. They helped to clarify the position of the church, and may have pressed the issue unduly.

Two conference ministerial meetings in 1911 and 1912 failed to bring agreement. The Kansas-Nebraska Conference, meeting in October 1912 at West Liberty, considered this question, "What does this conference believe the Bible teaches on the subject of holiness?''

In answer the following statement was adopted:

"Resolved, That we believe that the Bible teaches that without holiness no one can be a child of God (Heb. 12:14; II Tim. 1:9; I Cor. 12:13), and that each believer should so order his life as to meet the conditions for fuller growth in holiness (II Cor. 7:1; II Pet. 3:18; II Cor. 3:18), and that we should trust the Lord for a constant keeping and look forward to a completeness in holiness at His Coming (I Thess. 5:22-24 and 3:13)."

D. D. Zook was present at the first session of this conference, but after hearing the discussion he left and did not return. He felt that the conference had hurled a dart at the very heart of the Bible teachings on holiness, "a thrust at the fundamental principles of salvation." The conference had indeed attempted to check the extreme emphasis on the "second blessing" as a fundamental requirement of salvation, but also had reaffirmed the historical Mennonite position.

D. H. Bender had been ordained bishop at Pennsylvania on February 9, 1912. It was charged by the followers of D. D. Zook that Zook was not accepted to go through the lot. There is no document to tell whether this is true. But it may be. The men who did go through the lot were D. H. Bender, J. A. Heatwole, J. M. Brunk, and L. O. King. Zook's friends would probably have voted for him. Two days before the ordination the four bishops of the conference examined the candidates. One can understand why they might have decided not to admit D. D. Zook to the lot. For that same week he had spoken at the ministers' meeting. The Erb diary says, "His talk brought out many questions and controversies." The integrity of these bishops was at stake.

After the conference made its decision, D. D. Zook and those who agreed with him could either make less of an issue of the second blessing, or break their Mennonite fellowship. That the first was an option is shown by the fact that when the schism came, a number of people, including Deacon B. F. Buckwalter, who believed in the second blessing, remained in the Pennsylvania Church.

So in this schism no one was driven out of the church. But on December 29, 1912, Zook announced publicly his decision to withdraw from the church. Fifty members, including J. M. R. Weaver, went with him. It was claimed that Zook had no intention of splitting the church, nor of building another church. But these fifty people had to have a place to worship. A site was chosen one mile east of Pennsylvania, on the banks of the East Emma Creek. By May their church was ready for use.

The East Emmet Church, as it was called, did not affiliate with any other denomination, but continued under congregational government. A statement of creed was written, much like the Dordrecht Confession. Concerning the Holy Spirit, however, it says, "The baptism is always subsequent to regeneration." The premillennial viewpoint in prophecy was urged, and foot washing and nonresistance only recommended. This congregation gradually found that its members lived in Newton, and so it was disbanded and the building taken down in 1963.

This schism of 1913 can only be viewed as a tragedy. Families and friends were torn apart. The testimony of both churches in the community was hurt irreparably. An appalling number of people of Mennonite parentage have been lost to the Mennonite Church and often to Christianity. Each group needed the other. If that which the majority considered fanatical could have been avoided, and the second blessing not made an essential to salvation; and if the other group could have been more patient, with a little less insistence on legal correctness in orthodoxy, then the historian might have a different story to tell.

It is good to know that no one felt the two churches should have two cemeteries. Through all the years of their coexistence side by side, East Emmet funerals were held at Pennsylvania. It was especially gratifying that when D. D. Zook died in 1948, his funeral should have been in charge of Earl Buckwalter. Both churches, together with the Hesston congregation, joined in the use and the upkeep of the cemetery. In the earlier years this was a community burying ground. Tombstones here bear not only such names as Zimmerman, Hess, Hershberger, Byler, Schrock, Burkhart, Grove, and Heatwole, but also such as Deschner, Rodenbaugh, Dillman, Onstott, Perkins, and Umholtz. It has been well kept by sextons M. M. Zimmerman (from the beginning to 1926), John Roupp (1926-1950), and Lloyd Rodgers (1950-   ). There is plenty of room for the burial requirements of many years. The cemetery now lies alongside the new Interstate 35 highway. By vote of the Whitestone and Hesston congregations, the cemetery in 1972 was named East Lawn.

*East Lawn Cemetery
now includes the site
of the Pennsylvania
church building*

By the year 1960 the coming of some young families again cramped the facilities of the church. Accepted standards of living made it intolerable to have a church in which there were no toilet facilities. A new building was projected. Two factors entered into the decision to move to a new location. One was the difficulty in getting adequate water and sewage disposal at the old location. But the deciding factor was a survey which showed that more than half of the members lived in Hesston, and for most of the rest distance would not be a hindrance if the new church should be built in Hesston.

The site chosen in Hesston was in a developing section, a location that would serve a large number of people without intruding on already organized churches. A fund drive was successful, ground was broken on September 9, 1963, and the dedication service was on June 13, 1965.

Many of the members felt that the church should have a new name. The congregation was two generations removed from the migrations which brought most of the charter members from Pennsylvania to the plains of Kansas in the 1880s, and the name always required explaining. After considering many possibilities, a committee recommended Whitestone Mennonite Church as being descriptive and not likely to become outdated. The name relates to the architecture, as the front of the new building was finished in white stone. One member pointed out that this name would relate also to a scriptural phrase in Revelation 2:17.

The change of location has been vindicated by developments. With good facilities available, the congregation joined with the other churches of Hesston in efforts to reach unchurched families of the community. A number of new members, some who moved from Catlin and other Mennonite churches, but also some new believers from the community, now make up the congregation. Several were lifelong residents here, former pupils of the Pennsylvania Sunday school who had never been converted and brought into the fellowship of any church. In the ten years, 1962-1972, the membership increased from 100 to 213.

The old Pennsylvania Church building was sold and dismantled. The grounds became a part of the cemetery. In 1971 a seven-foot replica of the front of the old church was erected at the east end of the church site. Before it is the following plaque, written by Earl Buckwalter:

> *PENNSYLVANIA CHURCH*
> *1886 MENNONITE 1964*
> *was founded by hardy pioneers from Pennsylvania*
> *and other eastern states who tamed a virgin prairie*
> *while wrestling with inherited traditions and faith*
> *sometimes overzealous in conviction on divine truth*
> *but with vision to chart new paths in church program*
> *flexibility to adjust to cultural change aggressiveness*
> *in missions and unselfish dedication in giving of sons*
> *and daughters to christian service, the work begun*
> *and carried on here is perpetuated as the white-*
> *stone mennonite church.*

Music has had an important place in this congregation. There were singing schools as early as 1885. Most of the members have been able to participate in four-part singing. Songbooks used have been chiefly *Psalms, Hymns, and Spiritual Songs, Gospel Hymns, Church and Sunday School Hymnal, Life Songs 1* and *2, Sheet Music of Heaven, Church Hymnal,* and *The Mennonite Hymnal.* Of many song leaders these stand out in the author's memory: R. J. Heatwole, R. M. Weaver, Emma King Risser, Elmer Hartzler, and Edna Miller Byler. Later leaders have included Alice, Albert, Ralph, Lois, and Martha Buckwalter, Oliver Miller, Ethel and Eldon Risser, Howard Hershberger, D. D. Stoltzfus, Marvin and Edwin

Schrock, and Dale Martin. In 1965 a Hallman organ was installed, which most members feel has contributed to the atmosphere of worship without doing harm to the tradition of congregational singing. "Special" singing — quartets and choral groups — have been appreciated in this church since 1900.

Since John S. Coffman dissipated the prejudice against evangelistic meetings, a long list of preachers have labored in periodic "series of meetings." This has been the chief, but by no means the only means for the ingathering of new members. Outstanding to this end were the meetings by J. M. Shenk in 1892, with thirty-two accessions, and by J. E. Hartzler in 1906, with seventy confessions and forty-five accessions.

As at other places throughout the church, the Bible Normal was a very effective teaching instrument in the first quarter of this century. The first one lasted for ten days in 1903. George R. Brunk was the moderator, and other speakers were Noah Metzler of Indiana, J. M. Shenk of Ohio, and Andrew Shenk of Missouri. The last one was in 1926, with H. A. Diener and H. J. King as instructors.

The Sunday school began against difficulties. The Amish had been used to Sunday school in Mifflin County, Pennsylvania, but for some of those from Lancaster County this new thing seemed to be worldly. For some time they merely sat as observers. When R. J. Heatwole, probably the first superintendent, asked, "Would it not be nice if you also had a class?" one replied, "Yes, but we are not used to it." Later they did join a German class. But prejudice and fear died slowly, and even then some participated little in the discussions. The last German quarterlies were ordered in 1918.

At first Sunday school and preaching were held every two weeks in the morning. Then on the alternate Sunday there was only Sunday school, held in the afternoon. For a short time in 1890 Sunday school was always in the afternoon. In November T. M. Erb wrote in his diary, "This was the first time we had Sunday school right after church." This enabled the ones not interested to go home right after preaching. Not for the same reason, but from preference, this order of the two services has persisted through the years. After January 1, 1891, the Sunday school was evergreen.

Noah Eby, a Sunday school superintendent, felt the need for a meeting to promote the Sunday school. In June 1900 such a meeting was held. As far as is known, this is the first such meeting in the Mennonite Church. It was decided to continue such meetings as a quarterly event. Almost without interruption these quarterly conferences continued for more than fifty years, to April 1951. The programs varied greatly. For instance, the one in July 1929 was a memorial for T. M. Erb and J. M. R. Weaver, longtime ministers and teachers of the congregation.

One of these meetings, June 1912, was attended by Vachel Lindsay, America's "tramp poet," who at the time was helping John G. Longenecker in his wheat harvest. In his story of his experiences among the Mennonites he wrote: "I have never heard better discourses on the distinctions between the four Gospels. The men who spoke were scholars."[5] The chief speaker was the studious reader, J. M. R. Weaver. Lindsay also got the mistaken idea that the Mennonite men who experienced the second blessing went without neckties.

Missionary and service interest has always been strong at Pennsylvania-Whitestone. As early as 1901 returned missionary W. B. Page visited here and fanned missionary enthusiasm. The quarterly missions offering was one result. For many years a mission secretary of the Sunday school brought reports of mission happenings and needs.

The congregation proved to be a reservoir of witness talent. L. Ellen Schertz went to India in 1905. In addition to those already mentioned, Allen Erb was a leader in the church's witness in Colorado (now in his retirement at Schowalter Villa he is again an active supporter at Whitestone); Silas Horst had a long ministry in Iowa, and his brother Rufus at Kansas City. Cecil Miller and his wife served in East Nigeria and in St. Louis. Lena Horst, Martha Buckwalter, Emma King, Esther Buckwalter, and Susie Reiff filled big needs at the Kansas City Mission; Elizabeth Longenecker served at the Children's Home at West Liberty, Ohio; Elsie Byler and Martha Heatwole helped in the orphanage at Hillsboro, Kansas; and Grace King with her husband, Vernon Shellenberger, were for a while in charge of Welfare Home at Argentine, Kansas. Dorothy Schrock Kratz was a missionary in the Chaco country of Argentina. Albert Weaver has represented Mennonite General Conference on the Schowalter Foundation, and Howard Hershberger on the Board of Overseers for Hesston College. James Hershberger served as a pastor in Arkansas and at Spring Valley, and is the administrator of Schowalter Villa. Few congregations of this size, probably, have furnished the Mennonite Church with so many workers for its program.

And so, the "Pennsylvania" era of this congregation established a church and a Christian testimony on a rural frontier. This church was influenced by a movement that it could not absorb without great loss, but it did survive. The "Whitestone" era, just begun, has shifted to an urbanized setting. Here it will have to demonstrate whether it can absorb the influences of affluence and cultural change.

3. *West Liberty, McPherson County*

The first nine Old Mennonites in western McPherson County arrived between 1880 and 1882. They were the following men and their wives: David D. Yoder, J. C. Bontrager, S. C. Miller, and Matthias Cooprider; also Miss Maggie Bontrager, who later married R. C. Yoder. The Coopriders came from the settlement six miles west of Marion; the others all came from Lagrange County, Indiana. These people formed the nucleus of the West Liberty Church, the fourth of the congregations of the central Kansas Mennonites to be organized.

They had been preceded to this neighborhood, however, by a group of Amish Mennonites, the first of whom, John Schlatter, arrived from Iowa in 1872. When minister John Zimmerman came from Iowa in 1877, the Amish Mennonites organized a congregation. In 1886 they built a meetinghouse about three quarters of a mile south of the Santa Fe Trail, and a mile south of the present West Liberty Church.

The building of this church resulted in a schism among the Amish. About five families preferred to worship in homes, and they organized an Old Order Amish congregation. The church-house group continued until 1904, when they moved to Harper County (see Crystal Springs Church, p. 282).

The Mennonite congregation was organized in 1883 at the home of S. C. Miller by Bishop Daniel Brundage. The charter members were the nine named above. The last of them, Mrs. S. C. Miller, died in 1940. The group bought the Liberty School, where they had been participating in a union Sunday school. On the fourth Sunday of each month the Mennonites had charge of the Sunday school and preaching, Bishop Brundage being the preacher. He would drive the twenty miles in all kinds of weather in his crude cart.

Possibly because this building was only a half-mile from the Amish Mennonite Church, after eight years it was decided to move it to a site on the D. D. Yoder farm, one-half mile north and a mile west. But they anticipated difficulties in getting across Wolf Creek, and so John Slabach offered a site only a half mile north, where the church now is. Slabach gave a long-term lease for two acres without cost to the church. The Mennonites were a bit surprised at his generosity, since he was Amish, and the two groups were not always in agreement. But Slabach was dissatisfied with three Amish requirements of long, square-cut hair, hooks and eyes instead of buttons, and the "shunning" of people under church discipline. Shortly after giving the lease, he and his family joined the Mennonites.

D. D. Yoder was hired as janitor at $45 per year. His daughters had the task of filling the kerosine lamps and shining the chimneys. The door of the building was toward the east. Coats and hats were placed on a table just inside the door. The dimensions of the former school building were 20 x 32. It was four miles north and four miles west of Inman.

Since the new school, built two miles southeast of where the first one was, was named South Liberty, it was decided to call the church West Liberty Mennonite Church.

Some of the charter members had said, "We will never have a congregation in this wild region." At this time there were only a few houses, mostly of sod. Prairie chickens were numerous, and there were a few antelope. Rich, black soil could be purchased for six dollars per acre and up. But Bishop Brundage was untiring in his visits, and in seventeen years the growth was 800 percent. By 1892 the building was too small and there was agitation for the construction of a new meetinghouse. The location being only a lease, the two acres were deeded for church and cemetery purposes to the West Liberty Mennonite Church Association (the language of an attorney), and a state charter was secured with the following as the first trustees: Samuel Y. Yoder, Henry Schlatter, D. A. Miller, C. Sumy, and J. C. Miller.

The new church was constructed in 1892 at a cost of about $1,200, plus donated labor. It was 36 x 48 feet, again with entrance from the east. There were two double doors leading to cloakrooms, one on the south for the men and one on the north for the women. A mothers' room was between these two cloakrooms.

The first West Liberty Church as improved in 1912

The present West Liberty Church

Double doors, again, led from the cloakrooms into the auditorium. As the pulpit was on the east end of the room, those who entered went straight against the gaze of the assembling congregation. The floor rose sharply so that the back seats were on a level with the raised platform. One had the feeling that it took a good deal of will and effort to climb into that congregation. Some of the people said they liked to see who was coming in on time. There was no other way to get into the room.

While the new church was being built, services were held in the Amish meetinghouse. The two groups worshiped together, alternating in conducting the services.

In 1912 the congregation entertained the Kansas-Nebraska Conference. In preparation the building was raised, and a basement dug beneath it. There was a pipeless furnace, and a cement porch on the east end. Thus remodeled, the building served the congregation until the middle of the century.

John Slabach not only donated the land for the church and cemetery. He also gave $250 toward the cost of building, but on condition that the church was built on the corner of his farm, and not at another site that was considered. He had adapted some of his practices when he joined the Mennonite Church. But he wanted to be certain that the West Liberty Mennonites would not deviate from Old Mennonite faith and practice. He tried to write into the deed that if this church ever ceased being an Old Mennonite Church, the land would revert to the former owner.

He did not succeed in this, but he did succeed in having the name "Old Mennonite" placed in the gable end of the church.

In the early days the address of the people in this community was Monitor, a small trading center one mile east and one mile north of the West Liberty Church. Here at one time were a post office, two stores, and two houses. People often walked in two or three miles to shop and get their mail. When the stores were closed the community wanted to keep its post office, and Henry Hostetler, a son-in-law of John Slabach, moved it into his home. A woman on a star route hauled the mail from Conway for $98 per year. She drove a one-horse rig. Later the post office was moved to New Monitor, one mile west of the church. After 1906 the community was serviced by rural delivery from Conway, Inman, and Windom.

The first Mennonite settlers buried their dead in the Amish cemetery, a mile south and half a mile east of the West Liberty Church. This they continued to do until the new church was built in 1892. At this time a cemetery was started on the west side of the church. The first burial was that of Alph Yoder, a child who died in 1893. But the earliest date on any tombstone in the cemetery is 1879. This body, with its grave marker, must have been moved from another burial place. The West Liberty Cemetery is exceptionally well kept. John Zimmerman and Phares Loucks are remembered as careful sextons and caretakers. Edd Showalter and J. F. and Etta Brunk are among those who have contributed to a trust fund for maintenance.

Early in this century, but still in the horse-and-buggy days, sheds were built north and west of the church to protect the horses from the rain, snow, and wind. When the horses quit coming to church, and the sheds fell into disrepair, they were torn down.

The program of the church at West Liberty has been similar to that at Spring Valley. Some beginning dates have been as follows: Mennonite Sunday school organization, about 1884; first ordination of minister (S. C. Miller), 1885; first deacon ordained (D. D. Yoder), 1887; first evangelistic meeting (J. S. Coffman), 1888; first resident bishop (S. C. Miller), 1890; first district conference (Kansas-Nebraska) at West Liberty, 1890; first church building erected, 1892; first membership record book, 1898; first baptism in the church (instead of Wolf Creek or Little River), 1902; first Bible conference (by S. G. Shetler and D. H. Bender), 1908; sewing circle organized, 1909; first teachers' meeting, 1912; first singing school (at Wolf Creek School by T. J. Cooprider), 1912; first foreign missionary sent out (Florence Cooprider — later Friesen — to India), 1916; weddings in the church, after 1923; individual communion cups, 1943; first church bulletins, 1947; first constitution, 1948; organization of Mennonite Disaster Service, 1952; first church council, 1955; first salaries paid to ministers (John Duerksen and Clayton Beyler), 1959; first use of budget plan, 1956; first Every Home Plan for *Gospel Herald*, 1968.

Some of the evangelists who followed J. S. Coffman in evangelistic meetings at West Liberty were, in the earlier years, D. D. Miller, Noah Metzler, L. J. Miller, and D. J. Johns. Those serving after 1910 included the following: S. C. Yoder, E. D. Hess, J. W. Hess, C. F. Derstine, John Thut, H. A. Diener, J. A. Heiser, Jess Kauffman, Fred S. Brenneman, Gideon G. Yoder, P. A. Friesen, Oscar Burkholder, and E. S. Garber.

Before West Liberty had a resident minister, the congregation was served by the pioneer bishops Daniel Brundage, Daniel Wismer, and B. F. Hamilton. In 1885, S. C. Miller was ordained by Bishop Brundage. When he heard that he was voted into the lot, he felt he could not accept a call to the ministry. But a hired man urged him to yield himself to the lot, and he did so.

Five years later he was ordained to the office of bishop. Matthias

Cooprider was also in the lot. When the two men had taken their books, one of which contained the lot, Bishop Hamilton, who was officiating, proceeded to open the books. In the book of S. C. Miller he found nothing. Then he looked in the other book. But here also he did not find the lot, and he became so nervous that his hands shook. After a bit of hesitation he looked again in Miller's book. This time he found the lot, and proceeded with the ordination.

In 1886 Miller went to Ness County to take a homestead and improve his financial condition. While there he shepherded a small group of Mennonite settlers. But in 1888 he moved back to West Liberty. Once en route to Ness County he was overtaken by darkness and had no place to stay, as houses were very scarce on the prairie. He unhitched, tethered his horses, and lay under his buggy to sleep. He heard and even saw some wolves. He asked God to give him such sound sleep that if the wolves did attack, he'd not be aware of it. When he awoke, the sun was up and all was well.

When Miller was ordained, the use of tobacco had not yet become an issue in the Mennonite Church. His diary often refers to his buying cigars, even after he was a bishop. Once while waiting for a train he was walking back and forth smoking a cigar. He noticed that people were staring at him. Suddenly the thought struck him that the people thought it inconsistent for a plain-dressed, bearded man to be puffing a cigar. He threw the cigar away, and never used tobacco again.

In 1910 the Millers moved to Jet, Oklahoma, where they lived until he died in 1938. In his last years he was hard of hearing, and he spent most of his time in prayer and Bible reading. From August 29, 1936, to August 29, 1938, the day he became confined to his bed, he read his New Testament through thirty-two times. Both he and his wife were buried at the West Liberty Cemetery.

Matthias Cooprider was the second minister ordained at West Liberty. He also was ordained in 1885, probably by Brundage. When Cooprider came to Kansas in 1878 from his native Clay County, Indiana, he settled in Marion County near Canada, near the home of the widow Susan Brunk. As a young man he had joined the United Brethren Church. In 1862 he joined the Union Army and served three and a half years. He marched through the Shenandoah Valley of Virginia, and it is interesting to speculate whether he had a part in raiding the farms of the Mennonites with whom he would later be so closely connected.

Cooprider married in Indiana, but his wife died after three sons were born. Two of these — John and Walter — lived. Cooprider married again and another son — Thomas J. — was born. When this boy was eight years old the family hit the migration trail to the West — the father and his three sons by covered wagon and the mother, who was not well, by train. In about a year Mrs. Cooprider died, and was buried in the same burial ground where Henry G. Brunk and his three children are resting.

Then in January 1878 Cooprider married Susan Heatwole Brunk, a marriage unbroken for 31 years. A rather complicated family resulted. Cooprider had the three sons from two different Indiana wives. Mrs. Cooprider had the two sons and two daughters from her first marriage. His children, and her children, unrelated to each other, lived together in the same home. Then Matthias and Susan together had three more children — Lucy, Charles, and Nettie. Then two of Mr. Cooprider's sons were married to two of Mrs. Cooprider's daughters — Henrietta Brunk to John Cooprider, and Minnie to Walter Cooprider. And all of this complex family and many of their descendants were for many years active members of the West Liberty congregation.

In 1880 the reestablished family moved from Marion County to western McPherson County. But after Cooprider's ordination they moved to Spring Valley, where he assisted in the ministry for eight or ten years. Then they moved back to West Liberty, where Cooprider witnessed faithfully until his death in 1920, at eighty-four, the oldest minister in the district.

One problem of Matthias Cooprider related to his Civil War military service. As a former soldier he was entitled to a pension of $30 per month. This pension he received from the United States government from the time of his discharge from the Union Army to the time of his death. However, after his ordination some of the members felt that it was inconsistent for a nonresistant Christian to receive a military pension. The question does not seem to have been raised when Cooprider's qualifications for the ministry were approved. But some members kept making an issue of it.

Five years after the ordination, in 1890, the Kansas-Nebraska Conference, in a session which Cooprider attended, received this question: "Is it right for a brother to receive pension for services in the war?" The conference took the following action:

"Resolved, that it is right to receive pension. Soldiers receive home from the government (160 acres of land), and if such a soldier would become a brother in the faith, we would not think of asking him to give up his home.

"The United States government, of its own accord, has obligated itself to give pensions, and if a pensioned soldier accepts the faith, we have as little right to deprive him of his pension as we would have to prevent the other from keeping his home."

It seems that some persons continued to bring up this question. But it is significant to note that in the ordination for bishop in 1890, Cooprider was admitted to the lot; he was considered qualified for the highest office of the church.

Throughout the consideration of this question Cooprider placed himself in the hands of conference. He expressed himself as willing to give up his pension if conference should decide that was best.

The third man ordained to the ministry at West Liberty was George R. Brunk, stepson of Matthias Cooprider. The ordination was in 1893. Brunk was a tall stripling, twenty-one years old, still living with his mother and stepfather. He read extensively, often until he heard the roosters crow. Through self-education he qualified himself for a distinguished career of leadership in his denomination.

George had been converted at the age of seventeen under the preaching of John S. Coffman. But after a year or two, worldly ambitions began to grow, and church attendance, Bible study, and prayer were neglected. He has described the experience:

"There came an overwhelming sense of being forsaken by the Spirit of God. I labored hard and long in self-abasement and prayer to be restored, but the heavens were brass and the earth was iron and Satan plagued me with the Scripture, 'if they fall away, it is impossible to renew them to repentance.' My Uncle R. J. Heatwole had much to do with keeping me from drifting before conversion. So now, through all this struggle, I was ashamed to let him know. He lived thirty miles away and we seldom saw each other, but he got the news by way of the throne. One night in a dream he saw me standing and Satan wrapping me from my feet upwards with cords of heavy rope. In spite of all I could do, he at last fastened both my hands. Then my Uncle, in his dreams, saw me turn my eyes to him for help, and when he sprang to help me, he awakened. But early the next morning he hitched up his work team and drove, taking all day for the thirty-mile trip. We went out alone and he told the dream with the response, 'Uncle Reuben, you

have told me how I am, better than I could tell you!' Through his
help and guidance I was saved from absolute despair and, finally
brightly saved."[6]

In 1898 George R. Brunk was ordained to the office of
bishop by lot for the Spring Valley and Catlin congregations. It
was a double ordination, with T. M. Erb being ordained bishop
for the Pennsylvania congregation at the same time. It took place
at Pennsylvania and was occasioned by the declining years of
Bishop B. F. Hamilton. Brunk never served as bishop at West Liberty, although his residence and membership were there. He was
probably the second single man to be ordained bishop in the Mennonite Church. (J. N. Durr became a bishop at the age of twenty.
Brunk was twenty-six, and it was not until two years later that he
married Katie Wenger of Harrisonburg, Virginia.

Brunk served as minister at West Liberty until 1907, when he
helped to start a new community at Protection, Kansas. But he
was fearful of the future in western Kansas, and in 1910 became
part of another kind of frontier colony at Denbigh, Virginia. There
he lived until his death in 1938.

There may have been another reason for the move to Virginia. Brunk had become very conservative in theology and in
church standards. He waged a strong battle, for instance, against the
wearing of neckties by men. Since at this time the situation in the
Kansas churches seemed to be satisfactory, he felt a leading to move
East and assist there in stemming the tide of worldliness. On a
later occasion he remarked to a Midwestern friend, "I moved to
Virginia to help stop the drift in the East, and now, behold, conservative Kansas is drifting." As the founding editor of the *Sword
and Trumpet,* his influence for conservatism became churchwide.

The fourth minister ordained in the West Liberty congregation
was Charles D. Yoder, a son of Deacon D. D. Yoder. At the time
of his ordination in 1895 he was a 23-year-old schoolteacher. He
served the church faithfully for many years. One of his former members thus described his interests and concerns:

"Bro. Yoder, keenly feeling the responsibility grow heavier
the burden became heavy for the welfare of the young people who
each Sunday filled the back benches of the church. He taught the
junior classes a few times. . . . His concern for the young people
was realized by the interest he aroused in opening a mid-week
mission class, in connection with the mid-week prayer services

Charles D. Yoder and wife, Susanna Heatwole, with their oldest children, Lawrence and Phoebe

His encouraging words concerning higher education prompted a greater interest in the young people to launch out for a wider spiritual and secular education."[7]

Charles Yoder was injured while cutting hedge on his farm, and after a long illness died in 1923.

The fifth man ordained to the ministry at West Liberty was Allen H. Erb, the eldest son of Bishop T. M. Erb in Harvey County. He moved to West Liberty when he married Stella Cooprider in 1912. His ordination was promoted by the conference officers, and the vote at West Liberty was almost unanimous in giving the call. The ordination was in October 1912, and he served with the other ministers of the congregation. In 1916 he accepted a call to serve as administrator of the Mennonite Sanitarium at La Junta, Colorado. There through the years he became a foremost promoter of Mennonite hospitals and nursing homes. He directed the building of the first Mennonite hospital at La Junta, got under way the publicly owned but church-administered hospital at Lebanon, Oregon, and promoted a new idea in care for the elderly at Schowalter Villa, Hesston, Kansas. He was ordained bishop for the Colorado churches in 1937, and served as moderator of Mennonite General Conference 1943-1947.

The next man to be ordained to the ministry out of the
West Liberty congregation was Maurice A. Yoder, son of Deacon R
C. Yoder. The occasion of his ordination in 1923 was the failing
health of C. D. Yoder. The ordination, conducted by D. H. Bender
was by voice of the congregation. He secured his release in 1926
to pursue further education. He became a teacher of biology at Hess
ton College. He served as pastor of the Hesston congregation fo.
five years, 1939-1944.

In 1933 Yoder was severely burned when a blow torch exploded
in his shop. Both of his legs were later amputated, but he
courageously continued his teaching and preaching for many
years. He died in May 1973.

Later in the same year of Yoder's ordination, 1923, Joseph
G. Hartzler was ordained to the ministry by lot. He was born in
Allensville, Pennsylvania. Both Hartzler and Charles Yoder
were married to daughters of the pioneers R. J. and Margaret
Heatwole. In 1925 Hartzler was ordained bishop, again by lot.
The service was at the Pennsylvania Church in charge of T. M.
Erb, D. H. Bender, and H. A. Diener. He was immediately given
bishop charge of West Liberty and Spring Valley, and of Pennsyl
vania in 1930. The last of these he served until 1947; the other two
until the overseer plan went into effect in 1960.

The last man chosen for the ministry from the West Liberty
membership was Menno M. Troyer, ordained in 1927 by voice of the
congregation, following nomination by Bishop Hartzler. At that time
he was still single. In addition to the pastorate at West Liberty, he
later served as secretary of the South Central Conference.

Before M. M. Troyer left for La Junta, Colorado, in 1959
Kenneth I. Smoker devoted three years, 1953-1956, to the ministry
at West Liberty. For two years after Troyer left, Clayton Beyler
and John P. Duerksen, of the Hesston College faculty, took care
of the preaching appointments and other necessary pastoral work
In 1961 Edward Birkey, formerly pastor at Manson, Iowa, came t
West Liberty on part-time support. He earned part of his living
by the administration of a rest home in Inman until 1973.

Between the time that S. C. Miller left for Oklahoma in 191
and J. G. Hartzler became bishop in 1925, bishop oversight wa
given by T. M. Erb, D. H. Bender, and H. A. Diener.

The first deacon ordained for the West Liberty congregation wa
David D. Yoder, one of the charter members. He was ordained b

J. G. Hartzler in the pulpit at West Liberty

lot in 1885, probably by Bishop Daniel Wismer. Yoder, a year and a half after his ordination, made a move which cost him his office. He had gone security on the note of a brother-in-law, a member of the Church of the Brethren. When the creditor called on Yoder for payment, to gain some time he signed his property over to his wife. He did not intend to evade his obligation. Even though he acted on the advice of some of his brethren, others objected to what he had done. The congregation was about equally divided on the matter. The case was referred to conference, which restored his fellowship in the church, but took away his position as a deacon. He was not embittered by this action, however, for on his death his will included a $500 bequest to the West Liberty Church for foreign missions.

To fill the place left vacant by the D. D. Yoder episode, J. C. Hershberger, not later than 1887, was ordained by lot as deacon, with S. C. Miller officiating. But again there were troubles. The Amish were accustomed to having deacons preach; Mennonites used them only to open the meeting or to give testimony to the sermon. The people of West Liberty had both Amish and Mennonite feelings on the subject. Hershberger himself wanted to preach, but some of the older members objected. So he used the opportunity to give lengthy testimonies following the sermon, even if several ministers were present. The conference was consulted, and they advised that when a minister is present the deacon "shall not speak so long as to occupy the time belonging to the minister."

Furthermore, Deacon Hershberger performed a marriage ceremony, a function traditionally reserved for the bishop, in the home of the deacon and in the presence of the bishop. This brought criticism.

The congregation had a rule that no member dared to raise any point of dissatisfaction dated from before the latest communion service. A minority faction was lining up with the deacon on the above matters. One Sunday Bishop Miller asked all those dissatisfied with questions before the congregation to rise. J. C. Hershberger and seventeen other members arose. Since the matter of their dissatisfaction was from before the latest communion, the bishop expelled the entire group.

This threw the congregation into turmoil. D. J. Johns and J. S. Hartzler were called from Indiana to adjust the difficulty. The expelled group were received back into the brotherhood, but J. C. Hershberger was not given his office. His membership was without prejudice, however, for twice after this he was admitted to the lot once for minister and once for deacon, but he was not chosen.

The congregation, after these two unhappy experiences, did not try to fill the deacon's office until 1891, when R. C. Yoder was chosen by lot. This ordination was very successful. Rube Yoder was an influential character, a leader in church and community. He was highly appreciated as a Sunday school teacher. He was both a farmer and a dealer in horses, which he shipped and sold at auction in Belleville, Pennsylvania. And so he was widely known. He served the congregation faithfully until his sudden death in 1917. He gave to the church two minister sons: S. A. Yoder, who pastored churches at Harper, Kansas, and Leetonia, Ohio; and M. A. Yoder, whom we have noticed as one of West Liberty's pastors.

To fill R. C. Yoder's place Jess R. Brunk was ordained by bishops Erb and Bender in 1917. The ordination was by lot. But Brunk died in middle age, in 1924.

The next deacon to serve West Liberty was Oliver E. Hostetler, who was ordained in 1925, the choice again being made by lot. The services were in charge of D. H. Bender and Harry A. Diener. He was known especially as having ability and good judgment in handling the financial affairs of the church. His death came after a short illness in 1936.

The last deacon ordained for West Liberty was Roy Zook, who was called to this office in 1937. This ordination was by J. G. Hartzler and H. A. Diener. Zook served until he moved with his family to Kansas City in 1946.

In a seven-year period, 1917-1924, the congregation lost by death the following ordained leaders: R. C. Yoder, Matthias Cooprider, David D. Yoder, Charles D. Yoder, and Jess R. Brunk.

Only in recent years has this congregation given its ministers a regular salary. But needs have been met from time to time. For instance, in 1940 three congregations under J. G. Hartzler's bishop care gave him a car, and in 1947, on the 25th anniversary of his ordination to the ministry, he was given a new Bible and his wife was presented with an electric iron.

West Liberty gave to the church many workers for a varied ministry. T. J. Cooprider, who taught school for forty terms, often ed in congregational singing, and served the Kansas-Nebraska Conference both as moderator and secretary. He was frequently in the ot for the ministry but was never chosen.

S. Enos Miller was the deacon at Protection, Kansas, and taught biology at Hesston College for eleven years.

J. F. Brunk — one-armed Joe — was the first superintendent of the Kansas City Mission and helped to establish the Mennonite Sanitarium at La Junta, Colorado. He served at the Old People's Home at Rittman, Ohio, preached at Peabody, Kansas, and opened a mission in Hutchinson. He was a born promoter.

Florence Cooprider was the first female missionary doctor of the church, her field being India. After her first term she was married to P. A. Friesen, and together they served many years in India. After retirement they served in Denver, Colorado, and at Greensburg, Kansas. In her later retirement years she was cited by the Mennonite Board of Missions for her pioneer accomplishment in Mennonite medical work. She resides at Schowalter Villa.

Stella Cooprider, the wife of Allen H. Erb, was for many years in the General Sewing Circle Committee of the church.

Lydia Heatwole, daughter of R. J. Heatwole, was a pioneer of Mennonite nursing education, sometimes called the Florence Nightingale of the Mennonite Church. She received special recognition by the Colorado State Board of Nursing.

Chris E. Miller and wife served for eight years as superintendent and matron of the Mennonite Children's Home in Kansas City.

Edward Yoder, the youngest son of D. D. Yoder, served as deacon and minister in mission work in Kansas City.

Phoebe (Phebe) Yoder, a nurse and a teacher, daughter of C. D. Yoder, had her mission vision marvelously fulfilled in her call to Tanganyika (Tanzania), Africa, where she served under the Eastern Mission Board for more than thirty years. She moved to Schowalter Villa in 1973. Willis Yoder, her brother, has been effective as a rural missionary in northern Alberta. Vera Yoder, later Schrag, another daughter of C. D. Yoder, did relief work under the Mennonite Central Committee in India and China. Ruth Yoder, married to Emerson Miller, was a relief worker in Poland and the Netherlands.

Lester Zimmerman is a teacher at Goshen College.

Another form of outreach, into the more immediate environment, was Sunday school and preaching in Rice County, the next county west of McPherson. Andrew Shenk visited here in 1892 a family that had not been visited by any Mennonite minister for eight years. The next year it was reported that monthly services were held by the brethren from West Liberty, twenty miles to the

Phoebe Yoder among her beloved African friends

east, and that there were nine members here.[8] Ten years later there was a Sunday school in Rice County, where George R. Brunk preached every two weeks in a schoolhouse for "a miscellaneous assembly of Catholics, Methodists, Campbellites, Adventists, etc."[9]

Space is lacking to give a more complete picture of West Liberty's outreach into the world.

Records of the giving at West Liberty do not go back further than 1888. There were Sunday school collections, with totals as low as seventeen cents. That was the day of the "penny collection," used for Sunday school expenses. In 1928 church expenses were met by a tax on land — ten cents an acre on land owned, four and a half cents on rented land. Delinquent taxes could be worked out in janitor work at two dollars per week. Supplemented by a tax on the laboring man, this tax system lasted into the 1940s. In the latter part of the fifties a general treasurer was chosen to handle all funds, and since 1965 the budget plan for distributing funds has been used. For many years full or partial support of the congregation's missionaries was supplied. For a number of years per capita giving has exceeded $100.

The largest membership was about 170 in 1918. However, that included nonresident members in Reno and Ness counties. But the next year letters were given to fifty or more members when the Yoder congregation was organized. The membership in 1972 was 41.

In 1949 a new church building was dedicated. Funds for this began to accumulate in 1939. Building began in 1948. An additional acre of land was donated by Uriah Slabach. After a homecoming service on September 5, 1948, the old building was razed, and a temporary roof over the old basement furnished a meeting place during the construction. Ground was broken, not with shovels, but with the heavy earthmovers of Marvin and Ralph Hostetler. The new L-type frame building was dedicated on June 5, 1949. The cost was $18,000 in addition to contributed labor and special projects.

In July 1973 the congregation observed, in all-day services, the ninetieth anniversary of its founding. Sermons at the morning and afternoon sessions were given by Truman H. Brunk, a son of George R. Brunk, and Edward Birkey, the present pastor. In a vesper service at six p.m. Menno Troyer, a former pastor, conducted a memorial service in the church cemetery.[10]

For ninety years the West Liberty congregation has been a witness to the community and the world. Relations with the neighbors have not always been friendly, as when during World War I George Cooprider was tarred and feathered when he offered himself in place of his ailing father, who had refused to purchase war bonds. And as we have seen, before 1900 there were some unfriendly relations within the church. But such days seem long past.

The problem of the church now is the new economic and social order. Mennonites are no longer chiefly farmers, with sons following fathers in raising wheat. The congregation has produced fifty-one schoolteachers, eleven nurses, seven doctors, three foreign missionaries. Young people enter business and the professions, which has scattered them into most of the states and provinces. Any farmer who remains needs a much larger farm to make a living. So old homesteads are being wrecked.

West Liberty is a rural church, far from cities. The people are no longer there in substantial numbers. The congregation is made up of the older ones. Where there are no children and young people, there are poor prospects for growth of a church. Some at West Liberty fear that it is a church with only a glorious past.[11]

4. *Pleasant Valley, Harper County*

The Pleasant Valley Mennonite Church is located on Highway 160 near the east edge of Harper, Kansas. Harper County is in the southern tier of Kansas counties. This is an excellent agricultural area, and the members of this congregation have been farmers for the most part, with specialization in dairying, poultry, and haymaking. Harper has only 2,000 people, but even from the beginning a minority of the Mennonites were in various businesses, trades, and professions. Over the years these have included coal and feed, creamery, ice plant, building, implements and appliances sales, teaching, medicine, mail service, and others. Young people from Pleasant Valley have scattered over the world in a variety of services.

J. S. Coffman, pioneer Mennonite evangelist who visited scattered groups of Mennonites on the frontier, came to Harper in 1886. He found there two families from Wayne County, Ohio — the Ed Chatelians and B. A. Gerbers; Elam Rohrers, who had moved here from Harvey County; and a young woman who later became the wife of Lem Rohrer. Coffman's four meetings in a schoolhouse were the first public Mennonite meetings held in Harper County.[1]

Later that same year Jacob Zimmerman came from Pennsylvania; also a young lady named Susan Horst from Maryland, who shortly became Zimmerman's wife. In 1887 came J. G. Wenger and Susan Detweiler from Morgan County, Missouri, and Lizzie Brenneman, Wenger's niece, from Wayne County, Ohio. Susan Detweiler was the first Mennonite schoolteacher in Harper County, teaching at Prairie Queen and Planet schools.

These early settlers began to have Sunday meetings in their homes. Taking turns, all would gather at one place, eat their dinner together, and then have a service. They would have Sunday school, then have Scripture reading, and sometimes some brother would have an exhortation. In 1888 they began to meet at the Pleasant Valley school, three miles east of Harper.

At about the same time Bishop B. F. Hamilton, of Peabody, organized the group into a congregation. The fifteen charter members were J. G. Wenger, Jacob Holdeman and wife (from McPherson County), Jacob Zimmerman and wife, Lem Rohrer and wife, Elam Rohrer and wife, Ben Gerber and wife, Rebecca Chatelian, Sarah Gerber Beyler, Lizzie Brenneman, and Susan Detweiler.

The congregation met in the Pleasant Valley School for a decade. In the absence of a minister, J. G. Wenger or some other brother would read a printed sermon. In 1897 a church building was constructed across the road from the Pleasant Valley School, and automatically, it seems, was given the name of Pleasant Valley Church. This first church was a frame building 28 by 40 feet, with sheet tin siding embossed to look like brick. Conference was held in the uncompleted church that fall. T. M. Erb wrote: "We all were to church, it being full. Had dedication services, no strange preacher came, so Brother Hinkle talked a while, then I closed. Had not much of a Sunday school, it being too late."[13]

In those days it was common practice to ask for help in church building, and the *Herald of Truth* in 1897[14] ran such an appeal, signed by Andrew Good, T. M. Erb, E. M. Shellenberger, and J. G. Wenger.

Until 1907 the congregation averaged about forty members. For economic reasons chiefly, the membership was rather mobile. But there was missionary spirit. In the 1890s a Sunday afternoon Sunday school was held at a schoolhouse in Harper. Some of the members regularly attended three Sunday services.

In 1895 a cemetery was laid out a half mile north of Pleasant

Valley. The first burial was that of Salome Gerber (Mrs. Fred Beyler), who was laid to rest on June 1, 1897, the day after her death. This was the first death in the congregation. The funeral was in the Pleasant Valley School, as the church was not yet built. B. F. Hamilton preached in German and T. M. Erb in English.

This cemetery is maintained by the church, but has been available for community use. Families having members buried here are expected to make an annual payment toward cemetery care. In 1900 Tom Millsap was buried here. In 1933 his grave was in the way of a traffic lane, and so the few remaining bones were moved to another part of the cemetery. The first concrete vault was used in the burial of H. E. Hostetler in 1952.

Sol Plank, who died at 96, and James T. Hamilton, who lived five months longer, were the oldest persons buried in this cemetery. Five men and boys buried here were killed in automobile accidents. In April 1956 three men were buried who died "with their shoes on": Ammon Ramer from a heart attack; Sam Troyer killed by a falling tree; and Clayton Gerber, who died in a car-truck wreck. Sam Troyer was a casket-bearer for Ammon Ramer. On the way to the cemetery he said, "We don't know who will be next, it may be me." One week later he was buried, and two weeks later Clayton Gerber was carried to his grave.

The Sunday school has always been important at Pleasant Valley. Among early superintendents were T. M. Erb, J. G. Wenger, B. L. Horst, M. B. Weaver, R. M. Weaver, B. A. Shupe and Sam Schmidt. Later superintendents were D. J. Unruh, S. A. Yoder, John S. Hamilton, Leo Hostetler, Sam Troyer, Chancy Hostetler, Loren Gerber, Lee Unruh, Dwight Hostetler, and Urs Hostetler.

There was a separate primary department from about 1915. Superintendents have included Rena Balmer Glassburn, S. A. Yoder, Bertha King, Phoebe Hamilton, Amanda Gerber, Florence Detweiler, Alta Hostetler, Dewey Hostetler, and Mervin Troyer.

By 1915 the church had grown so that a larger building was needed. There was some talk of moving the location to Harper, just east of where the church now stands. But the final decision was to rebuild at the same site. In early spring 1915 the old church was dismantled and a new building, 36 by 52, with a basement, was erected on the same spot. There were anterooms at the pulpit end and also at the entrance end, with a gallery above them. The new

The 1915 Pleasant Valley Church as remodeled in 1937

building was heated by a furnace, and had electric lights. The total cost was $2,400. In May this building was dedicated, with Daniel Kauffman, of Scottdale, Pennsylvania, preaching the sermon.

In 1937 more room was needed. So additional classrooms were provided at the rear by building two-story towers at each corner, and the auditorium was enlarged by moving the pulpit back. This remodeling was financed with a wheat crop from eighty acres which the church rented and farmed.

In 1952 the congregation constructed a parsonage at the east edge of Harper on Highway 160, just west of where a decade later they were to build a new church. The parsonage cost almost $12,000. Waldo Miller, who became the first partially supported pastor of the Pleasant Valley Church, moved into this parsonage in September 1952.

The church attendance continued to grow. Sixteen babies were born into the families of the congregation in 1953 and 1954, and there was insistent need for a nursery, rest rooms, and more classrooms. In 1954 a building committee was appointed. The next year a building fund was started. But the new church came slowly. The question of moving to town came up again. The chief argument was better utility connections. But there was a strong objection. The money pledged was not sufficient. Was there need for as large a building as was being proposed? In view of world need, was it right to spend so much for a building? The tension was high, and there was more delay. Finally in April 1962 it was decided to move ahead on a building to cost about $120,000. Bonds were floated to raise the last part of the money.

By Easter, 1964, the congregation moved into the new, but uncompleted, building. The dedication was held on July 19, 1964, with James Detweiler, former pastor, preaching the sermon. Since then the completion of the basement has gone forward and equipment added. In 1967 an electric organ was installed, paid for by a few brethren.

The Pleasant Valley congregation has had an unusually large number of ordained leaders in the eighty-five years of its history. The first bishop was B. F. Hamilton, who organized the congregation in 1888. He lived at Peabody, where he served as head of the Catlin congregation. Some time before Bishop Hamilton's death in 1898 he turned over the bishop responsibility at Pleasant Valley to S. C. Miller, who lived in McPherson County at the West Liberty Church. He served until T. M. Erb was ordained bishop in 1898. In 1901, when Pleasant Valley found itself without a minister, S. C. Miller spent several months taking care of the pulpit need at Harper, after which he again returned to West Liberty.

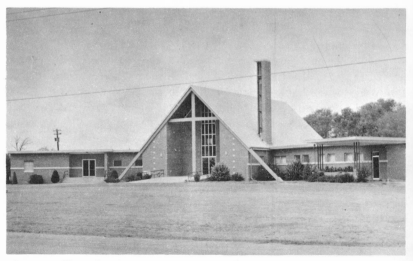

Pleasant Valley Church built in 1964

T. M. Erb moved from Newton to Harper in 1895 and became one of the ministers of Pleasant Valley. He was in the creamery business in Harper, and was influential in developing the dairy industry through the sale of hand separators to the farmers. He was active also in civic affairs, having been elected councilman of the fourth ward in 1898. He was ordained to the ministry before coming to Harper. In 1898 he was chosen by lot to the office of bishop in a service in Harvey County. He immediately took over the bishop responsibility at Pleasant Valley as the only resident bishop this church ever had. He moved back to Harvey County in 1900, but continued bishop oversight at Harper until 1910.

During this time S. C. Miller had moved to Jet, Oklahoma. From 1910 to 1928 he again served as bishop at Harper. He died in 1938.

D. D. Miller, who was ministering at Manchester, Oklahoma, was ordained as bishop at the Pleasant Valley Church in October 1927. He gradually took over the bishop oversight at Harper. He moved to Protection, Kansas, soon after he became bishop. He served Pleasant Valley until 1941, when he moved to Ohio. In 1974 he was in retirement at Greencroft Villa, Goshen, Indiana.

D. D. Miller's successor as Harper's bishop in 1941 was Milo Kauffman, of Hesston, Kansas. He served until 1945, when he ordained G. G. Yoder, pastor at the nearby Crystal Springs congregation, to serve as bishop of the Harper County churches. Yoder served for nine years in this capacity.

In 1954 the South Central Conference replaced bishops with overseers. Milo Kauffman, as overseer for Kansas churches, gave Pleasant Valley supervision for a period of ten years. From 1964, for a bit less than two years, Howard Zehr, the executive secretary of the conference, performed this function. In 1966 Ivan Lind became the Kansas overseer, and had oversight of the congregation until 1969.

The first minister of Pleasant Valley was Jacob Holderman. (Contemporary records spell his name "Holdeman," but his children used the "r.") He had been a minister at Spring Valley, but sold his farm in McPherson County in 1888, and moved to Harper in time to be listed among the charter members. He moved to Oklahoma in 1891. He later joined the Brethren Church, and died at Reedley, California, in 1911.

T. M. Erb's creamery at Harper about 1898. Erb stands in shirt-sleeves in the middle of the doorway. The cans in the ve-hicles brought cream from hand-turned separators on the farms. Butter was shipped in the wooden tubs on the dray wagon.

Andrew Good, the second minister, as the Mennonite settlement in Page County, Iowa, disintegrated, moved to Harper in 1891 with his daughter Ida and an adopted son Noah. Good was very active in the ministry at Harper. For a few years his daughter was courted by Daniel G. Lapp, a young minister at Roseland, Nebraska, who came to see her once a year. The wedding was held at the home of J. G. Wenger on February 22, 1898, with T. M. Erb officiating. Good had preached his farewell sermon at Harper on February 19, and he and Noah went to Nebraska to live with the Lapps. He was back at Harper for a short time in 1902. He died at Roseland in 1930.

Ephraim Shellenberger was born in Juniata County, Pennsylvania, in 1837. He was ordained at Freeport, Illinois, about 1878. He had also lived in Ohio and in Harvey and Ness counties in Kansas. He came to Harper from Ness County in 1893. In 1897 he moved back to Ransom, Kansas. He returned to Illinois in 1900 and died at the age of eighty-one.

Simon Hetrick was a minister at Harper by October 1894, for at that time he is listed among the ministers attending conference at Spring Valley, and his address is given as Harper. By June 1896 he was across the line in Oklahoma at the German Springs Church, where he was visited by T. M. Erb.[15] His address was Milan, Oklahoma, at the time of the conference at Harper in 1897.

George Hinkle was born in Russia in 1853. He joined the Pleasant Valley Church in 1896. Evidently he was fully accepted, for in October 1897 he was ordained to the ministry by the united voice of the church. His preaching was mostly or entirely in German, as English was difficult for him. A number of his children were members here for many years. Hinkle is on the list of Harper ministers attending conference as late as 1901. In 1902 he was listed, but with the address of Waldron. In 1907 the conference took the following action: "Whereas, that George C. Hinkle has united with another denomination and has withdrawn from us, therefore be it resolved, that we take his name off our ministerial list." The Harper historian has Hinkle's testimony that he belonged to the Methodist, Salvation Army, and Free Methodist denominations.

Ben Horst came to Harper from Maugansville, Maryland, early in the 1890s as a single man. In 1894 he married Leah Detweiler, who had come to Harper from Versailles, Missouri. After living in Oklahoma for nine months they moved back to Harper; here, with the exception of eight months at Olathe, Kansas, and Fairbanks, Texas, they lived until 1908. Horst was ordained to the ministry in 1902. In addition to preaching he taught a Sunday school class from June 22, 1902, to the close of 1907 without missing a Sunday, except February 4, 1906, when, according to the record, there was no Sunday school. In 1908 the Horsts moved to Comanche County, and in 1909 to Terra Bella, California. He died at Reedley in 1914.

Ben Horst was the only minister at Pleasant Valley when he was joined in January 1906 by Noah E. Ebersole. Ebersole had been ordained in Roseland, Nebraska, in 1900. He was at Harper about fourteen months. In later years he remembered that the Kansas-Nebraska Conference was held at Harper the fall of 1906. Later that winter Perry Shenk of Oronogo, Missouri, held meetings at Harper, and there were four confessions. There were about forty members here at that time.

Noah Ebersoles and Deacon Jacob Zimmermans moved to Protection, when that congregation was started in 1907. Ebersole later served in the ministry at Berea, Birch Tree, Missouri, and at Catlin, Peabody, Kansas. At the latter place he was buried.

By far the longest and most significant pastorate of the congregation was that of R. M. Weaver. The youngest son of David Weaver, the first minister of the Pennsylvania congregation at Newton, he was ordained at the Pennsylvania congregation in 1907 to preach at Pleasant Valley, and moved to Harper. This was the beginning of a service of forty-five years, thirty-eight years in the

R. M. Weaver, who more than any other one man was the builder of the Pleasant Valley congregation

capacity of pastor. During this period the membership increased from about forty to about 170. He had served before his ordination as a Sunday school superintendent and a song leader in Harvey County, and gave special encouragement in these two areas at Pleasant Valley. He was a lively preacher and a respected administrator.

Reuben and Ella (Neuhauser) Weaver had fourteen children — seven boys and seven girls. The two oldest ones, however, died of diphtheria before they moved to Harper. Weaver lived in an era before Mennonites were giving ministerial support, and he had a struggle to support his large family and at the same time to pastor a growing congregation. But he believed in Christian education and managed to send most of his children to Hesston College for part of their high school work.

Mrs. Weaver died in December 1925. His second wife was Lydia Gerber, who bore two daughters. Weaver was released from his responsibility as pastor of the Pleasant Valley congregation in 1946. In 1952 he preached his farewell sermon, and the congregation gave him a love offering of $1,000. He retired at Hesston, Kansas; his second wife died in 1955, and Reuben died at Newton in March 1957, at the age of over eighty-two. He was buried in the Pleasant Valley Cemetery.

Jacob P. Berkey came to Harper from Manchester, Oklahoma, in 1910. He was a one-armed man, but was able to do heavy work in such places as the Harper Ice Plant. He was used widely as an evangelist. He held meetings at Yellow Creek, Salem, and Nappanee in Indiana, when death was already getting a firm hold on his weakened body. He preached only one sermon after his return home from that trip. He died at La Junta, Colorado, in September 1916, at the age of forty-two, and was the first minister to be buried in the Pleasant Valley Cemetery.

James T. Hamilton, the son of Bishop B. F. Hamilton, was born in Illinois, and lived in Oregon, Minnesota, and Missouri after his marriage. While living at Alpha, Minnesota, he was ordained deacon. In 1906 he was ordained to the ministry at Oronogo, Missouri, for service at the Berea Church, Birch Tree, Missouri. However, after ten months at Birch Tree he returned to Oronogo. In 1912 the Hamilton family lived briefly at Plainview, Texas, and then came to Harper. He took his turn preaching at Pleasant Valley, but after 1919 was not listed as a minister. However, he and his family have made a significant contribution to the church, at Harper and elsewhere. His son John was the congregation's first historian. James T. Hamilton died in 1971.

Henry J. King, born in Missouri in 1891, moved to Harper in 1916. He was ordained to the ministry in 1921, and along with preaching at Pleasant Valley, did considerable evangelistic work. He was called to Arthur, Illinois, in 1938, where he helped to build a strong congregation in an Amish community. After serving one year at Bloomington, the Kings returned to Harper in 1959. But a call came from Greensburg, Kansas, where King was pastor until 1963. From January 1964 until August 1965 he served as interim pastor at Pleasant Valley. They retired at Schowalter Villa, Hesston, Kansas.

John Thut is another minister who had a significant broader ministry based at Harper. He was in failing health for many years. A native of Ohio, he was ordained to the ministry at Bluffton in 1909. In 1910 he moved to La Junta, Colorado, to Harper in 1926, and to Clearwater, Kansas, in 1943. He died in 1951, and was buried at Pleasant Valley. Thut's special interest was biblical prophecy, on which he did a great deal of speaking and writing. His book on *Basic Trends in Prophecy and History* was published in 1944.

Stephen A. Yoder, born in 1889, is the son of Deacon R. C. Yoder of the West Liberty congregation. In 1915 he was married to Esther Lehman of Columbiana, Ohio. They lived in McPherson County until 1921, when they moved to Harper County, where Stephen was a schoolteacher. In December 1927 he was ordained to the ministry, with the plan that they should move to Protection, Kansas, to serve in the pastorate there. This move was never made, but for some time he did drive to Protection on Sundays to preach there. He was also active in promoting the Sunday school work of the conference. He participated actively in the ministerial work at Pleasant Valley. However, in 1935 he was called to serve in the pastorate at Leetonia, Ohio. He was ordained as bishop in 1951. He resigned as pastor in 1959 and retired from the ministry in 1963. In his retirement he lives at Goshen, Indiana.

Wilbert R. Nafziger, born in Nebraska in 1908, was married in 1936 to Sara Flisher, a nurse. Wilbert was in relief work in Spain most of 1939. Because of war conditions his wife was not permitted to travel to Spain, and so Wilbert returned home to Idaho. In 1941 they were invited to come to Harper. In June Bishop Milo

Kauffman received them by letter into the Pleasant Valley congregation and Wilbert was ordained to the ministry. From September 1942 to September 1943 they were released for administration in the Civilian Public Service program. In February 1946 Nafziger was installed as pastor of Pleasant Valley at the request of R. M. Weaver, who felt that a younger man should take this responsibility. This installation was in charge of Bishop G. G. Yoder.

Early in 1947 Nafziger was asked by the South Central Conference to give one half of his time to serving as field secretary of the conference. The congregation consented to this arrangement. He continued to serve as pastor until 1952. He left Harper for the West in 1956, where he served pastorates at Winton, California, and Salem, Oregon. In 1967 he became superintendent of the Mennonite Home for the Aged at Albany, Oregon. In 1973 he retired at Lebanon, Oregon.

Samuel E. Miller, whose home was at Middletown, Pennsylvania, was ordained at Harper in August 1941, but not for the Pleasant Valley congregation. Miller's wife was Ella May Weaver, daughter of R. M. Weaver. They were under appointment by the Mennonite Board of Missions and Charities for mission work in Argentina. It was Board policy that missionaries should be ordained by their home conferences. And so at Ella May Miller's home church her husband was ordained to a missionary ministry by bishops Milo Kauffman and H. A. Diener. The Millers served among the Toba Indians in northern Argentina until forced by family illness to return. Samuel turned to teaching Spanish at Eastern Mennonite College and Ella May is experiencing a very fruitful broadcast ministry on the women's program, *Heart to Heart.*

It has been noted that the Waldo E. Miller family were the first to occupy the new parsonage at Harper. They were called in March 1952. Waldo was born at Windom, Kansas, in 1919, and was married to Neva Beck in 1942. On June 22, 1952, he was ordained at Pleasant Valley by G. G. Yoder and Earl Buckwalter. Waldo was the first partially supported pastor here. At first the support was through special designated offerings. But after January 1955 he was given $240 per month, plus the use of the parsonage.

In 1958, although the congregation wished the Millers to stay for another three-year term, Waldo accepted a call to Maple Grove, a congregation of three hundred members at Belleville, Pennsylvania, where they began serving in July 1958. In 1960 he was ordained bishop. Later he served a term as moderator of the Allegheny Conference. Although he had some serious health problems, he continued in the pastorate at Maple Grove until August 1972. At this time he became pastor of the Inter-Mennonite Fellowship at Hesston, Kansas.

The acting pastor at Pleasant Valley between July 1958 and September 1959 was Merle Bender, who at that time was Director of Development at Friends University at Wichita and was free on Sundays to come to Harper to preach on Sunday morning. He had been ordained earlier at his home church, East Fairview, Milford, Nebraska, for service at the Eureka Gardens mission church in Wichita. He had also done development work for Hesston College, and for Bethel College, North Newton, Kansas.

James Detweiler came to Harper from Elida, Ohio, in September 1959. He had been ordained at Elida in 1953 to be pastor of the Central Church there. At Harper he received partial support: $275 per month for three years, then $50 more for car expenses and $25 for secretarial work. He lived, of course, in the parsonage. He earned additional income by helping dairy farmers and with some cows of his own. His pastorate here was caught in the debate concerning the new church; he worked vigorously for the building program. In January 1964 he moved to Manson, Iowa, to be pastor there, and to Metamora, Illinois, in 1971.

After the interim pastorate of H. J. King, following August 1964, the congregation did not have a pastor for about a year. About twenty different ministers supplied the pulpit during that time.

In 1966 came another in the long succession of Pleasant Valley preachers. In January of that year Howard Zehr and Milo Kauffman took a vote to extend a call to H. Eugene Herr to serve as pastor of the congregation. The vote was almost unanimous. Herr accepted the call, to be effective in the fall of the year.

Herr came to Scottdale, Pennsylvania, from Lancaster County, Pennsylvania, in 1954 and became assistant pastor of the Kingview congregation in East Scottdale. In May 1955, after eight months as assistant, he became pastor. He was ordained to the ministry on May 15 by Bishop J. L. Horst. In 1958 he began a denomination-wide ministry as secretary of youth work under the Mennonite Commission for Christian Education, with his office and residence at Scottdale. It was from this assignment that he was called to Pleasant Valley. His youth work came to a fitting conclusion in the Mennonite

Youth Fellowship Convention held at Estes Park, Colorado, in August 1966. From this convention the Herrs — Eugene, Mary (Yutzy), and three children — came to the parsonage at Harper and Eugene was installed as pastor on August 28 by Ivan R. Lind, with the sermon being brought by Allen H. Erb. Herr was the first pastor at Pleasant Valley to be fully supported by the congregation. In the fall of 1970 he moved to Indiana to become director of education in the Goshen College congregation.

Millard Osborne came to the South Central Conference in 1970 to assume the duties of Conference Minister. There is no fixed conference office, and it was decided that he should have his residence at Harper, and operate from there. He and his family are members of the Pleasant Valley congregation, but he has no responsibilities as a minister in it.

Robert O. Zehr, who grew up in the Conservative Mennonite Church at Greenwood, Delaware, was ordained to the ministry in September 1964 by John E. Wenger and Howard J. Zehr at Madisonville, Louisiana, where he served as pastor. He came to the pastorate at Pleasant Valley in January 1971. In June of that year he was invited to give pastoral service also at Crystal Springs, a rural Mennonite congregation nearby. The church council recommended and the members approved that he should preach at Crystal Springs twice a month on Sunday morning and once on Sunday evening. In 1974 he serves as conference moderator.

Pleasant Valley has had five ordained deacons. Jonas G. Wenger was the first one, and he was probably ordained here in 1888 or 1889. He was in the feed and coal business in Harper, where he was highly respected and deeply loved for his self-forgetful concern for others. The author remembers him as being called "Uncle Jonas." It was a treat to be able to ride on the high seat of the delivery wagon with Will Detweiler, who worked for him. In 1902 Wenger went to Rittman, Ohio, to take charge of the Mennonite Old People's Home there. He returned late in 1904. In 1915 he moved to Hesston, Kansas, where he died in 1922 at the home of his niece, Lizzie Brenneman Hershberger.

When Wenger went to Ohio, Jacob Zimmerman was ordained deacon in 1903. The Zimmermans were charter members of the congregation. In the spring of 1907 they moved to Protection, Kansas. After a number of years he died there.

Emanuel C. Weaver was not ordained for service in the

deacon's office at Pleasant Valley. He was ordained in Marion County, and is listed as a deacon on the conference record as early as 1892, with his address as Peabody. He came to Harper County in 1900, and attended conference as a deacon from Harper in 1902. During the years he was here, he assisted in the work as called upon. He was the father of Menno B. Weaver, who served several years as Sunday school superintendent.

Henry E. Hostetler, born in 1867 in Elkhart County, Indiana, moved with his father to Cass County, Missouri, at the age of thirteen. At seventeen he was converted under the preaching of John S. Coffman and united with the Sycamore Grove congregation. In 1888 he started his lifetime vocation of farming in the West Liberty community in Kansas, where he married Saloma Slabach. They lived together sixty-three years, and had seven sons and seven daughters. In 1908 they moved to Protection, and in 1909 to Harper, where they spent their remaining years on a farm across the road from the Pleasant Valley Church.

In 1913 he was ordained deacon by lot. He was active in many church and community activities. He died in 1952, and Saloma died two years later.

Harold Sommerfeld moved to Harper when he was married to Ida, one of the Hostetler daughters, in 1931. He was a schoolteacher, and, after 1943, a farmer. He was ordained deacon to assist his father-in-law in 1944. He shared in the lot of 1945 when a bishop was ordained for the Harper churches, and Gideon G. Yoder was chosen. In 1946 he bought a publishing and printing business at Hesston, Kansas, which he operated until 1973. He has also served as deacon of the Hesston congregation. When Sommerfeld moved away, the Pleasant Valley congregation was moving to administration by a board of elders and has not ordained another deacon.

The congregation first adopted a constitution in February 1959. It was revised twice, the last time in 1968. Three major Boards make up the governing body — elders, trustees, and education — with the chairman of each Board serving with the pastor and a congregational chairman as a council which coordinates all other Boards and committees. Lyle Bauer served as the first congregational chairman, Charles Bickel as the first chairman of the board of elders, Delbert Hostetler as chairman of the board of trustees, and Bernice Hostetler as the first chairman of the Board of

Christian Education — the first woman to serve on a major committee of the church. In August 1969 the position of adult-youth superintendent was abolished, with this responsibility assumed by the Board of Christian Education. Ellis King was the last adult-youth superintendent.

Since 1962 the Pleasant Valley Church has been incorporated.

The Pleasant Valley congregation has been a loyal supporter of conference and denominational affairs. It has been noted that the first meeting of the Kansas-Nebraska Conference held here was in 1897. Later meetings here were in 1906 and 1915. The South Central Conference met here in 1924, 1938, and 1950. Pleasant Valley helped Crystal Springs entertain the conference in 1932 and 1943. Conferences were big get-togethers in those days, and until quite recently, with sessions devoted to missions, young people, women's work, Christian education, and other special interests. Large tents were sometimes used, and this church was the first to use a public-address system in such a big conference assembly. Pleasant Valley was also the first to charge for the meals. Lodging was in the homes. A large house like the Hershberger-Hostetler home across the road from the church could take care of a dozen or more.

In 1958 Pleasant Valley sponsored the conference, but on the campus of Hesston College, because of the facilities available there. In 1960 the two Harper churches entertained the Extension Convention of the conference, with the sessions held in the high school at Attica, next town to the west. In 1965 the Extension Convention met again at Harper, but this time in the new church. In the Sunday morning service 714 people were seated where they could see and hear the speakers.

The area stewardship conference and Hilfs Plan (mutual aid) meeting were held at Harper in 1964.

Something different from the usual series of evangelistic meetings was the Experiment in Depth directed by Lyman Coleman at the year-end of 1966.

Many of the young people of Pleasant Valley have attended our church schools — Hesston, Goshen, Eastern Mennonite College, and Goshen Biblical Seminary. Some went to Bethel College, a General Conference Mennonite school at Newton. The specialized agricultural interests of the community took some young men to Kansas State University at Manhattan.

This congregation has experienced the spirit of change in the

Mennonite Church during recent years. In 1959 the wedding ring issue came up. It was not decided by default, but was accepted by vote of the congregation. Now ring ceremonies may be used in church weddings.

In the earlier days the weddings were in the homes — either of the bride or the minister. The first church wedding was that of John Bauer and Maggie Bickel, on November 1, 1914, in a regular Sunday morning service. The first church wedding for which invitations were given was that of Gideon G. Yoder and Stella Hostetler, on August 31, 1936. Almost all weddings are now of this type. In 1961 there was a wedding in the regular morning service. The bride came from a non-Mennonite broken home. She was baptized after which the minister announced that this was also the day she had chosen for her wedding. The groom came forward and they were married without the usual attendants. A few weddings have been held in the church with only immediate families attending.

A few members have chosen not to observe foot washing in connection with the communion service.

Since 1965 some of the younger women have discontinued the wearing of the conventional devotional covering.

Not the least of the contributions of Pleasant Valley to Mennonite witness have been the workers scattered over the world, among them J. N. Weaver, at CARE headquarters in Philadelphia; Dale Weaver, relief worker in Korea; Reuben Yoder, music director at Eastern Mennonite High School; Calvin King, pastor at Colorado Springs, Colorado; Phoebe Hamilton, teacher at Iowa Mennonite School; Esther Thut Beck, missionary to Japan; Helen Hostetler Miller, interracial ministry at Cleveland, Ohio.[16]

5. *Crystal Springs, Harper County*

In 1890 there were twelve Amish Mennonite settlements in Kansas. Of these Crystal Springs is the only one that has survived as a congregation. With the exception of the Amish group in Harvey County which merged with the Pennsylvania congregation, the remaining Amish settlements came to nothing.

However, the settlement at Crystal Springs dates only from 1904. Beginning in 1902, the Amish Mennonite congregation in western McPherson County (see West Liberty, p. 250) began to move to Harper County, eighty-five miles to the south. There were some cultural differences between the Mennonites and Amish Mennonites.

The Amish had rules somewhat stricter than those of the West Liberty group. For instance, one sister recalls that Bishop John Zimmerman would not let her commune because her coat had buttons on it, rather than hooks and eyes. On other matters, like the use of tobacco, the Amish were more tolerant. Another sister remembers that her grandmother, the wife of the bishop, smoked a pipe, and the children would gather around her to see her blow the smoke into the air. Perhaps the Amish, the smaller group, felt sensitive about having a church only a mile away from West Liberty.

But there were economic pressures also. The General Conference Mennonites were moving in, and land prices were going up. There were farms available in a community seven miles west of Harper, for when the Strip of Oklahoma opened up, many Harper County farmers had crossed the state line to take claims. The M. A. Troyer family was the first to move from McPherson County to Crystal Springs, in 1902. By 1904 all the families but one had moved away, and services were discontinued at the McPherson church.

The Amish Mennonites who moved from McPherson County first met in the Nebo Schoolhouse, a mile north of Crystal Springs. But they dismantled the building they owned in McPherson County, and shipped the lumber by rail from Hutchinson to Harper. The benches, pulpit, doors, windows, and frames were hauled down in wagons. The church was rebuilt on a site donated by Joas Yoder, three quarters of a mile south of the Crystal Springs Santa Fe Railroad station. The dedication was held on January 29, 1905. At this time the little town consisted of a post office, a blacksmith shop, a store, a stockyard, a depot, two grain elevators, and four dwellings. Some years later the railroad changed the name of its station to Crystal, but the congregation is still Crystal Springs.

The congregation was organized in 1904 with twenty-seven charter members. They were M. C. Bender and wife, Joe Eash and wife, David Eash, John Eash and wife, C. Reber and wife, John Reber, Daniel Reber, Dave Reber, A. J. Stutzman and wife, Edward J. Shettler and wife, A. D. Troyer and wife, M. A. Troyer and wife, Katie Troyer Yoder, Katie Reber Troyer, A. A. Troyer, J. D. Yoder and wife, and J. J. Zimmerman and wife. J. J. Zimmerman was the pastor. The last survivors of these charter members are Fannie Stutzman, Katie Troyer Yoder, and Katie Reber Troyer.

Part of the services were conducted in German for several years after moving. The first bishop to serve the congregation in Harper County was Joseph Slagell, who lived in Lyon County at that time, but later moved to Hydro, Oklahoma. The women were active in sewing circle work almost from the beginning of the congregation. During the first years they met in homes; in 1919 they began meeting in the church. A Sunday evening young people's meeting was begun also in the early years.

The first evangelistic meetings were held in 1909, with the former Amishman D. D. Zook of Harvey County serving as the preacher. Twelve new members resulted from these meetings.

In 1910 the congregation lost about one third of its members. In 1909 John D. Kauffman, the sleeping preacher,[17] visited at Crystal Springs and the next year nineteen members moved to Shelbyville, Illinois, where a number of Kauffman's followers had gathered. And on a Sunday morning in July seven additional members were expelled from fellowship.

The longtime leader at Crystal Springs was J. J. Zimmerman, who had been ordained in McPherson County in 1894. Preceding him in the ministry there was his father, John Zimmerman, who had been ordained in Iowa; also Jacob Stutzman, ordained in 1884, and S. J. Swartzendruber, ordained minister in 1889, and bishop in 1890. David J. Yoder, ordained in Ohio, was the only deacon to serve the congregation in McPherson County. J. J. Zimmerman moved to Harper County in 1904, and was alone in the ordained leadership of Crystal Springs until Joas Yoder, son of Deacon David J. Yoder, was ordained deacon in 1906. Zimmerman served the congregation some fifty-five years, passing on in 1954 at the age of nearly 90 years.

However, during those years and since, a number of ordained persons have served the congregation. In 1907 Samuel Detwiler, a minister from Logan County, Ohio, came to the settlement. In 1910 Joseph Mast, a minister from Holmes County, Ohio, moved into the community. He was ordained to the office of bishop that year, and served several years in that capacity. About 1914 I. G. Hartzler of East Lynne, Missouri, began serving here as bishop, and continued until 1925. Harry A. Diener, Hutchinson, Kansas, succeeded him in bishop oversight, and served for 21 years.

Edward J. Shettler was ordained to the ministry in 1919, but moved to Kalona, Iowa, some years later. In that same year David

Geil, a deacon from South English, Iowa, became a member of the congregation, moving to Gulfport, Mississippi, about five years later. In 1924 D. Y. Hooley, a minister, and D. C. Schrock, a deacon, both from Jet, Oklahoma, joined the forces at Crystal Springs.

Gideon G. Yoder was called from Parnell, Iowa, to serve the congregation as pastor in 1936. He was ordained minister in 1937, and bishop in 1945. Donald E. King was ordained to the ministry in 1942 and served for a short period. In 1947 Glen Whitaker, a minister and son-in-law of J. J. Zimmerman, located near Crystal Springs and assisted in the ministry for a few years. In 1948 Clarence Burkholder was ordained as deacon. At the same time, his wife, Dorothy Burkholder, was ordained deaconess, the only woman in the South Central Conference to have held that office. The Burkholders have served to the present time (1973).

Recent pastorates have not been lengthy. Lowell Nissley was called and licensed in 1951; he was ordained in 1952. Alvin Kauffman was called to be pastor in 1955, serving at first under a license. But in December of that year he was ordained and served until he moved to Hesston in August 1964. In that year Earl Buckwalter, a retired pastor and bishop of Hesston, Kansas, became an interim pastor, and served the congregation until 1971, living for most of that period in the parsonage in Crystal which had been built in 1952. Following his return to Hesston, the congregation cooperated with the Pleasant Valley congregation in sharing the services of Pastor Robert O. Zehr. The two congregations continue to explore other possibilities of joint activities.

When the Western District Amish Mennonite Conference merged with the several Mennonite conferences of the Western states in 1920-1921, Crystal Springs became a part of the Missouri-Kansas Conference, which later changed its name to South Central. Crystal Springs hosted the Western A. M. Conference in 1910, and the Missouri-Kansas Conference in 1932.

Planning for a second church building began in 1926; J. D. Yoder donated an acre of land on the west side of the cemetery near the old church building. To raise funds for the new building, members were assessed 2 percent of their property evaluation. Many also donated one to two acres of wheat. The old building was wrecked in 1928; the new building was made of lumber and covered with stucco. The old seats and the pulpit, made by hand for the building in McPherson County, were placed in the basement of the new church and are still in use there.

Dedication services were held on September 30, 1928, with D H. Bender preaching the sermon. Funds received on this day com pleted the payment of building costs. Ministers at the time were J J. Zimmerman and D. Y. Hooley. There had been good recovery of the losses of 1910, and the membership in 1928 stood at 112

A Sunday school library was begun in 1928. Prayer meetings were held weekly for many years. These functioned as midweek fellowship meetings, and there were separate meetings for children and juniors. Other active organizations have been the Women' Missionary and Service Auxiliary (now Commission), Mennonite Youth Fellowship, and a Ladies' Chorus.

Many of the young people attended the Mennonite church colleges. Thirteen became nurses, and some became hospital staff members. Marie Naffziger administered the hospital at Greensburg Kansas, for a number of years. The service motive has always been emphasized at Crystal Springs.

When the conference set up the area overseer plan in 1955 Milo Kauffman became the overseer at Crystal Springs. The local administration is in the hands of a church council, which is com posed of the ordained members of the congregation, the church treasurer, the chairman of the board of trustees, the chairman of the Sunday evening program committee, the president of the women's organization, the director of music, the mission representative, the head usher, and the adult Sunday school superintendent. This council assists the pastor in guiding the program of the church.

Financing is through the budget system, with strong emphasis on the biblical principles of stewardship. Whereas in 1910 the total giving was $38, by 1958 the giving amounted to $10,000; giving in 1971 was $13,551.

Some joint meetings have been held with Pleasant Valley, which is six miles away in Harper. Joint quarterly Sunday school conferences were held for twenty-two years, between 1911 and 1933. In more recent years there has been cooperation in victorious life conferences, Bible conferences, and a Bible school in Harper. The sharing of a pastor may augur increasing cooperation between these two congregations.

The membership at Crystal Springs reached a peak of about 140 around 1945-1947. In 1972 there were sixty-six members. A few years before, the pastor reported the baptism of the youngest person in the congregation. A congregation without children or young people has no future unless younger married people become a part of the fellowship. The membership decrease has been explained by the departure of the youth to find employment. Because of changes in farming methods in this agricultural community, larger acreages are farmed by fewer people. There is little industrial employment, and the service professions tend to take the younger people away.[18]

6. *Argentine (Mennonite Gospel Mission), Kansas City*

Metropolitan Kansas City, a city of 600,000 at the junction of the Kansas (Kaw) and Missouri rivers, straddles the state boundary between Missouri and Kansas. In the first half of the nineneenth century a transportation break was located here, with traffic for the West and the Southwest being transferred from the Missouri River to the Oregon and Santa Fe trails. With the coming of the railroads, Kansas City was still a great center, with lines branching in all directions to Chicago, Detroit, St. Louis, the Gulf Coast, southern California, Colorado, the Pacific Northwest, and Minnesota. It is the largest metropolis, with the exception of St. Louis, in the northern part of the South Central Conference.

There are three Mennonite congregations in greater Kansas City, the Kansas City Mennonite Fellowship on the Missouri side (see p. 138) and the Argentine and Rainbow Boulevard congregations on the Kansas side. All three have some common sources. The first has been described among the Missouri churches, and Rainbow Boulevard, as an active congregation today, will have a separate treatment (see p. 349). The story of the Argentine Church has a continuous history back to the Mennonite Gospel Mission of Kansas City, being the one outreach of that mission which has a congregational status today.

Conviction that there ought to be a Mennonite mission in Kansas City dates from 1904. Three brethren independently expressed this conviction in letters to one another. The concern was brought to the contiguous conferences. The Kansas-Nebraska Conference appointed D. G. Lapp and T. M. Erb to a committee to take up this concern. The Missouri-Iowa Conference appointed J. M. Hershey and D. F. Driver. L. J. Miller, of the Sycamore Grove congregation of the Western Amish Mennonite Conference, also served

n this committee, as representing the interest of the congregation osest to Kansas City.

This committee met in the city on December 24, 1904, at the ome of G. L. Autenrieth; he and his wife were the only Menno- ites living in the city. The committee drew up a resolution advis- g that the two conferences establish a mission.[19]

In February the group chose a location at Seventh and Pacific, n abandoned Methodist Church. This was for many years the sidence, the meeting place, and the base of outreach for the Kan- s City Mennonite Gospel Mission.[20] Trustees were appointed, ith T. M. Erb serving as president and J. M. Hershey as cretary-treasurer. J. F. Brunk was appointed superintendent. T. . Erb went home from this meeting feeling that "God has aciously guided us in the work."[21]

In April the Brunks moved in. The first prayer service was held n April 20, and the first Sunday school was held with thirteen resent on April 23. That evening George J. Lapp began the first ries of meetings, and the next Sunday there were thirty-two resent.

In May J. F. Brunk was ordained to the ministry by Daniel auffman. The trustees "found the mission in good running rder."[22] A congregation was organized. There were fifty-seven pro- ssed conversions in the first year, of which sixteen became members f the Mennonite Church.

J. F. Brunk and wife, first workers at the Kansas City Mission

The purpose of the mission as expressed by the trustees at this time went as follows:

1. *To preach and teach the gospel.*
2. *To put homeless children in Christian homes.*
3. *To provide clothing and food for the worthy poor.*
4. *To provide free medical aid for the afflicted poor.*
5. *To welcome all classes, especially the poor and needy.*

A characteristic of this mission was the establishment of branches and stations. This began the first summer. Mrs. Mildred Koppenhaver, who lived in Argentine, a suburb six miles southwest of the mission base, became a member and offered her home for the holding of a branch Sunday school. The attendance there soon reached almost fifty, and J. B. Brunk, who had joined the force of workers, bought a storefront building in Argentine at 3105 Strong Avenue. The first floor was the meeting hall, and the second floor a residence for the J. B. Brunks. This station was called the Free Gospel Mission. J. B. Brunk was ordained to the ministry in February 1906.

Other workers of the mission in this first year were Sadie Hartzler, Emma Daren, and Sylvia Miller. Mrs. Koppenhaver brought as many as twenty-two children with her to Sunday school in Argentine. J. D. Charles came from Lancaster County, Pennsylvania, to be a worker, and his first task was to build up a Sunday school library of 130 volumes. [23]

In 1906 J. F. Brunk resigned his responsibility at Kansas City to take up the promotion of a Mennonite sanitarium at La Junta, Colorado. C. A. Hartzler, from Sycamore Grove, became another worker. J. D. Charles was appointed superintendent, but he was not ordained to the ministry until May 4, 1908. [24] Both J. F. Brunk and J. B. Brunk left Kansas City. In the fall of 1906, also, both of the sponsoring conferences instructed the trustees to deed the Kansas City properties to the Mennonite Board of Missions and Charities, and in 1907 the mission passed under the administration of that Board, so that there would be a greater churchwide interest in this mission.

The term of J. D. Charles as superintendent terminated in 1909, when he moved to Hesston, Kansas, to serve as dean of the new school established there that year. C. A. Hartzler succeeded him at Kansas City, moving his residence from Strong Avenue to

The mission building in Argentine. Workers lived on the second floor.

Seventh Street. The Board wanted to sell the building in Argentine, but when no buyer appeared, E. C. Bowman and wife, who had joined the force of workers, were given its use as a home. Bowman revived the Sunday school at Argentine in 1911, an important step in the light of later developments toward a permanent work in Argentine.

In 1912 C. A. Hartzler took up a pastorate in Illinois, and the Board called J. D. Mininger to be superintendent of the Gospel Mission. This proved to be a very important appointment. Mininger had been trying to farm in Colorado. But the work of a city missionary was more to his liking, and suited his talents much better. He was the obvious man for the place, and he spent the rest of his life here, a total of twenty-nine years. It was the kind of continuous administration that the mission required, if it was to be successful. The program never became static under the leadership of this Spirit-filled, imaginative, courageous, never-tiring man.

As a youth in the Franconia Conference of eastern Pennsylvania, Jacob D. Mininger had convictions for mission work, and after his marriage to Hettie B. Kulp he spent four and a half years as superintendent of the Mennonite Old People's Home, Marshallville, Ohio.

He was ordained to the ministry in Colorado in October 191
by T. M. Erb. But the real turning point in his life was in May
1912 when he and his wife began a missionary career in Kansas
City that hardly has a duplicate in Mennonite Church life. He died
January 4, 1941, while still very much in harness.

Mininger was a good preacher and Bible teacher. He spoke
with great earnestness. He used much material from his reading, but
he had made it his own. He was in great demand in his denomina
tion as an evangelist and Bible conference instructor. He was a
churchman, serving as a conference and church board official. He
loved his church with a deep loyalty. He was a writer of books and
tracts on mission work and on victorious living. He was a family
man, bringing up in a difficult city environment three children who
have served God and the church: Ruth, teacher of literature at
Eastern Mennonite College; Paul, General Conference moderator
president of Goshen College, and chief architect of the revised struc
ture (1971) of the Mennonite Church; Edward, chairman of the
Health and Welfare Committee of the Mennonite Board of Missions

J. D. Mininger was a strong personnel man. He knew how
to pick the men and women who could do the things which he saw
should be done. And he could challenge their loyalty and organize

*J. D. Mininger, long-term
pastor at Kansas City*

hem into an effective team. Some of those who worked on his eam were Allan Good, H. A. Diener, Edward Yoder, William Smith, R. P. Horst, C. E. Miller, Philip Kreider, Freedley Schrock, Paul Erb, Samuel Nafziger, Martha Buckwalter, Lena Horst, Emma King, Mary Stalter, Vera Hallman, E. C. Bowman, Bernice Devitt, Anna Schweitzer, Ella Zook. In addition he drew into the Kansas City program practically all the active Mennonite evangelists.

Of the multiple facets of the program only some can be mentioned.

In the summer of 1913 an extensive evangelistic campaign was launched, with a score of extra workers involved. The means used included tent meetings in the area of the mission and in Argentine, house-to-house canvass, noon meetings at Armour's and the Union Pacific shops, singing in hospitals and institutions, a chapel service in the state prison at Leavenworth. The chief evangelist in this campaign was S. E. Allgyer, assisted by Abner G. Yoder, Perry J. Shenk, and Allen H. Erb.

Especially in the earlier years, a great deal of help was given to the poor: clothes, food, fuel, and transportation to doctor, hospital, or church.

There was much visiting: of Sunday school pupils, shut-ins, the sick, people who called to ask for help. New converts needed constant encouragement. Funerals were conducted: a notable one in 1918 was that of Mrs. William Smith, who was converted at the mission. Her husband accepted Christ at her funeral, and became an outstanding Christian worker. He later married Anna Diller, one of the mission workers, and in 1923 he was ordained to the office of deacon — a deacon who really "deked," said Mininger. In 1941, after Mininger's death, Smith was ordained to the ministry, as his successor. However, he died in 1942.

New places of witness were opened up as there was opportunity. Following a Bible class held in homes of Armourdale, halfway between Argentine and Seventh Street, a vacant hall in that area was rented in 1924, and services were held there for a time. An empty building in a needy place was always a challenge to Mininger. In 1925 a Sunday school was opened in North Kansas City, Missouri, called Midway, in a former dance hall. There was no church in the area. A Bible school flourished, and in one series of meetings there were thirty-six confessions. The witness continued here to 1930.

A summer Bible school at Morris. Edward Yoder and William Smith stand at the extreme right of the picture. Other teachers that year were Mabel Berkey, Allan Weaver, Mamie Yoder, Vernon Allison, Sadie Bissie, Rachel Horst, Dollie Landis, and

Morris is a suburban community west of Argentine. A Sunday school was opened here in 1931. First it was conducted in the public school, but later in a donated building called the Morris Gospel Hall. There were a number of baptisms here, and a congregation was organized in 1946, with sixteen charter members. Edward Yoder was the pastor. In 1951, however, a flood from the Kaw River damaged the hall so badly that the work at Morris was discontinued.

The Mennonite Gospel Center was established on the Missouri side at 1238 Washington Street in 1946. Edward Yoder urged the opening of a work in this needy apartment house section, and he and his wife were placed in charge. A building was purchased and was remodeled into a chapel and classrooms on the first floor, and apartments on the second floor to house the workers and the VS unit who had been sent by the Mennonite Relief and Service Committee to begin aid service at the Kansas City General Hospital. A congregation was organized, and the Morris members were transferred here in 1951. Edward Yoder served until 1952. He was followed by Frank Raber, who came from Detroit. In 1954 Raber was moved to the Argentine pastorate, and John T. Kreider became pastor at the Gospel Center. The population here was transient, which brought the opportunity to serve many people, but made it difficult to build up a stable membership. In 1960 the name was changed to Community Mennonite Church. But attendance declined, and the work was closed in 1961. From the service unit developed the Kansas City Mennonite Fellowship (see p. 138).

Like some other city missionaries, the Miningers found the institutional mission, the "Mennonite hotel," a difficult place to raise a family. For a short time they lived at Blue Springs, east of the city. Later, after the Seventh Street property was sold, the Miningers established their home on the north side of Kansas City, Kansas, in Quindaro. Here they lived at the time of his death.

In Quindaro, as everywhere else, this mission-hearted man saw work to be done. A building became available across the street, and in July 1939 a summer Bible school was opened here, and was followed by a Sunday school. Mininger operated this school with the help of workers who came over from Argentine. When Mininger died, William Smith, who also lived in Quindaro, continued the work. And when Smith died, in 1942, others continued the Quindaro station for some years.

Special services of varied types were an important asset to the

Kansas City Gospel Mission. During World War I several hundred conscientious objectors, Mennonites and others, served sentences at the Disciplinary Barracks at Ft. Leavenworth. Kansas City was the nearest Mennonite Church, and J. D. Mininger accepted the responsibility of being pastor to these prisoners. Each Saturday for many months either Mininger or another minister from the mission rode the trolley to the prison, visited those in the hospital, and preached to those who were not in solitary or busy at assigned work.[25]

Taking care of homeless or neglected children was considered one of the purposes of the mission from the very beginning. A day nursery was first proposed. Many requests for child care came to the workers. Allan Good, who had joined the staff in 1913, became much interested in this phase of the work. In 1914 a Children's Welfare Board was organized and considered the possibility of having a "receiving home." J. D. Mininger had already placed a number of children in Christian homes. Finally, in 1917 the Mission Board purchased a house at 1620 South 37th Street, in Argentine. This building was remodeled in 1934 and 1952. Many hundreds of children have been cared for here or placed in foster and adoptive homes. The nature of this work has changed somewhat with the changes of the laws and with the needs in social welfare. In January 1972 the name was changed to Argentine Youth Services, Inc. The work is only with boys referred by courts and welfare departments. By 1973 the emphasis was on giving such help to parents as would make it possible for boys to return to their own homes. For those who need to be kept in a "home," a fourth group home was

The Children's Home in Argentine, Kansas, now the office of Argentine Youth Services

opened. These family-like living units have proved to be a more successful way of meeting needs of the boys. The Board of Directors is considering opening a fifth unit for girls. There are no longer any children at 1620 South 37th. The building is being used as office space by Argentine Youth Services and other organizations providing community services.

Superintendents who have served in this children's work are the following: Allan Good, 1917-1919; Bernice Devitt, 1919-1921; C. J. Freyenberger, 1921-1923; Earl Hartzler, 1923-1924; J. D. Mininger (with assistants), 1924-1932; A. Lloyd Swartzendruber, 1932-1938; Floyd M. Sieber, 1938-1947; Fred Swartzendruber, 1947-1950; Glen Yoder, 1950-1964; Jake Birkey, 1964-1967; Carl Gusler, 1968-1970; Larry Wenger, 1970-1973; Eugene A. Miller, 1973-.

The building is owned and the work is sponsored by the Mennonite Board of Missions. Immediate control is by a Board nominated locally and approved by the Health and Welfare Committee of the Board of Missions. Workers have been mostly from the Mennonite Church, some being, up to September 1972, Voluntary Service workers appointed by the Board of Missions. In past years the workers and the children have attended the Argentine Mennonite Church, which is only three blocks down the hill. Many of the youth through the years were baptized and became members of the congregation.

The Home Department of the Argentine Church was organized in 1934, and became exceedingly effective in reaching many shut-ins. While Katie Saltzman was superintendent in 1950, the enrollment reached 160. Some of these shut-ins were brought to church. The expansion of this home visitation was limited only by the number of workers.

The weekday Bible school was another service into which a great deal of effort went. Children from the Argentine public school were excused to go to the Argentine Mennonite Church nearby for a period of Bible teaching. This began in 1926 with an enrollment of 35. This pioneer effort was in its forty-sixth year in 1972-1973.

All this is preliminary to the history of the Argentine congregation. Up to 1946 the work at Argentine was a part of the Mennonite Gospel Mission. But at that time the mission work was continued at Morris and on the Missouri side. The congregation in Argentine became an indigenous congregation, no longer administered by the Mennonite Board of Missions.

In August 1920 the mission building on Strong Avenue was sold. The place of worship was moved temporarily to an empty churc at 1521 South 18th Street. The Board decided that Argentin should have a permanent place of worship, for church use alone the workers were to have a separate place of residence. In Novem ber 1921 the place of worship was moved to another church a 3713 Powell Avenue, which was nearer to the Children's Home Attendance increased at this location.

The next year it was decided to erect a church building in Ar gentine. A site was purchased at 3701 Metropolitan. Favorabl to this location was its nearness to the Children's Home, for th Home family needed to walk to church; and to the Argentine Schoo which made possible a weekday Bible school program, envisione just at this time.

L. A. Weaver, a builder in the congregation, served as forema for the building of the church. Volunteer labor came from Ontari Iowa, and Missouri churches. The building was dedicated on Febru ary 21, 1925, with S. C. Yoder preaching the dedication sermor The following day Rufus P. Horst was ordained to the ministry b D. H. Bender. Horst was to be an assistant to Mininger in the mis sion program. His ordination was called for by a vote of the congre gation. By this time the work on Seventh Street had been dis continued, and the Argentine Church was considered the base o operations for the mission, with Mininger as pastor.

The first wedding in this church was that of Claude Wise an Louise Jones, which was solemnized February 11, 1934. Louise wa a convert at Midway.

When J. D. Mininger died in 1941, Deacon William Smith wa ordained to the ministry to serve as mission superintendent, an Edward Yoder was ordained as deacon. When in the next yea Smith also died (his wife thought from working too hard), Yode was ordained as pastor of the congregation and superintendent of th mission. In this same year, 1942, Samuel Nafziger was ordained a deacon of the congregation and served two years, moving in 1944 t Kalona, Iowa, to teach in the new Iowa Mennonite School.

In February 1946 the Argentine Mennonite Church was organize by bishops J. C. Driver and W. R. Hershberger, of Cass County, Mis souri. R. P. Horst was asked to be the pastor, and Roy Zook, deacon who had just moved to Kansas City, was received as th congregation's deacon. Edward Yoder continued to be mission super intendent, with primary responsibility at Morris and the Gospel Center. In 1947 Levi C. Hershberger was ordained to serve as an additional deacon. Since there were many preaching appointments in June 1948, Norman Teague, who had grown up in the Children's Home, was licensed for the ministry and served for three years. In July 1949 Glen and Lois Yoder came to Kansas City, from Protection, Kansas, to assume direction of the Children's Home, and Glen was received to serve in the ministry. A church council helped to administer the congregation.

Beginning in 1947 plans began to be discussed for enlarging and remodeling the church. Dan King, a builder in the congregation, was appointed chairman of a building committee. The completion of this building program was observed February 18, 19. 1950, as a twenty-fifth anniversary of the organization.

The congregation had developed through the years with a rather conservative discipline. Now rules were applied in a way that built up tensions. Rufus Horst resigned in 1952. But since he still held his employment in a hardware business where he worked since 1919, he remained in the congregation. Frank Raber was moved over from the Gospel Center. But after three years his health broke, and he resigned the pastorate. D. Lowell Nissley came from Crystal Springs, at Harper, Kansas, in 1955, to take over the leadership. In November 1957 thirty-one members withdrew from Argentine, and with Nissley's leadership formed the Grace Mennonite Chapel (see Rainbow Boulevard, p. 349).

Horst and Glen Yoder then served for a time as copastors. In 1960 Yoder was chosen to serve as interim pastor. In January 1964 he was named pastor, but in June 1964 he moved to Maumee, Ohio, to head the Sunshine Children's Home.

In July 1965 John Paul Wenger came from Goshen, Indiana, and was ordained and installed as pastor on August 8, 1965. He resigned in October 1966.

For twenty months the congregation had no pastor. The pulpit assignments were under the direction of the church council. The congregation elected a pastoral committee — Vernon Allison, Jake Birkey, and R. P. Horst — to seek another pastor. Through the counsel of the area overseer of the conference, the council arranged for Paul Bender and wife, schoolteachers from Greenwood, Delaware, to meet with the congregation Thanksgiving weekend in 1967. The congregation later voted to call them to the pastorate. They moved into the parsonage at 3711 Metropolitan Avenue, on June 25, 1968. He was installed and licensed in July 1968. This also proved to be a brief pastorate, with Bender resigning in August 1970. The Benders moved back to Delaware in July, 1971.

John M. Landis, Hesston, Kansas, after driving to Kansas City for the weekends for a number of months, accepted the call to serve as an interim pastor, and moved to Argentine in the summer of 1972. John Heyerly served here between ministries at the Kansas City Fellowship and Protection.

The membership in 1972 was sixty-two.[26]

7. *Protection, Comanche County*

In 1906 R. J. Heatwole, long a lay pastor of the Southwestern frontiers, learned at Coldwater, Kansas, of a tract of 4,200 acres near Protection in Comanche County, Kansas, that would be available for colonization by March 1, 1907.[27] He no doubt spread the good news of plenty of good land at a low cost. In the older communities there were those who felt the need for more land: like Alvin Selzer, at Canton, Kansas. He was a cattleman who said Canton was too crowded. He wanted acres for his cattle to roam over. The move to Protection fulfilled his desire, for he owned, eventually, over 2,000 acres of land there.

The first Mennonites to come to Protection were Noah Ebersole and Jacob Zimmerman, a minister and a deacon from Harper, a few counties to the east. Getting in on the ground floor of the opportunity in the early spring of 1907, they purchased a number of good homesteads in Collier Flats south and west of Protection, planning to sell to other settlers.

After building rather crude homes, they went back to Harper and returned by train on March 7 with their families and possessions. A congregation was definitely in their thinking, for on March 10 they met to plan a Sunday school, and on March 17 the first services were held in the Murray Schoolhouse, District 42, two miles south of Protection.

Other settlers quickly followed. Within a few months Ben Horst, another minister, moved with his family from Harper. In the late summer of 1907 Alvin Selzer came from Canton. About the same time came N. E. Miller and his large family from Tuleta, Texas, and the Jacob Stutzmans from Nebraska. George R. Brunk, a bishop, and Henry Hostetler, both from McPherson County, came in August to

The first house the Selzers built south of Protection

A wheat-harvesting outfit on the Selzer farm

put out their crops.[28] Others who came in that year were John Schrock, a deacon, and family, from Louisiana; C. W. Miller, a minister, and family; Will Weaver; Mose Shenk; and Joe Landises, all from Canton. The Brunk family also seems to have come by October.

For on October 6, 1907, seven months after the first arrivals, the congregation was organized with thirty-two charter members. There was no lack of ordained leadership: George R. Brunk was the bishop, N. E. Ebersole and Ben Horst were ministers (Chris Miller was no longer preaching), and Jacob Zimmerman and John Schrock were deacons. Besides these men and their wives, the charter members were: Joe, Noah, and Ida Zimmerman; Noah and Pearl Schrock; Mrs. Nora Selzer; Chris and Katherine Miller and children: Charles, Ray, Ella, and Fannie; Will Weaver, Mose Shenk, Joseph and Rosena Landes, N. E. and Sophronia Miller and children: David, Howard, and Baldwin.

Of these charter members, the only one still living at Protection in 1973 was Nora Selzer. Those still living elsewhere are Noah Schrock (a deacon in Indiana), Mose Shenk (Schowalter Villa, Hesston, Kansas), Ray Miller (Newton, Kansas), and David D. Miller (Greencroft Villa, Goshen, Indiana).

Other families joining the community by 1909 were the Henry Hostetlers and the S. E. Millers from McPherson County; the John Bakers, from Jet, Oklahoma; the Henry Bakers and Dan Troyers from Holmes County, Ohio; the Wes Troyers, the L. C. Millers, the Alf Millers, and the Elias Millers (the last three the sons of N. E. Miller) from southern Texas. By 1912 there were fifty-four members.

Skeptics raised   objections to people leaving good homes and well-established churches and moving to marginal farming country full of sagebrush, jackrabbits, and duststorms. The early years were hard; crop failure is always a possibility in western Kansas. A common saying was that at Harper the rain comes fifteen minutes before it is too late; at Protection, fifteen minutes after it is too late! Another saying was, that of those who came to look at this country, some believed everything that was told them, some believed half of it, and some, none of it.

Not all the settlers stayed. After a few years, Bishop Brunk moved to Denbigh, Virginia, and Henry Hostetler moved to Harper. These were substantial families, and their leaving hurt. Several families moved to Hesston for the schooling of their children. After 1909 there was a sharp drop in the membership. When asked if he

*George R. Brunk I and wife,
who helped to start the
Mennonite congregation
at Protection, Kansas*

didn't get discouraged when so many of the others were leaving, one of the early settlers who remained replied, "I guess we were the only ones who didn't have sense enough to leave." But those who stayed, most of them, now have good homes, granaries full of wheat, pastures and barns full of cattle, and a thriving church. Of the thirty-one families in the church in 1949, all but one were descendants or related by marriage to four of the pioneer families of 1907-1909.

At the first business meeting of the congregation, on April 8, 1908, a committee was appointed to find out how soon a meeting-house could be built. This committee reported on July 7 that a new church would cost $1,200 and it was decided to take subscriptions at once. The building was to be 32 by 42, including ante-rooms. Building was to proceed as soon as enough money was in sight. Alvin Selzer donated three acres from the corner of his farm, five miles south of Protection. One acre was to be used as a cemetery. The ground was staked out on August 5, and building proceeded immediately, with both funds and labor donated by the members.

The only controversy which arose among the members while planning the building was the location of the entrances into the assembly room. Everyone but one sister wished to enter from the rear of the room. She was deeply convinced that this would be a grave mistake, for the young folks, she thought, would run in and out during services if they could do so without everyone seeing them.

So the church was built with the entrances on the two sides of the pulpit. Whether the frustration of masculine judgment in this decision is the reason or not, the tradition grew up at Protection that only men should attend the annual business meeting of the congregation and make the decisions. Now, however, all members are urged to attend.

The seating capacity of the church was 150. A well was dug in the churchyard. The church building was completed in three months, and the dedication was on November 1, 1908, with India missionary Mahlon C. Lapp preaching the sermon. That God's protecting hand was over the young congregation is shown in this incident. The church was lighted by kerosine lamps, and in this first service one lamp did not burn properly. That week Noah Schrock, the first janitor, discovered that by mistake gasoline had been put into this lamp! Electric lights were not installed until 1929. Before the dedication a dozen hymnbooks (probably *Church and Sunday School Hymnal*) were purchased.

The congregation was early accepted for membership in the Kansas-Nebraska Conference, and before the first church was finished they had invited the conference to meet here. A brief effort was made to have the new Western School located at Protection. But the business meeting of April 8, 1908, passed the following motion: "The church hath decided not to make anymore effort in the future to locate the Mennonite college at this place."

All the minutes of the congregation's business meetings over these years have been kept in one ledger book.

On October 3, 1908, just before a national election, "George R. Brunk (bishop) and Jacob Zimmerman (deacon) are appointed to investigate the several candidates now running for office in the county, state, and United States, and report their choice to the voters of the church." Evidently Mennonites were voting then and were open to advice by their leaders.

"Burying is to begin in the northeast corner for members and families. . . . Outsiders commence to bury on southeast corner" (December 29, 1908).

"A poll tax on each member and a tax levied on total valuation of membership — to pay church expenses" (December 29, 1908). "Drop the assessment and take collection for church expense" (December 21, 1909).

"A decision was made to put up a sign to stop camping and

messing up the church property" (September 27, 1910).

D. S. Troyer elected "ventilator" (December 26, 1911).

Janitor hired for the year at $75 (December 30, 1924).

In 1917, to prepare for the holding of the district conference, the church building was remodeled. The length was increased by twelve feet, a basement was dug under the whole structure, the platform was raised fourteen inches, and an eight-foot porch was placed on the east end.

In the spring of 1942 the pulpit was changed from the east end to the west end, and the seats were turned around facing the pulpit. This put the entrance in the rear instead of the front of the church.

At the 1917 conference session, many people came believing they were coming to a dry part of the country. During the last service a big rain fell, and cars were unable to go far on the dirt roads. The Selzers hauled people to their home until their car got mired in a ditch. Some walked barefooted through the rain and mud; many spent the entire night in the church. The Selzers accommodated thirty-some at their place, a few in the barn on the

Youth group at Protection in 1913. Some identifications in second row: third from left, Mary Miller, later a teacher at Hesston College; second from right, Nora Miller, later nursing instructor at La Junta Nursing School; first from right, Alta Mae Eby, who was visiting there (later Mrs. Paul Erb).

hay. All guests were given breakfast the next morning before starting homeward. Mrs. Selzer, remembering, says, "It was fun."

During World War I, in 1918, one Sunday evening during services four men entered the church with a large flag which they nailed to the wall behind the pulpit, then went on their way. Some time later the flag disappeared. Ten years later the men apologized for their act.

During the winter of 1954-1955, a three-bedroom parsonage was built in Protection with donated funds and labor. The pastors since that time have lived there. Open house and dedication of the parsonage were united in one occasion.

After much informal discussion of building needs, the trustees and the council began in May 1960 to formulate plans. In February 1961 by an 87 percent majority the congregation voted to move ahead. In August 1962 a constitution was accepted. In December of that year Aaron Willems, Ralph Baker, and Eldon Schultz were elected to investigate building needs, and by May 1963 this committee reported a survey they had made. In July another committee — Ernest Selzer, Vernon Loucks, and Verlin Kuhns — was asked to study the cost of remodeling the old building. This committee presented its findings in February 1964. The congregation voted, by an 82 percent majority, to build a new church rather than to remodel.

The following committees were elected: Building — Verlin Kuhns, Ora Baker, Lester Selzer, and Aaron Willems; Finance — Eldon Schultz, Truman Selzer, Chester Baker, and Jake Helmuth. The decision to build in Protection came in September 1964, and in May 1965 a city block on the south edge of town was purchased for $3,500. The building plans were approved in September by a 75 percent vote. The structure was to be of cement blocks, with brick veneer, ground level, with no basement. The assembly room was to seat 190, with overflow to handle up to 300. The building plans included twelve classrooms, a study, a library, a kitchen, a fellowship hall, and a nursery.

In April 1966 the members voted to have $25,000 cash in hand before ground was broken. This amount was soon raised, and groundbreaking ceremonies were held on May 29. Construction began immediately.

On April 2, 1967, the nine months of actual construction culminated in a dedication service. Members had contributed an estimat ed 12,000 hours of volunteer work, saving at least $25,000 in labor costs. The actual cash cost of the building was $97,000. Peter B. Wiebe preached the dedication sermon, interim pastor Wesley Veatch led in the act of dedication, and district overseer Ivan R. Lind led in the dedicatory prayer. Others who participated were Verlin Kuhns, chairman of the building committee; Charles Schweitzer, former pastor; Milo Kauffman, former overseer; Alva Swartzendruber, former bishop; Earl Buckwalter, former overseer; D. D. Miller, former bishop and pastor; and Sanford E. King, moderator of the South Central Conference. Recognition was given to Sanford Oyer, former pastor who helped to organize and promote the building program, S. Enos Miller, the oldest member of the congregation; and Mrs. Alvin Selzer, the only charter member still living in the community.

The church continues to use and maintain the cemetery at the old church location. The first person buried there was N. E. Miller, charter member, whose funeral was held on May 21, 1910, with the service in charge of T. M. Erb, then serving as bishop. The burials here totaled, as of August 1972, fifty-four. All of these were members of families closely related to the church.

Membership grew slowly until it reached 100 in 1964. Since then it remained at that figure or slightly above it. Clayton Beyler wrote in 1949: "The Mennonite community at Protection has been formed chiefly through families moving in from other congregations and from the growth of these families. . . . Mennonites as a rule . . . were able to keep the entire family within the church. As a colonization venture the community at Protection has proved a success. . . . One weakness in our growth in the Mennonite community at Protection has been our failure to win converts by evangelization outside our own group."[29] In a congregation in which many of the young people are related, a number of marriages have brought into the church mates from non-Mennonite background. But perhaps an equal number of marriages have taken Mennonite mates into other churches.

The women of the church organized the sewing circle about 1912. At first these meetings were held in the homes. Often they sewed garments for distribution by the new Kansas City Mission. Later sewing machines were purchased and placed in the church basement; since then, the sewings have been held in the church. A junior sewing circle for the girls was organized in 1941. The names of these organizations, of course, have been changed with the changed terminology and types of work in the churchwide organizations.

A Young People's Bible Meeting was organized in 1907, at the same time as the Sunday school. Junior meetings for grade school children began about 1946. In 1935 a joint semiannual Sunday school conference was started with the Greensburg and Larned congregations. In 1940 Larned dropped out, and after a few years Perryton, Texas, took Larned's place. The three congregations took turns in playing host. In later years the joint conference was discontinued.

A summer Bible school has been conducted each summer since the mid-1930s, with an average attendance of seventy-five. Mary Miller was the first superintendent. Every child in the community was urged to attend. Even when the church was still in the country, many from Protection were enrolled. The last few years before the new church was built, the Bible school used the Protection School building.

Soon after the church was organized the youth group met during the week for fun and recreation and often gave programs. First the group was called "Young Folks." It included the youth and married couples until they were parents of several children. After 1935 the group was called the Literary, and since 1952 it is known as Mennonite Youth Fellowship.

A Ladies' Fellowship was organized in 1954. Membership includes the younger homemakers of the church and community. Its purpose is Christian fellowship. The programs center around Bible study and homemaking.

A Ladies' Bible Study Class was organized in 1957 at the home of Mrs. S. Enos Miller in order to supply a need for more Bible study. It is open to any woman in the community regardless of age. The first course was "The Sermon on the Mount" from Mennonite Broadcasts. Meetings are held once a month in the homes of participants.

The Protection and Perryton Youth Fellowship had a retreat together at Boiling Springs State Park, Woodward, Oklahoma, the summer of 1965.

Both men and women have participated in relief canning, and in 1963 the men and women helped in cleanup in the Arkansas River flood at Dodge City.

Evangelistic meetings, sometimes in the early days in connection with Bible normals, have been an annual feature of the church program. The first meetings were held in March 1908, by C. D. Yoder. The first Bible normal was held in the same year by David Garber and D. G. Lapp. Later evangelists and instructors have included L. J. Miller, S. C. Yoder, D. A. Yoder, J. W. Hess, J. S. Shoemaker, J. M. Kreider, C. F. Derstine, J. A. Ressler, E. M. Yost, Allen Erb, G. G. Yoder, E. S. Garber, Samuel Janzen, Richard Birky, and Elam Hollinger. Also Fred Erb, Richard Yordy, Paul Miller, H. J. King, George R. Brunk II, Edward Stoltzfus, Nelson E. Kauffman, Calvin King, James Horsch, J. J. Hostetler, Ed. Miller, and John Willems.

Other important meetings were the first Sunday school conference, held in August 1911, with J. A. Heatwole as a visiting speaker; and the fiftieth anniversary program in 1958, with D. D. Miller, George R. Brunk II, Milo Kauffman, Clayton Beyler, and Alva Swartzendruber, as speakers.

Administrative responsibility in the congregation has always included the ministerial leaders. But from the beginning, and increasingly through the years, non-ministers also have been involved. At the first business meeting, on April 8, 1908, C. W. Miller was elected treasurer and N. E. Miller, clerk or secretary. Three additional directors, or trustees, were also elected. They were Henry Hostetler, Jacob Zimmerman, and John Schrock. The trustees at the time of the building of the church in town were Bill Bayne, Will Rempel, and Eldon Schultz.

In April 1956 a church council was organized. Three elders were elected to serve on this council, together with other elected persons. The elders have assisted the pastor in administering the spiritual duties of the church. Their term of office is three years, with one elder elected each year. The first elders were Crist Beyler, Aaron Willems, and Roy Selzer. The elders at the time of the church dedication were Victor Beyler, Chester Miller, and Glenn Selzer.

Good leadership, both ordained and lay, has been a favorable factor in the growth of the Mennonite community at Protection.

Bishops have served as follows: George R. Brunk, 1907-1910; T. M. Erb, 1909-1911; S. C. Miller, 1911-1928; D. D. Miller, 1926-1941; Alva Swartzendruber, 1941-1950; Earl Buckwalter, 1950-1954. Of these, only Brunk and D. D. Miller were resident pastors. Both transferred to bishop responsibilities elsewhere: Brunk at Denbigh,

D. D. Miller and wife, Maggie, church leaders at Protection for many years

Virginia, and Miller at Berlin, Ohio. When the conference changed to overseer administration, Milo Kauffman served as overseer 1955-1964. He was followed by Howard Zehr, 1964-1966, and I. R. Lind, 1966-1969. A Kansas Area Overseer Committee, composed of Edward Yutzy, John Lederach, and Gideon Yoder, provided oversight of the Kansas churches in 1969-1970, prior to the beginning of the Conference Minister position by Millard Osborne in 1970.

Of the ministers, N. E. Ebersole was the only active minister for a time after George R. Brunk left in 1910. Ebersole moved to Peabody, Kansas, in 1923. Ben Horst moved to California in 1910. George Landis lived here briefly from about 1910 to about 1913. L. C. Miller was ordained in 1922 and sent to a pastorate at Limon, Colorado. D. D. Miller was called to be pastor at Manchester, Oklahoma, where he was ordained in 1918. The next year, however, he returned to Protection to serve his home church as a minister. He was ordained bishop in 1926. Charles Schweitzer was ordained minister in 1935; he served until 1953, when he moved to Moscow, Kansas, to serve as pastor in another denomination. Glen Yoder, after being ordained in his home congregation in Cass County,

Missouri, taught school near Protection 1945-1947, and assisted in the ministry. From Protection he went to Kansas City to head up the child welfare program there. Clayton Beyler was ordained here in April 1944 at the request of the Mennonite Board of Missions and Charities, to do relief work in India and China, where he served two years. He then preached at Protection, 1947-1948, after which he joined the faculty of Hesston College, where he became dean in 1971, serving until his sudden death in October 1973. Simon Hershberger made his home at Protection in 1948, and preached occasionally until his death in 1949.

In September 1954 Sanford Oyer, of Fisher, Illinois, who had married Virginia Lee Baker, a Protection girl, was installed as pastor and he served until after ground was broken for the new church in 1966. He supplemented his support with a thriving automotive business. He served on the Executive Committee of the conference, and headed the local ministerial association. He moved to Wooster, Ohio, to a full-time pastorate there.

Wesley Veatch, a Disciples of Christ minister, began serving as interim pastor in August, 1966, preaching three Sundays a month. Nevin Miller, of Hesston, preached the fourth Sunday. Veatch assisted in the dedication of the new church, and filled in until Alvin Beachy arrived from Lenoir City, Tennessee, in August 1967. In addition to teaching school at Coldwater, Beachy was ordained on November 5, and installed as pastor of the Protection congregation. In 1970 Beachy moved to Indiana to become pastor of the North Leo congregation. In January 1971 Robert Yoder moved from Shedd, Oregon, and served until his resignation in 1972. From July 1972 the congregation was served part time by Dave Robinson, a Friends pastor from Coldwater. In June 1974 John Heyerly became pastor.

Of the deacons of this congregation, Jacob Zimmerman died in 1917, just as the church building was being remodeled. John Schrock moved away about 1922. S. Enos Miller was ordained deacon by S. C. Miller in 1918. This was the first ordination in the congregation. Miller moved to Hesston in 1920 to teach there, and returned to Protection in 1931. He died in 1971, at the age of ninety-seven, and was followed a few months later by his wife, Ursula. Charles Schweitzer was ordained deacon in 1922.

There are some changes in the observance of the church ordinances. Previous to 1958 the semiannual communion service was held on Sunday morning. Since then, it is sometimes conducted on Sunday evening. Earlier, foot washing was held following the communion service. More recently it is conducted in a separate service, sometimes in the evening. The holy kiss is practiced in connection with the foot washing service.

Believers' baptism is practiced, but most of the children ask for this ordinance between the ages of eight and twelve. The majority of the older sisters wear the prayer veiling in worship. Since 1960 some of the younger sisters wear it only at certain times — some only at baptism.

This congregation is still chiefly agricultural, as there is no industrial employment. The majority of the farmers are landowners. But farms are larger, and it is hard to get more land. Some are turning from wheat to dairy and beef cattle. Others have wheatland in Colorado — a kind of "twilight" farming. Since some of the young people must move away to make a living, the congregation may not grow much more. But the church at Protection should live for many years.[30]

8. *Hesston, Harvey County*

Possibly the most spectacular growth of congregations in the South Central Mennonite Conference has occurred at Hesston, Kansas, in Harvey County, only three miles from the pioneer Pennsylvania Church. Hesston is within the circle of the four original congregations of central Kansas. But up to 1909 there was no Mennonite congregation in Hesston. Three Mennonite families lived there at that date, but they were on the northwestern border of the Pennsylvania community. There was no prospect of another Mennonite church in that area.

But the founding of a Mennonite school in the West and its location at Hesston brought students and new families to the town, and a congregation was organized on October 3, 1909, several weeks after Hesston Academy and Bible School opened its doors. The organization was effected by Bishop T. M. Erb, who was also business manager and one of the prime promoters of the new school. The following were the twenty-six charter members: Mr. and Mrs. D. H. Bender from Scottdale, Pennsylvania; Mr. and Mrs. C. Hertzler, Mr. and Mrs. A. L. Hess, and Mr. and Mrs. C. M. Hostetler, from the Pennsylvania Church; Mr. and Mrs. C. W. Miller and daughter Fannie and son Ray, from Protection, Kansas; Mr. and Mrs.

Abram L. Hess, pioneer for whom the town of Hesston is named, and donor of land on which Hesston College was built

J. D. Charles from Kansas City; Mr. and Mrs. J. A. Cooprider and their daughters Stella, Grace, and Ruth, from West Liberty; Mr. and Mrs. J. M. Brunk and Roy Ebersole, a student, from La Junta, Colorado, Mr. and Mrs. J. T. Landes and their daughter Rosa, from Spring Valley; J. B. Kanagy from Allensville, Pennsylvania. Of these charter members, in 1974 only Ruth Cooprider Zook is living and holding membership in the Hesston congregation.

On the same day, the Sunday school was organized with J. M. Brunk as superintendent, J. D. Charles as assistant, J. B. Kanagy and Roy Ebersole as choristers, and Stella Cooprider as secretary.

The congregation was received into the Kansas-Nebraska Conference a week later in the regular 1909 session at the Pennsylvania Church. The first communion service was held on April 2, 1911.

The school at first was careful not to disturb the congregational stability of the nearby Pennsylvania Church, or "PA.," as it came to be called by the students. Services at Hesston were held on Sunday afternoon and evening. By the summer of 1911, however, the regular services of the congregation were changed to Sunday morning. For many years, students and Hesston members attended special services at Pennsylvania. Students often walked part way on the railroad tracks to make the distance shorter. It was a place for young people to go on dates.

T. M. Erb served as bishop until 1912, when D. H. Bender, who was the principal of the school, was also ordained as bishop. The ordination was at Pennsylvania, in charge of Albrecht Schiffler, assisted by T. M. Erb and David Garber. Four men were in the lot. Bender was bishop of the congregation until he resigned in 1930, both as bishop and as president of Hesston College. Harry A. Diener was then a non-resident bishop until Milo F. Kauffman, Bender's successor as president of Hesston College, was ordained by lot to the bishop's office. He served until the congregation accepted the new overseer pattern of the South Central Conference in 1954.

The first pastor at Hesston was J. D. Charles, dean of the college. With the president of the college as bishop and the dean as pastor, it is evident how interlocked the administration at Hesston was. This was accentuated by the fact that for forty-seven years the congregation worshiped in facilities rented from the college. There was needed very little formal congregational organization. There

Milo Kauffman, for many years president of Hesston College and bishop of the Hesston congregation

A winter scene of the Hesston College campus. There were only three buildings for decades: Green Gables, a dormitory; the Ad Building, with offices, classrooms, and a chapel which served the congregation as a church; and a small frame gymnasium.

was little business, other than for someone to agree on the annual rent to be paid the college: this was $175 for many years. There was no constitution until 1933. No church records were kept before that time. Someone must have made some decisions. But it is only a matter of memory who it was, and what the decisions were. Pastors were always full-time faculty men, and could give only marginal time to ministering to the congregation.

Pastoral terms during this period were as follows: J. D. Charles, from the beginning to the time of his death, 1923; Noah Oyer, Charles' successor as dean, 1923 (ordained September 30)-1924; I. E. Burkhart, 1924-1925; D. H. Bender, 1925-1928; I. E. Burkhart, 1928-1934; Milo Kauffman, 1934-1940; M. A. Yoder, 1940-1943; Jess A. Kauffman, 1944-1949; John P. Duerksen, 1950. Partial support was given to the pastor from 1944.

Between 1951 and July 1952 the congregation had no pastor. Deacon Harold Sommerfeld coordinated the church program and chaired the worship services. Ministers of the community, of whom there were several on the faculty, were invited to occupy the pulpit.

Ivan R. Lind was given one-third support as pastor in 1952-1958. Full support was first given to Edwin I. Weaver, whose term was cut short in 1959 by a call to a Mission Board assignment in Nigeria. Peter B. Wiebe's pastorate extended from 1959 to 1972, almost thirteen years; only the fourteen-year term of J. D. Charles was longer. However, one year of that time Charles was on leave for graduate study. In 1972 Richard J. Yordy came from Illinois to become pastor at Hesston. Wiebe moved to Smithville, Ohio.

The congregation purchased a parsonage in 1958, but sold it again when Pastor Wiebe preferred to purchase his own home in the country.

Peter Wiebe found that the growth of the congregation made assistance in the pastorate imperative. So Jerry Weaver was licensed as assistant to the pastor in June 1965. He was followed by James Horsch, who was ordained in 1966 for this assignment. Horsch went to Mennonite Publishing House, Scottdale, Pennsylvania, in 1968 for editorial work, and Wiebe had no assistant until Duane Beck, a son of the congregation, arrived to spend a year as a pastoral intern. He was followed by another theological student from the congregation, Ronald Brunk, who interned at Hesston for a year, to 1971.

These assistant pastors have been fully supported by the congregation.

Following the traditional Mennonite system of a threefold ministry, B. F. Buckwalter, the deacon at Pennsylvania, was "borrowed" for deacon functions at Hesston in the first years. Then E. W. Byler, a deacon from Bethel in Missouri, moved to the community and was accepted as the deacon. J. L. Shellenberger also moved in from Spring Valley and served as called upon between 1920 and 1926. S. Enos Miller, who came to teach, had been ordained as deacon at Protection. A. N. Troyer was the only deacon to be ordained by the congregation. He was ordained in 1933 and died in 1954. Harold Sommerfeld had been ordained deacon at Pleasant Valley, Harper, Kansas, and when he moved to Hesston in 1946 to go into business, he was welcomed to serve as a deacon, and he coordinated the church program for a time when there was no pastor.

A constitution, first adopted in 1933, has been revised five times since then. One revision provided for a church council. The 1957 revision changed the council to a board of elders. Harold Sommerfeld was the first chairman of this Board. Other members of this first Board were Clayton Beyler, Justus Holsinger, M. A. Yoder, and Chester Osborne. The later revisions replaced the bishop with an area overseer, in line with conference action, provided for a full-time supported pastor, and dispensed with the office of deacon. The congregation secured a state charter in 1966.

The congregation for many years met in the chapel-auditorium which served the school. At first this was the first floor, north wing, of Green Gables. This, of course, was all one room. When the Administration Building was erected in 1919, the auditorium moved to the entire west side of the main floor of that building, now used for offices. The raised platform, large enough for all programs, was across the south end of the room, with the pulpit in the middle. Often the crowds attending filled the hall that ran through the middle of the building. The privilege of using classrooms for Sunday school, of course, gave the congregation much better educational facilities than most churches of the time had.

In the late forties, planning was begun for a new place of worship. The erection of Hess Hall had made available a larger room for mass meetings and for regular church services after 1950. But its use as a gymnasium by the school made it rather unsatisfactory for a place of worship. The congregation at last was feeling a responsibility for providing its own meeting place.

The growth of the church through the years made it clear that a better meeting place was imperative. These are some membership figures: 1909 — 25; 1920 — 111; 1932 — 120; 1937 — 185; 1940 — 190; 1950 — 343; 1961 — 401; 1971 — 525. Many of the new members were transfers from other Mennonite churches.

Several factors contributed to the rapid growth of the congregation. One was the growth in enrollment of Hesston College, from a mere handful in the beginning and again during the Depression, in the thirties, to over 400 in 1972. Another factor was the development of Hesston as a retirement center, especially in the rapid growth of Schowalter Villa, founded in 1961 and with a guest list of 103 in 1972, a number of whom belong to the congregation and many of whom attend its services. But by far the greatest factor is the development, through Mennonite initiative, of industry which gives employment to a large number of Mennonites who have made their homes in Hesston or the nearby countryside. The population of the town of Hesston has more than quadrupled within thirty years.

We have noticed the rapid growth of the Pennsylvania congregation when it moved to Hesston as the Whitestone Church. The factors noted above contributed also to the growth of Whitestone. There is in Hesston a third Mennonite church, intended to be inter-Mennonite, but largely made up of General Conference Mennonites who live in the community (see p. 354). The concentration of Mennonites in the area has made Hesston a leading center for Mennonitism in the Midwest. This is especially true of the (Old) Mennonite Church, and still more so, of the South Central Conference. This gives the Hesston congregation unusual influence and responsibility.

And so it was apparent, early in the forties, that the congregation which was for so long using college facilities needed a church building. And yet, since the college needed better chapel facilities and classrooms for the Bible Department, a plan of cooperation was devised in which the cost of construction would be shared by the Hesston congregation and the Mennonite Board of Education. The building would be available to both the church and the college, with maintenance also shared.

The new building was to be on the campus; it would have a

The Hesston Corporation, manufacturers of farm machinery, produced a windrower among other contributions to agriculture. This machine introduced a new era in hay farming. The corporation, with branches in Italy, France, Utah, Illinois, and Wisconsin, has over 1,100 employees at the main plant in Hesston.

sanctuary, classrooms to the rear, and an educational wing extending to the side. Ground was broken on June 14, 1953, and the educational wing was built first. The builders were Mennonites — F. G. Roupp and his son Paul. This wing was completed in 1954. The next year work was begun on the main part of the building which was dedicated on May 27, 1956. E. M. Yost preached the dedication sermon. However, the first service in the new church was the funeral of its builder, Frank G. Roupp, who had died suddenly after seeing this last contract through to completion.

The sanctuary has a total seating capacity of 690. The cost of the project was $187,000, of which the congregation paid $110,000. The remainder was paid by the Mennonite Board of Education.

The continued growth of the congregation has posed continued problems concerning facilities. A divided Sunday morning service has become a necessity, and there has been experimentation on the format of this divided service. At this writing (1972) the nine o'clock service is of the usual type and is attended chiefly by the resident members and their families. At ten o'clock there is Sunday school, with classes in the church building and in the various college buildings. At eleven o'clock there is a less conventional and more varied type of service. Most of the students attend this hour.

The congregation has also shared with the Board of Education in the cost of the new Music Hall erected in 1971. The basement of this building, which has a floor space equal to the present sanctuary, is designed for the youth program and other educational and social purposes of the congregation. It is air-conditioned, and can be used for larger summer meetings.

Until 1940 the Hesston Mennonite Church met expenses by membership assessments. Monthly offerings were taken for various causes in the church program. In the business meeting on January 1, 1940, it was decided to discontinue the assessment program and have a schedule of freewill offerings for every Sunday morning. This plan was used until 1952. At this date the budget system of giving was adopted. A stewardship enlistment program was carried through in 1964, using the materials prepared by Daniel Kauffman, Stewardship Secretary of Mennonite General Conference. The budget adopted in 1952 was $24,367. By 1972 this had increased to $87,352. The per capita annual giving has grown to $164.

A few outstanding events and features in the life of the Hesston congregation may be noted.

A. L. Hess and C. Hertzler were the first owners of automobiles, in 1911 and 1912. D. H. Bender bought one in 1914. But he had to go to Wichita to have lights and speedometer installed. The first owners of cars frequently used them to help their neighbors. D. H. Bender's diary notes that he "brought Mrs. M. D. Landis and infant son from Bethel Hospital," and that he took a wheel of C. Hertzler's Ford to Newton for him. Cars did not become common until 1916.

The first funeral was for Mrs. Adeline Egleson in 1911. It is not certain that she was a member of the congregation. The second funeral was of Mrs. Samuel Wenger in 1914. She was a member. The congregation never started a cemetery. Most of the dead have been buried in the Pennsylvania Cemetery, which is now jointly administered with Whitestone. Its name was changed to East Lawn Cemetery in March 1972.

The first marriage of members was that of James A. Kauffman and Mabel Erb in 1912. The first marriage in the church auditorium united Paul Erb and Alta Mae Eby in 1917. This was in the

North Lawn, the music building on the Hesston College campus

Administration Building, before construction was completed, and the audience sat on rough board seats.

On a frosty night in 1918, when the war spirit was at its height, several men of the community raised a flag on top of the pavilion, a little shelter at the center of the campus. The next morning D. H. Bender took the flag down, folded it, and called a responsible person in the community and told him he could have it if he would call for it. On another occasion a mob from McPherson came fully organized to tar and feather the leaders of school and congregation. They stopped at a farm north of town to get details about where the leaders lived. The farmer immediately announced the presence of the mob in the community, whereupon they left and returned to McPherson without carrying out their plans.

The first strictly Mennonite summer Bible school was conducted by Noah Oyer at Hesston in 1923.[31] Since 1960 the summer Bible schools have been held jointly with the other churches in town, each contributing teachers, pupils, and facilities.

A tragic accident was the drowning of Ellen Hertzler, youngest daughter of C. Hertzler, when a canoe capsized in the mill race at Goshen, Indiana, in 1933. The funeral services were held both at Goshen and at Hesston.

In 1940 Bishop Milo Kauffman presented the question of using individual communion cups. The congregation approved this change. Other changes included the first use of church bulletins about 1942 and in 1942 the first consecration services for children born into homes of members of the congregation.

In the fall of 1955 the foot washing service was, for the first time, held separately from the communion service. Communion continues to be observed at the time of the regular Sunday morning service, twice a year, and is well attended. The foot washing service has been held at different times, usually Wednesday or Sunday evening near the time of the communion service. It is not attended by all the members.

Congregational singing of the church has always been without instruments. In 1963, however, it was agreed to permit the use of an organ for weddings, funerals, and perhaps other special services. The next year the congregation voted to purchase a pipe organ. This was installed in 1965, and is used regularly for prelude, offertory, postlude, and special numbers. Congregational singing continues to be unaccompanied at this writing.

Air-conditioning was installed for the pastor's offices and the Mothers' Room in 1968. A proposal for air-conditioning in the sanctuary was voted down, possibly as a reaction of younger people against a growing affluence.

A Women's Council, the first in the South Central district, was organized under the leadership of Pastor Edwin Weaver in 1958. A constitution was drawn up in 1966, later revised and adopted. The council functions in a vital way in the life of the church. From the beginning women have served on the faculty of Hesston College. This has tended to give them an influential part of congregational and conference life, particularly in Christian education, where they have served as teachers and superintendents, and in sewing and service groups, where they have given the conference real leadership. At this writing (1972) the secretary, the treasurer, and the secretaries of literature and girls' activities of the conference Women's Missionary and Service Commission are from Hesston. Lois Amstutz, of this congregation, is one of a number of members who hold responsibilities in the denominational organization. She is a member of the Overseas Missions committee of the Board of Missions. Mrs. Elva Dyck became a member of the Hesston College Board of Trustees in 1973.

The traditional Mennonite head veil is no longer used by all the women. Some use another form of veiling in church; others are bareheaded. Few wear hats in church.

When the city of Hesston was first incorporated in 1921, T. M. Erb became the president of the council. As business manager of the college he was concerned to protect and promote the interests of the college. The office was nonpolitical. He resigned this office in May 1922.

In recent years Harold Dyck, of the Hesston congregation, served as mayor of the city. At this writing he is also a representative in the state legislature.

The trend in recent years has been toward a more congregational form of church government. The term "subject to the will of the congregation" appears frequently in the constitution and in the minutes of church proceedings. As elders and church officers, laymen are increasingly responsible for the standards and the life of the church.

The mission spirit has always been strong at Hesston. Outreach is the largest item on the budget. Various missionaries have been totally supported. Several members have become career missionaries; Milton Vogt gave his entire life of service to India, and is buried in Bihar. The congregation has worked with the college in mission projects in Newton, Hutchinson, and Wichita. Many young people have given voluntary service in our own and in other countries.

Some people in the conference think of Hesston as being a place of affluence. The members of the congregation here recognize the challenge of using prosperity for the extension of the kingdom.

What has become Mennonite Disaster Service (MDS) had its beginning in a suggestion made by Dr. F. S. Brenneman in a Sunday school class at Hesston in 1950. It was first called Mennonite Service Organization (MSO). The first opportunity for service came during a flood in Wichita. Some of the men quipped that MSO stood for Mighty Soaked Outfit. This organization soon became inter-Mennonite and nationwide. John Diller of Hesston has given years of effective leadership as a contact man and area coordinator.[32]

9. *Yoder, Reno County*

Since Yoder is one of the more common names among Mennonites, one might suppose that the Yoder Mennonite Church in Reno County, Kansas, took the name of some prominent member of the church. But the church gets its name from the village of Yoder, one mile to the south; it was in a store building in this village that the congregation was first organized. Then one might think that the village got its name from some Mennonite settler. Wrong again. When the Missouri Pacific Railroad built a branch line northwest from Wichita in 1887, it located a station on the farm of Eli M. Yoder, who later built a store here, and the place took his name.

But Eli Yoder was never a Mennonite. He was the son of an Amish bishop who lived near Baltimore, Maryland. In 1874 Eli went West, and bought 320 acres of land twelve miles southeast of Hutchinson, Kansas, from a man who had homesteaded it. He married a girl named Mary Young, who was not Amish, and he left the Amish Church. When Amish families came to this area about ten years later, Eli did not unite with them, but rather wanted to conceal his Amish origin. He moved to Hutchinson in his later years, where he was a justice of the peace.

Four months after Yoder came West he was followed by E. F. Peachey, whose father was also an Amish preacher, probably in the "Big Valley" of central Pennsylvania. Peachey had never joined the Amish Church, and like Yoder, he did not join the Amish who later came to the Yoder community. He lived on a homestead claim south of Yoder, but soon gave it up. He married a Miss Moore. Later he went to Colorado to work in the mines. He was baptized by the Baptists. He remembered his Amish home training with appreciation.

In the fall of 1874 John Naftzinger, a young Amish lad from Maryland, came to Kansas to visit his uncle, Eli M. Yoder. He married Emma Young, sister of Mrs. Yoder, and bought a farm. He also left the Amish Church, of which he had been a member, and would not come back when an Amish community developed in this area.

The first Amish families to come to the Yoder community were those of Christian H. Miller, a minister, and his son, Christian C. They came to Kansas from Shelby County, Illinois, in 1883.

The same summer three Amish families came to Partridge, southwest of Hutchinson. They were the Christian Bylers, from Indiana, and the Christian E. Bontragers and the Abraham Nisleys, from Shelbyville, Illinois. Bontrager was a bishop, the leading Amish bishop in the Amish churches of Kansas for a long time.

In 1884 other Amish families came to Reno County. They came

from Illinois, Indiana, Ohio, and Pennsylvania. Family names were Bontrager, Yoder, Miller, Schrock, and Stahly. The reasons for coming were chiefly economic: cheap land, milder climate, easily worked soil. They were too late for homesteads, but proved-up claims and railroad land were available for a few dollars per acre. The Santa Fe Railroad had been built to Hutchinson and beyond, and the new settlers came in by train.

Life was primitive and rigorous, although the Amish were urged to build roomy houses as soon as possible, so that there would be places to have church. First houses were often dugouts or sod. The roof was made of poles, blue-stem grass, and sod. Cows would pasture on the grass roofs. As long as there were buffalo, someone had to stay at home to shake a sheet at the heavy beasts to prevent their crashing through the dugout roof. One man brought his wife from Illinois and showed her their house — a dugout. She said, "You expect me to live in that?" and started to weep. But they lived there and raised a family.

For fuel the settlers burned dried buffalo chips, which they gathered on the prairie, and stacked along the house. They also burned cornstalks, and corn, when it was very cheap. When meat was scarce they ate rabbits. They took their wheat to Murdock for grinding, where there was a mill on the Ninescah River. They could make the round trip in a day. They had green vegetables in the summer, and buried cabbage and apples for the winter. They used rope beds, with ticks of chopped straw, or perhaps of goose feathers. Trundle beds for the children could be kept by day under the big beds. They made most of their own clothes, sometimes spinning their own wool.

At first mail was brought daily from Wichita by a pony hitched to a two-wheeled cart, and distributed from some farmer's house, later from a post office in Yoder.

From a small start the churches grew and multiplied. By 1918 there were six Amish congregations of about seventy-five members each — two in the Partridge community and four in the Yoder community.

These churches placed great stress on old customs and the manners of the fathers. They held their church services in private houses, and they did not accept automobiles, telephones, and electricity in their homes. They ruled that tractors could be used for belt work but not for pulling field implements. But more serious, they refused, in the Yoder churches, to allow Bible teaching through Sunday schools. Tobacco, for smoking and chewing, was freely used among them. There were reports of low moral standards, drunkenness, and some lawbreaking among the young people.

Some parents wanted better spiritual privileges for their children. They asked for Sunday schools and were refused. Out of these tensions came the beginnings of a Mennonite church at Yoder.

Two families, the A. O. Millers and Will Schrocks, became members at West Liberty, twenty-five miles north of Yoder. They moved to western Kansas, but soon returned to Medora, a town between Hutchinson and West Liberty. With help from Hesston, they began in the winter of 1917 to hold services in the school at Medora, and other families from Yoder attended, and were applying for membership at West Liberty.

War sentiment at Medora, however, stopped the services there. Pastor C. D. Yoder of West Liberty and D. H. Bender and L. O. King of Hesston decided to interview the Amish ministers at Yoder. A meeting was arranged for March 1, 1918, and about twelve Amish ministers and bishops discussed the situation at length with the Mennonite ministers and some interested members. Not much was accomplished. That same evening L. O. King and C. D. Yoder held services in the home of D. J. Yoder, some forty being present. The children that were there caused the group to announce Sunday school for March 10.

Fifty were present that first Sunday. The Sunday school was organized by D. H. Bender and B. F. Buckwalter from Hesston. Buckwalter was appointed as superintendent and D. J. Yoder as secretary-treasurer. By this time ten persons from Yoder had united with West Liberty. They were D. J. Yoder and wife, J. E. Yoder and wife, Jerry Schrock, Clarence Schrock, Abe F. Miller and wife, and Dan J. Headings and wife.

There was great joy in the prospect of a Sunday school at Yoder. The meetings were held at the Harmony School, one mile south of Yoder. The first teachers were D. H. Bender and wife, Esther Good, Emma Risser, Edward Yoder, and Silas Horst, all from Harvey County. Edward Yoder spent the summer in the community as separator man for thresherman J. E. Yoder.

On July 4, with 143 people present, the first baptismal service was held, with T. M. Erb officiating. These eight people were baptized: Tobias, Manasseh, and Aaron Yoder, Joseph Kauffman, Samuel and Mary Beachy, Barbara Hostetler, and Elizabeth Bontrager. They were received as members at West Liberty.[33]

By this time Harmony School was too small, and from July 21 on, the Sunday school met at the Laurel School, two miles northeast of Yoder. Other teachers from Hesston and West Liberty joined the teaching staff. And other members were received from time to time — by letter, confession, or baptism.

Opposition grew, and in spite of the pleadings of Gladys Van Buren, the teacher of Laurel School, the Amish directors ordered the building vacated after January 26, 1919. For the next three Sundays the service was held in a tenant house on the J. E. Yoder farm. But this was much too small.

Then A. M. Switzer, a businessman in Yoder, offered the use of an empty store building. The first service was held there on February 23. An offering of $60 was lifted to pay the rent and to buy some lumber to make benches. On February 28, evangelist C. F. Derstine arrived and preached seven sermons. At these evening meetings Amish boys who did not dare to come in stood outside to enjoy the singing.

On March 2, just a year after the work started, the attendance was 156.

L. O. King and family moved to Yoder on March 28. He had been ordained some years before for the congregation at Manchester, Oklahoma. He had also served at Peabody, and lived briefly at Hesston. He was installed as pastor at Yoder, and served faithfully until his sudden death on December 3, 1940.

On April 18, 1919 (Good Friday), a separate congregation was organized and named Yoder Mennonite Church. Three services were held that day, with addresses by T. M. Erb, D. H. Bender, J. D. Charles, and C. D. Yoder. There were sixty charter members, most of them transferred by letter from West Liberty. Five more were added that day, the result of the Derstine meetings.

The evening meeting on April 18, 1919, was in the nature of a business meeting. B. F. Buckwalter was asked to serve temporarily as deacon. And by a unanimous rising vote it was decided to proceed immediately with the building of a church. All necessary committees were elected that night, and within twelve days a second meeting was called, at which a building site and building plans were approved. The site was on the northwest corner of the J. E. Yoder farm, one mile north of Yoder. L. O. King was a car-

The Switzer building in Yoder, Kansas, where the Yoder congregation was organized. Note the crowd of Amish boys.

penter, and gave his full time at first to the erection of the new church. He never received a salary for his work as pastor. After the church was built he purchased a farm north of the Arkansas River, and made his living as a dairy farmer.

First communion services were held on May 4, 1919, with D. H. Bender and T. M. Erb officiating. On August 17 the building was far enough along that services could be held in the basement. The dedication was held on December 7, with D. H. Bender preaching the sermon. The same week a Bible normal was held at the church, conducted by C. Z. Yoder and J. M. Brunk. The locating committee had been made up of A. F. Bontrager, J. E. Yoder, and Clarence P. Schrock. The building committee consisted of D. J. Yoder, A. F. Bontrager, J. E. Yoder, A. J. Miller, and John G. Kauffman. The first trustees were D. J. Yoder, chairman; D. J. Headings, secretary; and J. H. Kauffman, treasurer. The members of the first finance committee were J. H. Kauffman, A. F. Miller, and Sam M. Miller.

In February 1921 Harry A. Diener and family moved to this community from Proctor, Missouri, the Ozark mission field. He assisted in the ministry until February 1923, when he was ordained to the office of bishop by lot. The ordination took place at the West

The Yoder Church as it appeared in 1919

Liberty Church, and C. D. Yoder was also in the lot. The purpose of the ordination was to give assistance to T. M. Erb and D. H. Bender in their bishop district. But Diener also assumed bishop charge of the Yoder congregation. In March 1963 a special service was held in recognition of his having served forty years as bishop. During this time he was widely used in the conference and denomination in various administrative assignments. He was moderator of General Conference 1939-1941. In August 1964 he was released by the Yoder congregation to serve as interim pastor at Sycamore Grove, Garden City, Missouri. In October 1965 he went to Gulfport, Mississippi, and was pastor of the Gulfhaven congregation until December 1970.

In September 1971 Diener requested, and was granted, retirement from official responsibility in the Yoder congregation. In appreciation for his fifty years of service here, the congregation conferred on him the title of bishop emeritus. During this time he suffered three great personal losses. One was the accident in which his car struck and killed an 18-month-old son in 1929. Another was the sudden passing of his wife, Amanda, in November 1958. The third was the burning of his farm home in April 1960, with the loss of all contents, including records, books, and sermon outlines.

His later years were brightened by his marriage to Anna Kreide Bender. In 1973, in his eighty-sixth year, he lived in the smalle house on his old farm, keeping busy in helping with the dairy work making garden, reading, and doing much visiting.

The first ordination to the ministry at Yoder was that o Clarence A. Bontrager in October 1927. He was ordained for the work at Lyman, Mississippi, where he served three years. Whe he returned he assisted at Yoder until his death following an accide in 1934. In July 1938 his younger brother Andrew was ordaine by lot to the ministry, and in 1973 was still preaching as called upo

In 1942 and 1943, within a year's time, five young men o the congregation were ordained to the ministry. Edward Diener, so of Bishop Diener, was called by voice of the congregation in Marc 1942. He later served pastorates at Clarence Center, New York; Hart ville, Ohio; and Pettisville, Ohio. Leroy Schrock, who had earlie given six months to the Kansas City Mission, was ordained whil in Civilian Public Service at Downey, Idaho, in January 1943. He was ordained for the Exeland, Wisconsin, congregation, movin later to Glen Flora nearby, where he still is pastor. Richar Showalter was ordained in June 1942 for a pastorate at Perryton Texas. He is now engaged in psychological counseling. In Novembe 1942 Donald King, son of L. O. King, was ordained to assis Gideon G. Yoder at Crystal Springs, Harper, Kansas, where he ha been laboring for over a year. He left Crystal Springs for seminar training at Goshen, and then held pastorates at Pigeon, Michiga and at Whitestone, Hesston, Kansas. He later became a hospita chaplain at Lebanon, Oregon. In February 1943 Sanford E. King oldest son of L. O. King, was ordained to serve as pastor-superin tendent of the Hutchinson Mission. He served there when the mis sion became the Pershing Street Church. During this ministry h served also on the Executive Committee of the Mennonite Board o Education and as moderator of the South Central Conference. Afte his Pershing Street ministry closed in 1967 he served as interi pastor of the General Conference Mennonite Church at Kingma Kansas. He died in March 1974.

Rudy M. Bontrager was ordained by lot to service as deacon i October 1923. This was the first ordination at Yoder Church. Bon trager served until his death in 1929. The next year Deacon D. C Schrock moved to this community from Crystal Springs, and serve the congregation as deacon until his death in November 1960

Levi Headings was ordained as deacon in 1935.

In June 1951 Edward Yutzy was chosen by lot to assist Harry Diener in the ministry. When Diener was released to serve at Sycamore Grove, Yutzy, in August 1964, was installed as pastor. Since 1969 he has given all his time to the work of the congregation and the conference.

In August 1946 Daniel Kauffman answered the call to serve the congregation at Cherry Box, Missouri, and was ordained for the pastorate there. Later he was ordained as bishop, and served a number of years as overseer of the Missouri churches.

In 1931 the Yoder and the West Liberty congregations cooperated in beginning mission work in Hutchinson. Through the donations, contributions, and sacrificial labors of many, the mission grew into the Pershing Street Mennonite Church, with a church building and a parsonage. A number of the Yoder members became members at Pershing Street.

In 1944 the congregation celebrated its twenty-fifth anniversary in an Easter weekend meeting. Visiting speakers included Edward Yoder, Scottdale, Pennsylvania, and H. S. Bender, Goshen, Indiana. By this time the membership had grown to 313, most of whom were farmers. About this time a large military base was established west of Yoder. This changed somewhat the character of the community, and many families, both Amish and Mennonite, moved away. The period of rapid growth was over.

One by one the usual activities of a Mennonite congregation were begun. In 1918 Emma Risser organized a sewing circle which met in homes until 1921. A reading circle began to meet in 1929, with Anna E. King as the chief promoter. This developed into a youth fellowship by 1956. Summer Bible school began in 1936, and a Christian Workers' Band in 1938.

In 1948 the Yoder congregation was host to the South Central Conference. The meetings were held in a tent. Special guests at this conference were two Mennonite ministers from Europe: Pierre Widmer, from Grand-Charmont, par Montbeliard, Doubs, France, and Christian Schnebele, from the Thomashof near Karlsruhe, Germany.

In 1950 discussions began on the enlargement of the church building. In a special meeting in 1951 a study was reported which showed the need for more auditorium room and classrooms, indoor rest rooms, and a larger entrance. A remodeling program was approved and a building committee appointed. On December 31, 1951, the plans were approved, and a finance committee was appointed. Work was begun in April 1952.

An intermediate department of the Sunday school was organized in September 1952, but for lack of room did not begin operating until the completion of the remodeling in January 1953. Dedication services were conducted on Easter Sunday, with the sermon preached by B. Charles Hostetter, Mennonite Hour Broadcast preacher. Other speakers were J. H. Kauffman, S. E. King, A. J. Kauffman, J. J. Bontrager, and H. A. Diener. In 1965 the church basement was further improved with a ceiling and partitions for classrooms.

The South Central Conference in 1953 was held in the 4-H Building on the State Fairgrounds in Hutchinson. The Brunk Brothers Revival Campaign was conducted at the same time. Conference sessions were held during the day, August 18-21, and the evangelistic sermons were preached each evening in a large tent, continuing to August 30. Working together in hosting these meetings were the Yoder, Hutchinson, West Liberty, Hesston, and Pennsylvania congregations.

The spring Mission Board meeting and the sewing circle meeting of the South Central Conference were held at Yoder in April 1955. The Yoder congregation hosted the conference again in August 1956, but on the Hesston College campus.

A church library was started in the fall of 1956. In 1962 the business meeting decided to purchase individual communion cups.

In 1963 the Extension Convention of the conference, which was the successor to the Mission Board meeting, was held in the Haven High School auditorium, with the Yoder congregation as the host.

The convictions on stewardship and the administration of the congregation's giving have grown through the years. The first Sunday school offering, on May 5, 1918, totaled $2.29. By 1944 congregational expenses had grown to about $900 a year. By 1968 this was about $6,000. An increasing amount has been given to outside causes. Through the years a missionary has been supported. MYF and the primary and intermediate departments have supported missionary children. The business meeting in 1965 decided that one treasurer should handle all church funds. Total giving in 1971 was $48,000, of which $29,000 went to causes other than local expenses.

Since 1966 a church council has assisted the pastor in spiritual administration. The first council consisted of Tom Egli, Edward Roth, and Willard Diener.

The fiftieth anniversary was observed April 4-6, 1969 — a half century after those sixty-five eager believers meeting in Switzer's store were organized into a new congregation. Now there were 271 members, not as many as twenty-five years earlier. But former members were serving the Lord in a variety of callings in twenty-four other states and in three foreign countries. Many were occupying important posts in the program of the Mennonite Church.

In the Yoder congregation itself half of the families no longer had their income directly from the farm. Only 20 percent got all their income from the farm.

Serving on the anniversary program were several of those who had come over from Harvey County to help start the Sunday school at Yoder: Silas Horst, Emma Risser, and Paul Erb. A number of the sons of Yoder who served at other places were on the program: Daniel Kauffman, Leonard, Missouri; Edward Diener, Hartville, Ohio; T. E. Schrock, Clarksville, Michigan; Fred Schrock, Goshen, Indiana; Leroy Schrock, Glen Flora, Wisconsin; Clayton Diener, Hesston, Kansas; S. E. King, Hutchinson, Kansas; Kenneth Bontrager, Denver, Colorado. Guests attended the anniversary from fifteen states. T. C. Yoder was the song leader. And the anniversary closed with a communion service in charge of Harry A. Diener.

The membership in 1971 was 295. Of the original members, only seven were still attending the Yoder Church in August 1972.

An Amish community as a mission field! It was that in 1918. It was difficult to make the break. Jake Yoder lost most of the members of his threshing ring. But the results seem to have been worthwhile. Many were brought into an assurance of salvation. "I never knew that one could know he is saved," said Rudy Bontrager. The moral tone of the community has improved. An evangelistic note has gone out to all the world through preachers, teachers (TAP), relief workers (Pax), missionaries, and medical people. The product of the rich Arkansas Valley supports missions, churches, schools, social services, and hospitals in many places. A mission point in 1918, Yoder has become one of the stronger congregations of the South Central Conference. There have been changes in operation, facilities, and in personnel. But the movement is forward.[34]

10. *South Hutchinson, Reno County*

Hutchinson, a city of 40,000 in central Kansas, lies between two rural churches — West Liberty and Yoder. These two congregations joined their resources to start a mission here in 1931, at the bottom of the Great Depression. As the country Mennonites, rich in farm products for which they hardly had a market, came to town to shop, they became aware of many destitute people in Hutchinson who were in need of food and clothing. They observed, also, that there was unmet spiritual need, particularly in the southeast part of the city.

Alf B. Miller and J. F. Brunk (the same one-armed preacher who helped to start the Kansas City Mission and the La Junta Sanitarium) were appointed to survey the needs and find a location. Distributions began, and these opened the door for a Sunday school. In August 1931 a school was opened in a four-room house at 203 East Park Street. Within a year this was too small, and the Church of the Latter Day Saints at C and Plum streets was secured for afternoon services. Two men and their wives took vows at the first baptismal service in March 1932.

By December 1932 thirty-three people had requested baptism. The church was filled to overflowing, and there was talk of building. Dan Headings, Alf Miller, and Henry Cooprider were appointed as a building committee. In the summer of 1933 thirteen lots at C and Pershing were bought at a sheriff's sale. A basement meeting place took shape, mostly with donated labor and materials. One man gave a carload of cement. The basement church was dedicated August 27, 1933, with Bishop George R. Brunk, brother of J. F. Brunk, preaching the sermon. It was the place of worship for eight years.

By 1935 the drive-in help was not sufficient. Paul and Gertrude Roupp were appointed to be resident workers. In 1936 Paul built a parsonage beside the basement. In 1937 the Hutchinson Mission Mennonite Church was organized with forty-one charter members. The congregation was received into the South Central Conference, and the mission went under the sponsorship of the Conference Mission Board.

In 1939 Paul Roupp returned to his building work at Hesston, and Dan and Susie Headings moved into the parsonage to carry on the mission work for the next twelve years. Relief was less necessary now, and the effort went into visitation, prayer meetings,

The basement church and mission home on Pershing Street in 1933

The Pershing Street Church built in 1941

Bible school, sewing classes, personal work. Preaching was still done by ministers from the country churches. Harry A. Diener and J. G. Hartzler gave bishop oversight to the work. There were baptisms in homes and hospitals, and the church grew. Young families from the country began to make Hutchinson their home church. The first summer Bible school was conducted in 1937, with Mary Miller directing. The enrollment was 205.

In 1941 a church was built on the basement walls, and was dedicated that same year. Material and furnishings of the extinct

Milan Valley congregation at Jet, Oklahoma, were moved to Hutch-inson and went into this church. Dan Headings and others gave of their carpentry skills. The cost of the building above donated ma-terial and labor was a little over $2,000.

In 1943 Sanford E. King, Sunday school superintendent, was ordained and began a 25-year pastorate. He lived in Hutchinson, but not in the parsonage, and supported himself, first in the oil business, and later in the sale of investments. Several other families occupied the parsonage for short periods and gave marginal time to the work until 1956, when the house was remodeled into a Church Activity Center and used for classrooms, pastor's study, MYF activi-ties, and sewing circle.

Sol Zook ministered to the congregation as deacon for a number of years until his death in 1954.

A faulty furnace caused heavy fire damage to the church building on February 11, 1953. Restoration cost about $5,000.

"In 1941 the first of 22 semi-annual Sunday school conferences was held. Themes for these conferences revolved around the home, personal evangelism, spiritual resources, and challenges to mission outreach."[35]

After this year, however, the attendance in both Sunday school and summer Bible school declined somewhat. Transportation furnished to neighborhood children was tapered off, and only those came who were interested enough to walk. There was also, accord-ing to Dwight King's thorough study and analysis, "a stronger thrust toward the total church program."[36] The church membership grew steadily. Although the majority of these lived in Hutchinson and South Hutchinson, an increasing number of families in the church lived in a widely scattered area outside the city. As it got larger, the congregation became less directly attached to the Pershing Street neighborhood. And this area of the city was not growing as were some other areas.

Annual evangelistic meetings were an integral part of the church program, involving the services of many of the denomination's leading evangelists. Some of these were city campaigns in which other churches cooperated. Myron S. Augsburger held two weeks of meetings in Convention Hall, which were well attended; there were a number of confessions. Likewise with a campaign held by George R. Brunk (II) in a tent on the State Fairgrounds.

The annual business meeting in 1962 asked the Men's Fellow-

Dan and Susie Headings, who served in the mission home from 1939-1951

ship to initiate a program for a building fund. Factors leading to this action were inadequate Bible school and Sunday school facilities, bad acoustics in the church, need for more room in the Activity Center for social events, and a growing feeling that the church plant was drab and unattractive.

A members' meeting in May 1963 appointed a committee "to evaluate present property, study effect of relocation, investigate possible relocation in South Hutchinson or other likely location."[37] It was clear that the Pershing Street Mennonite Church had outgrown its facilities and did not feel tied to the location in southeast Hutchinson. This would be a primary concern of the congregation during the next decade, for there were many problems involved of location, financing, the church's mission, leadership, and attitudes of members.

Dwight King, son of the pastor, in the year 1963-1964 made a case study from a sociological point of view of the Pershing Street situation and problem. The study received some subsidy from the church, and the members cooperated in various ways. The conclusions of the study probably aided the congregation in thinking through the problem during these years.

In October 1964 a building committee was elected, and a consulting architect prepared a plan. The committee reported in November

1965 and the congregation accepted the report as a basis for future planning. In March 1966 the congregation adopted a plan for raising $80,000, the estimated cost of the building. There was to be a five-year pledge campaign, and an attractive booklet was prepared to aid in the campaign.

There were problems in translating the plan into a new church building. Sanford King had successfully led the congregation to this point, but he felt led to resign in 1967, although he retained his residence, business, and church membership in Hutchinson. Gideon G. Yoder came from Wellman, Iowa, to serve as the first full-time pastor. He was installed on September 17, 1967, by Allen H. Erb, overseer, assisted by the retiring pastor, Sanford E. King. He did not push the building program, as he felt it important to give priority to a study of mission. His two annual reports to the congregation probed concerning the purposes of the congregation, which he felt had to be clarified before proceeding with a building program. He concluded his interim pastorate in 1969, moving to service in the inter-Mennonite congregation at Hesston, Kansas.

Calvin King and family came to Hutchinson in November 1969 to serve in the pastorate at Pershing Street. A different parsonage had been purchased at 820 East A Street. In extending a call to King, the council said they would be expecting him to push for a new building in the near future. This he did, and building got underway in 1971 on a new site at 808 South Poplar Street in South Hutchinson. There is only one other church in South Hutchinson, and the new location is easily accessible to all the members.

The new church is a brick structure, with an auditorium seating 200, fourteen classrooms, a kitchen, and a fellowship hall.

The first service was held in the new church on Good Friday, March 31, 1972. It is now known as the South Hutchinson Mennonite Church. A celebration service and open house was held on the afternoon of May 7, with special groups and the congregation participating. An offering of appreciation was taken for the South Central Conference.

South Hutchinson in 1972 had 150 members. The per member giving in 1971 was $238.

The church has a new organ. Pershing Street had an organ for a number of years, even though, when it was purchased, "a number of the members," says Alf Miller, congregational historian, "especially the older ones, refused to help in purchasing it, because of the many calls for money needed to carry on missionary work, and because we didn't want to be an influence to other congregations or be an offense to those who object to instruments in worship."[38]

In 1971 South Hutchinson cooperated with First Mennonite (General Conference) to establish a VS unit in Hutchinson at 211 West 11th. In 1972 the unit had three men working at the two hospitals as ambulance drivers, and three girls and one man working at Friendship House, a day-care center for small children.

In the summer of 1972 summer Bible school was held cooperatively with the South Hutchinson United Methodist Church, using facilities and teachers of both congregations.[39]

11. *Greensburg, Kiowa County*

Greensburg, at the western edge of south central Kansas, is in wheat and cattle country. It has 2,000 people. Four large natural gas booster stations afford employment to several hundred men. It is 100 miles west of Wichita, and thirty miles northeast of Protection.

Before 1932, there were three Mennonite-related congregations in the Greensburg area: Church of God in Christ, Mennonite (Holdeman), the largest; General Conference Mennonite (Bethel), without a pastor and at the point of disbanding; and Krimmer Mennonite Brethren, a small but robust group. There were no (Old) Mennonites here.

E. M. Yost had been pastor of the Church of God in Christ, Mennonite congregation six miles southwest of Greensburg. He was ordained as a young man, and had preached for ten years. But he gradually found himself in serious disagreement with some of the doctrinal positions of his church. He was asked to discontinue preaching in the Greensburg area. But he felt a personal call to preach the gospel. Early in 1932 Yost attended a Mennonite ministers' conference at Goshen, Indiana, and took wide counsel concerning his problem.

After consultation with the Executive Committee of the Missouri-Kansas Conference, arrangements were made for C. F. Derstine, dynamic Mennonite evangelist, to conduct a series of meetings in the town of Greensburg. The meetings were held in a large skating rink. Large crowds attended for a period of three

*E. M. Yost, founder of
the Greensburg congregation,
pastor, bishop, evangelist
— a man of great talents*

weeks. Help came from Hesston, Hutchinson, and Protection, including bishops H. A. Diener and D. D. Miller. This was in April 1932.

In the middle of the meetings E. M. Yost and wife were received into the Mennonite Church. By the end of the series, eight others, all from the Bethel Church, became the nucleus of a Mennonite congregation at Greensburg. The building, now called the Tabernacle, was rented for six months and a Sunday school with seventy-five enrolled was organized. Derstine held another series the next fall, and the membership was forty in 1933.

By November of 1932 the little congregation, in spite of drought and economic depression, had purchased a lot and constructed a basement as a church home. I. E. Burkhart, of Hesston, preached the dedication sermon.

After several years, in 1937, another more adequate meeting place became available. The Greensburg schools had moved to a new plant, and the old building on the north side of town was for sale. Some saw possibilities of its being converted into a church building. The basement was sold and the two-story brick structure with a full basement was purchased for $2,000. The remodeling of this building for church use was in stages, and was not completed until 1965. Walls were removed, the roof was lowered, a new entrance was provided, a new floor laid, and a new heating plant purchased. Much of the labor for this remodeling could be furnished by the members. Extensive remodeling in 1953 cost $5,800. There was further remodeling in the basement from 1963 to 1965.

A first dedication was held in 1937, with Allen H. Erb preaching the dedication sermon. At the dedication in 1953 E. M. Yost preached. The congregation rejoiced greatly when this work was completed. The working together at a common task drew the brotherhood together and was a real means of strengthening the congregation.

The membership climbed steadily until a peak of 92 was reached in 1941. Then the war, with its military draft, and the moving away of a number of families, brought the number to a low of 56 in 1946. By 1972 membership had climbed again to 88.

The bulk of the early membership came from the Church of God in Christ, Mennonite. The Krimmer Mennonite Brethren group had now disbanded, and a few families joined the Calvary Church, as the new church was named. In 1962 the Faith General Conference Mennonite congregation, meeting south of Greensburg, was invited as a body to become a part of Calvary, with full rights and duties. This invitation was not accepted, but a number of GC families did become members of the Calvary fellowship, both before and after 1962. The Faith congregation was disbanded, and Calvary in 1965 became the Greensburg Mennonite Church. One (Old) Mennonite family, the Noah Zimmermans, moved from Protection in 1936.

E. M. Yost, the first pastor, was ordained bishop in 1943. H. A. Diener served up to that time. Because Yost was away from home a good deal in evangelistic work, Samuel Janzen, a student at Hesston College and formerly a member of the General Conference Mennonites, was ordained in 1942 to assist him.

In 1944 P. A. Friesen, former missionary to India who had recently helped to organize a congregation in Denver, Colorado, held revival meetings in Greensburg. Negotiations were begun which resulted the next year in an exchange of pulpits: E. M. Yost moved to Denver to begin his significant career of leadership in the Colorado churches, and P. A. Friesen moved to Greensburg. He became bishop and copastor with Samuel Janzen, and Mrs. Friesen, as a practicing physician, opened the way to further Mennonite involvement in the community. Friesen laid down his official responsibilities in 1950, and later retired at Schowalter Villa, Hesston, Kansas, where he died in 1967.

Mennonite Church at Greensburg, Kansas

In 1955 Samuel Janzen moved to Glenwood Springs, Colorado, to administer the Valley View Hospital for the Mennonite Board of Missions and Charities. He had already served five years as hospital administrator at Greensburg. His successor, both as pastor at Calvary and as administrator at the hospital, was Robert Keller, of Illinois. He was the first pastor to receive a regular salary from the congregation.

After Keller left Greensburg in November 1955 Calvary had no resident pastor. Eugene Garber, a student at Hesston College, served as a licensed minister at Greensburg during the 1956-1957 school year, commuting to Greensburg each weekend. H. J. King, long a pastor in Illinois, came in March 1960 for meetings and then remained and was installed as interim pastor. The interim lasted until June 1963. Then Calvin R. King, of Ohio, was ordained and installed and pastor. He also served, and received part of his support, as chaplain of the hospital. After six and a half years at Greensburg, King moved to a pastorate at South Hutchinson. Succeeding him in both the pastorate and the chaplaincy at Greensburg was D. A. Raber, formerly pastor at Tenth Street in Wichita.

After Bishop P. A. Friesen retired in 1950 Earl Buckwalter served as bishop until 1954. Then Milo Kauffman assumed oversight under the overseer plan of the conference.

The congregation has had only one deacon, A. F. Willems, who was ordained in January 1937.

Evangelists who have served include J. D. Mininger, Nelson Kauffman, Maurice O'Connel, B. B. King, H. J. Zehr, Wilbur Yoder, John Duerksen, Kenneth Good, Richard Yordy, Roy Bucher, Frederick Erb, Roy Koch, Edward Miller, and James Detweiler.

A Bible Conference was held in 1936, with Paul Erb as instructor. Jess Kauffman conducted the summer Bible school in 1938. S. G. Shetler spoke in a young people's institute in 1937. Alva Swartzendruber had a Bible study February to March, 1947. J. C. Wenger lectured on Mennonite history in 1946.

Three former members — Wesley Jantz, Paul Holdeman, and Wallace Jantz — have served elsewhere in the ministry.

One of the most effective ways in which the congregation has related to the community is through the hospital. Greensburg was thirty miles from a hospital of any kind, and fifty miles from adequate facilities. Dr. Florence Friesen and other Mennonites encouraged the building of a hospital. The community voted to match federal funds and build a 20-bed hospital.

Who should operate the hospital? Several years earlier E. M. Yost had a vision of the possibility of the Mennonite Church operating a hospital in the Greensburg area. Dr. Florence Friesen's skill and devotion helped to build up the reputation of Mennonites as being persons concerned about the physical and spiritual welfare of humanity. At the suggestion of another doctor and with the support of community leaders, the Mennonite Board of Missions and Charities was contracted to operate the hospital. Wesley Jantz, who was serving as assistant administrator of the Mennonite Hospital at La Junta, was appointed administrator. As a son of the community, he was well known by its people. Lydia Diener was the first Superintendent of Nursing Services.

The hospital was dedicated and formally opened on March 5, 1950. It has given efficient service to the community. The Mennonite congregation also has profited by the location of the hospital here. Several families have moved here for hospital employment. As many as 15 percent of the hospital employees have been Mennonites, and they have participated actively in the church. Two of the pastors have doubled as hospital administrators, and two others as chaplains. This has helped the small congregation to support its pastor, and has enriched the witness of the church.

After Robert Keller's term as administrator, Marie Naffziger held this position for many years (1959-1971). She had earlier served as Director of Nursing Service (1953-1959). She was succeeded by Jerry Unruh in the administrator's office.

Greensburg cooperated with the churches at Larned and Protection in biannual Sunday school conferences. When Larned dropped out, Perryton, Texas, took its place. These contacts through the years have been a mutual help to these isolated congregations.

A highlight for the congregation was the twenty-fifth anniversary on December 1, 1957. All the persons on the program had had a leading part in the life of this church: E. M. Yost, A. F. Willems, Earl Buckwalter, C. F. Derstine, Samuel Janzen, P. A. Friesen, H. A. Diener, Eugene Garber. Derstine followed this program with another series of meetings.

In 1964 the Faith Mennonite Church donated their relatively new pews and pulpit furniture to the Calvary Church. In that same year the business meeting voted to join the youth fellowship in buying a used piano "to be used only in the basement." However, the next year a new piano was purchased for the auditorium. In 1966 a public-address system was installed. A parsonage was purchased in 1960.

The congregation has a constitution, which provides for a Board of Elders to give counsel to the pastor.[40]

12. *Zion, Wichita, Sedgwick County*

Located in an area of black housing, Tenth Street Mennonite represents an attempt of the South Central Conference to develop an integrated church. In January 1952 a group of forty students from the Hesston College YPCA surveyed a section of Wichita's inner city to determine the interest of the people in attending a Sunday school if one were started. Of the 600 homes contacted, seventy expressed interest in the Sunday school.

Further contact with the people in the area was established through Sunday afternoon visitation. There were Bible stories, with singing and fellowship. Among the first students involved were Viola Steiner, Elizabeth Yoder, Merle Springer, and Leonard Bechler, with James Kratz directing the project. The homes were visited to get acquainted with the parents as well as the children. Several people accepted Christ.

This work was continued through the summer. That autumn the Cleveland Street Mission was begun with a Sunday school, meeting in the Hutchinson Branch of the YMCA on Cleveland Street. More than sixty children attended the first service. D. A. Raber served as superintendent. Mothers soon visited the service, and an adult class was started. Afternoon visitation was continued to make contact with the families of Sunday school pupils.

After several months Wednesday evening clubs were formed — the "Golden Promise Club" for girls and the "Sun Ray Club" for boys. The clubs were an excellent method of contact and gave children something to do in their spare time.

In 1953 a summer Bible school was held, with an enrollment of over 200. Bible school became an annual part of the program. In 1954 the Voluntary Service unit at Eureka Gardens helped with the teaching.

As the Sunday school grew, so did the interest of the people. With the attendance of adults came the need for a minister. In 1956 D. A. Raber, the superintendent of the mission, was licensed to serve as a minister. He moved to Wichita and gave full time to this opportunity and responsibility, with financial support from the conference mission board. They began holding Sunday evening services in their home at 1227 North Grove. In June 1957 Raber was ordained to the ministry and continued to give leadership for about four years.

The first person baptized was Norma Brown Hughey, who became a member of the church in June 1957. By January 1958 seven persons had been baptized. Attendance at the Sunday school went up to eighty.

The Cleveland Street Y was only a temporary home for this growing work. In January 1957 the South Central Conference had purchased a house at 1103 North Piatt, on a lot 150 feet by 216 feet, with ample space for a future church building. This house was to serve as a parsonage and a place of worship until other provisions were made.

On Easter Sunday 1957 the first service was held in the parsonage. Since the new church would face around the corner, on Tenth Street, the name was changed to Tenth Street Mennonite Church. Prayer groups and Bible studies were held in homes of participants, and the clubs continued. The Hesston Y no longer directed the work, but students and faculty continued to be involved in the program. In the summer of 1957 Merle Bender and his family came to assist in the youth program.

Plans were made for a new church building and submitted to the Executive Committee of the conference. The cost was to be about $27,000. A building fund was set up. The committee had decided that building could begin when the congregation had raised $2,500. In January 1958 the following building committee was appointed: Harry Weaver, Levi Headings, John W. Brown, Merle L. Bender, and D. A. Raber.

Ground was broken on June 29, 1958, by John W. Brown, Milo Kauffman, Merle Bender, Mrs. Dorothy Toms, and D. A. Raber. Milo Kauffman was the speaker. Actual work did not begin until August. Service and labor were donated by several local men and members. On April 5, 1959, the completed church was dedicated, with 250 people present. H. H. Bookers, pastor of the St. Paul A. M. E. Church of Wichita, delivered the sermon. The litany of dedication was led by Pastor D. A. Raber. The Men's Chorus from Hydro, Oklahoma, sang. So now for the first time the Tenth Street Mennonite Church had its own building.

In August the congregation was received into the South Central Conference by a unanimous vote.

In 1960 a spirit of disunity began to manifest itself. The doctrine of sinless perfection became an issue for a time, and attendance fell off. The pastor was willing to step aside, and the conference Executive Committee appointed a church council to lead the congregation. This council consisted of Perry Stutzman, chairman, Stanley Kuhns, Willard Conrad, and Curtis Burrell. Merle Bender was appointed as interim pastor, and he served until November 1961.

At that time Lynford Hershey came to be pastor at Tenth Street. He had been serving as unit leader in VS work at Portland, Oregon, which had projects where interracial cooperation was a feature. He threw himself into the work at Wichita, he said, "not because he feels the Negro needs him, but because he needs to express his faith by evidencing lack of prejudice as a Christian."[41] In January 1962 Hershey was installed as pastor by Milo Kauffman, and in October of that year he was ordained to the ministry by Milo Kauffman and Clayton Beyler.

Under Hershey's leadership the church program grew. A library was started. The Bible school of 1962 had an unusually high enrollment of 246. A Mennonite Youth Fellowship was started, and

Women's Bible Study. The congregation worked with the Wichita Council of Churches in a released-time Bible school. Each Wednesday morning ninety-five fifth-graders from the Ingalls Public School were released in three shifts for instruction at the Mennonite Church. Several women in the church taught the classes.

The church council became a Board of Elders to assist the pastor. The church adopted a "Statement of Membership." In 1964 the membership stood at thirty-five, and a monthly budget of $280 was adopted.

Hershey belonged to the Wichita Ministerial League, which is predominantly black; to the Fair Housing Committee, whose main object is to obtain a fair housing ordinance in a city which ranked in the highest ten for the existence of discrimination; to the Community Council, whose main purpose was to build a better community through the school. Hershey wanted to identify with his members and their needs. He associated with the men, taking them out for coffee and conversation. He encouraged the white families in the congregation to move into the ghetto.

In February 1966 Earnest Kauffman, an ordained deacon from Beemer, Nebraska, was installed as an assistant to the pastor. Howard Zehr, overseer of the Kansas Mennonite churches, preached in this service.

In the spring of 1966 Hershey was granted a 15-month leave of absence for the development of a church camp in the Coast Range of Oregon. Sam Williams was asked to serve as pastor during this leave. Near the end of that period Williams, who was a black man, felt a call to continue as pastor at Tenth Street. Hershey therefore asked to be relieved of his commitment to return to Wichita. The congregation agreed to this, and called Williams to continue in the pastorate. This was early in the summer of 1967. In a few months, however, Williams resigned, and Hershey was contacted about coming back. But he was now committed to continued work in Oregon, and could not come.

Milo Kauffman filled in as interim pastor. Jim Dorsey, who was serving as VS director in Wichita, served as pastor for a few months in 1968. The unit occupied the former parsonage. A new parsonage was purchased late in 1968 at 2320 Random Road.

In May of 1968 the Kansas Mennonite Disaster Service accepted a block clean-up assignment in cooperation with the congregation. This came from a new realization by MDS that some chronic

John Powell and family during their Wichita days

conditions in our inner cities are as worthy of help as the communities struck by sudden disaster. In 1968 summer Bible school was canceled because of a lack of teachers. Instead the Mennonite Brethren people at Hillsboro invited 17 children to live in their homes and attend Bible school in the church there. Later in the summer these hosts visited the families of the children in Wichita.

Late in 1968 John Powell, who had assisted in Mennonite pastoral work in Detroit, came to take the pastorate at Tenth Street. Powell grew up in Alabama and is a graduate of Tuskegee Institute. The VS unit and the congregation cooperated in a house-to-house survey of the church community, conversing on how the church can help to solve some of the community problems. One completed project was the paving of an area for a basketball court. Powell served as director of The Brother's House, sponsored jointly by Brotherhood Presbyterian and Tenth Street Mennonite. The Brother's House offered music, recreation, opportunity for dialogue, and courses in black history. There were attempts at spiritual renewal, but some of the congregation wondered whether there was too much emphasis on black power and the social gospel.

The church lost its leadership again when Powell went to Elkhart to work on the Minority Ministries Council of the Mission Board. The congregation was uncertain about what it could do, with only seven supporting families. A committee was elected to function as the church leaders and to secure someone to serve as minister. They first chose William Raines, a warm, evangelical white man who had attended Grace Seminary at Winona Lake. Serving in 1972 was Carl Henderson. He has been a resident of Wichita for a number of years and is a black ordained minister. The congregation now holds the title to the property, and seeks to be more indigenous in fellowship and outreach. In 1973 James Lark, veteran black leader, came from California to serve an indefinite period, helping the congregation to evaluate its mission and plan its future. The name was changed from Tenth Street to Zion.

This attempt at an interracial fellowship is hard to evaluate. Tremendous effort and a good deal of financial investment have gone into this work. The two longer-term pastors, D. A. Raber and Lyn Hershey, both were hard-working and effective shepherds, even though they worked at times amid great discouragements.

Great credit should go to the lay persons who came in to be a part of this congregation. The Kuhns family lived in the ghetto for a number of years. Grace Roth, a schoolteacher in Wichita, was actively and helpfully involved. Stutzmans and Conrads were faithful commuters. There have been some faithful and long-term members from the community. Among these the James Holt family deserves special mention as a stabilizing influence in the church. The attempt has been noble, and much good has been done. The years to come will have to determine the net results.[42]

13. *Rainbow Boulevard, Kansas City, Wyandotte County*

Rainbow Boulevard Mennonite Church was formed in 1964 by the merger of Grace Mennonite Church, South Central (Old) Mennonite Conference, and Kansas City Mennonite Church, General Conference Mennonite, Western District. The merged congregation is now affiliated with both conferences, and contributes to the financial needs of both.

First for our purposes here we must consider the history of Grace Mennonite Church.

In November 1957 thirty-one members, including the pastor of the Argentine congregation, withdrew their membership with the purpose of organizing another Mennonite congregation in the Kansas City area. The first three Sundays of December they met in the Youth for Christ building. The next Sunday they met with the Kansas City Mennonite Church. After that they met in a Christian day school building, until after the purchase and remodeling of a church building was completed.

The church building was purchased for $20,000 from the Church of Christ. It was a frame building with an auditorium, an educational wing, and a nursery wing. The remodeling put a large window between the nursery wing and the main room. In 1960 pews were installed in place of the folding chairs.

On charter day, January 4, 1958, there were thirty-nine members: the thirty-one from Argentine, four received by baptism, and four by letter. Of these, fifteen were children of members, one was from a non-Mennonite church, and four had been won from non-Christians. The first name of the brotherhood was Grace Mennonite Chapel, but during the first year the name was changed to Grace Mennonite Church. Family names in the group were Buller, Elkins, Gray, King, Heineken, Kauffman, Lewis, Nation, Nissley, Sanvold, and Troyer.

The first meeting was held in the new building on August 17, 1958, with sixty-two present. The location was in Mission, a densely populated area on the south side of Kansas City, across the line in Johnson County, Kansas. The building was dedicated on December 7, one year after the Charter Day Service. Milo Kauffman, the area overseer; Marcus Bishop, a Denver pastor; and Stanley Bohn, the pastor of the Kansas City Mennonite Church, were the speakers. Five new members were added in this service, bringing the total to forty-three. The congregation had been received into the South Central Conference in August.

The first trustees were Emery King, Lester Wise, and Frances Heineken. Members of the first Church Council were Melvin Buller, Dan King, Ora Troyer, and Roy King, Sr.

The highest membership, forty-eight, was reached in 1960. After 1961 the membership declined slightly. Some moved away, two returned to the Argentine Church, and some went to other denominations. It was difficult to interest people near the church, as none of the members lived nearby. But some people were won to

The building purchased at Mission, Kansas, for the use of Grace Mennonite Church.

Summer Bible school at Grace Mennonite in 1959

Christ. One from outside the Mennonite fellowship showed a real change in his life and gave a good testimony before his death. One who had been out of fellowship showed a real interest in the work. Two others who had not been attending are now active in the merged congregation. Of the thirty-nine charter members, eighteen are members of the merged church.

D. Lowell Nissley was the only pastor of Grace. He was fully supported only one year, 1960-1961. After the merger he was associate pastor until August 1964, when he accepted a position with Mennonite Aid, Inc., at Goshen.

The Sunday school enrollment reached eighty-five at the highest. A group of about a dozen young people were active in MYF. The women were active in WMSA program. The men of the four (Old) Mennonite churches in the city met monthly until 1961. The church had a strong library program, with some 900 books read through the five years. The library of 471 volumes was moved to Rainbow Boulevard after the merger. The highest enrollment in summer Bible school was sixty-four, in 1962. The 1963 summer Bible school was a union school with Kansas City Mennonite. The church participated in camping programs at Rocky Mountain and Laclede, Missouri.

The sermon followed the Sunday school. Sometimes it was short, with a discussion period following. The *Church Hymnal* was used. An organ was placed in the church in 1959, but was not usually used to accompany singing. Sunday evening and midweek meetings were regular.

Evangelistic meetings were held by E. M. Yost, Marcus Bishop, Edward Miller, and B. Charles Hostetter. There was a seminar by Horace Dean, and weekend Bible studies by Calvin Redekop, Clayton Beyler, and Milton Brackbill.

Grace cooperated with other Mennonite churches of the city in Easter Sunrise hilltop services, and in mother-daughter banquets. There were always New Year watch-night services, and for the first few years, monthly fellowship meals. There were periodic child dedications.

A very meaningful communion service, usually candlelighted, was held at least twice a year. Foot washing, usually on a midweek night, was not joined in by all. The prayer veiling was not required, and a small percent of the women continued its use. The holy kiss was not practiced. Anointing for healing was called for on several occasions.

The pastor performed three marriages, all ring ceremonies, one at Grace, and two at larger churches. Counseling preceded the weddings.

Unity marked the church life. Discipline, including excommunication, was administered by the pastor, in cooperation with the church council.

The budget plan of financing was used, with members committing themselves to "intended" giving, not pledges. There were contributions for Hesston College, South Central and General Conferences, district and general mission boards, the Mennonite Hour, and the American Bible Society. The highest budget, in 1960-1961, was almost $10,000, and the per member giving in that year was $184.

The pastor fellowshiped with local pastors in a ministerial alliance.

The Kansas City Mennonite Church, the other party to the merger, was organized in January 1957. The Western District Conference purchased a building across the street from the University of Kansas Hospital. The conference also promised funds for a pastor. A full-time pastor, Stanley Bohn, was installed in August 1957. In November of the same year, on Charter Day, there were forty-three members who agreed to assume the responsibility of being the church. In 1961 volunteers from other congregations helped them to build an educational wing.

Men from Grace and Kansas City Mennonite, working together in May 1960, in disaster service after a tornado at Meriden, Kansas, began to discuss the inefficiency of their two groups, so much alike, spending most of their resources in self-preservation, and how together they might give a more effective witness in their city. Exploration was made for merger possibilities. Cooperative programs were planned and study committees were organized.

In the summer of 1963 came the joint summer Bible school. In August both church councils divided into smaller study committees. The combined church councils on January 19, 1964, chose officers for the first year of the merged church. The first service of the two congregations together was on February 2, 1964.

The official merger service, on March 1, 1964, was an all-day affair, with a fellowship meal at the noon hour. Leonard Garber represented the South Central Conference and Arnold Funk represented the Western District Conference. The speakers were Arnold Funk and Milo Kauffman. The name adopted by the merged congregation was Rainbow Boulevard Mennonite. Stanley Bohn was continued as the pastor, and services continued where Kansas City Mennonite had been worshiping.

When Stanley Bohn left in October 1965 for an assignment at Newton, Kansas, the pulpit was supplied for a number of months by Don Houts, from the Methodist Seminary. Gary Schrag came in August 1967 to serve as pastor. He was ordained in October 1967 by Arnold Nickel, representing Western District, and James Hershberger, representing South Central. Schrag resigned as pastor, effective September 1971. Kenneth Rupp, of Beatrice, Nebraska, was installed as pastor in October 1972.

The membership of the merged congregation in 1969 was 157. In 1972 there were ninety-eight resident members and forty-three nonresident.

The congregation participates in community work, among the poor, both white and black, in the Rosedale area, with some twenty other denominations and churches, in the "Cross-lines Community Project."

Since late in 1969 the congregation meets in the nearby building of the Rosedale Methodist Church, since its own facilities have become inadequate.[43]

14. *Inter-Mennonite Fellowship, Harvey County*

The Hesston Inter-Mennonite Fellowship was organized when Mennonites of several branches living in and near Hesston felt the need of a church home where they lived. The desire to explore the significance of inter-Mennonite fellowship in a congregational setting also existed.

On May 14, 1967, a group of interested families began meeting in the commons area of Hesston High School. These meetings continued for two and a half years. On February 22, 1970, the fellowship moved into the present facility in Hesston, which was purchased from the United Methodist Church of Hesston, when that group built a new church on the edge of town.

The congregation was formally organized December 3, 1967, with thirty-seven charter members. The majority brought letters from General Conference Mennonite churches, and the remainder from (Old) Mennonite churches. Two youths were baptized on the charter-signing day.

The fellowship was accepted as a member of both the Western

District of the General Conference Mennonite Church and the South Central Conference of the (Old) Mennonite Church on November 4, 1972, when these two conference districts met jointly for the first time, on the Bethel College campus, North Newton, Kansas.

Membership in December 1972 was sixty-two, with the total church family numbering over 100, which includes a large number of children and youth. At least five different Mennonite, Methodist, and Catholic backgrounds are represented within the fellowship.

Family names of members and regular attendants include the following: Bachman, Blosser, Chaple, Derksen, Duerksen, Ensz, Friesen, Graber, Habegger, Holle, Janzen, Jantzen, Jantz, Juhnke, Klassen, Krehbiel, Koehn, Loewen, Miller, Martens, Prouty, Regier, Rempel, Rilling, Schmidt, Siegrest, Small, Yoder, Zimmerman.

Occupations of family heads include the following: administrator (Rehabilitation Center), church conference employee, factory employee, farmer, lumber company employee, mechanic, mortician, MCC administrator, minister, painter-artist, physical therapist, Mental Health Center employee, purchasing agent, railroad employee, sales clerk. Areas of employment include Hesston, Newton, and Moundridge. The congregation has two adult and two children representatives serving in Africa, two in France in language study, and one couple returned from Africa.

In 1969 forty-three members contributed a total of $11,370. or $264 per member. In 1970 forty-nine members contributed $12,154, or $248 per member. In 1971 fifty-six members gave $13,963, or $249 per member. The 1972 operating budget was $5,763. The congregation supports the programs of both conferences to which it belongs. It has been self-supporting since its beginning.

In its program the fellowship has stressed prayer, individual witness in the daily walk, and relating to the needs of the fellowship, as well as the community and the world at large. Laymen lead the worship services, and everyone has an opportunity to share concerns, experiences, and joys in the Sunday morning worship services. Youth serve in various capacities: playing the piano, taking the offering, singing in either a junior or a senior choir, presiding in a Sunday morning worship service. At various times the congregation meets in different homes for Bible study. Numerous activities, such as the Ministerial Alliance, community hymn-sings, community summer Bible school, World Day of Prayer, and Thanksgiving Day services, are shared with the United Methodist and the other (Old) Mennonite churches of the community.

The first couple years the congregation did not have a pastor, but depended for leadership on members of the congregation. In the summer of 1969 Gideon G. Yoder became pastor. Yoder was an (Old) Mennonite, but had been a pastor of both (Old) Mennonite and GC Mennonite churches. Yoder died unexpectedly in August 1971, and for another year the congregation did not have a pastor. Waldo E. Miller was installed as the second pastor in September 1972. He had served pastorates at Pleasant Valley, Harper, Kansas, and at Maple Grove, Belleville, Pennsylvania.[44]

SCATTERED MEMBERS IN THE SOUTH

CHAPTER  8

SCATTERED MEMBERS IN THE SOUTH

1. *Oklahoma*

Oklahoma was not for many years, like Missouri and Kansas, an open frontier, inviting settlers to come in and turn its wilderness into farms and cities. Anyone who had the courage and the stamina to endure the conditions in the undeveloped lands in pioneer days could go to Missouri and Kansas. There was nothing to prevent him but drought and heat and grasshoppers and poverty and homesickness.

But Oklahoma was for many years closed to the hordes pushing west. It was reserved for the Indians. The very name of the state is a Choctaw word for Red Man. The policy of the federal government was that here the Indians could come and stay, without fear of being driven out by the white man.

As early as 1819 the government began driving the Indians of the East and South over the "trail of tears" to the "Indian Territory." Various tribes were given their land allotments between the Arkansas border and the semiarid desert, between the Kansas border and the Red River. In 1834 the eastern part was set apart for the Five Nations as "Indian Territory"; in 1850 the western part was parceled out to other tribes as "Oklahoma Territory." Here, however, thousands of white settlers managed to crowd in.

Two developments worked against sole Indian occupancy. One was the railroads. The Katy (MKT — Missouri, Kansas, and Texas) first crossed the state in 1872, followed by the Frisco, the Santa Fe, and the Rock Island. Settlement and business follow railroads. The other development was the driving of cattle from the Texas pasturelands to the railheads in Kansas. The Chisholm Trail and others, sending 500,000 Texas steers north annually in the seventies, became roads that had to be serviced. Within a few years the white settlers killed off five and a half million buffalo, and the Red Man faced starvation.

Pressure mounted to allow free settlement on the fertile lands of the two territories. And step by step the government yielded. As a method the "run" was developed. In this unique plan for giving land away, the landseekers are camped along the edge of the tract about to be deeded to them. All have registered at a booth. The object is to be the first to set a white stake on a quarter section of land. The race starts at noon. A bugle sounds and rifles crack the starting signal. They are off — in carts, buggies, spring wagons, heavy wagons, prairie schooners; on bicycles and horseback, and even on trains. The racers have maps and an idea of where they want to go. Most of them are able to drive their stakes, and get a free home.

The first run was in 1889. There were others in '91, '92, and '93, and 1901. The whole area was open to settlement after 1904. For Mennonites, the important one was in 1893, for in this one the Cherokee Outlet, sometimes called "The Strip," was opened. This was a great tract, 200 miles long and 57 miles wide, next to the Kansas border. The run was on a Saturday, September 16. More than 100,000 people were in this race to claim the rich prairies of northwestern Oklahoma Territory. It was the greatest of all the runs.

Mennonites of the various branches were in the front ranks. They came from Iowa, Nebraska, Kansas, and Missouri. Nearly all got their quarter section, but a few lost out to challengers — perhaps "sooners" who sneaked across the line ahead of the signal.

But many of them were widely scattered. What about building churches? In May 1894, eight months after the run, T. M. Erb and R. J. Heatwole visited some of these pioneers in the eastern part of the "Strip." Across the line there were small frame houses, sod houses, and tents, as far as the eye could reach across the level prairie. Along the Santa Fe, between Newkirk and Guthrie, there were Mennonites at five points. Along the Rock Island they were at seven points between the state line and Kingfisher. There were from one to four families at a place. In three weeks T. M. Erb preached eighteen sermons, two of them in German. They held services in homes, in a rude log house, in schools, in a Presbyterian church. They slept on an outer porch and on a riverbank, beside a fire they had built. They traveled 800 miles, half of it in a wagon. At times they were forty-five miles from the nearest railroad station.[1]

In 1907 the two territories became the state of Oklahoma. By that time there were thirty-seven Mennonite congregations of the various branches in the area of the Cherokee Outlet: 17 General Conference, 12 Mennonite Brethren, 4 (Old) Mennonite, 2 Old Order Amish, and 1 each of the Krimmer Mennonite Brethren and the Church of God in Christ, Mennonite. The (Old) Mennonite churches were at Manchester, Jet, Hydro, and Newkirk. Only Hydro survived the second decade of the century.

In 1894 the Kansas-Nebraska Conference passed a resolution adding Oklahoma to the area served by the conference.[2]

The Red Man was largely submerged by the tide of white migration. In 1972 only one percent of Oklahoma's population was Indian.[3]

There is nowhere in the Mennonite records any hint that Mennonite settlers, from Germantown to this settlement of the last stand of the Indian in the West, had any feeling that they were doing wrong in acquiring deeds of ownership for land that the Indians claimed as theirs. There was no questioning of the right of government to grant land titles, and of settlers to accept such title, as it was handed down. Mennonites, as well as other Americans, seemed to believe that the United States had a right and a duty to overspread the continent and make a home for the multiplying millions. "Manifest Destiny," a phrase coined about 1845, became a slogan to assert that God "had designed a unique geographical arena for the American experiment." The American urge to expansion had something of a religious fervor. Colonization was considered a divine mission. This is seen in the zeal of the pioneering Mennonites in starting Sunday schools, building churches, and scattering evangelists over the frontier. They evidently never had a thought that they were wickedly stealing land from the Indians.

As we see it now, Mennonites do share a collective guilt for violating the tribal ownership of land, for killing the buffalo upon which Indian life depended, and for breaking the treaties which were given to protect Indian rights. Only recently in Arizona and Mississippi and Canada, but not in South Central territories,

have (Old) Mennonite missions to the Indians recognized our obliga-
tions to the Red Man. General Conference Mennonites expressed
this obligation much earlier, so that today they have in Oklahoma,
for example, four Indian congregations strong enough to join in
hosting the Western District Conference.[4]

To ask what kind of practical restitution Mennonites might
now make to the descendants of the Indians whose lands we and
other white Americans took is of course to pose a deep puzzle.
The buffalo herds cannot be brought back. Our minds and our wills
hardly seem ready for proposals to restore lands to tribal ownership,
to say nothing of the practical difficulties that would imply. But we
can begin by trying to see the historical process through Indian
eyes. We can acknowledge the wrong that was done. And at least
we can be careful not to see in the pioneering of our forefathers
only the heroic deeds, the wresting forth of new churches and new
communities in the quest for religious freedom. We can try to see
the other side: our forefathers' failure to see that they were benefiting fairly directly from the destruction of other people's lives
and communities — as we are still benefiting.

2. Arkansas[5]
a. Peach Orchard, Clay County

John Hartzler and Levi Miller went from the Amish Mennonite
community in Cass County, Missouri, in 1895 to northeastern Arkansas. They must have settled between Delaplaine and Peach
Orchard, for these two towns three miles apart in the level country
along the Black River are both given as addresses. They organized a church and Sunday school there. Since there was no
building in which to hold services, C. S. Weaver, J. B. Mishler, and
J. B. Schrock were appointed to attempt to build a meetinghouse.
They received $14.75 from the Howard-Miami congregation in
Indiana.[6]

This settlement does not seem to have lasted long. A minister,
Peter Zimmerman, moved from Delaplaine to Roanoke, Illinois, in
1897.[7]

b. Bentonville, Benton County

The ministry of the White Hall congregation at Oronogo,
Missouri, extended across the line into Benton County, Arkansas.
Appointments were filled, sometimes regularly, in several commu-

nities where members lived. One of these communities was at Bentonville, where Fred and Jane Young lived for a few years in the late 1920s. Their daughter Florence attended Hesston College and Eastern Mennonite College. She became the wife of Sanford G. Shetler, of Johnstown, Pennsylvania.

c. Conway, Faulkner County

In 1958 a group of Mennonites from Buchanan County, Iowa, and a few other places moved to Vilonia, about ten miles east of Conway, Arkansas, about sixty miles north of Little Rock. They lived there only five years before returning to Iowa.

Dale Dorsey, who lived in Conway in 1964, met Wayne Yoder, pastor of the Buffalo congregation, Mountain Home, Arkansas. Dorsey grew up in Mississippi, and in 1949 was ordained to the ministry. He knew nothing of the Mennonites, but from his own Bible study he had developed convictions against war and race prejudice. He and his family have been received as members of the South Central Conference. The Dorseys hold services in their home, and he has held meetings in some Mennonite churches. They sponsor daily Mennonite Hour radio spots and several tract racks in the community. One daughter is teaching in the Christian day school at Sarasota, Florida. [8]

d. Other Mennonites in Arkansas

These are a few of the places in Arkansas where Mennonites moved into the state as frontiersmen to establish homes and, if possible, churches in new areas. Other places were Springdale, Wynne, Siloam Springs, and Jonesboro.

Other Mennonite groups are in the state. The Conservative Mennonite Conference has congregations at El Dorado, Mountain View, and Timbo. At Mena there is a strong congregation of Amish Mennonites related to the Hostetler group at Shelbyville, Illinois. There is a small Beachy Amish group at Mountain View. There are several Old Order Amish groups in the state.

3. Louisiana
a. General

Probably the first Mennonites to see the state of Louisiana were European immigrants who landed at New Orleans, a seaport and the chief city of the state. From here they would find their way north by Mississippi River steamboats. Thus in 1839 Christian Reesor and his two brothers and sister from France came to America.[9]

In 1872 Jacob Kauffman traveled from Osage County, Kansas, to New Orleans, where he met Christian Mourer, the leader of a group of fifteen Amish who lived there. The group observed communion on Easter Sunday of that year.[10] Two years later John F. Funk corresponded with Mennonites who were resident in New Orleans.[11]

But early Mennonite settlements in Louisiana were not permanent. European immigrants who may have landed here passed this state by as they sought homes farther north. Not till near the end of the century did the tide of Mennonite migration turn back to the Acadian country.

b. Roseland, Tangipahoa Parish

John S. Coffman took his evangelistic message wherever Mennonites had settled. And so in the early spring of 1895 he came to Roseland, Louisiana, a new town on the Illinois Central seventy miles north of New Orleans. A little group of ten members worshiped here in the West End Schoolhouse. Their minister was J. T. Nice. Another family head was J. C. Kornhaus. Coffman preached here from February 19 to March 3.

Coffman, in a letter to the *Herald of Truth*,[12] honestly described this vegetable country and expressed a hope that others would leave their large northern communities to make a strong settlement here. But this did not happen, and like so many frontier settlements, this one soon scattered.

4. Texas

Rose Lambert was married to David Musselman in Elkhart, Indiana, in the home of her father George Lambert on October 4, 1911. Rose, a member of the Mennonite Brethren in Christ Church, had been a missionary in Armenia for several terms. David had been raised in a Mennonite home in Pennsylvania but at the time of his marriage was a Methodist. A few days after the marriage ceremony the Musselmans moved to Victoria, Texas, where they stayed until the following March, when they moved out to their ranch about twenty miles north of Victoria. Here they came to the settlement which Musselman had helped promote. The settlement was Salem, with its general store operated by Abner Stoltzfus, who had been ordained by the Mennonites. The Chris Stahleys had come there from Indiana; two Gerber families had moved in from Indiana also. The Newcomers had come from Kansas. The Frank Colemans were there a short time. Mrs. Coleman was a Stoltzfus and a Mennonite. A Brethren minister, Grandfather Fike, and some of his family were members of the community. In the early years of the settlement, the settlers built a church in Salem but it was a community church supported by Mennonites, Brethren, and Brethren in Christ. Eventually the congregation came under the supervision of the River Brethren. Only a few of the original settlers remain there. Among them is Rose Lambert Musselman and her son and family, with the address Star Route, Inez, Texas.[13]

EXTINCT CHURCHES IN THE SOUTH

CHAPTER

EXTINCT CHURCHES IN THE SOUTH

1. *Yoder, Arkansas County, Arkansas*

As the Mennonite frontier pushed to the west, there were those who thought they saw opportunity in the South. One of the earliest settlements was in Arkansas County, in Arkansas state. Stuttgart is forty-five miles southeast of Little Rock. There were two different Amish Mennonite settlements there, both of which became extinct.

The first immigration began in 1880. Most of the first settlers came from Hickory County, Missouri. Family names were Springer, Stutzman, Stahley, Schulz, Roth, Nofziger, Rich, Yoder, Scheffel, and Beck. Others came from Butler and Fulton counties in Ohio, Tazewell County in Illinois, and Henry County in Iowa. They used the German language in their worship services. Jonathan Beck was ordained to the ministry and Jacob Yoder was ordained as bishop.[1] The group became too large for meeting in homes, and a meetinghouse was built by 1886, six miles southeast of Stuttgart, called the Yoder Church. Beck died in 1890. Daniel Roth, ordained in 1885, also died in 1890 from a lightning stroke.

The first burial in the cemetery adjoining the church was the daughter of Joseph R. Roth.[2] There were seventy members in 1890. By 1897 that membership had been reduced to fifty-one. The members were scattered over the flat ricelands, but the Sunday school attendance was ninety. The report to the Western A. M. Conference in 1902 listed Jacob Yoder as bishop, and John Augsburger and Samuel Summer as ministers. There were still fifty members in

1904.[3] Another minister of these years was Fred Gingerich. But by 1920 the settlement died out, and the meetinghouse was moved to Pryor, Oklahoma. The Yoder cemetery continued to serve the Lutheran and former Mennonite community and today is large and well-kept. Names on tombstones which are thought to be of Mennonites include Eichelberger, King, Lantz, Nofsinger, Oesch, Rich, Roth, Schultz, Scheffel, Sommers, Springer, Stahley, Sutter, Yoder, and Zimmerman.

Not all of this community moved away. Quite a few remained in the area, and their posterity are still there. The Methodist Church in the community has members named Roth, Stahley, Nofsinger, Gingerich, Zimmerman, Yoder, Meyers, and Schultz.

The second wave of Mennonite immigration to this area began in 1925, this time chiefly from Iowa. By 1928 a dozen families had moved in, most of them in 1926. The Iowa families were those of Joe Eiman, Manass Brenneman, William J. Schrock, Simon Gingerich, Solomon C. Ropp, Thomas and Leroy V. Miller, and Lloyd Knepp. Three families came from Indiana: Almon P. Hostetler and John and Noah Smucker. These settlers were attracted by the good land and the profitable rice farming. The families were Amish Mennonite, Conservative Amish Mennonite, and Old Order Amish. But there was no minister, and they had preaching only when there were visiting ministers. They did hold Sunday school in the Yoder Schoolhouse. They lived in the same area that the earlier group had — between Stuttgart and Almyra.

But four of the families moved away after two years, and the outlook was not bright for developing another church. By 1931, when the Depression was on, all were gone except the Schrocks and the Leroy Millers. Participating in their Sunday school was a small group of Disciples of Christ. At the close of the Sunday school each Sunday they would have communion, as is the rule in their denomination. About once a month there would be a visiting Disciples minister, who would hold morning, afternoon, and evening services. The Mennonites would participate in these services, except the communion. It was a rewarding fellowship.

By 1934, however, the Disciples group was scattered. The Schrock young people were grown up, and their teenagers wanted the companionship of the Baptist young people in Almyra. So the Sunday school in the Yoder school was discontinued. The Schrocks eventually joined the Baptists. The Millers attended the Methodist Church in

Stuttgart, and Leroy taught a men's class. In the evening they attended the Baptist Church regularly. They enjoyed the fellowship in these churches. But they loved the Mennonite Church and wanted their children with them in that church. So, although they liked Arkansas, and had to sell out in these Depression times for a fraction of what their land was worth, they moved back to Iowa in 1937. Today they are happy to see their son J. John J. serving as pastor of the large East Union Mennonite Church at Kalona, and their daughter Grace as a teacher at Iowa Mennonite School.[4]

This incident may illustrate why, when a church begins to disintegrate, the members are likely to scatter rapidly. They want their families to find a church home in a stable community.

The Mennonite Church still holds title to the acre of land where the Yoder Church stood, and many Mennonites remain buried in the Yoder cemetery. But no Mennonites live there, although in 1972 the Stuttgart newspaper ran an appreciative story on the Mennonites who were once a part of the community.[5]

2. *German Springs, Alfalfa County, Oklahoma*

The first (Old) Mennonite congregation to develop in the Cherokee Strip was at German Springs, located about ten miles west, and across a wide valley, from Manchester, Oklahoma. The church was about the same distance southeast from Waldron, Kansas. It was thirty miles south of Harper, Kansas, just across the state line.

Among the early families were M. H. Yoder, Christian Butz, Sam Kuhns, Henry Schmidt, and Hiram J. Yoder. Simon Hetrick was the first minister. The group constructed a sod church building, sixteen by thirty feet, with a good floor and seats. Gifts were received for the lumber needed.

The people lived at first in sod houses or dugouts. Most of those staking out claims in Oklahoma were limited in resources and had a hard time getting started. The sod in that area was not sufficiently matted to make waterproof walls. And so dugouts were more popular. Hetrick wrote in 1895: "We have not been able to put up a house yet, and live in a dugout in the hillside, 8 x 12 feet, and have a tent to sleep in. . . . A few times we had four inches of water in our little house. We have no floor in it."[6]

Grant Foreman has written: "The dugout or sod house stands out in the amazing saga of early Oklahoma as a symbol of the resourcefulness, fortitude, and adaptability of those early settlers who conquered the territory almost unarmed except with courage, irrepressible optimism, and patience."[7]

In February 1895 the group was asking for help. Cattle were dying of starvation, and many families were living on flour gravy and bread. Some men and women had no shoes. Supplies were taken to them from Harper. In July 1895 it was reported that 23 families, 109 persons, received help in buying flour, cornmeal, molasses, seed potatoes, and garden seeds from the $106 contributed for German Springs.[8] In the last three years of the century, however, there were bumper crops throughout the Strip country, and many settlers were able to pay for their homes.

There were seventeen members at German Springs in 1895 and they had two Sunday schools and preaching every Sunday. In 1896 they had thirty-three members. In 1897 they had services only three times a month, as Hetrick went to Milan Valley, twenty-five miles south, to preach once a month. At German Springs they had a service every Wednesday in the homes.

The next year Hetrick moved to Milan Valley, and there was no minister at German Springs. There were twelve members and four applicants. By 1902 George Hinkle, a man of Russian background, who had been ordained at Harper in 1897, lived near Waldron, and served as a minister at German Springs. He spoke mostly in German. There were twenty-one members at German Springs in January 1904. Hinkle resigned about 1906, and joined another denomination.

In 1905, when Bishop T. M. Erb was at German Springs, probably for a baptismal service, he recorded a lingering bit of frontier violence: "An excitement tonight after services when a man started to fight one of the converts. After a few blows we got it settled and went home all rather scared."[9]

In 1907 L. O. King, a native of West Liberty, Ohio, was ordained in Harvey County, Kansas, by T. M. Erb for service at Manchester. He married Erb's oldest daughter, and drove overland in a wagon to Manchester. He served there for three years. There were nine converts in meetings held by Perry Shenk. Some time in that first decade of the 1900s a frame church replaced the sod building.

But gradually the few families at German Springs moved, some to Harper, Kansas, and the church was closed. A cemetery had been started beside the church. The first burial was that of Jacob Bechtel late in 1896.[10] This became a community burying place, and there was need for it to be continued as such. So about 1920 Paul Erb, president of the Kansas-Nebraska Mission Board, which held title to the building, signed a quit-claim deed to the property. The building was torn down. But the cemetery, still used for burial, is well taken care of by a cemetery association.[11]

3. *Milan Valley, Alfalfa County, Oklahoma*

Christian Bontrager and two friends staked farms in Alfalfa County, Oklahoma, in the Cherokee Run in September 1893. Their claims were thirty miles south of German Springs, across the Salt Fork of the Arkansas River, and twenty miles from the Great Salt Plain, where the settlers could scoop up a salt supply for their cattle. They were near a country store and post office called Milan. This disappeared when the railroad came through and a nearby station was called Jet.

In the spring of 1894 John Bontrager, father of Chris, bought out one of the friends, giving $150 for 160 acres of land. Four families — the two Bontragers, Noah Troyer, and Philip Zimmerman, all from McPherson County, Kansas — were the first settlers, in 1895. In March 1896 there were twelve members who were visited every month by Simon Hetrick, pastor at German Springs. Bishop T. M. Erb of Harper, Kansas, also drove fifty-five miles across the country — with his ponies, fording the river (see p. 21) — to guide the new settlers into a church life. The people lived in dugouts, about twelve by fourteen, and half out of the ground. Dirt floors made it possible for the children to dig ponds and scrape roads without going outdoors.

In 1897 Hetrick moved to Milan Valley, and a church was organized with sixteen members. The first church services had been held in the dugouts of the settlers. But in 1898 the first frame church building was constructed on a corner of J. C. Bontrager's farm. It was sixteen by twenty-four feet, and cost $175. Philip Zimmerman was ordained deacon in May, 1899, by T. M. Erb. J. M. R. Weaver came to hold evangelistic meetings.

In 1901 Deacon Tobias Hershberger moved in from Tennessee. In the spring of 1902 the George B. Landis family migrated from Canton, Kansas, and Landis and Simon Hershberger were ordained to the ministry by T. M. Erb and S. C. Miller. Miller now had the bishop oversight, and frequently drove his dun-colored ponies the 150 miles from McPherson County. In 1904 the little church was moved

John C. Bontrager and son Abe, about 1897, standing in front of the sod-house dugout in which the first services of Milan Valley Mennonite congregation, Jet, Oklahoma, were held

a half mile north to a site donated by N. E. Miller.

But the building was too small. N. E. Miller and G. B. Landis had brought large families to Milan Valley, and with two new ministers prospects were good. In 1908 a new and larger church was built on the Miller farm site, although the ill health of Mrs. Landis took this family to California, and the Millers were going to Protection. Forty-two members communed in 1904. J. M. R. Weaver preached at the dedication of the new church.

In 1910 S. C. Miller bought several farms at Jet and moved down. This was his home to the end of his long and fruitful life in 1938. Several new families came in, and from 1910 to 1924 the membership ranged from forty to sixty. There were many children and young people. The congregation was strong enough to host the Kansas-Nebraska Conference in 1913. D. Y. Hooley assisted for a while in the ministry, between residences in Texas and Kansas. Deacon Hershberger died in 1918. Other deaths contributed to the growth of the small cemetery back of the church.

Evangelists holding revival meetings in the early years included Jacob Winey, Andrew Shenk, Perry Shenk, Charles D. Yoder, D. D. Zook, J. E. Hartzler, D. J. Johns, and D. D. Miller (of Indiana). In 1904 C. D. Yoder baptized the following: Melvin Landis, Lewis and David Miller, Carl Hershberger, Sam Garber, Rebecca and Nettie

S. C. Miller (1853-1938) lived at Milan Valley 1910-1938. He served as bishop here and for various congregations in Kansas.

Garber. In 1905 T. M. Erb baptized Abe Bontrager, Abe Garber, Howard and Baldwin Miller, Alvin, Emmon, and Dan Yoder.

Family names occurring in the records include Eash, Yoder, Hostetler, Hamilton, Troyer, Cooprider, Fischer, Boyts, McPherson, Pugh, Schrock, Kuhns, Auras, and Osborne.

Record books that have been preserved reveal that in the annual business meetings on January 1, there was continued interest in keeping the church house and grounds in good condition. A janitor was paid from $50 to $100 a year for his work, although during the thirties members took turns in doing this work. Money for church expenses was raised through assessments. A sample assessment was ten cents per acre for land owned and five cents for land rented. The total for a year was from $100 to $150.

In the early 1920s Sunday school attendance ranged from 50 to 80. There was a quarterly Sunday school conference. But in the Depression families moved away, and only the bishop, minister, and deacon were left. After the deaths of the bishop and the deacon, church services were discontinued. The church building was dismantled in 1941 by men from Pleasant Valley, Crystal Springs, and Yoder, and moved to Hutchinson, Kansas, to be reassembled as the Pershing Street Church. There were only three members left at Jet. Simon Hershberger, like a faithful captain, was the last to leave. He spent the rest of his days at Protection, Kansas.[12]

4. *Lake Charles, Calcasieu Parish, Louisiana*

Lake Charles is two hundred miles west of New Orleans and thirty miles north of the Gulf Coast. It is a seaport, an important business center. The farming land here is adapted to rice growing.

A. B. Kolb, of the *Herald of Truth* staff at Elkhart, Indiana, stopped at Lake Charles in 1897 to appraise its possibilities for Mennonite settlement.[13] The first settlers moved in from the north in 1898. By 1901 there were twenty-two members. The ministers were Jonas Nice and Andrew Good. The group applied for membership in the Missouri-Iowa Conference and was accepted.

In 1902 J. T. Wise is reported as the minister.[14] The group decided to build a church house. Chosen as trustees and a building committee were James Miller, C. C. Schrock, and John Sehrick. The church was built between Lakes Charles and Iowa, which was the post office of some of the members. It was opened for services in July 1902. A Sunday school was organized.

Andrew Shenk came in February 1903 to adjust some difficulties in the congregation. A few families came from Austell, Georgia, in 1905. The highest membership was about 40.[15]

The third wife of J. N. Durr, well-known Pennsylvania Mennonite bishop, was Sarah B. Gsell Leidig, whose family was active in the Lake Charles fellowship. Until her death Bishop Durr lived at Lake Charles, the only resident bishop the congregation ever had.

Rice farming did not prove as profitable as had been hoped. For this and other reasons the congregation slowly disintegrated. There were eight members in 1936. The E. G. Leidig family, who were at Lake Charles until 1954, were the last Mennonites in the community.[16]

5. *Newkirk, Kay County, Oklahoma*

The third Oklahoma (Old) Mennonite congregation that lived for a few years in the area of the Cherokee Outlet was at Newkirk, just across the Kansas line and almost straight north of Oklahoma City. The settlers here, however, did not come in with the Cherokee Run, but bought land a decade later.

Beginning in 1904 a number of families from Sterling, Illinois, moved to Newkirk in an attempt to have a Mennonite church and community there. Some of the family heads were John F. Weber, Abraham Frey, David Ebersole, Daniel Frey, Daniel Ebersole, John Frey, and Frank Kreider. They organized a Sunday school in 1905 with forty-five present. D. M. Ebersole was the superintendent.

A church was organized with fifteen members in March 1906 by T. M. Erb. They planned to have preaching once a month. Two months later Erb was there for one of these appointments, and preached to a schoolhouse full of people.

The congregation was further organized in November 1907 when Daniel Ebersole was ordained by lot to the office of deacon. Chris Reiff had been ordained to the ministry for Newkirk in September, in the same service at the Pennsylvania Church in which L. O. King had been ordained for Manchester and R. M. Weaver for Harper. Reiff moved to Newkirk in November 1907. He was pastor of the church there until its discontinuance a few years later. Twenty-three members communed in April 1908. Reiff returned to Harvey County when the families who had moved to Newkirk all returned to Sterling, but not all of them to the Science Ridge Church from which they had come.[17]

6. *Tuleta, Bee County, Texas*

The first Mennonite settlement in south Texas was made near Normanna, in Bee County, sixty miles north and west of Corpus Christi. In 1905 Peter Unzicker, a minister from Illinois, came here and acquired a large tract of land, on which he laid out the town site of Tuleta. In January 1906 there were six Mennonite families there, with a total of fourteen members.[18] A congregation was organized in January 1907 with twenty-four members.[19] Minister D. S. King moved from Larned, Kansas, in December 1906 and Minister J. M. R. Weaver from Newton, Kansas, in February 1907.[20] Other early ministers were D. Y. Hooley and C. L. Ressler. Other family names in the colony included Miller, Schrock, Hamilton, Overholt, Shellenberger, Neuhauser, Teuscher, Holderman, Gingerich, Kauffman, Hostetler, Swartzendruber, Eash, Shenk, and Zook. By 1913 there were eighty-one members, and a little later, 104.[21] But war conditions after 1915 and a severe drought in 1917 caused many families to move back to the north. Some families remained, however, even when there were no longer any ministers.

In 1927 E. S. Hallman, for the benefit of his health, moved from Saskatchewan to Falfurrias, Texas, one hundred miles south of Tuleta. During the four years he was there, he and H. Frank Reist alternated in filling preaching appointments at Tuleta. By 1932 the membership there was about thirty. They asked Hallman to come to Tuleta as the regular pastor and provided a parsonage with sufficient land for pasture and small crops. While he was there the high point of church activity was reached when all of the young people confessed Christ and were active in the work of the church.

In 1936 Tuleta became the home base of the South Texas Mission outreach to the Spanish-speaking people in this area. T. K. Hershey and William G. Detweiler were sent to investigate. They reported a good evangelizing opportunity. Twenty-six years earlier, Simon Del Bosque, the first Spanish-speaking convert, had become a member at Tuleta. He was now a valuable help in translating, opening up contacts, and serving as a bridge between the missionaries and the Spanish-speaking people.

In 1937 Hershey came to get the new work started. The David Alwines also came from Johnstown, Pennsylvania, to help. He was self-supporting, operating a service station at Pettus, near Tuleta, and working with Spanish-speaking people at Helena, twenty miles farther north. In midsummer the Amsa H. Kauffmans arrived from northern Indiana, and went to Laredo to study Spanish. Regular services were held on Sunday afternoons in the Spanish schools in Normanna, and were translated by Del Bosque. On January 2, 1938, the first baptismal service was held at Normanna, three miles south of Tuleta. Seven were baptized and a total of twelve were received into the church. The ages of these ranged from twelve to ninety. By the end of the year the mission workers were able to preach in Spanish, and in December the Normanna Mennonite Mission was organized by E. S. Hallman, with H. F. Reist, A. H. Kauffman, and David Alwine participating. On January 1, 1939, A. H. Kauffman was ordained to the ministry. H. F. Reist's ordination sermon was translated for the Spanish-speaking people.[22]

The Hallmans continued their service at Tuleta until in 1950, when they retired to Akron, Pennsylvania. They had observed their fiftieth wedding anniversary in their home at Tuleta in 1943, and the fiftieth anniversary of Hallman's ordination was observed at Kitchener, Ontario, in 1947.[23]

The center of the South Texas Mission shifted to the south and west, where the present churches are, and migration from Tuleta to the north again set in. In one week Hallman issued ten church letters to members moving away. So by 1957 there were only nine members in Bee County.

7. Manchac, Akers, and Madisonville, Louisiana

Southern Louisiana has millions of acres of marshes and swampland. People live along canals and other waterways, often traveling by boat. Many of these people live by the sale of fish, shellfish, and furs. The state produces annually over a billion pounds of fish, crabs, and shrimp, and about 40 percent of America's wild fur pelts come from this region.

One of these fishing communities is called Akers; another name is Pass Manchac. The congregation was known by both names. It is located in Tangipakoa Parish on the waterway that connects Lake Maurapas and Lake Pontchartrain. The village is built on stilts, among bayous, moss-laden oaks, and palmettos. Akers is the only place in America where people came to a Mennonite church by boat.

Mennonites came to this community on the west side of Pontchartrain, forty-five miles northwest of New Orleans, because Henry Tregle, who was converted at Des Allemands, owned a fishing dock at Akers, and spent months at a time here plying his fisherman's trade. Henry was an eager Christian witness, and he conducted a Sunday school on the porch of a two-room house. In 1942, one year after his conversion, Tregle was ordained to the ministry by E. S. Hallman. He built a small chapel, twenty by twenty-six feet. A lumber dealer gave $675 worth of lumber for $150. The total cost of the chapel was $652. Enough help came from Des Allemands and from northern churches to pay for the church.

Tregle preached for three years without any converts. Ninety percent of the people here were Catholics. Then in 1945 Richard Showalter held meetings and there were twelve converts. One of them was George Reno, who soon became assistant superintendent. He rowed five miles to get to church. Tregle got a vision of tent evangelism, and in 1951 Reno became pastor of the church at Akers. Hugo Succow had been ordained deacon in 1946.

One of the places where Tregle put up his tent was at Madisonville, on the north side of Lake Pontchartrain, in St. Tammany Parish. The longest bridge in the world, 25 miles, joins this community to New Orleans. The population was growing here. And with the building of a paved highway (U.S. 51) through Akers, that community was somewhat broken up. Some houses were dismantled and moved to Madisonville. A church was needed here also. The Chester Morse family offered a site, and with the help of the Des Allemands and other interested people a meetinghouse, 24 x 44, was erected. But Akers and Madisonville were considered as one congregation.

The service in Tregle's tent meeting was integrated, and the church at Madisonville was started on that basis. But the whites would not come when the blacks were there. And so the membership of the blacks was moved to a town close by and services were held there for them.

At Tregle's invitation Kenneth Smoker moved in from Pennsylvania to be pastor at Madisonville. He was there six years. Voluntary Service workers helped with Bible school at both Akers and Madisonville.

Henry Tregle went to a pastorate at Three Brothers, Arkansas, in 1957. But he has again returned to southern Louisiana and is attending and doing some preaching in a full gospel church at Pointe En Chien, where he lives, forty-five miles from Des Allemands.

All of the Akers members were attending at Madisonville, and in 1963 George Reno moved to Gulfport, Mississippi, to serve as pastor of the Crossroads Church. After his resignation in 1969 Reno moved to Venice, Louisiana, far down in the Mississippi Delta, and he conducts services in his home for some church members who live there, having moved from Madisonville.

Robert O. Zehr, from Delaware, became pastor at Madisonville in 1964, serving there until he moved to Kansas in 1971. He was ordained to the ministry at Madisonville by John E. Wenger and Howard J. Zehr in September 1964.

The *Mennonite Yearbook* for 1972 listed a membership for Manchac of twenty-one. But the secretary's report to conference in November 1972 revealed that this congregation was no longer active, and its membership was "delisted" from the conference total. One local family transferred to the Southern Baptists. A small nucleus of the congregation is alive at Manchac. Chester Morse, who donated the church land at Madisonville, received the land and the building back almost reluctantly. He has made repairs, and says the building is available to the Mennonites anytime they want to come back.[24]

Crossroads Bible Church, Harrison County, Mississippi

The Crossroads Bible Church, a Mennonite congregation in the South Central Conference, was both an outgrowth of CPS Camp 141, called Camp Bernard, and a mission outpost of the Gulfhaven congregation.

Camp Bernard was a Public Health Service 25-man unit opened in February 1945. Its purpose was to assist in the control of environmental diseases. When officials and groups in Harrison County were being consulted about the location of a Mennonite-controlled CPS camp in their community, they "spoke highly," according to Claude Shotts of NSBRO, "of the Mennonites who live in southern Mississippi. For this reason public relations should be good."[25] A transient and Boy Scout camp was made available for Camp 141, which carried on a very effective program of sanitation and health care for a little over two years, until March 1947. The camp was five miles north of Gulfport, about ten miles from the Gulfhaven Church.

The Health Service unit helped blacks as well as whites without discrimination. An after-hours project of the men was the improvement of the facilities of the North Gulfport Negro School, and the teaching of shop crafts to black boys. On Christmas Eve a caroling group sang for Negro homes, something that the blacks had never imagined could happen.

The CPS men attended services at Gulfhaven, but on Sunday afternoons they helped in an interdenominational Sunday school organized by the people of the community near the camp. Finally the Sunday school was operated by the Mennonite CPS workers. Ed Miller, one of the campers, was ordained to be assistant pastor at Gulfhaven, and he also assumed responsibilities for this community Sunday school.

Once a month the campers came to Gulfhaven to participate in a Sunday evening service, and once a month the Gulfhaven people participated in a Sunday evening service at the camp chapel. The Gulfhaven young people also joined in an evening of games and other recreation for the community youth each Saturday evening at Camp Bernard.

When the CPS camps were discontinued in March 1947, a VS camp was continued by MCC at this location, carrying on some of the same functions. When the campsite had to be vacated, the service unit moved a mile west. The new camp, called Camp Landon, was dedicated in April 1948, and the community program, though slowed down somewhat, continued its helpful ministry. At this time MCC turned the Sunday school over to the Mennonite Church, to become officially a Mennonite mission effort.

The end of the war made available some army barracks near Gulfport, and one of these was moved to a donated lot. A chapel, called Wayside, which had cost less than $200, was dedicated in May 1948, and worship services were again under way. But soon industrial development forced another relocation.

The new location was eight miles northeast of Gulfport, at the intersection of Three Rivers and Deadeaux Road. This was a beautiful location on a roomy, wooded yard in a rapidly growing community. With much help from other Mennonite churches and local personnel a building was constructed, with improvements being made from time to time. The persons who attended came from all walks of life: bookkeeper, nurse, schoolteacher, postman, plumber, airfield instructor, baker, printer, seamstress, housewife, auto mechanic, hospital worker.

The Camp Landon personnel attended and made a special contribution in music and teaching.

The church building was dedicated in June 1957, and the name of Crossroads Bible Church was chosen. Ed Miller was the pastor until April 1963 when he moved to a pastorate in Denver, Colorado.

In June of 1963 George Reno came from Akers, Louisiana, to become pastor. He retired from the pastorate in October 1968, but remained in the community for a while to serve the church through its youth program. Then he moved to Venice, Louisiana, to shepherd a few families there.

Harold R. Regier and wife, who had served in a General Conference Mennonite mission program at Camp Landon for seven and a half years, placed their membership at Crossroads in February 1969, and he was installed as pastor. But after a year's service he accepted a position with the General Conference Mennonite office at Newton, Kansas.

Both Ed Miller and Harold Regier carried on a radio ministry at Gulfport.

The membership at Crossroads was listed at thirty-seven in the *Mennonite Yearbook* for 1972. But during the year questions were raised about the ability of the congregation to continue. Proposals presented by Overseer John E. Wenger and Conference Minister Millard Osborne were not accepted. The building was rented to a Congregational Methodist group, and it was offered to them for sale. Crossroads has ceased to exist as a Mennonite congregation.[26]

CHURCHES IN THE SOUTH

CHAPTER

CHURCHES IN THE SOUTH

1. *Pleasant View, Custer County, Oklahoma*

In 1896, while Oklahoma was still a territory, B. B. Miller moved with his family from Kansas to the vicinity of Thomas, in what is now Custer County. The next year, 1897, W. C. Lantz and family moved here from Indiana. These were the first two Mennonite settlers in this new country, although some Old Order Amish had moved to Thomas in 1893.[1]

Farm products in those early days had to be hauled sixty miles east to the nearest elevator at El Reno. On the way the treacherous Canadian River had to be forded. Since the roads were rough and crooked, it took a week to go to town and to return. Neighbors lived several miles apart in little log houses. Sometimes herds of cattle, on the way from Texas to the Kansas railroads, went through the community — herds so large that it took several hours for them to pass. About every quarter mile there was a cowboy, riding along to herd the cattle and urge them along.

Bishop Joseph Schlegel, of Milford, Nebraska, organized here an Amish Mennonite church in March 1898 and had oversight for several years. There were ten charter members. In addition to the two founding couples, there were the following converts, who were baptized at that time: David Lantz, Edna Miller, J. I. Miller and wife, William Lantz, and Noah Miller. In that same year David Lantz and Edna Miller were married in the first wedding for the congregation. The first funeral was held in 1899, for W. C. Lantz.

It seems they had Sunday school right from the beginning. Services were held in the homes until 1902. Before they had a preacher of their own, occasionally they had a visiting preacher, and their Old Order Amish neighbors would join them in the special service. Differences were laid aside during those pioneer days when spiritual food was scarce. Almost all of these first services were held in German. Relations between Mennonites and Amish have always been friendly in this settlement.

Paul Glugash became a member of the church, and in the fall of 1899 he was ordained to the ministry by Bishop Schlegel. L. J. Miller, of Garden City, Missouri, assisted in the ordination, which was held at the home of A. B. Miller. In a few years Glugash moved away. About 1900 the oversight was transferred to another Bishop Joseph Schlegel, who had moved to Hartford, Kansas, from Thurman, Colorado, and finally, in December 1906, to this community in Oklahoma.

In 1902 a church building was erected across the road from the cemetery which is now used by the Old Order Amish. The building was small, only 24 by 24 feet. The first seats were merely boards borrowed from B. B. Miller's granary. This church was nine miles southeast of Thomas.

In November 1905 John Johns, at the age of twenty-three, was ordained to the ministry, and Lewis Eichorn was ordained deacon. L. J. Miller again assisted Bishop Schlegel in these ordinations.

By this time the language in the services had changed to English, although there were two German Sunday school classes until 1937.

By 1906 most of the families had moved to the Caddo Flat nearer Hydro. To make the church more central it was moved four and a half miles southeast, to a site on the farm of Bishop Schlegel. This location is nine miles northwest of Hydro, and twelve miles northeast of Weatherford. The church was named Pleasant View, for from the hill on which it stands one can see from ten to twenty miles in almost any direction. To the extreme southeast is a long butte.

Some additional family names by this time were Haas, Byler, White, Schantz, and Zook.

Revival meetings during these early years were held by Andrew Shenk of Missouri, D. D. Miller of Indiana, and N. E. Roth of Nebraska. Through these meetings not only Mennonite young people, but also some from outside families were brought into the church. The church grew steadily. A young people's meeting was started in 1909, with topics taken from the *Christian Monitor*.

In the spring of 1908 Deacon Lewis Eichorn and family moved to Guymon, Oklahoma, in a covered wagon — this left the church without a deacon. In 1909 and 1910 Bishop Schlegel, who by that time had very poor hearing, asked N. E. Roth to officiate in communion. In 1911 Minister Joseph Schantz moved to Nebraska. Bishop Schlegel died in July 1914. This left the care of the church to John Johns, who was a young man. Joseph Schlegel, the son of Bishop Joseph Schlegel, was ordained deacon in November 1914; he was 27 years old.

The little church could no longer accommodate the worshipers, and in the fall of 1915 the old building was enlarged. While this work was going on, meetings were held at Hopewell, a two-room schoolhouse. Here S. C. Yoder, Kalona, Iowa, held revival meetings. Large crowds attended, and there were fourteen confessions. In the spring of 1914, when Bishop Schlegel was ill, communion services were conducted by John Berkey of Hopedale, Illinois. He was given the oversight of the church after Schlegel's death. But Berkey was rather old and feeble, and the Western District Amish Mennonite Conference gave the oversight to I. G. Hartzler, of Cass County, Missouri. In 1918 four young men were drafted and had to report to army camps; they were Arthur Shantz, Henry Eichelberger, Ben Slagell, and Dan Slagell.

In August 118 John Johns, the young minister, died of a heart ailment. This left the church with only a deacon and a nonresident bishop. During the next six months Ed R. Herndon, a Brethren minister who lived close to the church, preached occasionally at Pleasant View. S. C. Miller, of Jet, Oklahoma, who was called to preach the funeral sermon of Johns, stayed several evenings for preaching services. D. R. Eyster, bishop of the Brethren in Christ Church near Thomas, also preached several times. When no minister was present, sometimes Deacon Slagell (the spelling of the name had now been changed) spoke, and other times the worship hour was spent in singing.

John Slagell, 25 years old and unmarried, was ordained to the ministry by Bishop Hartzler in February 1919. The next year he was married to Alice Schantz. John was the youngest son of Bishop Joseph Schlegel. In November 1919 Alva Swartzendruber,

Bishop Alva Swartzendruber and wife

who had moved to Oklahoma Territory in 1905, was ordained to the ministry. This gave the church youthful but capable leadership — two ministers in their twenties and a deacon in his thirties. In November 1922 I. G. Hartzler ordained a bishop. Alva Swartzendruber, at twenty-eight, was chosen by congregational vote, without the use of the lot.

The second church house became so inadequate for the increased attendance that a new building was constructed during the winter of 1924-1925. It was 34 by 54 feet, and had a gallery above the entrance and cloakrooms. It also had a large basement. On May 10, 1925, the new church was dedicated in an all-day service. J. A. Heatwole, of La Junta, Colorado, preached the dedication sermon. People came from Hydro and Thomas, and some had to stand. In the fall of 1927 the Missouri-Kansas Conference, to which Pleasant View now belonged, met here. It was the first time the congregation felt able to entertain such a meeting.

In May 1930 there were 129 members in the church, with one bishop, one minister, and one deacon. The deacon took his turn at preaching at the request of the bishop or minister, about every fifth Sunday. The attendance was at its highest in 1931, with an average in the Sunday school of 172 for that year. During the next few years — the Depression — the attendance diminished by about forty because four of the largest families left. They left for economic reasons. The coming of the tractor and combine made land and jobs hard to get, and it was hard to support large families. They moved to the East, where manual labor was more plentiful: two families to Delaware, one to Indiana, and one to Iowa. By 1942 the average attendance had again climbed to 164.

Almost from the beginning of this church, singing was an important part of the worship. John D. Miller and H. H. Haas, who both came in 1905, loved to sing and both taught singing in their young manhood. The Slagells, who came a little later, also loved to sing. The young people would often gather during the week to spend the evening singing. These were the only gatherings they had, until the twenties, when they started having social gatherings; they never organized a literary society. In 1932 a young men's quartet and a young ladies' octet were formed, which later developed into men's and ladies' choruses, directed by W. C. Schantz and Valentine Swartzendruber, and "chorus practice" almost replaced the singings of previous days. Singing by smaller groups has always been allowed and enjoyed in this church. To maintain interest in congregational singing, hymnbooks were changed frequently, and singing schools were held at the church every few years. In 1954 Chester Slagell organized a Men's Chorus which has continued to the present time. This group has presented programs locally, as well as in churches of Kansas, Colorado, and Arkansas.

The congregation has a strong mission and service interest. During 1925-1937 Phebe Waters gave her full time at the Hutchinson Mission. The Sunday school gave $5 per month toward her support, and the same amount in 1940 to support Katie Anna Swartzendruber Birky in mission work at Adair, Oklahoma. In 1938 five Pleasant View members went to Missouri to help in summer Bible school work, and each summer has found some teachers from Hydro, either in the Ozarks or in a city mission.

On Missionary Day in November there is usually a missionary program by the children. On this day they bring their quarter investment funds, a practice which was started probably before the twenties.

During the years 1942-1946 a number of the young men served in Civilian Public Service as an alternate to military service: Glen

Swartzendruber, Walter and Harold Slagell in California; Alva Yoder in Colorado and Montana; Leroy Miller in Colorado and New Jersey; Melvin Miller in Idaho; Ernest Schantz in Iowa; Allen Miller in Colorado; and Chester Slagell in Iowa and Mississippi, where he continued in a term of Voluntary Service.

Beginning in 1952 a number of young people were in drafted and/or voluntary service. Carl Eichelberger, Carl Dean and Daniel Slagell, and John Dale Schantz served in I-W at Pueblo, Colorado, later at Wichita, Kansas, or Reedley, California. Howard Stutzman served in the Kansas City General Hospital; Maurice Slagell was in VS at the Portland, Maine, General Hospital; and Maxton Slagell was in I-W service at Denver, Colorado. Doris Slagell gave a two-year term of VS as a teacher in San Juan, Puerto Rico, in 1964-1966. Kenneth Bailey spent two years in the Pax program in Israel during 1964-1966, and Keith Miller was a Pax worker in Bolivia beginning in 1967. Richard Thomas and Robert Stutzman served two years in VS in the hospitals at La Junta and Rocky Ford, Colorado, while Roberta Stutzman gave a year of VS in the migrant program at Surprise, Arizona. This kind of participation in the church's service program is continuing.

In 1964 the Pleasant View congregation, in cooperation with the Oak Grove and Zion congregations of eastern Oklahoma, assisted in building a church for a new congregation at Spencer, Oklahoma.

The Pleasant View Church as remodeled in 1972

In 1917 a sewing circle was organized. The circle met in homes at first, but now meets in the church building. This work was supported at first by each member bringing an offering to the sewing meeting, but it is now supported by a monthly church offering.

Wednesday evening Bible study meetings were organized in 1919, but were discontinued in 1926.

Complete membership records were not kept until about 1908. About one fourth of the members came from non-Mennonite homes. Some came from other denominations: Christian, Lutheran, Brethren, Old Order Amish. There were 167 members in 1972. Most work on farms, but there are also nurses, teachers, electricians, grain buyers, oil salesmen, carpenters, and mechanics.

Summer Bible school for children in Nursery through Grade 10 was held for the first time in the spring of 1942 with an enrollment of 130, and has been continued every summer since. The attendants have been not only children who attend the Pleasant View Sunday school, but those of other denominations of the community and the surrounding towns.

To provide more adequate Sunday school and summer Bible school classroom facilities, the church basement was remodeled in 1956. And a major remodeling in 1971-1972 constructed a new brick auditorium and remodeled the old auditorium for use as a fellowship hall. The new auditorium is air-conditioned. It does not have a basement. But in the old basement new classroom partitioning has been provided. A dedication and open house was held on March 26, 1972.

Joseph Slagell in 1962 asked to be relieved of his deacon responsibilities because of his age. His health steadily declined until his death on August 16, 1972. Bishop Alva Swartzendruber requested that because of his age a younger person assist him in the ministerial responsibilities. Chester Slagell was licensed to assist with the ministry of the church in March 1962. Then in July 1963, he was ordained to the ministry. Bishop Swartzendruber's wife, Mattie, passed away on February 14, 1968. In July 1969, Alva Swartzendruber took residence at Pleasantview Home at Kalona, Iowa, where he served as chaplain. After Alva Swartzendruber moved, Chester Slagell was named pastor, and in 1970 elders were elected by the congregation to assist the pastor.

The Pleasant View congregation has been privileged to have a number of couples observe their 50th wedding anniversaries: V. D. and Kate Detweiler, December 8, 1945, and their 60th anniversary in 1955; Jake and Mae Miller, December 26, 1959; Julius and Lizzie Miller, January 3, 1957; Joe and Emma Slagel on March 9, 1963; Levi and Mary Miller, July 26, 1964; Sam and Barbara Stutzman, November 5, 1966; and Alva and Mattie Swartzendruber, December 26, 1966.

In March 1973 the Pleasant View congregation celebrated its seventy-fifth anniversary. Through pictures and a drama it was emphasized that the people came here because the blue-stem land was calling. Former members from Florida, Pennsylvania, Indiana, Kansas, and Oklahoma told what the church here has meant to them. Speakers were the former bishop and pastor, Alva Swartzendruber, and the present pastor, Chester Slagell. Three hundred people enjoyed the noon meal in the fellowship hall. Among the historical displays, in one room two coal-oil lamps used in the 1898 building were burning.[2]

2. *Zion, Mayes County, Oklahoma*

Pryor is a town in eastern Oklahoma, forty miles east of Tulsa, the great oil center. It is the post office of the Zion congregation.

The first Mennonite settlers came here from Cass County, Missouri, in 1910. About fifty members came from there at this time. This migration was not exactly a schism. But those who moved were on the conservative side of several questions, and felt that Sycamore Grove was getting too worldly. The issues were not the telephone and the automobile, for some of these who went to Oklahoma were among the first to use these new inventions. In general, it was those who were followers of John Kauffman, the sleeping preacher from Indiana, who went to Pryor. Kauffman, in his sermons to the group, had advised them to leave. His last visit to Cass County was in 1910.

B. F. Hartzler, who had been ordained to the ministry at Sycamore Grove in May 1897, led the search for a new location. In August 1910 he went to Stuttgart, Arkansas, with the hope that someone from there would accompany him to Pryor, Oklahoma. No one could go, and so several men from Cass County met Hartzler at Pryor. A man by the name of Joe Miller helped them to locate farms. This had been Indian Territory land and was just becoming available to settlers. The land they bought was not cleared and was unimproved.

Some of the party moved in 1910, and others in the spring of 1911. These first families arrived in the following order: Christian

Hostetler, Sam Hostetler, Levi Hostetler, Pius Hostetler, Dave Hostetler, Ben Hartzler, Jake Kropf, Albert Kropf, Niles Yoder, Sam Schrock.

B. F. Hartzler was the minister of the group. A congregation was organized in September 1911. Bishop Jacob Yoder of Stuttgart was in charge, but he did not move to Pryor until March 1912. Services were held alternately in a temporary shed at David Hostetlers, in German, and at the Ogretta Schoolhouse, in English.

Additional members received by letter in 1912 were Bishop Yoder and his adopted daughter, Katie Rich, Rudy Sutter with his wife and son, T. K. Zook and son, and Jake Sutter. By 1920 all the members had left Stuttgart, many of them going to Pryor.

In the fall of 1912 Bishop Yoder purchased a nearly new building and moved it to an acre of ground that had been donated by Rudy Sutter for a church and cemetery site. B. F. Hartzler bought the windows and lumber needed to complete the building.

First officers of the Sunday school were Jake Sutter, superintendent; T. K. Zook, secretary; and Irvin Hartzler, chorister. For some years only men were allowed to teach Sunday school classes. The first marriage in the congregation was that of Jake Sutter and Nettie Kropf.

In June 1914 Bishop Jacob Yoder died. He was buried at Stuttgart, where his wife had been buried in 1903. Bishop J. C. Birkey of Illinois served the congregation as bishop until his health began to fail. Then he authorized B. F. Hartzler to administer the ordinances, which he did for many years; but he was never ordained to the bishop office. I. G. Hartzler was bishop from 1915 to 1937. In 1919 the church decided to ordain a deacon. Irvin Hartzler was chosen by lot and served, sometimes as the temporary pastor, until his resignation in 1963. He died in 1967.

Minister Sam Sommers was one who moved from Stuttgart in 1920. He died in 1923, and was buried in the Fairview Cemetery at Pryor.

Since all the members had left Stuttgart, many of them going to Pryor, it was decided to move the church building also. Five men took the building down, loaded it on a boxcar, and shipped it to Oklahoma. Here the house was erected again, with two anterooms added. In this building the congregation worshiped for forty-one years. After that it was used as an educational building until 1972.

A sewing circle was organized in 1927, meeting monthly in private homes. Ida Springer, who later was Mrs. Dan Sommers, was the first president.

In the spring of 1935 B. F. Hartzler began to fail in health. He consulted specialists in Kansas City, but in July he died in Cass County and was buried there. The vacancy in the ministry at Pryor was filled by the ordination, in June 1936, of Dan Sommers, the son of the former minister. For reasons of health he moved to Archbold, Ohio, in 1943.

When John Kauffman preached in Missouri, he charged that the conference — which was the Western A. M. — was leading them into worldliness. So the group at Pryor, called the Zion Amish Mennonite Church, was not much interested in conference membership, even though they were carried on the list of congregations in the Western A. M. Conference, and after that the Missouri-Kansas Conference. The members did not seem to be at unity on this and other matters, and after a few years the Hostetlers and Sam Schrocks moved to Shelbyville, Illinois, where their esteemed teacher, John Kauffman, came and was ordained as their bishop. Some of this group scattered and formed congregations at other places. But all of these are unrelated to any conference. It was an early nonconference movement.

Whatever may have been the attitude of B. F. Hartzler and his congregation toward conference after the Hostetlers left, it is significant that the only history produced by the congregation says concerning conference membership: "Until the year 1937 this church was known as the Zion Amish Mennonite Church. In this same year the church became associated with (what is now) the South Central Conference, (then) known as the Missouri-Kansas Conference. From this time on it was called the Zion Mennonite Church. Bro. Alva Swartzendruber from Hydro, Oklahoma, was serving the Church as Bishop at that time."

It seems clear that the Zion congregation before 1937 did not consider itself a member of any conference. When the Western Amish Mennonite Conference became a part of the other Western conferences in the early 1920s, Zion apparently did not feel a part of the merger, and kept the Amish name until 1937.

After Dan Sommers left, there was again need for a pastor. Nelson Histand, who was serving the Missouri-Kansas Mission Board at Culp, Arkansas, was invited to serve as pastor at Zion. He came in 1944, and in 1950 was ordained as bishop. After a decade of service Histand, because of failing health, asked for help, and in April

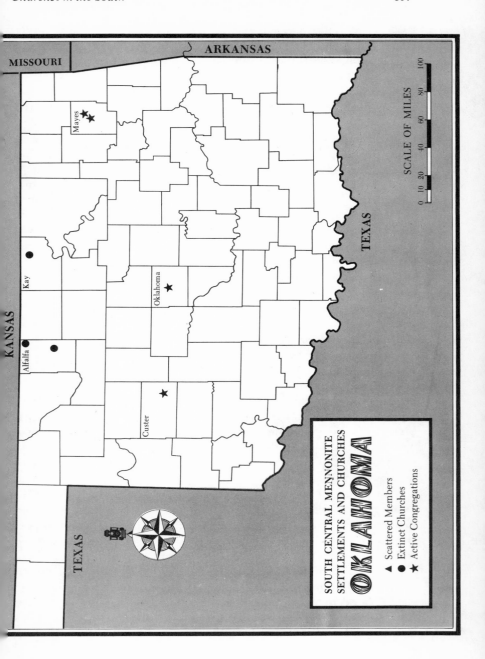

SOUTH CENTRAL MENNONITE
SETTLEMENTS AND CHURCHES

OKLAHOMA

▲ Scattered Members
● Extinct Churches
★ Active Congregations

SCALE OF MILES

0 10 20   40   60   80   100

1955 Walter Funk was ordained as assistant pastor. The next winter Histand resigned his pastorate, having been elected as overseer for the Oklahoma and Arkansas area by the Executive Committee of the South Central Conference. Funk was given full responsibility for the Zion congregation, and served until he resigned in June 1959.

In 1958 the congregation asked Richard Birky, who lived nearby at Adair, to serve as their bishop and to help in finding a pastor. John M. Troyer, a former member of Zion who was now serving as deacon of the Clinton Brick congregation in Indiana, accepted a call and was ordained to serve as pastor in December 1959 by Bishops Richard Birky and Harry A. Diener, with Menno Troyer assisting.

In the spring of 1964 Troyer, because of failing health, asked for the help of an assistant pastor. Alva J. Yoder was chosen from the congregation and ordained to the ministry in July 1964. Participating in this ordination were Bishop Birky, Pastor Troyer, Clayton Beyler, and Howard J. Zehr.

In August 1966 John M. Troyer moved to Arkansas, where he had accepted a call to be pastor of the Culp and Calico Rock congregations. After that, Alva J. Yoder served as pastor at Zion. Ralph Yoder, who was ordained as deacon in 1950 at Alpha, Minnesota, was installed as deacon at Pryor in 1964.

Through the years the church grew; the membership in 1972 was 148. The congregation had outgrown the meetinghouse. In the fall of 1959 a committee of six was appointed to investigate. Three plans for additional space were presented, and the congregation selected the one which was used. Ground was broken in February 1961. Men of the congregation did most of the work. First services were held in the new auditorium on May 7, 1961.

On July 23, 1961, was observed both the fiftieth anniversary of the church's organization and the dedication of the new building. It was an all-day service, with a fellowship dinner at noon. The dedication message was by a former bishop, Alva Swartzendruber. Other speakers were James Detweiler and Richard Birky. There was special music by the Eden quartet and a Pleasant Valley group directed by Reuben Yoder.

The new church was built alongside the old one, which was remodeled for an educational building. But in 1972 this old building was replaced by a new educational building, which was dedicated in April. Again there were all-day services. In the morning there was a message by Dale Dorsey, Mennonite minister living at Conway,

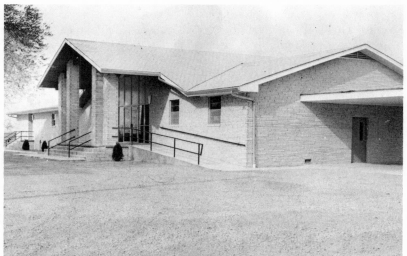

The old and the new meetinghouses at Pryor, Oklahoma

Arkansas. The dedication message in the afternoon was by Chester Slagell, now serving as overseer of the Oklahoma churches of the South Central Conference. The evening message was by Richard Birky.

In June 1973 Alva J. Yoder accepted a Mennonite pastorate at Macon, Mississippi. Succeeding him at Zion is William Briskey, from Altoona, Pennsylvania,[3] who was ordained minister July 22, 1973.

3. *Gulfhaven, Gulfport, Mississippi*

Early in 1920 a number of families from Colorado and Kansas became interested in some land for sale in the northwest part of Harrison County, Mississippi. It was cut-over pine land advertised in the *Kansas City Star* by a lumber company which had removed from it all the good virgin timber. That year four men — J. M. Brunk, Amos Rhodes, D. S. Weaver, and Oliver Showalter — investigated the possibilities of a Mennonite settlement here. They took an option on 5,000 acres near Lyman and Gulfport and proceeded to interest others.

Early in 1921 Deacon David S. Geil moved his family down from the Crystal Springs congregation at Harper, Kansas. Minister D. S. Brunk and wife had spent the winter of 1920-1921 at Long Beach, near Gulfport. In 1921 their two sons, both ministers, John M. and Jacob B., came, as did also John S. Ross and I. E. Hershey from Colorado, Paul Hershey from Missouri, and S. M. Buckwalter from Kansas. These all bought land and began building homes in what was called the Mennonite Colony, fifteen miles northwest of the commercial and tourist center of Gulfport.

From the very beginning the group was concerned about building a congregation. First they met on Sunday afternoons with a small Methodist group at Finley, on the Poplarville Road. Then they met in a shack until a church building could be constructed. The simple little structure in the center of the colony, lighted with Coleman lamps, was dedicated in January 1922. Bishop Andrew Shenk organized the congregation with twenty-eight adults and young people as charter members. The Brunk brothers were the ministers and D. S. Geil was the deacon. During this first year the E. J. Hersheys and the Walter Greenwoods came. By the end of the year there were thirty-nine members. The congregation chose a name, Gulfhaven, from a list suggested by the members, and it was accepted into the Missouri-Kansas Conference.

But during 1922, also, John M. Brunk was lost to the church through a moral lapse. In 1929 he died in an accident, and lies buried in the Gulfhaven Cemetery. Until 1927 J. B. Brunk and his father served the congregation. When J. B. Brunk left, D. J. Brand, a General Conference Mennonite minister who had moved into the community, preached for the group. In December 1927 Clarence Bontrager, of Kansas, was installed as pastor by Bishop I. G. Hartzler. He returned to Hesston College in 1929 to pursue his education.

A view of the original church building at Gulfhaven. Mrs. E. J. Hershey and Mary and Samuel are in the foreground.

Before 1930 other families came to Gulfhaven: Myrta Brunk, Earl Geil, Abram Eby, and Walter Rutt. The Jacob Yoder, Harvey Lantz, and Milford Miller families moved to the Kiln-Picayune area thirty miles to the west. But there was no church there, and their membership was at Gulfhaven.

Of great importance to the congregation were a number of families from other denominations who moved into the community and attended the Gulfhaven Church regularly. Besides D. J. Brand, the Sam and Ed Langenwalters represented the General Conference Mennonites. There were also such family names as Schanbacher, Nix, Cadle, Stayton, and Huston.

In its first decade this small congregation experienced many difficulties. The glow and the smoke from burning stumps could be seen far into the night as the land was being cleared. The land did not produce as had been hoped; these Northerners had to adjust to a different soil and climate and to new farming methods. They did not feel the kinship to the land felt by those who had always lived here. For this and other economic reasons, members went to town for employment. Some families moved away. When some members proved unfaithful, all the members suffered. It was only through the heroic struggle and diligence of the pioneers that the church has endured.

The Great Depression through the thirties was difficult for everyone. Houses were unfinished, and debts were hard to pay. But there were also hidden blessings in the struggle. By sharing burdens and problems, as well as all kinds of material things, the group became welded together to a degree that affluence cannot give.

Late in 1929 the Levi S. Yoder family moved into the community from Virginia. Yoder was an ordained minister, and he was asked to serve as pastor. He served until 1944, when the family moved back to Virginia. During these years, the years of the Depression, the congregation reached its highest total membership — 75 in 1940. This was due both to growing families and to people moving in. Among these new families were Milford Millers, Harvey Lantzes, Simon Millers, and John Detwilers. Several members of the local O'Neal family joined the church.

In the early thirties, Levi Yoder established a broom factory in the community that furnished employment for members of his family and a number of others. This was a real help during the Depression years. Paul Yoder during these years organized a community chorus. This proved to be good for community relations.

Clarence W. Geil, son of Paul and Cora Geil, was the first baby born in the colony. Russell Wenger and Edith Ross were the first couple married here. The first funeral was for Mrs. Walter Greenwood's mother, who lived with them. However, the first grave in the cemetery back of the church was Walter Greenwood's father, who was brought in for burial.

The women first organized as the WMSA about 1926, and during all the years since many women from various denominations have worked faithfully with the Gulfhaven women in sewing projects and in giving money and labor for relief and services.

Deacon David Geil died in May 1935. Before his death, however, E. J. Hershey in 1931 was ordained to the office of deacon by Bishop J. N. Durr. He served faithfully until his death in 1959. In 1934 Paul Hershey was ordained as minister to assist Levi Yoder. He became pastor and bishop in 1943.

In 1946 Edward J. Miller, who was a member of the CPS camp near Gulfport, was ordained to the ministry to assist in the ministry at Gulfhaven. During his ministry the church building was remodeled;

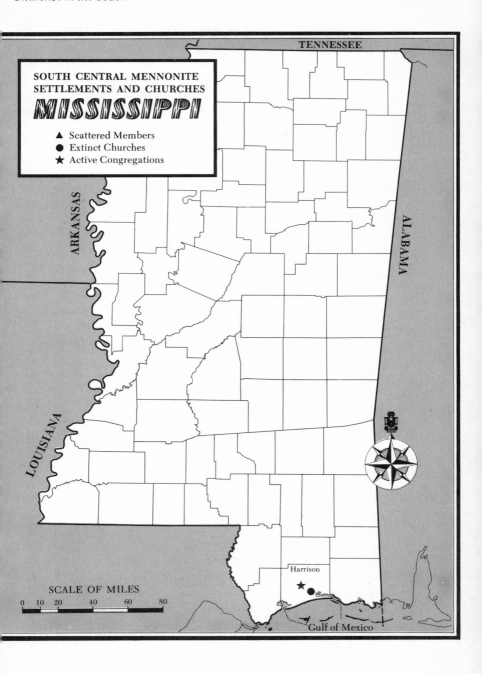

SOUTH CENTRAL MENNONITE
SETTLEMENTS AND CHURCHES

MISSISSIPPI

▲ Scattered Members
● Extinct Churches
★ Active Congregations

TENNESSEE

ARKANSAS

ALABAMA

LOUISIANA

Harrison

SCALE OF MILES

0   10   20   40   60   80

Gulf of Mexico

a library, three Sunday school rooms, and walks were added. He was responsible for much of the planning and the work himself. Dedication services for the new addition were held in August 1948. Miller was released by Gulfhaven in 1949 to become pastor of the new Wayside congregation at Gulfport.

In 1940 the first summer Bible school was held. Esther Detwiler came from Birch Tree, Missouri, to help organize the school, which was held in the church building. The next year it was moved to the Lyman School in order to accommodate more people. The school continued at Lyman until 1951. As a result of this effort many children from a wide area, and of many denominations, received Bible teaching. Attendance reached as high as 150. Even during the war years and gas rationing, the Lord always provided a way for the school to go on. After 1951 the school was held at Saucier, Mississippi, for a few years, and then it was moved back to the church, where it has been held every year since. The churches in Lyman and Saucier now conduct their own Bible schools.

Only three of the original farms near the church are still owned by members of the congregation. Members have been teachers, carpenters, and mechanics. The congregation has been fairly successful in keeping its young people in the community. The membership in 1972 was fifty.

In the early years a mission Sunday school was held one summer in the Lizana community. There has been an offering for missions on the first Sunday of each month for more than forty years. A number of young people served in CPS, VS, and I-W both at home and abroad. One couple has served two terms in relief work under MCC. In the early days of the work at CPS Camp Bernard there was close fellowship and cooperation with the work there. Likewise, when hurricane Camille in 1969 struck savagely at the entire Gulf Coast, and Mennonite Disaster Service came in to help overcome the damage, the congregation helped as much as its own hurts would permit. In 1973 Walter Rutt supervised MDS operations along the Mississippi.

In 1942 the first Gulf Coast Inspirational Conference was held at Gulfhaven. It took in the churches of Louisiana and Mississippi and has proved to be a real help to these small and isolated congregations. The conferences are held in May of each year. One thing that made it possible for Gulfhaven to host these meetings was the donation of the old Geil house, less than a mile east of the church, for use as a

*Harry and Anna Diener,
pastor, 1966-1970*

community center. The WMSA also met there. It was used for fellowship dinners and wedding receptions until the new annex was completed in 1967.

In January 1952 Paul Holdeman was ordained as pastor by Paul Hershey, and he served about two years before going to Denver for an MCC assignment. From 1959 to 1963 Paul L. Yoder, son of Levi Yoder, served the congregation as a licensed pastor. He moved to Colorado for a hospital assignment. In June 1964 Robert Yoder from Albuquerque, New Mexico, was made pastor and served one year before he answered a call from California. Between the ministry of Paul Yoder and the coming of Robert Yoder, Orlo Kaufman from Camp Landon preached for the congregation.

Although Paul Hershey had wanted to resign some years before, he continued to supply as pastor and preached during these years of change from one pastor to another. After the death of his wife, Martha, in 1962, in 1964 he married Christine Christensen, and several years later moved with her to near Chicago, and attends a Lutheran church there.

In 1966 Harry A. Diener, a retired bishop from Hutchinson, Kansas, came to serve as interim pastor. Although he reached his eightieth birthday while he was here, his ministry was so acceptable that the interim period lasted until 1970. In the fall of that year Lester Horst became the pastor. He was first licensed, and then ordained in May 1972.

In December 1966 the congregation voted unanimously to proceed with the building of an annex. Walter Rutt and C. W. Geil drew the plan and directed the work. Much of the work was donated. Ground was broken in January 1967, and on April 30 the first fellowship dinner was held in the new addition. A dedication was held in August, with a sermon by Nevin Bender, a dedication litany led by Harry A. Diener, and a dedicatory prayer by Paul Hershey. The new facility has provided two classrooms, a large sewing room — also used as a classroom, a well-equipped kitchenette, and indoor rest rooms.

The congregation celebrated its fiftieth anniversary on October 29, 1972. The mingling of past and present participants in the fellowship at Gulfhaven was a happy celebration of the successful founding of a new church community; the provision of a church home for settlers, VS and CPS workers, and tourists; the achievement of a spirit of love and concern in a wide circle of people; and the clear proclamation of the Christian faith in southern Mississippi.[4]

4. *Oak Grove, Mayes County, Oklahoma*

"God loves the hill country, for He made so much of it." So wrote M. Lena Kreider.

Adair, ten miles north of Pryor, is on the edge of the hill country which stretches away eastward to the Ozarks.

It was about 1928 when Monroe Hostetler, a layman who had served in maintenance at Hesston College for some years, was visiting relatives in eastern Oklahoma. Finding land up in the hills at a reasonable price, he purchased a home and moved into the community.

The Hostetlers had family worship in their home. One day several neighbor ladies happened in at worship time, and were asked to join the family in Bible reading and prayer. At that time there was no church in the community. There was a schoolhouse on the side of the hill below the Hostetlers where a Sunday school had been started a number of times but no one had been able to keep it going.

The ladies enjoyed the Hostetler devotions so much that they asked whether they might come often. As other neighbors heard about this, they too wanted to come. Finally Hostetler decided to use the schoolhouse and have a Sunday school. Soon the little building was filled and became the center of the community life. Hostetler was accepted as a capable leader.

When Hostetler suffered a stroke and was no longer able to conduct the Sunday school, it continued under the leadership of Mrs. Ray Rhodes. There were two other Mennonite families in the community — the Mahlon Bares and Chris Millers. The Baldwin Millers came up from Pryor to help. In 1940 the Richard Birkys moved to Adair. He was ordained in 1942 as the congregation's first minister. But six years later he had to take a Colorado pastorate for health reasons. Ivan Headings was ordained in 1947 to serve as pastor. When he felt called to leave, Roy Creason, a Baptist layman of the community, was asked to supply the vacancy.

The Birkys returned to Adair in 1955. The new Will Rogers Turnpike was being built five miles west of Adair, and Birky was able to buy for $500 a house that had to be moved. In a series of answers to prayer they were able to buy a tract of land to which to move the house, and to borrow the money to make all this possible. He made his living by hauling with a dump truck he had purchased.

It was necessary to move the Sunday school away from the schoolhouse, and for a time it was held under shade trees on the Mahlon Bare place. At this time, 1942, an acre of land one half mile south of the school was purchased and a building moved onto it. This was used as a church until 1953. Headings decided, since the school was not being used, that it might be a boost to the attendance to move back to the school. In the fall of 1956 there was serious planning for building a place of worship. A Thanksgiving Day offering amounted to $450, and with that and a great deal of faith they started on a 30 by 50 foot concrete block building. A site on Highway 28 four and a half miles west of Adair was donated by Roy Creason.

Men from Hydro and Adair helped with the foundation, the floor, and the roof. Everette Scheffel supervised the block laying. Most of the interior finishing was done by the Oak Grove group. Used pews were purchased for $10 each from a church which was getting new ones. The building had two classrooms at each end. The approximate cost, including a propane heating plant, was $3,000.

The church was dedicated debt-free on May 12, 1957. There was an all-day meeting, with a basket lunch at noon. Alva Swartzendruber preached the dedicatory sermon. There was special music by a men's chorus from Hydro, a male quartet from Zion, and solos by Indian pastor Davis from near the Arkansas line. Pastor

Birky led the congregation in a dedication litany. This was the closing paragraph of the litany:

"With memory of the past and vision for the future, realizing that we are 'compassed about with so great a cloud of witnesses,' we do here and now dedicate ourselves anew to the teaching of the Word of God and in both precept and practice by presenting our 'bodies a living sacrifice, holy, acceptable unto God, which is our reasonable service,' and do now declare this building built for the worship of God Almighty, separated and set apart from common and secular uses. We now dedicate this building to the sacred uses of God's people, as a place of prayer and worship, nurture, and Christian training, to the glory of God and the good of man, in the name of God the Father, God the Son, and God the Holy Spirit."

The congregation meets regularly three times a week; the prayer meeting is attended as well as any meeting. The women meet once a month for sewing for relief. The summer Bible school is a regular part of the year's program. In 1972 the sisters started a Bible study once a week. The ladies in the community are taking a good interest and there seems to be a real thirst for the truths of the Word. The congregation experiences a rich fellowship.

In 1967 an A-frame was built over the front entrance to relieve the flat appearance of the structure. In 1972 a room 24 x 30

Oak Grove Church

was built on the west side, including rest rooms and kitchen facilities. The sisters appreciate this for their monthly meetings. Though the congregation is small (38 in 1972), the pastor receives partial support. Those who know the story of this mission church from its beginning see the working of the Lord in providing for the needs of His children and giving spiritual light in the surrounding community.

One of the converts, a man who lost a leg in an accident during his teens, has given this testimony: "The Oak Grove Mennonite Mission has become very dear to me. It was here I accepted the Lord and was received into the church and later witnessed the conversion and baptism of my father. The faith and testimony of this congregation and the ministers who have labored here have been a constant source of encouragement and comfort — beginning with their prayers and concern for my soul's well-being and continuing until now."[5]

5. *Des Allemands, Saint Charles Parish, Louisiana*

Des Allemands is a town of a thousand people in the low country lying west of the Mississippi River levees. It is twenty-five miles west of New Orleans.

Bishop E. S. Hallman and family came here from Alabama in 1917. About the same time a colony of home-seeking Mennonites moved in from northern Indiana. Some Old Order Amish and Wisler Mennonites were among them. Some names in the settlement were Wenger, Grabill, Beachy, Ressler, and Slabaugh. In 1920 the Hallmans moved on to southern Texas.

Evangelization was not the primary motivation of this first settlement. But they did have services in their homes; even when they had no resident minister, they sometimes had visiting preachers. There was spiritual hunger in the hearts of their Catholic neighbors, and in those first years ten people were baptized and joined the Mennonite Church. Among the visitors who gave spiritual help was Bishop A. O. Histand, of Doylestown, Pennsylvania.

After four years the threat of flooding broke up the community. A few families were flooded; others feared the uncertainty of crops and the liability of high water. Chester A. Wenger, the father of John E. Wenger, who is now the pastor at Des Allemands, was one who knew he wanted to leave Louisiana, and he felt led to move to a place in the Lansdale area of eastern Pennsylvania. John was

eleven years old when they left Des Allemands, and he never forgot
the people there. When he was thirteen he promised the Lord he
would go back to Louisiana sometime.

There were members of the church at Des Allemands who needed shepherding, and the Missouri-Kansas Mission Board agreed to
continue work there. Ministers were sent in to preach and to visit.
Bishop Andrew Shenk was burdened for the remnant of those who had
been baptized by him. He saw Allemands as a fruitful mission field.
Arrangements were made for J. B. Brunk to make monthly trips
from Gulfport. He got other evangelists to help him.[6]

Lizzie Wenger was a devoted woman who had a burden for
the Des Allemands field. She spent time there trying to keep services going. In the summer of 1925 Brunk got William Jennings to
help in a series of evangelistic meetings at Des Allemands. But
there was no suitable meeting place. So Lizzie Wenger furnished the
money for the building of a tabernacle. Brunk and Jennings put
it up in five days. It was just a shell of a building, 28 x 20 x 7.
The screen walls kept out millions of mosquitoes. The interest of
the people was good.[7]

That fall S. E. Allgyer was sent south by the General Mission
Board to study the field as a place for a rural mission. Leidy Hun-
sicker of Blooming Glen, Pennsylvania, went with him to help with
the singing. They held a week's meetings at Allemands in the tabernacle.[8] In 1926 when Paul Erb and family stopped here, the tabernacle was still in use. But after a few years it was torn down.

Family names of the native people, many of them French, who
came into the Christian life in these years were Le Blanc, Tourell,
Schmell, Meyers, and St. Amant.

The real building of a congregation at Des Allemands dates from
1936, when John E. Wenger and his wife, Esther (Moyer), fulfilled the
promise he had made to the Lord. They did not move to Louisiana
to prosper financially; they knew they could do that better in Pennsylvania. But they had faith that if other people could live in the watery
country of Des Allemands, they could too.

John's parents went down in May to find a place for them to live.
In September John E. Wenger's sister Mabel and her husband, Lester
M. Hackman, whom the Lord had also called to the South, joined
the pilgrimage to Des Allemands. They found that Dad Wenger had
started Sunday school in some homes, the first Sunday school in the
area. Soon there were some faithful attendants.

There was a very small Presbyterian Church building in Des Allemands, which the newcomers bought for $200. This building was moved to a more suitable location. The Blooming Glen congregation in Pennsylvania took an offering to help pay for this venture. This little meetinghouse served the group until 1949.

Bishop E. S. Hallman was quick to back up the consecrated young people who had the vision of a church at Des Allemands. He asked their Pennsylvania bishop, A. O. Histand, to come to Louisiana and help to organize the church. In November 1937, John E. Wenger was ordained pastor and Lester Hackman, deacon, both by unanimous voice. In that year the congregation became a member of the South Central Conference. Evangelists came in to help in giving the gospel call. When James Bucher preached in 1940, Henry Tregle, Jr., was convicted and became a Christian.

Slowly the membership grew, and a larger building became necessary. In 1949, at Thanksgiving, a new meetinghouse, 30 by 60, was started. C. Z. Martin, of Columbia, Pennsylvania, was there for meetings, and encouraged them to move ahead. Three men from the CPS camp at Gulfport helped to put in the foundation. There was $800 in the building fund, and they ordered $1,600 worth of lumber. More help came from Gulfport, and then from Pennsylvania. The old church was enclosed in the new one, and not one service was lost during the building process.

By Christmas the unfinished building was in use, with sheets hung on the front walls. Enough money came in to make it possible to keep buying material. The total outlay for the building was $5,500. The indebtedness when it was finished was $1,400.

That spring, in 1950, Jacob Rittenhouse held meetings, and that fall, Richard Birky. Within that year there were fifteen new members, all new family units. The attendance grew to more than one hundred. It was clear that now the people had confidence that the Mennonites would stay, and not leave them. The church growth was chiefly from people of the community, as is seen by the family names on the membership list: Comardelle, Waterman, Bergeron, Arceneaux, Alphosine, Trauth, Champagne, Cortez, Matherne, Folse, Monier, Mecum, Cornwell. Local talent was used for teaching and youth activity.

The summer Bible school has always been important here, for many children come whose Catholic parents do not allow them to attend other services. In one year in the fifties, in a total of 162,

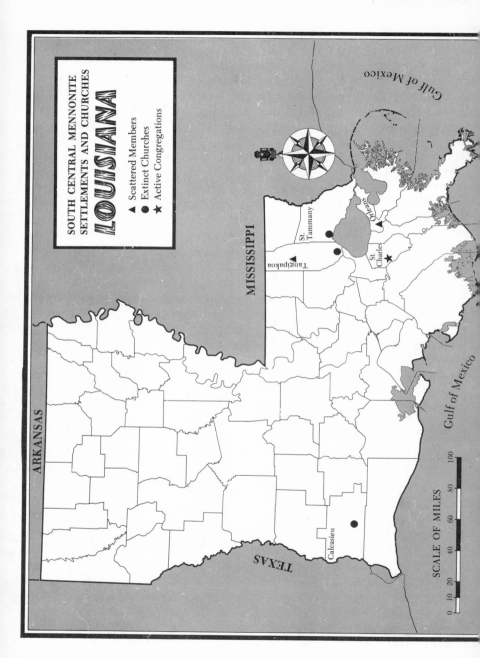

SOUTH CENTRAL MENNONITE
SETTLEMENTS AND CHURCHES

LOUISIANA

▲ Scattered Members
● Extinct Churches
★ Active Congregations

MISSISSIPPI

ARKANSAS

TEXAS

Gulf of Mexico

Gulf of Mexico

St. Tammany

Tangipahoa

St. Charles

Orleans

Calcasieu

SCALE OF MILES

0 10 20 40 60 80 100

there were 92 Catholic children enrolled.

Room was a problem. Classes were held in a tent and in nearby homes. Adjoining lots became available and were purchased by the church. In 1960 a 35 by 55 foot addition was built to the back of the church. This provided classrooms, an assembly hall, and a kitchen.

In 1957 the congregation began financial support of its pastor. This was pushed by the conference, and the challenge was taken up by the people. This has made the pastor more free to meet the spiritual needs of the church. The expanding building program has been paid for by the church. Total contributions in 1971 were about $9,000.

In 1965 hurricane Betsy struck the Louisiana coast with record force and destruction. Winds were up to 150 miles per hour. There was a tidal wave beyond New Orleans. Many buildings were washed away, and few roofs did not need repair. Des Allemands became a base of operations for Mennonite Disaster Service. Army cots were placed in the church for the workers, and they were fed in the church kitchen. Later the men could be housed nearer their work in New Orleans. Pastor Wenger directed this reconstruction, which gave a strong Christian testimony. One crew worked largely for blacks and were rewarded at one home with a chicken dinner. In the total MDS project 287 persons, local and from the north, participated between October 1965 and February 1966.

There are only a few blacks living near Des Allemands. They have testified that if all people would treat them as the Mennonites do, it would be easier to get along.

Chester Wenger and wife, the patriarchs of the congregation, died in 1959 and 1943 respectively. The membership in 1972 was ninety. Many more than that have been baptized. Some have died, moved, or proved unfaithful.

John E. Wenger continues as pastor in 1974. He has given time also as overseer of churches in Mississippi. Lester Hackman continues as deacon. In August 1972, by unanimous voice of the congregation, Marvin LeBlanc was ordained to the ministry, and became assistant pastor.

There have been discouragements and setbacks in the work at Des Allemands. But on the whole it appears to have been one of the most successful mission extension efforts of the South Central Mennonite Conference.[9]

6. Bethel Springs, Baxter County, Arkansas

All of the Mennonite churches in Arkansas which now belong to the South Central Conference are in the mountainous north central part of the state. They represent mission outreach rather than home-seeking migration.

The first of these, and the matrix of them all, is Bethel Springs, located in the settlement in the White River country called Culp, about one hundred miles north of Little Rock. Culp was across the river from Calico Rock, the largest town of the area. Until 1966 there was no bridge across the river, only a somewhat primitive ferry. Culp was a typical isolated Arkansas mountain community, with a little travel by wagon on rocky roads. Most people walked on paths and long trails over the hills and through the forests.

The Mennonite Church was introduced into this part of Arkansas through Maude Buckingham. In 1922 this remarkable Arkansas woman hitchhiked to Colorado with her husband, Edward Buckingham, who was severely ill with tuberculosis. At La Junta he could go no farther, and he was taken to the Mennonite Sanitarium, which had been built by the Mennonites for the help of such persons as he.

The Buckinghams were professing Christians, but Edward had never been baptized. Before he died, he was helped to a clear faith, and was baptized. His wife was given a job in the sanitarium to earn money for the payment of their bill. Soon she united with the Mennonite Church. Then she decided she wanted to take nurse's training. But she had not gone to high school. So she went to Hesston College, in Kansas, and in 1926 finished in three years the high school course. Then she went back to La Junta and in 1929 finished the nurse's training and became a registered nurse.

Maude Buckingham was eager to return to the Ozarks to help the people whose needs she knew so well. She came in 1930 to Mountain Home, where she worked with a good doctor. She married John Douglass, who had a four-year-old daughter by a former marriage. She started a Sunday school, using old helps sent by her Kansas friends. But she wanted to go deeper into the mountains, where the needs were greater. Finally in 1932 the family bought a little mountain farm at Culp. Working with her hands, Maude helped her husband to put up a cabin and some shelters for their stock along a rushing mountain stream. She used her medical training as a nurse and registered midwife. The nearest doctor was at Batesville, forty miles away, which was utterly beyond reach for a poverty-stricken com-

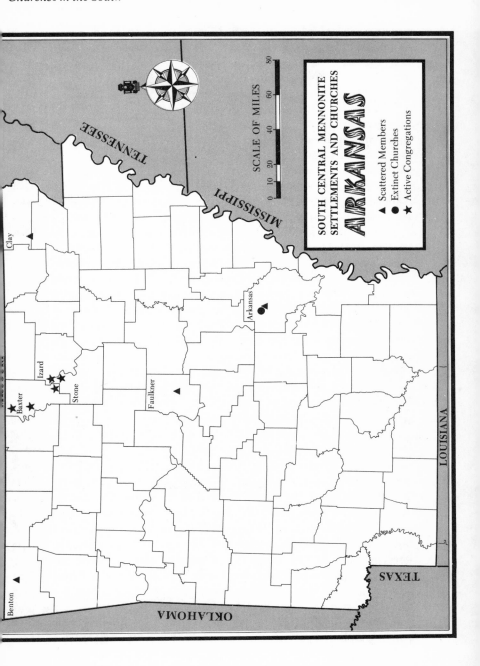

SOUTH CENTRAL MENNONITE
SETTLEMENTS AND CHURCHES
ARKANSAS

▲ Scattered Members
● Extinct Churches
★ Active Congregations

SCALE OF MILES

0 10 20 40 60 80

TENNESSEE

MISSISSIPPI

Clay

Arkansas

Izard

Baxter

Stone

Faulkner

LOUISIANA

Benton

TEXAS

OKLAHOMA

munity. So, to meet the needs, she was also a doctor, even a veterinarian. When her daughter Darlene was one month and one day old, she was out again on the mountain trails, calling on the sick who needed her. Her skills became a legend in the community.

But the area was largely unchurched, and Maude Douglass started a Sunday school at the City Rock School. She distributed literature, trying to supply Bibles to homes that had none. However, she found some opposition. The Pentecostals wanted to take over the Sunday school at City Rock. Maude simply transferred elsewhere. Near her home was a log cabin which the government had built as a cannery. A Sunday school was started here, and at other schoolhouses — Table Rock, Casteel, New Hope, and others. She made appointments for ministers who came. When the Paul Erb family stopped on their way to Mississippi, Erb was the first Mennonite to speak in a little church at McPhearson. At all these services people packed the buildings.

By 1935 the Missouri-Kansas Conference became interested. Earl Buckwalter, on his way to the annual session at Versailles, Missouri, took his wife and several others with him to spend the weekend at Culp. They reported to conference the opportunities of this field. A committee was appointed for further investigation: Earl

Attendees at Table Rock Sunday school, some of whom became charter members at Bethel Springs

Buckwalter, J. R. Shank, and L. J. Miller. That fall Shank and Miller preached for a week at Table Rock. Each month thereafter J. R. Shank came from his Missouri Ozarks to Arkansas for a weekend of four or five days. He preached at Canning Cabin, City Rock, Casteel, New Hope, McPhearson, and Martin Springs. He walked many miles, calling on people in their homes.

The first confession was at McPhearson in July 1936. The first baptisms were in the creek in front of Canning Cabin: three were baptized and one received on confession of faith. Land was purchased for a church, and volunteer labor put up the frame building, 24 by 30, that was named the Bethel Springs Mennonite Church. Mrs. Douglass and another woman built a sandstone fireplace. Amos Gingerich preached the dedicatory sermon on April 18, 1938. His son-in-law, Nelson Histand, was ordained to serve as pastor of the little congregation, which now numbered seven.

Three more acres were purchased, and a mission home was built beside the church. Support for the pastor came from the Missouri-Kansas Mission Board, and eventually from the churchwide Mission Board at Elkhart. Efforts were made to start enterprises which could furnish employment. One was a mission farm, a donation from Lewis Strite, of Virginia. Maude Douglass had already tried to demonstrate some improved farm practices.

Two teachers came to teach in the one-room mountain schools, and living with the people as they did, they made a fine contribution to the church. First was Richard Showalter, who taught a couple years at Casteel. Succeeding him was Mae Strubhar, who spent eleven years in the field, first at Casteel and then at McPhearson. They conducted Sunday schools, walking many miles to get from place to place.

The church added members; by 1940 there were twenty-nine members. Some of the early members who eagerly took responsibility in the little fellowship are: Viola Wheat, Alice Freeman, Russell Poole and family, Everett and Zella Higginbotham, Alice Harris and son Walter, Earl Wyatt, and Stanley Curtis and family.

In 1941 the Histands moved to Pryor, Oklahoma, and Frank Horsts, who had helped in a summer Bible school at Culp in 1940, came to lead in the work at Bethel Springs. They served here nineteen years, until May 1960.

One way of meeting community needs was the opening of the Bethel Springs School at Culp. Public schools were poor. It was felt

*The former Bethel
Springs School now
serves as the main
building on the Ozark
Mennonite campground*

that a Christian school, with Christian teachers and supported by the church, could be effective in bringing pupils to a Christian commitment and in building Christian character, besides giving good educational opportunity. The school started in 1944 as a grade school, with Dorothea Martin as the teacher of twenty-four pupils. Miss Martin lived that year in the mission home with Mae Strubhar, who had been appointed to do visitation work.

The first three terms were held in the church building. A new school building, constructed by the Mission Board and completed for use in 1947, provided classrooms and living quarters for the teachers. By 1953 the school had twelve grades, with a total of forty-nine pupils. Patrons were asked to pay what they could, but obviously the school required a good deal of home missions subsidy. Edwin Alderfer was principal of the school 1951-1955. Other teachers at the school during its history include Helen Alderfer, Erma Grove, Arletta Selzer, Lydia Burkhart, Ted and Arlene Walters, Albert and Lois Buckwalter, Eli Miller, Kathryn Slaubaugh, and Carl Metzler. Some of these became missionaries in other fields. Several pastors of the Bethel Springs congregation had responsibility also in the school. Among these were Glen Yoder, Menno Ebersol, Arlin Yoder, and Paul Martin.

The building of a bridge across the river to Calico Rock made better public schools available, and Bethel Springs School was closed in 1965. The building and grounds are now administered by the Ozark Mennonite Camp, which by 1969 was offering a full summer's program of camps, retreats, and workshops. For several years the Beachy Amish used the building for a nine-week Bible school during the winter months.

Another service to the community at Culp was the medical clinic, operated beside the church. This was a natural development of the medical work of Maude Douglass. Also of Ruth Cressman, a nurse and midwife, who came to this field about 1940. She married Clifford Strubhar, who managed the mission farm from 1948. She did good work until her early unfortunate death.

The first personnel in the clinic were John and Mary Detwiler. Mary had seventeen years' experience as a nurse in India. They were succeeded by David S. and Rhoda Wenger, who served, he in maintenance and she as a nurse. The parsonage burned down in 1946. A new medical clinic was dedicated on May 20, 1951. Speakers on this occasion were Dr. Saltzman from Mountain Home, Mrs. Ware, the county nurse, Frank Horst, and J. D. Graber. When Dr. Grasse came to Calico Rock, and the bridge made his services available to people across the river, the need for a clinic at Culp existed no longer.

Summer Bible school was a regular feature of the Bethel Springs program. Workers came from various communities to help with this. Numerous gospel teams visited the area.

Beginning with nothing in the middle thirties, the membership was sixty-one by 1950. But that was the peak. Better roads and bridges made it easier to get away, as well as to get to. Employment opportunities were few, and so, many people moved away. There was a good deal of argument about mission policy. Some felt that the work became overorganized and overadministered. Capable people came in as workers, and the local untrained people were afraid to express themselves. A number of the members now live across the river, and it was natural that they should transfer to the Mennonite Fellowship in Calico Rock when it was organized.

Whatever the causes, there were only eight members at Bethel Springs in 1972. But four other churches in Arkansas may be thought of as resulting from Bethel Springs: Mt. Joy, Buffalo, Three Brothers, and Calico Rock.

John M. Troyer came from Pryor, Oklahoma, in 1966 to be

pastor at Bethel Springs and Calico Rock. Troyer moved to Indiana in 1967. After that Manasseh Bontreger, pastor at Mt. Joy, also gave oversight to Bethel Springs. Floyd Miller was selected as lay leader of the Bethel Springs group.

Maude Douglass is still active. But even she is at Calico Rock. She is night nurse at the hospital there, taking care of the needs of people who know and trust her.[10]

7. *Mt. Joy, Stone County, Arkansas*

Mt. Joy is a Mennonite congregation twelve miles southeast of Culp, Arkansas, on the same side of the White River. It was near a small post office called Optimus, but is now on a rural route from Calico Rock, which is across the river, and the chief town of the area.

In the summer of 1945 two ladies of the Optimus community asked Frank Horst, pastor at Bethel Springs, to hold services for them in the schoolhouse east of the Optimus store. This he did; he had regular Sunday services, both morning and evening, as well as a midweek meeting. And that same year they had a summer Bible school.

Soon after this John and Mary Detwiler came to Culp to work in the clinic. During their stay they helped in the work at Mt. Joy, John as superintendent and Mary as a teacher. Others of the school staff came to Mt. Joy, among them Dorothy Horst, Marie Kauffman, and Edwin and Helen Alderfer. Edwin was superintendent of the Sunday school for three years.

Early in 1948 Nelson E. Kauffman, then bishop of the Arkansas field, asked the M. E. Bontregers, Goshen, Indiana, to consider Arkansas as a place to serve. He was proposing that they be responsible for their own support. They visited the field, and felt that the Lord was leading them there. So in December 1948 they arrived and unloaded their belongings into an old log house. In February 1949 Bontreger was ordained and installed as pastor of the group which soon after took the name of Mount Joy. He built a house and has found ways to make a living.

The Willard Barges came from California in 1952, and stayed until 1961. The Barges and Alderfers made a real contribution to the congregation. Both men served on the building committee for the new church house, which was dedicated in May 1953.

A few other families moved in. The Emanuel A. Millers came in 1962 and are still serving there. Vernon and Arlene Cross came in

Manasseh E. and Mary Bontreger, who gave a quarter of a century to the work in Arkansas

1964. He was licensed to preach and installed as pastor in August 1964. When the Crosses returned to Indiana in 1966, Bontreger again assumed leadership of the congregation. At times through the years, when there was no pastor at Bethel Springs, he shepherded that congregation also. His long-term service has been a real asset to the work in this field.

A number of people have come into the church at Mt. Joy. Some have left the state for economic reasons and some returned again to sinful living and are out of church fellowship. Some who became Christians here are members of the church in other states where they have located. And there are members of other churches who attend at Mt. Joy, as it is the only active church in the community.

Mt. Joy is the nearest of the Mennonite churches to Blanchard Springs, a state park facility which has at times served the conference and the area churches as a campground. The natural beauty of the area makes it a wonderful place for a retreat. [11]

In March 1974, when Bontreger retired and moved back to Indiana, the building was sold to the community, and services are being continued as there is opportunity.

8. *Buffalo, Baxter County, Arkansas*

Buffalo Mennonite Church is near Buffalo, a small town fifteen miles southwest of Mountain Home, Arkansas. This is in the northern tier of Arkansas counties, a region which is changing into a resort and industrialized area because of dams which have created two large lakes — Bull Shoals and Norfolk.

Clarence Horst and family moved to Mountain Home from Virginia in July 1945. He was equipped to make his living with a hatchery. But they had come with a Christian witness purpose. The first service was a Sunday school held following a summer Bible school in July 1946 at a schoolhouse in Buffalo. The group moved to the Lone Pine Schoolhouse in July 1947. The first baptism was performed in June 1947, with Nelson E. Kauffman as the officiating bishop. The first communion was in September 1947.

A meetinghouse was begun in October 1947. It has an attractive native stone veneer, and a full basement. Many local residents donated labor. Sanford Eash, of Millersburg, Indiana, supervised construction. At its dedication in May 1948 R. P. Horst preached the sermon.

Clarence Horst was licensed as the first pastor in September 1947 and ordained in February 1950. His service continued to August 1958 when ill health made him seek a different climate. During their years at Mountain Home the Horsts hosted many Eastern friends who were traveling through. Fred Meyer, of Rittman, Ohio, served as a licensed pastor for the year following Horst's departure. Marvin Miller, who had earlier taught school at Buffalo, commuted from Hesston College during the spring and summer of 1960 as a temporary pastor. James Hershberger was the pastor from October 1960 to September 1963, operating as a licensed minister.

The second longer-term pastor at Buffalo has been Wayne Yoder, who came from Goshen, Indiana. He was licensed in March 1964 and ordained in August 1966 and was the pastor as of 1973.

Preaching services were first held in 1946. Sunday evening services were begun in 1947. There was an active youth group, many of whom are now in Christian service in local congregations from Connecticut to Oregon, as well as in mission outreach in northern Alberta.

Services in 1973 consist of the usual Sunday morning and evening programs; Tuesday evening adult prayer meeting; Wednesday evening youth Bible study; monthly WMSC, GMSA, Boys' Club, Youth Fellowship; and Sunday afternoon visitation of shut-ins.

Though the congregation is small, it has reached out. Summer Bible school and monthly preaching services were begun at Rea Valley, eight miles to the west, in 1948, and continued to 1956. There was a summer Bible school at Three Brothers in 1949, and Sunday school began in 1951. This work has since developed into a separate congregation. Girls' work in sewing and boys' in woodworking, as well as an active youth program led by teachers of the Christian day school, served as outreach, since most of those involved were not Christians. Present local outreach includes summer Bible school, helping in the operation of Ozark Youth Camp at Culp, plus home visitation. The congregation cosponsored a weekly Mennonite Hour broadcast from a local station until March 1972. A Heart to Heart Club meets every two weeks, GMSA, Boys' Club, and WMSC once a month, and the youth Bible study once a week.

In the early days of the witness here, need was felt for a Christian day school. A schoolhouse, including a lodging for the teacher, was built on the hill about 200 feet above the church house. Marvin Miller was the teacher, 1950-1952; Gladys Selzer (now the pastor's wife), 1952-1953; Clayton Gerber, 1953-1955; and Ada Clemens, 1955-1956 (last year of operation).

A nursing home named Resthaven was built by Baxter County at Midway, which is seven miles northwest of Mountain Home, near Three Brothers. It was operated by the Mennonites for five years, 1951-1956.

At first this congregation carried the name of Mountain View because of the lovely Ozark prospect to the south and west. But a city of Mountain View is forty miles to the south, and as the church became better known, the name became confusing. So in 1965 it was changed to Buffalo, from the town and the river nearby.

In the spring of 1968, after nearly two years of prayer and discussion, the congregation acted to bring a better realization of the privileges and responsibilities of church membership. Because of a sizable proportion of inactive, disinterested, and unresponsive members, it was decided to dissolve the congregation. Then a congregation was to be re-formed, including only those who were willing to commit themselves to a minimum pledge of membership. These, in asking for membership, declared that they:

1. Are born-again, Spirit-led Christians.
2. Will attend church regularly.

3. Will give faithfully.
4. Will accept responsibility when asked.

The congregation has had as many as twenty-nine members. In 1972 the recommitted congregation numbered only eleven. In its early years the congregation enjoyed a great surge of interest. It weathered seasonal labor migrations. Now it is thought that the community is being stabilized by increasing industrialization in the county. With a hard-surfaced road to Buffalo in prospect, retirees as well as younger families are being attracted and moving in. The location is strategic and the church can expect increased attendance. The Buffalo Church sees the Spirit of God at work.[12]

9. *Calvary, Mathis, San Patricio County, Texas*

The congregations in south Texas which belong to the South Central Mennonite Conference are, with the exception of United Mennonite at Premont, predominantly Latin in membership. They have been established in areas which are also predominantly Latin in population, and are the result of the mission organized by the Mennonite Board of Missions (Elkhart) in 1938.

The background of this mission to the Spanish-speaking people of south Texas was the reception of Spanish-speaking Simon Del Bosque into the congregation at Tuleta, Texas, about 1916. In 1920 D. H. Bender and S. E. Allgyer made a tour of investigation in south Texas, beginning at Brownsville, near the Mexican border. Nothing came of this except the knowledge that there was a ripe foreign mission field within the borders of the United States.

In 1929 Amos A. Schertz and his family moved to Falfurrias. Later his son Arthur and his wife, Dorothy, conducted Sunday school at La Gloria and then at Falfurrias among the Spanish-speaking people. Many of these were Mexicans who came across the border to do seasonal work on the farms and ranches of the United States. Some returned to Mexico in the off season, but an increasing number stayed in the various communities of south Texas, so that some towns and cities had a Latin population as high as 80 percent. In the state of Texas by 1930 there were about a million and a half "Mexicans," as they were then called, and most of these lived between San Antonio and the Rio Grande.

About 1935 T. K. Hershey, missionary on furlough from Argentina, was convicted that mission work ought to be done among these Spanish-speaking people in south Texas. The Mennonite Board of Missions, in its annual meeting in that year, passed a resolution favoring a mission in the Southwestern part of the country, and asked Hershey and William G. Detweiler to make an investigation of the field.

The story of this investigation and the resulting mission at Normanna has been told in the history of the extinct church at Tuleta (see p. 378). The work did not develop as Hershey envisioned it. He thought the mobility of the people ruled out church building at fixed centers. He proposed preaching at various places, and then expected those who were converted to carry the gospel back to Mexico. And so in that first decade services were held in Helena, Normanna, Mathis, Benavides, Premont, and Falfurrias. In 1940 a Spanish Mennonite conference was held at Normanna, with members present from Falfurrias, Tynana, and Helena.

But experience soon showed that in spite of the people's following the seasonal employment, it was necessary for the missionary to live among them, to help them with their economic, social, and spiritual problems. This meant church building at certain fixed centers. And it meant that strategy required the missionary to live in the larger centers of Latin population.

After the David Alwines had moved to Ohio, to work among the Spanish people there, the Amsa Kauffmans moved in 1937 to Premont, from which as a center they worked in the surrounding towns. At one period they drove to Mathis Sunday after Sunday, 55 miles one way, to get the work under way there.

Mathis is in the Nueces Valley, and has been called the vegetable center of south Texas. It is thirty-five miles northwest of Corpus Christi and one hundred and fifty miles from the Mexican border. There were a number of interested people here, and it seemed to be a logical center for the mission outreach in south Texas.

The Calvary Mennonite Church (La Iglesia Menonita del Calvario) was organized in 1944. A house was purchased to serve as a meeting place and as a home for the missionaries. By 1945 there were fifty baptized members.

In 1946 the Kauffmans were recalled to Indiana, to serve in their home church there. The Frank Bylers, under appointment for Argentina, served a short time at Mathis while they were in language study. Then the William G. Lauvers, former missionaries to Argentina, were appointed as missionaries in Texas. In this year the congregation was received into the South Central Conference. This pattern was in effect for a number of years: administration and financial support from Elkhart, but conference membership and fellowship in the South Central Mennonite Conference.

In 1948 Eldo J. Miller succeeded Lauver. Services were held in the Miller home, with attendance as high as sixty-three. A small church, 20 by 24 feet, was built.

T. K. Hershey, now a retired missionary, was in charge briefly in 1950. In 1951 the J. Weldon Martins, after language study in Saltillo, Mexico, took over the work at Mathis.

Elvin Snyder, another former missionary in Argentina, was teaching at this time in Yorktown, Texas, eighty miles from Mathis. Snyder and his family drove to Mathis each Sunday for several years to help in the services. He knew well the situation in Mathis, and the Mission Board had asked him to make suggestions for the work there. He pointed out the following needs of the Spanish people, beyond the message of salvation:

1. Kindergarten fcr preschool children to teach them English, readying them for first grade.

2. Maternity and medical facilities for the Latin mothers.

3. Housing which will enable the families to put down roots in Mathis and to form a church.

4. Recreation for Spanish-speaking children in connection with the public schools.

In 1952 the first VS workers were sent to Texas from Elkhart, and began to turn Snyder's recommendations into program. The VS ministry to the economic and social and health needs of the people has made Mathis and other churches illustrations of a ministry to the whole man.

In Mathis a kindergarten was begun which prepared Spanish-speaking children for going to the English public schools. This opened the way into many homes and made good relations with officials of the town. The summer Bible school was given the use of the public school building.

As a response to the great need for better housing in Mathis, a block plant was brought from Michigan in March 1953 and in May the first house was made from the blocks produced. In this year, too, a house was purchased for the pastor.

Nurse Lela Sutter came in July, and appalled by a 50 percent infant mortality in the town as a result of untrained midwives, she promoted the idea of a maternity home. In February 1954 ground was broken for a two-bed, 30 by 40, flat-roofed maternity home, built by the construction unit, and ready for dedication in August. The Bible school enrollment this year reached 160. Four members of the construction gang were loaned for building at Grants, New Mexico.

In July 1954 Paul Conrad and Ann Burkholder, after the completion of their VS term, were back in Mathis for further service as a husband-and-wife team. Ann taught in the kindergarten, and Paul earned their living by working for the lumber company, where he could facilitate arrangements for home-building. He was also Sunday school superintendent. The Conrads were on the way to becoming permanent Texans.

The next year, 1955, was another milestone in Mathis history. T. K. Hershey and wife arrived in January to substitute for the Weldon Martins, who were again studying language in Mexico, this time at Torreon. *Luz y Verdad*, Lester Hershey's evangelical message originating in Puerto Rico, began to be broadcast from Station KCCT, in Corpus Christi; this could be heard in the whole mission area. The Roman Catholic sisters in Mathis started a kindergarten, but there were plenty of applications to keep the mission kindergarten full, and some pupils who were drawn away came back again, in spite of threats from the priest.

The biggest event in 1955 was the building of the educational wing of a new church. Paul Conrad was chairman of the building committee, and Lester Kropf came from Oregon to be foreman for the VS construction unit. Ground for the 32 by 56 structure was broken on January 16, with T. K. Hershey making the main address. The cornerstone was laid on February 13, and the building was dedicated on April 17, thirteen weeks after the groundbreaking. A series of meetings followed, conducted by David Castillo, a Mennonite pastor from Colorado, who was born in Monterrey, Mexico, and who had joined the Mennonite Church in Chicago.

In 1956 the church building program went ahead in the construction of the auditorium, with a seating capacity of 250 persons. This building was dedicated on August 10, and for the first time this growing congregation had an adequate plant for its work. In this year a Board of Directors was appointed for Mathis — a group of brethren from Premont and Tuleta to help plan the expansion of the south Texas work.

There were three series of evangelistic meetings in 1956: by Victor M. Ovando, a Mennonite pastor native to Nicaragua, but then from Defiance, Ohio; by Mario O. Snyder, missionary-to-be in Argentina; and by Lester T. Hershey, radio pastor from Puerto Rico. In the summer of this year the first camp was held at Lake Corpus Christi, a large lake near Mathis, the largest freshwater lake in Texas.

By January of 1956 the maternity home could report the birth of 204 babies since its opening, an average of thirteen per month. Since the home had a follow-up program, many homes of the community were opened to the ministry of the church through this means.

In addition to summer Bible school and evangelistic meetings, the congregation was involved in other activities aimed at reaching the community for Christ. Every Saturday night a prayer meeting was held in some community home. Adults and youth who could read Spanish participated in Bible studies in community homes. The group met with the pastor, Weldon Martin, to study a passage of Scripture, and then each shared the lesson in the home of a neighbor. In 1956 a church bus was purchased with funds donated by a Virginia businessman, Dwight Hartman. This helped to boost church attendance. In 1955 a church council was formed to involve the members in congregational decisions. The Lord blessed the witness. During the years 1951-1957 fifty-five were received into church membership.

On January 1, 1956, the Mathis congregation began services in Alice, Texas. Paul Conrad and Weldon Martin held Sunday afternoon services for about a month. Then in February Sam Swartz, from Premont, began to assist Paul Conrad in Sunday morning services.

The Martins were granted a year's leave and spent July 1957 to July 1958 in Virginia. Upon returning to Texas in 1958, the Martins were assigned to the beginning work in Corpus Christi. Don and Marilyn Brenneman left the Corpus Christi work to help in the Spanish Church in Chicago.

In May 1957 Paul and Ann Conrad were granted a short period of Spanish study in Saltillo, Mexico, in preparation for assuming leadership of the Mathis congregation. Paul was licensed to the ministry and installed as pastor the Sunday before the Martins left in July.

The first marriage in the Calvary Church was that of Vanita Horst, of Columbiana, Ohio, and Raul Tadeo, who were both serving as VSers in Mathis.

Another kind of service to the community was the sheltering of three hundred temporary refugees in the church when hurricane Carla struck the Mathis countryside in 1961. Mennonite Disaster Service workers came from the Mennonite churches of the North and helped in cleanup and rebuilding. This demonstration of the spirit of brotherhood by people they had never seen gave further content and support to the gospel which was preached by the missionaries and the VS workers.

Paul Conrad was ordained to the ministry by Earl Buckwalter and Weldon Martin in January 1962. The congregation was growing: the membership was now 130. But members were scattered, and Pastor Conrad and family spent several weeks visiting Mennonite families that were following the cotton harvest as far as Lubbock, Texas. To give him assistance Samuel Hernandez, later a pastor in Oregon, was licensed for a year.

Senora Adan Garcia, Ann Conrad, and Romiro Garcia smile their greetings from a Texas cotton field

In 1963 the Maternity Home joined operations with the Mathis Hospital, and the Health and Welfare Committee of the Mission Board assumed operation of the hospital. But in 1965 the hospital was closed because of financial difficulties.

In August of 1965 a Servanthood Work Camp was held. Four young people from Kansas and Iowa joined with seven from Texas in ten days of fellowship and work. Five days were spent in brightening up with paint the ten-year-old church building. They were invited to homes of members for some meals, tasting new foods and making new friends. One evening they attended a service at the Corpus Christi Church. Another evening they spent at Lake Mathis, and on a third they attended a football game in which one of the camp members played. Saturday they took a trip across the border, and fellowshiped with the Munoz family in Reynosa. Over the last weekend they gave programs at Premont, Alice, and Mathis. It was a worthwhile experience of fellowship and service.

The kindergarten has continued with an average enrollment of fifty. Its service in preparing the children to go to school has been greatly appreciated by the public school. And the church continues to reap benefits from this program. Nancy De Leon, who attended the kindergarten at Mathis, went on to graduate from Mathis High School, and was graduated from Hesston College in 1970. The following persons have taught in the kindergarten more than one year: Ann Burkholder Conrad, Sarah Yoder, Delores Bohn, Rachel Liechty, Ruth Keeler, Rachel Snyder, Ruth Zimmerly, Irma Guzman, and Elizabeth Martinez.

Voluntary Service has continued to be an invaluable part of the program at Mathis, and later at Alice, Premont, Robstown, and Corpus Christi. Besides the block-making and construction, the kindergarten teaching, and the medical services, the unit members gave training in shop, sewing, and crafts, supervised recreation, did housekeeping and bookkeeping for the unit, taught in Sunday school and summer Bible school, and gave a constant example of the far-reaching implications of the lordship of Christ. From 1952 to 1972, one hundred and thirty persons have been a part of VS in south Texas, at five locations.

It was during 1967 that the Mennonite Youth Fellowship, together with the MYF at Chapel of the Lord, in Premont, sold watermelons and had a bake sale to help build a recreation facility in Mathis.

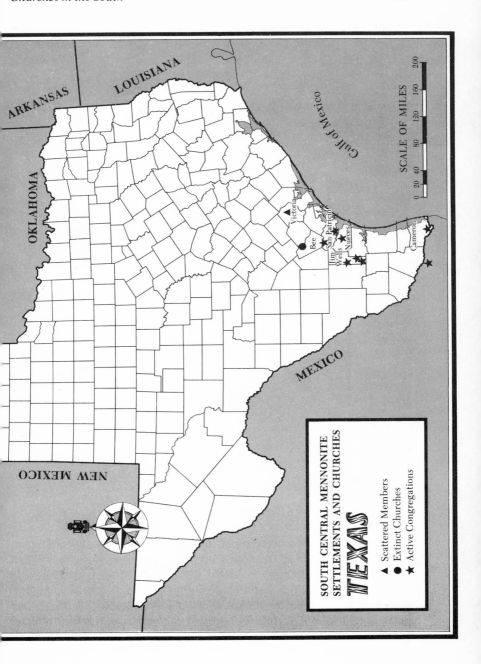

SOUTH CENTRAL MENNONITE
SETTLEMENTS AND CHURCHES

TEXAS

▲ Scattered Members
● Extinct Churches
★ Active Congregations

Victoria

Bee

San Patricio
Jim Wells
Nueces

Cameron

Gulf of Mexico

SCALE OF MILES

0 20 40   80   160   200

MEXICO

NEW MEXICO

ARKANSAS

LOUISIANA

OKLAHOMA

Young people of Mathis have attended our church schools. Among others, Samuel Hernandez, Lupe De Leon, Jr., Verardo Gonzales, Irma Guzman, Lupe Garcia, and Pedro Cavasos went to Hesston College.

Paul Conrad took a furlough from the work in Texas in 1968. Adolfo Saldivar succeeded him in an interim pastorate at Mathis. In 1970 the congregation got its first Latin pastor. Atancio Paiz was licensed in August to serve as pastor in his home congregation. Gilbert Perez, a young man of the congregation, was subsidized by the conference for two years of study in Rio Grande Bible School, which is conducted by the Church of the Brethren in Harlingen. In 1972 Perez was licensed to serve the congregation at Taft.

Other Mathis youth have been active in Christian service. Samuel Hernandez, after a year as assistant pastor at Mathis, and following study at La Plata Bible Institute in Puerto Rico, Hesston College, and Christian Bible Institute, served under the Latin American Fellowship, teaching and ministering, at La Paz, Baja California. He located in Woodburn, Oregon, in 1964 and established an independent Evangelical Spanish Church there. Early in the seventies he was appointed to serve under the Pacific Coast Conference in the only Spanish-speaking ministry to the more than 20,000 Mexican-Americans in the Willamette Valley of Oregon.

Lupe De Leon pastored the Chapel of the Lord, Premont, Texas, for a short time, studied at Hesston College, and returned to south Texas for service at Corpus Christi. In 1970 he became Associate Executive Secretary for the Minorities Ministries Council, Elkhart, Indiana. In 1973 he graduated from Goshen College and entered Goshen Biblical Seminary.

Lupe Garcia spent 1970 and 1971 as a VSer connected to the Mennonite Mission in Sinaloa, Mexico. In 1972 he moved to Elkhart, Indiana, to direct the High-Aim program, which sends minority group young people to Mennonite high schools. He continued his studies at Goshen College.

Tomas Mendoza, who moved with his family to Brownfield, Texas, for economic reasons, is preparing for the ministry in the Baptist Church.

In 1971 the membership at Mathis had fallen a bit to 117. Limited employment possibilities there cause members to move elsewhere. Some of them may become members of other denominations in their new locations.

J. Weldon Martin, former pastor at Calvary, returned to that responsibility in 1972. The adults of the congregation are active and there is growth in decision-making by the lay members.

Calvary was the host for a south Texas hymn-sing in January 1973 and for an MCC Extension Committee Convention in November of that year.[13]

10. *United Mennonite, Premont, Jim Wells County, Texas*

The United Mennonite Church is in Premont, a town of 3,000, one hundred miles north of the Mexican border. It was formed by the merger in 1964 of the La Gloria congregation of the Mennonite Church and the Premont congregation of the Mennonite Brethren Church. Locally the congregation is one body for worship and the proclamation of the gospel, but it maintains a working relationship and identity with both conference bodies, supporting equally such programs as missions, relief, and education.

The Premont Mennonite Brethren (MB) Church had its beginning in 1928 when several families moved from Kansas and Oklahoma. A congregation was soon organized with H. H. Flaming as the pastor. Meetings were first held in available church buildings, but later the group erected a church in the town of Premont. The membership grew to nearly one hundred in the early years. However, isolation, hard times, and lack of employment prompted many families to move away.

In 1920 H. F. Reist, in search for a more healthful climate, moved from the presidency of Goshen College, in Indiana, to the Rio Grande country, settling first at Weslaco, near the border. In 1927 the Reists joined other Mennonite families near Falfurrias, a county seat ten miles south of Premont. For several years these Mennonites worshiped with a congregation of the Church of the Brethren. Reist shared the pulpit with the Church of the Brethren ministry, and later was the only minister. Reist was ordained bishop by the Mennonites in 1946.

In 1950 the Mennonites built a church at La Gloria, halfway between Falfurrias and Premont. The building cost about $6,000. Donated labor totaled 1,500 hours. On August 6, when the building was dedicated, Samuel C. Swartz, son-in-law of H. F. Reist, was ordained to the ministry, with Milo Kauffman preaching the sermon and E. S. Hallman officiating. As Reist gradually retired from active leadership, Swartz became the leader of La Gloria Church.

La Gloria remained small, however, and faced difficulties in carrying on a full church program. And so the members frequently worshiped and worked with the Mennonite Brethren in Premont in special meetings, revivals, Christmas programs, and summer Bible school. The possibility of some plan of merger was thought of from time to time, and this became a question of concern, discussion, and prayer.

Late in 1963, when the M. B. group was without a pastor, the time seemed favorable for action. Several meetings of the two councils led to a united meeting of the two congregations. In this meeting the United Mennonite Church of Premont was born.

On the first Sunday in March 1964 the two groups met in the M.B. Church for worship. Samuel Swartz was elected pastor and Paul Wohlgemuth, a layman, was elected moderator.

In 1965 the physical properties of the two churches were united when the La Gloria Church building was moved into Premont to become the church auditorium for the new fellowship. The M. B. building with an annex serves as the Sunday school department, library, and social center. Subsidiary organizations serving the congregation are the Sunday school, Ladies' Sewing Circle, Mennonite Youth Fellowship, and Christian Endeavor. There is a three-bedroom parsonage adjoining the church property. The church is located at S-W Sixth and Bernice streets in Premont.

The combined membership of the united fellowship was fifty-four in 1972. The total giving in 1971 was $4,800, about $100 per member. Congregational expenses totaled $1,884.

The congregation has six teachers, including the pastor, in the Premont and Falfurrias schools. Two members work in the Premont school cafeteria. Another member is a school trustee. Ezra Wohlgemuth, a member of the church, is the mayor of Premont. These persons and the Disaster Service workers, both local and from the North, have done a creditable job in giving a peace and service witness in the community.

The church council — composed of pastor, deacon, Sunday school superintendent, church secretary-treasurer, elected moderator, and elected members — meets regularly to conduct church business. The council makes recommendations on major matters for the consideration of the congregation.

Since the Mennonite Brethren baptize by immersion, the mode used at Premont is optional, and there have been no problems. In a

1972 baptism there were eight candidates. After a meditation on the meaning of baptism, some were baptized within the church by pouring. Then the congregation moved to an outside baptistry for the baptism of the others by immersion. The congregation had no difficulty in finding real meaning in both modes.

This is the first congregation to have dual membership in the South Central and Mennonite Brethren groups. The congregation feels the merger was the only solution to the problem of two small congregations. They appreciate the concern of both conferences. They have eliminated some of the confusion in the community about who the Mennonites are. There have been no serious problems in working together.

Mennonite Brethren family names in the group are Warkentin, Balzer, Flaming, Friesen, Wohlgemuth, Schuchert, Everett; (Old) Mennonite names are Swartz, Reist, Stoltzfus, and Schertz, with origins in Ohio, Iowa, Pennsylvania, and Illinois. Families from the community now in the church are Crockett, Hale, Lowell, Lanmon, Moss, and Whitcher. The only Spanish members are Walter Gomez and wife. Gomez is president of Mexican Mission Ministries, at Pharr, Texas.

One mile away from United Mennonite is the Chapel of the Lord, begun as a mission to the Spanish-speaking people of Premont. Chapel of the Lord has only a few Anglo members, including the pastor and his family. The Robert Reists came to the chapel to help with the mission in its early days. But the two churches belong to the same conference, South Central, and cooperate closely in the circle of Mennonite churches in south Texas. They merely serve two different ethnic, language, and cultural groups. But of their oneness in Christ neither group has any question.[14]

11. *Three Brothers, Baxter County, Arkansas*

Three Brothers is in Baxter County, Arkansas, eight miles northwest of Mountain Home, and only two miles from the Missouri line.

Clarence Horst, pastor of the Buffalo Mennonite Church, and the Mission Board of the South Central Conference worked closely with the Baxter County judge to help the county rest home become a reality. Rest Haven was dedicated in 1951. The Home was built by the county, and the Mennonite Church was asked to operate it. Many single and young married Mennonites from all over the United States have served at Rest Haven. They came from Maryland, Iowa, Indiana, Pennsylvania, Ohio, Kansas, Virginia, Missouri, and the

District of Columbia to serve the Lord and mankind in Voluntary Service under the Mennonite Board of Missions.

Their work was not limited, however, to caring for the guests at Rest Haven. They worked with the Buffalo Church in starting a Sunday school at Three Brothers, a little town nearby. Lewis Good, Jr., from Washington, D. C., was the first superintendent, doubling sometimes as the preacher too. Others who followed him were Menno Nisley, Hutchinson, Kansas; Bernard Wagler, Belleville, Pennsylvania; and Charles Greaser and Orville Stutzman, Hesston, Kansas.

Before the Sunday school, however, was the summer Bible school. In 1950 Wilbert Nafziger, secretary of the South Central Mission Board, sent to Clarence Horst enough volunteer Bible school teachers to supply three schools at the same time. One of these schools was at Three Brothers. Four teachers cleaned up an old two-room schoolhouse. A lady who lived near the school went with them to invite the pupils. At the end of that first Bible school the enrollment had reached forty-one. The second year the enrollment was fifty-nine. That fall a young mother of the community wrote to a Bible school teacher, "I would like to send my children to Sunday school, but there is none."

And so the VS workers became a Sunday school staff. During the first years the attendance was irregular, as people in this town did not have the churchgoing habit. The schoolhouse was painted inside and out, plenty of new seats were provided, and a sign by the highway announced that this was a church.

During the 1952 Bible school Wilbur Yoder, of Indiana, preached revival sermons each evening, and several adults accepted Christ. In 1953 Roy Selzer moved with his family from Protection, Kansas, to serve as a pastor at Three Brothers for a year. In 1954 George Mayfield, a young man from this community, was licensed for the ministry at Three Brothers. He served for a year and then went to school at Hesston College.

In October 1957 Henry Tregle, a minister from Akers, Louisiana, moved to Three Brothers. In December the church was organized, and Tregle was installed as pastor. The service was conducted by Clarence Horst, then serving as regional overseer. Frank Horst preached. Others participating were Manasseh Bontreger, David Wagner, and George Mayfield.

The sixteen charter members were George Mayfield, Faye Sis-

Henry, Lowell, and Nettie Tregle

ney, Thurman Sisney, Lois Dunbar, Sue Dunbar, Dee Dee Belts, Ruth Hamilton, Jim T. Hamilton, Estella Short, Henry J. Tregle, Nettie Tregle, Glenn Tregle, James L. Hamilton, Myrtle Hamilton, Lowell Tregle, and Minnie Sisney. During the next year ten other members were added to the church: Henry Tregle, Jr., Earnest Farrer, Mrs. Lou Farrar, Ronald Rose, Mary Ann Rose, Linda Rose, Mrs. Ray Smith, Clyde Chensworth, and Mrs. Frances Miller.

The work branched out. The women felt their prayers were answered as they found an avenue of service through WMSA, with Estella Short as president. Other highlights of the year were the first communion service and cottage prayer meetings. Olen Nofziger held meetings in the fall of 1955, with a number of decisions.

For nine years services were held in the old school building. In 1959 Pastor Tregle and Mr. Miller, a man of the community, started making cement blocks for a new church. As funds came in, the block pile grew. Land was given at the end of the Promise Land Road, one mile north of the old building. Everyone helped. The women cleaned and finished old benches donated by the church at Versailles, Missouri. The young people cleared brush and hauled rocks; fathers came after a day's work to help; those who couldn't work sent food. Men came from Louisiana and Kansas. A gospel team from Hesston came one weekend and did their bit on the building. This church at Three Brothers was built by many brothers — and sisters too. The new

building was dedicated on Easter Sunday, 1961, with a record attendance of ninety-one.

The church has found a witness point at Dugginsville, Missouri.
Henry Tregle concluded his pastorate in May 1969 and returned to
Louisiana. Jerry Strobel succeeded him. The membership in 1972
was nineteen. The church is developing something of its own worship and service pattern to fit the background of its people.[15]

12. *Alice, Jim Wells County, Texas*

Alice is a city of about 23,000 people, of which 75 percent are
Spanish-speaking. It is fifty miles west of Corpus Christi, about thirty
miles southwest of Mathis, and twenty-seven miles north of Premont. So it is pretty much the geographical center of the Mennonite
churches of the area.

The first Mennonite Church service in Alice was conducted January
1, 1956, by J. Weldon Martin and Millard Osborne of Mathis. In
August 1958 a VS unit came from Mathis to hold a summer Bible
school in a residential area on the west side of the city. The response
was good. For many children this was the first opportunity to study
the Bible. Regular Sunday school and Wednesday evening Bible
study under the leadership of S. V. Zapata followed. In November
Joseph and Norma Hostetler, VS workers, moved to Alice, followed by
Allen and Bernelle Kanagy. Both couples supported themselves.

In January 1959 Zapata was licensed for the ministry. A building,
14 by 28, was rented, and in October was purchased, from Sarita
Gonzales for $1,400. This was at 1413 Consuelo Street, and became
the first site of the Alice Mennonite Church. The adjacent lot was
purchased in January 1960. These purchases were paid with donations
from individuals and also by a gift of $50 per month from the La
Gloria Church near Premont. This illustrates how this Anglo church
promoted the development of the Spanish-speaking churches. The
property at Alice was all paid for by 1960.

In the winter of 1958-1959 a 14 by 28 addition was built to the
west side of the church. All of the labor was donated. This building,
now 28 by 28, had a seating capacity of eighty. The Sunday school
classes could be partially divided by curtains.

After their marriage in 1959, Raul and Vanita (Horst) Tadeo
lived in Alice and helped with the work there. First evangelistic
meetings were held in 1959, with preaching by Victor Ovando,
formerly a Catholic priest, born in Nicaragua. He has been in

evangelistic meetings several times at Alice. Sunday evening meetings also were begun in 1959.

Zapata moved to Premont in 1960 to help in the work among the Spanish-speaking there, and Allen Kanagy was called to the leadership role. The Richard Mussers moved in from Pennsylvania to help in the program.

Four ladies, all grandmothers, were the first persons baptized; that was in March 1962. They were Maria Luera, Fransisca Trevino, Hipolita Guerra, and Manuela Guzman. In September of that year the Kanagys moved to Corpus Christi, and Tadeo, after two years in school at EMC, was installed as the first full-time pastor at Alice. The property of the Kanagys was purchased in September 1963 to serve as a parsonage. In May of 1963 the church was organized and received into conference membership.

The church grew, and in June 1964 serious plans were being made for a new church building. The committee appointed to promote these plans consisted of Joe Hostetler, chairman; Raul Tadeo, and Richard Musser. In August a one-acre tract of land on Beam Station Road was purchased for $2,450. The congregation paid cash for this land, but was later reimbursed by the Board of Missions at Elkhart. The work at Alice was being administered as a mission, using a service program for building a church. The Spring Missionary Day offering of the South Central Conference in that year was designated for the Alice church building. The offering amounted to $10,125.

On November 15, 1964, ground was broken for the new church. Lupe De Leon and Paul Conrad, pastors of the Chapel of the Lord at Premont and Calvary at Mathis, participated. The church is brick veneer, triangular in form to symbolize the Trinity. Neri Bontrager, a builder from Elkhart, supervised the construction as a VS worker. Simon Hershberger, of Iowa, visited his daughter for several months, and donated a good deal of labor. The building is 92 by 36, and is to serve as the educational wing, with classrooms, when the main auditorium can be built. The building was dedicated in March 1965. The cost was $18,000. This included air-conditioning and folding chairs and tables.

Tadeo went to Goshen in 1967 to attend seminary, and Joseph Hostetler became interim part-time pastor while he was attending school at Kingsville, Texas, and then serving in the school system of Alice. He resigned in 1970, but not until July 1972 was this po-

Alice Church

sition filled by Ruperto Gudea. Gudea came from the Mennonite
Church in Chicago, and attended Hesston College. He had served
in Denver, and was pastor of the Mennonite Church in Defiance,
Ohio.

Since its organization the congregation has maintained a regular
program of Sunday school, preaching, and Bible study. A youth fellowship was organized in 1962, with Joe and Norma Hostetler as the
first sponsors. A kindergarten was opened as part of the VS program
in 1963, with Allie Kauffman as the first teacher, followed by Edith
Jantzi and Eva Yeackley. The women's group was organized in
October 1963 and meets monthly. In November 1965 a men's group
began monthly meetings. Romaine Sala, of Goshen, Indiana, conducted a music workshop at Alice for the south Texas churches in
November 1965. There have been clubs for boys and girls.

Beginning about 1967, the congregation has used the former
church building as a youth center, named Rancho Allegre. Voluntary
Service has supplied the staff members for the congregation to
operate the Center. Rancho Allegre meets a very real need in the
lives of youth in the immediate area.

The membership was twenty-eight in 1971, and is about three-
fourths Spanish-speaking Americans, most of whom were born in
Texas and were Catholics before joining the Mennonite Church.
There were thirteen members for the official chartering service on May
5, 1963. Nine were received by letter; the others had been baptized
in 1962. In March 1964 the Alice Mennonite Church received its

Certificate of Incorporation from the state of Texas. A constitution was adopted in June 1965. It provides for a church council, which meets monthly and reports to a bimonthly members' business meeting.

Communion is held since 1966 on the first Sunday evening of each quarter, along with a foot washing service. Public prayers are offered in both Spanish and English, with the worshipers usually in the sitting or standing positions. The prayer veiling worn by the women is usually of the style found in the Latin-American countries. The first funeral was held in the church in February 1966 for Mrs. Josefina Sanches, who was not a member of the church. A quartet from the church provided music. All ladies who attended wore veils.

It was at Alice that the need developed for modifications of the denomination's mutual aid system that would take care of members of low-income congregations. In a meeting there it was argued that the assessments of Mennonite Mutual Aid are more than the average family at Alice can pay. Pastor Hostetler passed this problem along to MMA, where it was agreed that those who may need help most are often the least able to afford it. So CHIP (Congregational Health Improvement Program) was devised, and Hostetler was able to offer to his members mutual aid through the plan of the church.

That year Roberto Luera found out what fellowship in the church could mean. Roberto suffered injuries in an auto accident. A new son was born while Roberto was working in the Ohio vegetable

Alice Church Council (l to r.):
Anita Gonzalez, Richard Musser,
Roberto Luera, Rita Charles, and
Joe Hostetler.

fields. And another son was hospitalized with a digestive ailment. Total expenses from these causes were almost $1,000. Of this amount the Mennonite Church, through its agency, paid 80 percent. MMA's catastrophe fund, supported by the Compassion Fund of the Board of Missions, took care of the amount above what the most needy members can afford to pay. The year's trial at Alice assured MMA that CHIP privileges could be offered to other low-income congregations; and the plan was extended in 1972 to include three additional congregations: Prince of Peace at Corpus Christi, Calvary at Mathis, and Chapel of the Lord at Premont. Serving as local consultants were Juan Cortez at Corpus Christi, Lupe Garcia at Mathis, and Maria Villarreal at Premont. Joseph Hostetler coordinated the whole south Texas CHIP program. By the summer of 1972, more than $10,000 had been donated to help finance CHIP.

One person whose testimony and quiet activity have influenced many to serve Christ is Mrs. Olivia Cantu. Olivia can always be counted on to do more than her fair share. Whether it be feeding a group of young people or teaching a class, it is always more important to her to serve others than to be served. Norberto, her son, and Elda, her daughter, are members of the church's youth group.

In the fall of 1973 Joe and Norma Hostetler moved to Kansas, where Joe joined the faculty of Hesston College. The Hostetlers had lived in south Texas nearly fifteen years, and they had contributed so much to the church life that they are greatly missed.[16]

South Central Extension in Mexico
13. Reynosa, Mexico

In 1957 the family of Mario Sanchez Munoz moved to the Mexican city of Reynosa, which is just across the Rio Grande, about one hundred miles straight south of Falfurrias. They came from the state of Coahuila, where Munoz in his childhood heard the gospel taught by Anglo missionaries. Munoz and his wife, Candelaria, had two sons — Ricardo and Alfonzo, and three daughters — Elizabeth, Ruth, and Maria Dina. In Reynosa they established a chapel for worship and to extend the gospel.

The radio program *Luz y Verdad* from Corpus Christi could be heard in Reynosa. It advertised the Bible studies directed by Don Brenneman. Five members of the Munoz family enrolled and made contact with the *Luz y Verdad* office in Corpus Christi.

When Weldon Martin took over the correspondence work, he

and Richard Fahndrich, the pastor at Chapel of the Lord in Premont, visited Munoz, and encouraged him in his evangelistic outreach. In a few months they brought Milo Kauffman and Nelson Kauffman to see the work being done by Munoz. In 1960 Mario attended the South Central Conference at Hesston, at which time the church in Reynosa was received as a member of the South Central Mennonite Conference.

Through the devoted efforts of this family, the evangelistic work prospered. After Alfonzo completed the *Luz y Verdad* courses, he enrolled in a Bible Institute in Saltillo, Mexico, where he graduated four years later. Maria Dina, as her part of the family effort, established a kindergarten and enrolled as high as 125 pupils. She is also a dressmaker, and has taught many girls in sewing classes. In 1967 she was married to Alfonso Ruiz, and her wedding

L. to r.: Paul Conrad, Timothy Conrad, Mario S. Munoz, Martha and Alfonzo Sanchez talk over plans for pouring a concrete floor for the El Banco Mission

was attended by many friends from the south Texas churches.

The witness in Reynosa is carried on at four places. The principal mission since 1962 is called Bethel, or Mina Street. A second, called Sinai, is in the Industrial Colony; and a third, called El Mesias, is at the Garcia Rojas Colony. Mario Munoz himself is the pastor of all these. The fourth place of witness, called Iglesia Cristiana Bethel, is at El Banco Colony. The pastor here is Alonzo, son of Mario, whose wife is named Martha.

These churches do not have a fixed membership count. The buildings are usually full, but not always with the same people. Most of them participate actively in the program, and the church has a vision of establishing more missions, even into other cities.

The churches of south Texas have aided in this work across the border. They helped build a small (14 by 20) new church in the Industrial Colony. For a special child dedication service which Elvin Snyder addressed in 1967, forty adults and seventy children were packed into this building. Other building projects are being carried forward as funds become available.

The South Central Conference has subsidized the work in Reynosa. For example, the 1968-1969 budget designated $1,200 for Reynosa.[17]

14. *Chapel of the Lord (La Capilla del Senor)*, *Premont, Jim Wells County, Texas*

Amsa H. and Nona Kauffman, missionaries appointed by the Mennonite Board of Missions to work among the Latins of south Texas, moved from Tuleta to Premont, Texas, in 1941. They began work in Benavides, thirty-five miles northwest of Premont, and in Falfurrias, nine miles south, where Arthur Schertz had started a Sunday school for Spanish-speaking people.

The work in Benavides did not prosper, and so the Kauffmans concentrated their earlier efforts in Premont and Falfurrias. In Falfurrias services were held in a small building which the Mission Board had purchased. But in Premont Kauffmans had made many friends and found many homes open for meetings. Two lots were purchased in Premont, and they moved the little church from Falfurrias to this site, thus establishing a meeting place for the Latin Americans in Premont.

In 1946 the Kauffmans left Texas, and the church building in Premont was sold to the Southern District of the Mennonite Brethren

Church, who have a number of mission churches in the Rio Grande Valley. J. P. Kliewer began the Mission Board work at Premont, assisted by Alvina Fast and Martha Foote. Later B. W. Vogt became responsible, and he was assisted by Ricardo Pena, a Latin worker who came on weekends from the Rio Grande Valley. This work continued until May 1948.

In June 1948 the H. T. Esaus came from Kansas to serve as full-time missionaries at Premont. Soon the small church building was too crowded. Esaus purchased four more lots, added two classrooms to the chapel, and built a parsonage. A bus was used to pick up children, and a garage was built to shelter it. When the bus was sold, the garage was converted into a recreation hall. By 1955 two more Sunday school rooms were added to this hall. Grass, trees, and shrubs were planted, so that the plot had a beautiful, spacious lawn.

But due to ill health, the Esaus had to discontinue their work. The property was their own, and they wished to sell to someone who could continue the mission work without interruption. Since the Mennonite Board of Missions (Elkhart) had been in this field before the Mennonite Brethren took it over, the Esaus offered the place to them in preference to another group. The offer was accepted.

By August 1960 the new appointees of the Board, Richard and Luella Fahndrich, came from Ohio to begin their new work in Premont. The next month Silvestre Zapata came from Alice with his trailer house to assist in the work; he sold Bibles for a living. Where once the mission had ministered mainly to children, and had been highly successful through Bible school, Sunday school, and clubs, the Fahndrichs directed their attention to adults and young people, hoping to make the Chapel of the Lord into a self-supporting congregation. The Robert L. Reist family brought their membership from La Gloria, and plunged into the work with the Fahndrichs. Soon, although the self-supporting status was nowhere in sight, the small congregation began to be more active as responsibilities were distributed to the various members.

In 1963 the Fahndrichs resigned to work in Mexico. S. V. Zapata had died, and so Robert and Ruth Reist were asked by the South Central Mennonite Conference, which was now administering this work, to take charge temporarily. With a half-dozen young men of the congregation they carried on for almost a year. Then a newly married couple from the Calvary congregation in Mathis, Lupe and

Seferina De Leon, accepted a year's assignment as pastor. At the end of this service they left for further training at Hesston College. In the middle of 1965 the Chapel of the Lord was without a pastor, and again Robert Reist assumed the responsibility, with five young men of the congregation giving excellent help.

However, both of the Reists were teaching school. So Keith and Rhoda Schrag, then living in Ohio, were invited to serve for a year at Premont. They stayed two years. The Schrags knew Spanish well, were excellent administrators, and brought many new ideas to the work. While the Schrags were in Premont, two more members of the congregation left for college, and three for VS and alternate service. But new members came into the church. With the arrival of a VS couple in April 1968 the load was lightened for the Reists and the Schrags. The VS couple assumed responsibility for maintenance, clubs, recreation, transportation, and teaching.

Teodoro (Ted) Chapa is one example of the active young people in this congregation. First his confidence had to be won. Ted remembers that when Keith Schrag came into one end of the recreation room, he slipped out the other. But he gradually opened his life to the workers and to Christ. He was baptized in July 1965 by Lupe De Leon. He finished high school in 1967, and the next January left for a year of Voluntary Service. He worked for a while in a home for boys in Denver, then in Frontier Boys Village in Colorado Springs. His period of service was concluded by speaking to many Mennonite youth groups about Voluntary Service. His visits to churches took him north as far as the Upper Peninsula of Michigan. Returning home, he served as youth minister in south Texas and then took a year of college at Hesston. All this prepared him for eight months of service in the denomination's youth office at Scottdale, Pennsylvania, helping to set up and to administer the Cross-Cultural Youth Convention held at Epworth Forest, Indiana, August 20-25, 1972. He continued in the planning and administration of the 1973 Youth Convention, under the Board of Congregational Ministries at Goshen, Indiana.

Keith Schrag, while pastor at Chapel of the Lord, also served as coordinator of the MDS clean-up work in McAllen, Texas, after the destruction by hurricane Beulah in 1967. Volunteers from Kansas, Texas, Oklahoma, Iowa, Ohio, Colorado, Montana, Indiana, Missouri, Virginia, Louisiana, and Florida completed almost one hundred jobs, which required almost a thousand workdays. Schrag's fluency with Spanish was a great asset, as many of the homeowners contacted preferred to speak Spanish. The Region III director was grateful to the conference and the congregation for allowing Schrag to be used in this way.

The Schrags terminated their services in September 1968 to take up a pastorate in Wichita, Kansas. Pastoral duties and responsibilities were delegated among lay members of the congregation, with a committee of three to act as leaders.

Damage done by hurricanes Celia in 1970 and Fern in 1971 gave additional opportunity for Mennonite Disaster Service. Men and a few women from many parts of the United States and Canada helped to clean up, but especially to rebuild. In the Falfurrias area Earl Boyts, of Harper, Kansas, was foreman of the project for many months, and operations were not phased out until February 1972.

In June 1969 Howard and Anna Beth Birky assumed pastoral responsibilities at the Chapel of the Lord. The Birkys, formerly of Goshen, Indiana, first came to south Texas in January 1968 as program directors for the Corpus Christi VS unit. They studied Spanish at Rio Grande Bible Institute in Edinburg, Texas.

Soon after the Birkys came to Premont, the congregation began to show signs of revitalization. New church council members were elected, the youth became more interested in church activities, and community activities for children and youth were started on weekdays. Voluntary Service continued to offer assistance by developing the club programs and by helping the Birkys in the overall church program.

The women in the congregation expressed a desire to become actively involved in Bible studies and sewing circles. Participation by the women in church activities grew steadily, and soon a representative from the women's group was asked to join the church council to represent the women's point of view and to relate to the council their concerns. The sewing group has supplied the church with additional funds for church repairs and other needs of the church. This group has held bake sales and clothing sales in order to raise funds for special projects.

Interest was also expressed by the young adults of the congregation in Bible study. Thursday evenings were soon looked forward to as a group of six or seven young adults met in different homes for prayer and Bible study, or for discussing new Christian literature.

The MYF became better organized and soon new service projects were undertaken; they became involved in south Texas area MYF activities. The VSers served as sponsors. The emphasis on witnessing around the country stimulated the young people to attend Probe 72 and Explo 72. The momentum of these new experiences prompted the MYFers to take part in weekly meetings of the local God Squad.

After serving the Chapel of the Lord for twelve years, the Robert Reists decided to return to the United Mennonite Church in Premont. The fruits of their work are manifested in the quality of the young men and women who have come up from the congregation. Their efforts have contributed to the growth of the congregations.

From a two-year term in VS at the Chapel of the Lord, Marc and Grace Miller late in 1972 began to work with Teen Challenge at Corpus Christi. Succeeding them at Premont were David and Melissa Schrock, from Orrville, Ohio.[18]

Early in 1973 the Birkys left south Texas. Howard took up training in bookstore management at the Provident store in Lancaster, Pennsylvania.

The congregation has learned that a willing and cooperative spirit can effectively strengthen both the individual and the group. People like the Esaus, Fahndrichs, Reists, Schrags, De Leons, and Birkys have contributed to the success of the congregation in developing stronger personalities, deeper spiritual commitments, and effective church and community programs.

15. *Prince of Peace Mennonite, Corpus Christi, Texas*

Corpus Christi is an important seaport on the Gulf Coast, the tenth largest in the United States according to tonnage. Its population is over 200,000. With at least half of the people being Spanish, that language is heard everywhere. The city is about forty miles southeast of Mathis, and a little farther straight east of Alice. It is one hundred and fifty miles from the Mexican border.

The Mennonite Board of Missions in 1956 sent Don and Marilyn Brenneman to Corpus Christi to bring a witness to middle-class Latin people, and to build an indigenous church. Don grew up in Argentina, and so he was at home with the Spanish language. After two years in Corpus Christi, the Brennemans went to a pastorate in Chicago and then to Argentina for missionary service there.

Beginning services were held in the Brenneman home at 4422 Kilgore Street. The very first service had only two attendants —

Don and Marilyn Brenneman. Later cafeterias of school buildings were rented: Prescott School and Chula Vista School. A house trailer was used for a kindergarten. In 1962 six lots were purchased on Horne Road as a site for a church building. First services in the new building were held in August 1962 and the building was dedicated on October 29. The congregation had been organized in April of that year.

J. Weldon and Lorene Martin came from Mathis to succeed the Brennemans in August 1958 and they served until March 1965. Elvin Snyder was then installed as pastor, serving 1965-1968. He terminated his services to travel to Argentina, where he had formerly been a missionary. William Hallman, another former missionary in Argentina, took over for two years. Paul Conrad, formerly of Mathis, was installed as pastor in September 1970.

Sylvestre Zapata never lived in Corpus Christi, but he came at times with his van to sell Bibles, and thus made a contribution to the work.

Voluntary Service brought a number of workers to Corpus Christi, beginning in 1959. Among them have been the Orlo Fishers, Allen Kanagys, Milford Lehmans, Julio Validos, Sue King, Linda Burkhart, Emma Metzler, Delores and Mardella Bohn. Projects included boys' and girls' clubs, kindergarten, and summer Bible school. Summer Bible school began in 1959, and was held in a public school building until the church was built in 1962. In Molina, a suburb, another Bible school was held in homes the summers of 1960 and 1961. The next two years pupils were transported from Molina to the Prince of Peace area. Then in 1964, again in Molina, the school was held in the kindergarten house, on the lawn, or in adjoining homes.

Robstown, a few miles west of Corpus Christi, has had VS workers since 1962, but no church had yet been organized there in 1972. The church has been present, however, in the James Miller family, who had their home there. Miller taught school. The VS and local personnel have been active in Sunday school and community work. Reconstruction after hurricane damage in 1971 by Mennonite Disaster Service, under foreman Leonard Peters of North Newton, Kansas, has given a good witness. Plans in 1973 call for the organization of a congregation here as soon as a pastor can be found. Bible studies have been started here.

Robstown has been thought of as an extension from the Prince of Peace Church in Corpus Christi.

In November 1972 the annual extension convention of the South Texas Church Council was held at the Chula Chula Cafeterium in Corpus Christi. Conrado Hinojosa of Brownsville was the moderator and Guillerimo Tijerina, of Archbold, Ohio, a native of Brownsville, served as guest speaker. MYF teams from Mathis, Brownsville, Corpus Christi, Taft, and Premont participated in a quiz on the Book of Ephesians, with Mathis taking first place. Seventeen persons had a joyful experience distributing 1,000 tracts, door to door, in the community. Representatives of six congregations organized for MDS work, with Wayne Hochstetler, of Robstown, being chosen as coordinator.

The Prince of Peace congregation hosted the 1958 persons registered for the convention. Nelson and Lois Kreider, of Taft, led the children's activities, and Gilbert and Elizabeth Perez, also of Taft, were in charge of the music. Weldon Martin, of Mathis, led in a communion service. The convention was a significant experience in togetherness for the Mennonite churches of south Texas. [19]

16. *Spencer, Oklahoma County, Oklahoma*

The James Posar family moved from Wichita, Kansas, to Oklahoma City in 1961. They wanted to continue to worship with Mennonites of their conference, and so drove seventy miles to Pleasant View, at Hydro, the nearest congregation. James urged that congregation to consider starting a new church at Oklahoma City. In May 1963 a committee was appointed to study the question of an outreach in the capital area. The committee consisted of LeRoy Miller, Bill Mast, Alva Yoder, Chester Slagell, and Ira Switzer (chairman). The congregations at Pryor and Adair were asked to help, and Joy Stutzman and Ralph Yoder were appointed to represent these congregations.

A study of the field led to a decision to locate the new congregation in Spencer, a growing suburb northeast of Oklahoma City. The Posars bought a home in this vicinity, and the first service was held in their garage in July 1963 with seventeen people present and Chester Slagell preaching the first sermon. Services were continued in this garage until a church building was constructed. The average attendance was about thirty. The sponsoring churches sent some people each Sunday to encourage the fellowship.

The search for a pastor led to John Otto, who was attending Hesston College. He was a carpenter and would be available to

Spencer Church

put up a church building as well as to give spiritual leadership. He moved to Spencer, and was given full financial support until the church was built and he had found other employment.

A site was secured and ground was broken in July 1964. The work was done by volunteers from the Spencer group and from the sponsoring churches. Construction moved rapidly, and by October 1964 the brick veneer building was ready for dedication.

On October 4 a multiple service was held. The congregation was organized with nine charter members: Henry and Annette Inge, James and Ethel Posar, William and Betty Mast, John and Edna Otto, and Mrs. Sylvia Brown. Chester Slagell read the covenant of membership. The congregation had decided that children who wanted to accept Christ but were too young for baptism would be called intermediate members. There were six of these.

A second service that day was the dedication of the new church building. Howard J. Zehr, conference secretary, preached the dedicatory sermon. More than two hundred persons were present, many from Hydro and Pryor.

In a third service for this busy day John Otto was ordained to the ministry by Alva Swartzendruber, bishop at Hydro. The ordination sermon was by Clayton Beyler, of Hesston College.

A youth organization was formed in November 1964 to serve the young people fourteen and above. It was in charge of James and Ethel Posar. In January 1965 the Spencer Mennonite Church was incorporated; the incorporators were Bill Mast, Henry Inge, and John

Otto. In May of that year a junior choir began practicing, led by Elvin and Janice Zurcher, who had come into the church in April.

The first summer Bible school was held in June 1965. There were eighteen staff members and 105 pupils enrolled. In August a servanthood work camp was held in Spencer, with a total of eight campers. They were involved in cleanup and painting; one day they cleaned the city hall. Bill and Betty Mast were sponsors and hosts of the camp.

This was a year of growth. Bill Masts had moved to the city, and a few other families came into the church. In August the congregation was received into conference membership. The Every Home Plan for *Gospel Herald* subscriptions was started in November, with ten families on the list. The year ended with a watch-night service, sponsored by the Ladies' Fellowship. Forty-seven people viewed the film *In His Steps.*

Membership and attendance suffered some loss in 1966. A few families moved away. The Posar family had some dissatisfaction, and transferred to another denomination. But some others moved in, and membership at Spencer remained fairly constant. There was a fifty percent increase in Bible school attendance in 1968.

John Otto resigned as pastor in August 1970 but continues in active membership. Bill Mast was called to serve as lay leader. Lay leadership was a good experience for the congregation. But by March 1972 they were again ready for a pastor-leader, and Moses Mast, who with his wife, Sadie, had moved to Spencer from Alberta, Canada, that year, was licensed and installed as pastor. In June 1973 he was ordained. The membership in 1973 was seventeen.[20]

17. *Calico Rock Mennonite Fellowship, Izard County, Arkansas*

Calico Rock is a town of about one thousand people on the east bank of the White River, about fifty miles below the Arkansas-Missouri border. In the early days the paddle-wheeled steamboats had their northernmost landing here, where there were calico-colored rock bluffs. It was the "landing at the calico rocks." Later this name was reduced to Calico Rock. The settlement here lost many of its people in a typhoid epidemic in 1897 and in a drought in 1901. In 1902 there were only three families left. The population increased when the Missouri Pacific built a line up the White River Valley.

In 1908 the first Baptist church was built in the town. It stood on the hill above the river, in the cemetery area. In 1961 this congregation built a new church in the east part of town. The old church building was sold to the editor and publisher of the local newspaper. The auditorium became a pressroom, and the classrooms became the printer's living apartment. Soon, however, the press was sold and moved from this old church, which now stood empty and deteriorating.

The medical needs of this mountain area had been publicized throughout the Mennonite brotherhood in the story of Maude Buckingham Douglass and the clinic in Culp, just a few miles across the river, but isolated by the lack of a bridge. It came as a conviction to Dr. A. Meryl Grasse and his laboratory technician brother, John L., that they ought to take their training and skills to this medically deprived area. But that meant going where the people were, which was Calico Rock rather than Culp.

In 1952 these two brothers came to Calico Rock and set up practice. John's wife, Mary Margaret, is a nurse, as is Meryl's wife, Gladys, and together the four served as a medical missionary team in the community. In 1954 a combination clinic and residence was built. In 1957 a neighboring house was converted into a three-bed hospital. These facilities were soon outgrown and by 1959 a new twelve-bed hospital and clinic was opened, called The Medical Center of Calico Rock.

In 1964 Dr. John M. Grasse, Jr., a cousin of the Grasse brothers, joined them at Calico Rock. His wife, Betty, was also a registered nurse; the clinic was building a strong team. In 1969 Dr. John M. left for psychiatric training and practice at San Marcus, in southern Texas. In 1971 a new wing increased the capacity to twenty-six beds. The Medical Center enjoys good community relationships. An auxiliary of eighty women raised $1,000 to furnish a room and a wheelchair. The staff feels a personal involvement with the patients and their families not only in medical matters, but in spiritual ones also.

In 1972 there was further remodeling of the clinic facilities, making available a new hospital record room, a physical therapy department, an enlarged reception room, a business office, a waiting room, and an emergency room. The number of patients admitted has increased from 524 in 1967 to 771 in 1971; and the number of employees from 25 in 1967 to 40 in 1972.

For fifteen years the Grasses and other staff members of the hospital worshiped and served with the other Mennonite congregations of the area — filling pulpits, teaching classes, and participating in programs at Mount Joy, Bethel Springs, Advance, Buffalo, Three Brothers, and other places. A number of the Bethel Springs members lived east of the river. And so when the movement began to form the Mennonite Fellowship in Calico Rock, it was really an outpost of the Bethel Springs congregation. The building of a bridge across the river in 1966 accelerated the migration from the national forest area around Culp into the town of Calico Rock.

In 1963 Meryl and John L. purchased the former Baptist church building on the hill. The building was remodeled and restored. Everyone in the community seemed to be glad to see this building return to its former use as a house of worship. Many helped by providing money and gifts, such as hardwood flooring, a wood stove, and a rug for the main aisle. And a fund was started for a new church.

Services were begun in this restored facility in the spring of 1964 with a vesper service as the main time of meeting. This enabled the same pastor to serve both Bethel Springs and Calico Rock, and many of the people attended at both places. In August 1966 John M. Troyer moved from Pryor, Oklahoma, into the Culp area. He began to hold services at both Culp and Calico Rock, preaching at each church every other Sunday. In November 1966 Chester Slagell, who was serving the conference as chairman of the Church Extension Committee, held a weekend meeting at Calico Rock and helped to conduct the fall communion.

During the next year several meetings were held concerning the setting up of a separate membership at Calico Rock. Finally, in the presence of the area overseer, M. E. Bontreger, it was decided that those who wish to transfer to Calico Rock may do so, and those who do not may retain membership at Bethel Springs. In a weekend service in August 1967 the Calico Rock Mennonite Fellowship was formally organized with fifteen charter members. Manasseh Bontreger presided and Chester Slagell, chairman of the Church Extension and Evangelism Committee of the South Central Conference, was the guest speaker. The dedication of the building, which had been in use for two years, was in charge of Pastor John M. Troyer. After this, regular Sunday morning services were held.

The new congregation called Gordon Schrag, of Goshen, Indiana, to serve as pastor. He and his wife, Laura, arrived in December 1967, and in January he was installed as pastor by Manasseh Bontreger. Schrag held former pastorates in Ontario and New York. Their oldest son, Keith, has held South Central pastorates at Premont, Texas, and Eureka Gardens, Wichita, Kansas. At Calico Rock they live in a parsonage which the congregation has purchased near the church.

A full church program with a church-council-type government and including a chaplaincy at the Medical Center are now being carried on. Membership is largely from the Medical Center personnel, although a few others have joined. There has been home-to-home contact with people not attending any area church. There have been evangelistic meetings held by Richard Birky, Adair, Oklahoma; Henry Fast, Marshall, Arkansas; and others. A number of accessions have resulted.

Already Calico Rock has the largest membership of the Arkansas churches — twenty-seven in 1973. This shows that the population movement to the towns and cities has affected the mountain people too. In 1966 the *Conference Messenger* said, "It becomes more and more evident that Calico Rock will become a center for Mennonite witness and church building."[21] This does not mean that scattered members will be forgotten. Dr. John M. Grasse feels that in order to minister to the small Mennonite congregations in Arkansas there will need to be some kind of itinerant ministry. He sees the need for VS workers in doing some of this. But at any rate the Calico Rock congregation represents a move toward putting church efforts where the people are. And it illustrates the importance and the possibilities of a lay ministry.[22]

18. *Evangelical Mennonite Church*
(Iglesia Menonita Evangelica)
Taft, San Patricio County, Texas

The church fellowship at Taft, Texas, began with Nelson and Lois Kreider, who had served in VS at Mathis, Texas, in 1958-1959. After teaching school for some time in south Texas, the Kreiders moved to Corpus Christi to work in the witness of the Prince of Peace Church there. After a few years a school-counseling opportunity became available in Taft, twenty miles northwest of Corpus Christi. After Kreider had worked as a school counselor in Taft for one year, he and his family moved to Taft.

During the first year of work there, the Kreiders became increasingly aware of the large percentage of persons in the town of 6,500 who did not attend church. Among the Latin-American community of about 3,500 it was learned that nearly eighty percent of the persons did not attend church. As the Kreiders prayed and kept alert to the possibilities of a spiritual outreach, a small church building, owned by the local Methodist church, became available for the starting of a Sunday school.

At this time Ruth Brubaker and Savilla Ebersole, who had each served in south Texas at Mathis for several years, were interested in further outreach and agreed to serve in the development of a Sunday school with the Kreiders.

On August 2, 1970, the first Sunday school was held. Twenty-one persons attended. The following day, August 3, hurricane Celia struck. The windows of the church were blown out and the doors were blown in and one wall was separated from the main supporting frame. But this apparent tragedy turned into a blessing. With the insurance money, a modest loan, and the help of the Mennonite Disaster Service not only was the building repaired but four Sunday school rooms were added.

After six months of work in the community, which involved a considerable amount of visitation, the attendance of the Sunday school grew to sixty-five. Some adults were beginning to attend by this time, and of these adults Elias Casas was outstanding in his contribution to the growth and development of the congregation. Casas, who had been a Christian for a long time, was searching for opportunities to serve and give witness to his faith in Christ and it was at this growing Sunday school that he found such an opportunity. It was through his witness and testimony that a number of his relatives and friends became interested in the fellowship and later became a part of the congregation. It was soon after Casas began to serve with the fellowship that he became a coleader in the work.

The next need for the fellowship was a full-time pastor. The Kreiders felt able to lead the children and youth, but the adults who were more fluent in the Spanish language desired a Spanish-speaking pastor.

After a brief search they found a young man by the name of

Fernando Perez from Mexico, who shortly before his introduction to the congregation had completed his work in a Bible seminary in Mexico. The congregation extended a call to Fernando, but the call was short-lived. It was soon after he took the pastorate that a problem concerning his immigration documents became apparent. After considerable time in working with the immigration officials of the United States, the papers were denied due to the permanency of the position.

Soon after the decision concerning Fernando, acquaintance was made with Gilberto Perez, who was reared in Mathis, Texas, and who was now completing his Bible work at the Rio Grande Bible Institute, at Edinburg, Texas. Near the end of Gilberto's study term the congregation extended a call to him and his wife, Elizabeth, and their two children.

On Sunday, July 2, 1972, Gilbert was licensed and installed as the pastor of the Iglesia Menonita Evangelica at Taft. J. Weldon Martin, pastor of the Mathis congregation, preached the commissioning sermon and Paul Conrad, pastor of the Corpus Christi congregation, gave the charge to Perez. Jesus Navarro, Jr., chairman of the South Texas Mennonite Church Council, issued the license to preach. Perez had served as pastor in one of the Mennonite Brethren mission churches during his training at the Rio Grande Bible Institute.

Nelson Kreider is presently serving as secretary of the South Texas Mennonite Church Council, which recommended the new fellowship at Taft for membership into the South Central Conference. The fellowship was officially accepted into the conference in June 1971.[23]

19. *Brownsville Mennonite Church,*
Cameron County, Texas

In 1969 Conrado Hinojosa, after spending six years at Archbold, Ohio, returned to his hometown of Brownsville, in the southernmost tip of Texas. His purpose was to do missionary work with his people, and he and his wife began visiting in homes. Services were held in one of the homes, and attendance was increasing. So they looked for another meeting place in that area of the city. They found a deserted shack on a lot which was largely a dump. Permission was secured to use this building, and some of the men helped to haul away three loads of trash and to put in new glass and apply some paint. Friends and brothers from other churches furnished some of the money.

The building was ready for use in February 1971 after three months of work. There were no seats, and so the people either stood on the sides or sat on stools which they brought. A gasoline lantern served for lighting. After a month they were able to buy some lumber to make seats, and to make the necessary deposit for electricity. A pulpit was given by a Methodist church. People were coming to church.

In February 1972 application was made for affiliation with the South Central Mennonite Conference. Hinojosa was licensed to preach, and he began calling the church a Mennonite church. He talked about baptism on confession of faith, and in April eight people were baptized by Pastor Tijerina of the Good Shepherd Mennonite Church in Archbold, Ohio. A family from Indiana began helping with the work. A women's group became very active in the church. None of the members had ever heard a Christian hymn or led in prayer, but now the Lord taught them to sing and pray. The church has a Sunday school superintendent and teachers and a church council, all from these new Christians. The group wanted to build a new church, and Simon Gingerich, of the Home Missions Office of the Mennonite Mission Board, was in Brownsville in December 1972 to help find a site.

The site which was purchased by the Mission Board was a five-acre tract in a growing residential district. Financial gifts came from Ohio and South Central congregations. When building began in January 1974, brethren from Ohio and Indiana joined local laborers, quickly constructing the beige block and brick Spanish-style building. The name chosen was La Iglesia del Cordero (Church of the Lamb). In the dedication on May 5, 1974, Guillermo Tijerina, of Premont, preached the sermon. The building includes a fellowship hall.

20. *South Texas Mennonite Church Council*

There was a growing concern among the churches in south Texas to seek methods of unifying the area. Many believed that in coming together as a group of believers to share concerns and discuss similar problems facing the congregations, the insight and program direction would undoubtedly benefit the individual congregations. However, in one of the early attempts made for a more organized and structured setting in which to meet together for these purposes, the believers ran into misunderstandings.

As early as in 1968 and 1969, the south Texas area had dealt with the possibility of forming an area council. However, the group atmosphere at that time prohibited any further developments, as some area people were not sure just what would be the function of such a council. Some were upset when one of the purposes proposed was that the council would be a decision-making body. This was interpreted that an area council would dictate local congregation decisions. Some felt that the local congregations should retain their autonomous entity and the formation of a council would threaten their power to govern themselves. Because of such feelings among many of the south Texas people, the possibility of forming an area council was abandoned for a while.

In 1970 another attempt was made to get some structured direction in the south Texas area for assisting the south Texas overseer for South Central Conference in dealing with programs in the area. Chester Slagell, the south Texas overseer, was present at one of the meetings and presented to the area persons attending a list of his concerns. However, the mood of the group present was more docile and not as suspicious as in previous meetings. At this time, the attitude changed to one of cooperation and after much discussion and soul-searching the consensus of the group was to work toward the possible formation of a council. It was reemphasized that the council was solely to serve in an advisory capacity, and only in dealing with programs affecting the area as a whole. Lupe De Leon, Jr., was elected as interim chairman to conduct another area meeting to lay the groundwork for the beginnings of an area council.

In the following meeting the congregations were asked to send interim delegates with voting power to make temporary decisions on actions needed in order to establish guidelines essential for the council to have minimum authority for executing its purpose. The group met on January 24, 1971, in Robstown, Texas. The group elected five area persons to serve in a constitutional committee responsible for drafting a constitution to serve as the guideline for governing the council. The five persons elected to this committee were: Lupe Longoria, Alice; Manuela Garcia, Premont; Lloyd Miller, Robstown; Chuy Navarro, Premont; and Paul Conrad, Corpus Christi. The committee met several times within a couple of months and was able to draft a constitution to be presented in March of the same year in Mathis, Texas. The interim area council met in Mathis and adopted the constitution. The next step was to select a nominating committee (provision for such committee had been included in the constitution) to present a slate of possible candidates to the May 2, 1971, meeting in Corpus Christi, Texas.

On May 2, 1971, Interim Chairman Lupe De Leon, Jr., opened the meeting with the roll call of the official delegates representing five congregations and one VS unit. With the adoption of the constitution in March, each congregation was to elect three representatives and one alternate to officially establish the council. The name officially adopted for this organization was: South Texas Mennonite Church Council. The election of officers was held and the first STMCC officers to be installed were: chairman, Chuy Navarro, Premont; vice-chairman, Israel Lozano, Alice; secretary, Nelson Kreider, Taft; and treasurer, Dan Miller, Alice, Texas.

The purposes of the STMCC were to promote and oversee church extension program in south Texas; to provide an avenue for area churches to receive counsel on individual congregational concerns; to promote MDS, WMSC, MBM, and MMA activities in south Texas; to give direction to VS projects not under any specific congregational administration; and to conduct and execute business pertaining to the area church program.

The standing committees created in council were: Camp, Church Extension, Nominating, Public Relations, and Scholarship. Most of the activity is being carried in these committees. The committees meet whenever it is essential for carrying out their purposes and give regular reports to the council in its quarterly business sessions. The executive committee, composed of the four officers, meet prior to each regular STMCC business meeting for preparing the agenda for the business meeting.

Since May 1971 the council has been active in executing the purposes outlined in the constitution. Area people serve on committees on a voluntary basis. The interaction which has transpired during the committees' meetings and during the business sessions, and planned area conventions, have richly blessed the area. The communication among south Texas people has greatly improved. There is more understanding and cooperation than ever before. Many unselfish hours have been donated by south Texas persons and hard work has literally been given in order to give the workings of the council its great success. Although south Texas is a poorly developed area economically, the south Texas churches support the council with donations and offerings in order to strengthen the work of the council. The present chairman, Chuy Navarro, has great expectations for the council. Navarro has been diligently working to keep the council active and to keep the spirit of brotherhood and cooperation alive in south Texas. Navarro is also serving as district representative on the Executive Committee of South Central Conference. For the first time in the organization of South Central Conference the Executive Committee has a native south Texan to serve as a member and give accurate account of south Texas needs and concerns. Navarro is a financial service worker in charge of the Financial Services Department of State Welfare in Falfurrias, Texas. He also is serving as a member of the Commission on Congregational Education and Literature, which is one of the commissions created by the Mennonite Board of Congregational Ministries.[25]

The council sponsored the fifth annual assembly of the Minority Ministries Council (Elkhart) at the Zephyr Encampment, Sandia, Texas, October 19-21, 1973. The Home Missions Committee of the Mennonite Board of Missions met at Corpus Christi, October 18 and 19. So the south Texas churches are very much in the denominational perspective.[26]

THE SERIES OF MENNONITE
CONFERENCES

CHAPTER 11

THE SERIES OF MENNONITE
CONFERENCES

In the series of congregational histories there have been numerous references to the conferences where they have or did have affiliation. Now we look at the conferences themselves, the South Central and the conferences which preceded in South Central territory.

1. *Missouri-Iowa Conference*

The Missouri-Iowa Conference was organized in 1873. The moving spirit was Bishop Daniel Brundage, of the Morgan County congregation, where the first session was held on October 24, 1873. In those first years it was called the Missouri Conference, as the member congregations were in that state. Later the conference included congregations in Iowa, Minnesota, North Dakota, eastern Kansas, Louisiana, and Texas.

Leaders in this conference, other than Brundage, included D. D. Kauffman, Daniel F. Driver, Daniel Kauffman, Andrew Shenk, J. C. Driver, J. M. Kreider, and J. R. Shank.

The conference met annually, alternating in the early years at Mt. Zion and Mt. Pisgah. It was one of the first conferences to urge the formation of a Mennonite General Conference, and in other ways was forward-looking.

A resolution of 1881 seems to be a good deal ahead of its time. "Missionary work is a matter of great importance and demands the immediate attention of the church. It was decided, however, that home missions demand our first attention, and that an effort should be made to spread the gospel over our own country before we attempt foreign mission work."[1] The conference had a district mission board for home mission work, organized in 1898, and a Sunday school conference, organized before 1905.[2]

This is one of the three conferences that were dissolved in 1920-1921 to make way for the organization of the Missouri-Kansas Conference. Its Dakota congregations became a part of the Dakota-Montana (later North Central) Conference; its Iowa congregation went into the Iowa-Nebraska Conference; the rest of the congregations became members of the Missouri-Kansas Conference.

2. *Kansas-Nebraska Conference*

The Kansas-Nebraska Conference for years was composed of the Mennonite congregations in Kansas and the one at Roseland, Nebraska. The first session was held at Spring Valley in Kansas, on April 14, 1876. Again, as in Missouri, Bishop Daniel Brundage led in the organization. Attending the first session were bishops Brundage and Henry Yother, two ministers, a deacon, and R. J. Heatwole, a delegated layman, who served as secretary. Heatwole, though a layman, served as moderator of a number of sessions. T. M. Erb, also, was elected moderator of conference before he was ordained to the ministry. From 1879 to 1890 the conference met for both spring and fall sessions; from 1892 on there was only an annual session, usually in October.

In 1879 the growing congregation at Roseland became a member of this conference and what had been the Kansas Conference became the Kansas-Nebraska Conference. The Roseland congregation was organized in 1880 of people who had migrated from Illinois and eastern Pennsylvania. Their leader was Albrecht Schiffler, who had been converted and ordained in Tazewell County, Illinois. The deacon was Samuel Lapp. Meetinghouses were constructed in 1882 and 1898. It was a strong church, with a great sense of mission. Well-known church workers who came from there were Noah Ebersole, the Lapp brothers — Samuel, Daniel, Mahlon, and George — Jacob Burkhard (the first Mennonite missionary to die in India), J. M. Nunemaker, C. U. and Chris Snyder.

The first session of the conference to be held at Roseland was in 1882; it met there frequently after that. By 1900 the membership at Roseland was nearly one hundred.

As the Western frontiers were extended, churches from other

states were received by the conference: Oklahoma (1895), Idaho (1900), Oregon (1900), Colorado (1904), Texas (1908), and New Mexico (1911). This created a problem about the name of the conference, until in 1906 action was taken changing the name "The Kansas, Nebraska, Oklahoma, Colorado, Idaho, and Oregon District" to "The Kansas-Nebraska District." Someone in 1899, when only three states were involved, suggested that it be called the "Kannebokla" Conference![3]

In 1905 the conference, in session at Hubbard, Oregon, took action to divide the conference, with the Rocky Mountains as the dividing line. This was the beginning of the Pacific Coast Conference.

Interesting actions of the Kansas-Nebraska Conference include the following: against the use of lightning rods (the first resolution); that voting at the polls is inconsistent with nonresistance; that tobacco should not be chewed in the house of worship; against taking pictures; that preachers should not preach too long; that part singing is permissible; that a General Conference would promote the welfare of the church; that the church should establish an orphans' home; that it is advisable to preach for other denominations; favoring the Chicago Home Mission; that the prayer covering need not be worn continuously; that a supported ministry is scriptural; favoring a church-owned publishing house; against powwowing; that ordination may be by consent of the congregation, without the lot; favoring both district and general mission boards, and a sanitarium at La Junta; favoring a school in the West; defining doctrinal positions, such as on Holy Spirit baptism.[4]

In the reorganization of conferences in 1920-1921, the Kansas-Nebraska Conference was dissolved. The last session was held at Spring Valley in 1920. The conference at that time had eighteen congregations, with a total of 797 members. The Roseland congregation went into the new Iowa-Nebraska Conference; the rest into the new Missouri-Kansas Conference.[5]

The Kansas-Nebraska Conference organized by conference action in 1905 a Home Mission Board. The first officers were L. L. Beck, president; R. M. Weaver, secretary; J. G. Wenger, treasurer. The Board was composed of representatives elected by all the congregations of the conference, so that every congregation had a member on the Board. These members made annual reports of congregational giving. When conferences were merged in 1920, new mission boards conformed to the new conference boundaries.

3. *Western District Amish Mennonite*

The third fellowship of churches whose dissolution in 1920 made a new alignment possible was the Western District Amish Mennonite Conference. This conference developed slowly during the second half of the nineteenth century among some thirty congregations. Largely congregational in form of church government, there were differences among them in doctrine, policy, and custom. They struggled with such questions as laxity in discipline, the wearing of buttons or hooks and eyes, and the shunning of excommunicated members. There were some meetings of ministers for fellowship and informal counsel. But in a meeting at Sycamore Grove in 1890 the Western A. M. Conference was organized. Leaders of this conference included J. C. Kenagy, J. J. Hartzler, L. J. Miller, C. A. Hartzler, and Joseph Schlegel, all in the area covered after 1920 by the Missouri-Kansas Conference. The Western District A. M. Conference had at the time of its dissolution thirty-two congregations, with 4,388 members in the following states: Illinois, Iowa, Missouri, Arkansas, Nebraska, Kansas, Oklahoma, Colorado, and Oregon.[6] Those in Missouri, Kansas, Oklahoma, and Arkansas ultimately became members of the Missouri-Kansas Conference.

The Western District A. M. Conference did not have a constitution, and its authority grew very slowly. At first resolutions were not voted on. German was the language used until after 1911. Reports were issued in both languages until 1920.

The official merger followed a growing sense of unity and brotherhood. Bishop Joseph Buercky, of Illinois, after a visit at Roseland, Nebraska, testified, "Here were no Amish nor Mennonites, but all Brethren in Christ."[7] All these conferences cooperated in Mennonite General Conference and the three general Boards. The Amish elected representatives on the local Boards of the Chicago and Kansas City missions. The Missouri-Iowa Conference in 1889 invited the Amish churches to meet with them.[8] All had similar problems, and their doctrines were the same. There was almost complete freedom of pulpit and of communion across conference lines. And so, although the conference reorganization is a credit to Daniel Kauffman and the other leaders who engineered the change, actually they were only writing into official unity the spirit which had been growing for many years.

However, the merger was not without its difficulties. There was much friction over church polity. The Amish were congregational; the Mennonites were more bishop-oriented. The Amish churches did not want bishop rule. Not till some years later did they feel comfortable in leaving "Amish" out of the name of the conference to which they belonged and so for a time the Iowa-Nebraska Conference used neither "Mennonite" or "Amish" in its conference name.[9]

4. *Missouri-Kansas Conference*

A merger of the Mennonite and the Amish Mennonite conferences was first accomplished in Indiana-Michigan, where the process was completed by 1916. The western merger involved the conferences west of the Indiana-Illinois line. In September 1919 the Kansas-Nebraska Conference appointed its committee to confer on this matter. In October Missouri-Iowa and Western District A. M. made similar appointments. Of the sixteen recommendations proposed by the conferring group, the tenth provided for five new conference districts: Illinois, Iowa-Nebraska, Missouri-Kansas (later, South Central), North Dakota (which became Dakota-Montana, and still later, North Central), and Pacific Coast. The recommendations were adopted by all the conferences, and in a referendum nine tenths of the members were favorable. The new conferences all held first meetings in 1921. Thus were brought together in this western area 7,500 members, 4,500 of them from the Western District A. M. Conference.[10]

The first session of the Missouri-Kansas Conference was held at West Liberty on August 20, 1921. J. M. Kreider was the moderator and the conference sermon was given by George R. Brunk. A constitution was drawn up and adopted in the next two years. There were thirty-five congregations and almost 2,000 baptized members.[11]

5. *South Central Conference*

In 1946 the Missouri-Kansas Conference, to recognize more adequately its congregations in Colorado, Texas, Louisiana, and Mississippi, changed its name to South Central. At that time it had grown to forty-two congregations with over 3,000 members. These churches were located in eight states, from Denver, Colorado, to Gulfport, Mississippi, from Hannibal, Missouri, to Perryton, Texas.

The next adjustment in conference lines was the organization in 1961 of the Rocky Mountain Conference. This new conference was comprised of the fourteen South Central congregations in Colorado, New Mexico, northwestern Texas, and western Kansas, with a total membership of about one thousand. This left the South Central Conference with congregations in Missouri, central and eastern Kansas, Oklahoma, northern Arkansas, southern Texas, southern Louisiana, and southern Mississippi. In 1972 there were forty-four congregations and something over 3,500 members. Over half of the congregations had fewer than seventy-five members. About a fifth of the members were in one community — Hesston.

Other South Central Developments

For years there was a Sunday School Conference, with its own officers and having its own sessions in the annual meeting. Then, to recognize the summer Bible school and other parts of the Christian education program, it became a Christian Education Conference. Then, following the pattern of the Commission for Christian Education of General Conference, and giving emphasis to year-round administration instead of an annual program of inspiration, the conference became a Christian Education Cabinet. In the constitution now in effect there are no standing committees, but the Executive Committee appoints ad hoc task forces for specific assignments.

Likewise the Mission Board became a Church Extension and Evangelism Committee, in some years conducting its own evangelism conference at a place and time different from the annual meeting of the conference. The treasury of the Mission Board and of the conference were coalesced into one. For almost fifteen years (1945-1959) Roy S. Troyer was the conference treasurer. He was not only a faithful and efficient custodian of funds, but was also an administrator who gave spiritual directions to policies.

The women's work of the district had its origin at the Pennsylvania Church in 1908. The women began meeting regularly to sew garments for mission and relief needs. This was related to the church-wide sewing work soon after it was organized in 1915. A district-wide organization was effected about 1930, but the larger slate of officers, such as functions today, dates from about 1936. Mrs. Allen (Stella) Erb, Mrs. Mahlon (Dorothea) Eigsti, Mrs. John (Ruth) Duerksen, Mrs. Roman (Marianna) Stutzman, and Mrs. Alvin (Beulah) Kauffman are persons from South Central who have served on the General WMSC committee; Beulah Kauffman moved on to Elkhart to become executive secretary of the work which after 1971 is carried on under the name of Women's Missionary and Service Commission, now functioning under the Board of Congregational Ministries.

Gradually the program of women's work came to realize that though women can sew, they can also do very well a great variety of services and spiritual life projects, like, for instance, the retreats for spiritual renewal.

The South Central Conference never developed a camp of its own. But camping programs have been carried on at various camps in Missouri and Arkansas, at Rocky Mountain Camp in Colorado, and, more recently, at the General Conference Mennonite Camp on the Ninnescah River west of Wichita.

The strong mission spirit among the people of the South Central Conference and its predecessors has been behind various mission beginnings: city missions at Kansas City, Wichita, and Hannibal; rural missions in the Ozarks of Missouri and Arkansas; work with minorities at St. Louis, in south Texas, and along the Gulf Coast; child welfare work in Kansas City; sanitarium and hospital work in Colorado, Kansas, and Arkansas.

A conference fund for building facilities for the aged was the first money raised for Schowalter Villa. This retirement home at Hesston, Kansas, was the first Mennonite home built without general solicitation but on the principle that for the greater part those who use the institution would eventually amortize the cost of construction. One of the purposes of the J. A. Schowalter bequest was providing for the need of retired church workers. To carry out this purpose the Board of Control of the Schowalter Foundation in 1958 purchased a site adjoining the Hesston College campus. The Mennonite Board of Missions through a Kansas subsidiary owns and operates the institution. The first members of this subsidiary were O. O. Miller, E. C. Bender, R. S. Troyer, and Allen H. Erb.

Some apartments were ready for occupancy in September 1961, with the main building completed early in 1962. Demand for this kind of lifetime care has increased, and the facility has expanded with more apartments, rooms, and nursing facilities. Ground was broken in November 1972 for a 27-bed nursing care addition.

The total number of residents since the 1961 opening to December 1972 was 183. The number of those who had been engaged in full-time church service was 56. The capacity of the Villa is 112.

The Villa strongly promotes rich and full retirement living and a vital Christian atmosphere. All are helped to attend public worship, but the service from the Hesston Mennonite Church can be brought into the rooms of those who wish it.

James Hershberger now gives full time to the administration of the Villa. Wilma Friesen was, in December 1972, the director of nursing. The Villa is licensed as a skilled nursing facility by the Kansas State Department of Health.

Hesston College is closely related to the conference. It was a conference resolution of 1907 which moved the Mennonite Board of Education to establish Hesston College, and the officials of the college have oftentimes been conference officials also. The campus facilities have again and again served the conference. The college increasingly became a chief center of conference life, but it was never owned or operated by the conference. Hesston College has had a tremendous influence on the conference, doctrinally, spiritually, and in the education of the young people.

The Conference Messenger is the organ of the conference. The following have served as editors: Glen Yoder, Sept., 1945-Aug., 1949; Jess Kauffman, Sept., 1949-May, 1953; J. P. Duerksen, Oct. 1953-Aug., 1955; Edward J. Miller, Nov., 1955-Sept., 1957; Clayton Beyler, Oct., 1957-Aug., 1959; Menno Troyer, Sept., 1959-Dec., 1961; James Detweiler, Jan., 1962-Dec., 1963; Harold Sommerfeld, Jan., 1964-Aug., 1964; Howard J. Zehr, Sept., 1964-Aug., 1966; James and Ruth Horsch, Sept., 1966-Aug., 1968; Ruth K. Duerksen, Sept., 1968-Aug., 1971; Harold Sommerfeld, Autumn, 1973-

The Conference Messenger, printed at Hesston by Jess Kauffman and Harold Sommerfeld, served through the years as a means of communication between conference districts, of relaying information from General Conference, the general Mission Board, Mennonite Central Committee, Women's Mission and Service Auxiliary, of keeping churches informed about work in the district, of providing a file of materials for later researchers.[12] As an economy move the conference discontinued this publication after August 1971. This was soon felt to have been a mistake, and irregular publication was resumed in the spring of 1972. "The South Central Story," an audiovisual report, was ready for use in February 1973.

The South Central Conference has cooperated in many ways with other branches of Mennonites. A common support of Mennonite Central Committee has brought speakers into the churches and found the rank and file of the membership working side by side in such projects as meat-canning and disaster service.

As noted earlier, disaster service had its birth in a Sunday school class discussion at Hesston in 1950. It soon became inter-Mennonite, and was organized by MCC into districts. John Diller and Marvin Hostetler have had an important part in area management, and Earl Boyts, among others, has served as a field foreman.

Another form of cooperation is in the annual ministers' weeks held at Hesston each winter, and now participated in by ministers and their wives of the General Conference Mennonites and the Mennonite Brethren.

Dual conference membership seems to be another form of inter-Mennonitism. The Rainbow Boulevard congregation in Kansas City and the inter-Mennonite congregation in Hesston now belong to both the South Central Conference (MC) and the Western District (GC); United Mennonite at Premont, Texas, belongs to both the South Central Conference and the Mennonite Brethren (MB).

Cooperation became closest in November 1972, when the South Central Conference (MC) and the Western District Conference (GC) held their annual sessions simultaneously on the Bethel College campus. Each conference met separately for its own business, but the groups met conjointly to hear reports of common interest, to receive the inter-Mennonite congregation into both conferences, to hear the various addresses, to sing and worship together, and to celebrate a final communion service. The two moderators presided in the joint sessions. Two thousand people attended the Sunday morning service.

The South Central Conference led in 1954 "in a revision of church polity by (1) the introduction of the office of regional overseer appointed by the executive committee of the conference in conjunction with the ministry of the region, (2) the introduction of a three-year term not only for the overseer but also for the local pastor, and (3) the suspension of further ordination of bishops."[13]

Not all congregations immediately accepted the new overseer plan, and there have been problems in securing overseers and in administering the plan. In 1971 the conference was divided into six administrative districts: South Texas, Gulf States, Oklahoma, Arkansas, Missouri, and Kansas. Each district elects a representative on a central coordinating and executive committee. This conference no longer ordains bishops, but has not yet fully solved the problem of how the congregations shall be supervised.

For a few years the conference had an executive secretary, who carried some supervisory functions. This has since given way to a conference minister, whose responsibilities have not yet been constitutionally defined. Millard Osborne, the first conference minister, began his full-time service to the conference in July 1970.

The South Central Conference was one of the first to have lay delegates helping to make conference decisions.[14]

Mennonite General Conference

The Missouri-Iowa and Kansas-Nebraska conferences were among the first to urge the organization of a Mennonite General Conference, in response to John F. Funk's proposal to establish a General Conference. Daniel Kauffman was moderator of Mennonite General Conference for four terms. Allen H. Erb was moderator for three terms. Other men from the South Central area to hold the moderatorship of the Conference for one term were D. H. Bender, H. A. Diener, and Milo Kauffman. General Conference met at Garden City, Missouri, in 1921 and at Hesston, Kansas, in 1933 and 1955.

Region III of Mennonite General Assembly

The reorganization of the Mennonite Church which was approved in 1971 divides the churches of the United States and Canada into five regions. According to this preliminary division southern Mississippi is in Region V; the rest of the South Central Conference is in Region III, which lies between the northern and southern boundaries of the United States, and between the Mississippi River and a line extended south from the Montana-Dakota boundary. How this will affect the district conferences is not yet clear. But the South Central Conference participated with the North Central and Iowa-Nebraska conferences in selecting delegates to the first meeting of the Mennonite General Assembly at Harrisonburg, Virginia, in August, 1973. The South Texas Church Council may be showing how congregations in a smaller area work together.

Mennonite World Conference

Through Mennonite General Conference, but also by sending its own delegates, the South Central Conference has participated with international Mennonitism in the Mennonite World Conference. The 1948 sessions of that body were held at Goshen, Indiana, and Newton, Kansas, where the South Central Mennonites assisted in the hosting of the meeting.

The tenth Mennonite World Conference will convene in Central Kansas in July of 1978, the thirtieth anniversary of its last meeting in the United States. The South Central Conference joined the

Southern District of the Mennonite Brethren Church and the Western District of the General Conference Mennonite Church in giving an invitation for this meeting to be held in Kansas.

New Frontiers

The Mennonite churches of the South Central Conference area have been pushing out to new frontiers: finding new areas for settlement, organizing new congregations and new conferences, establishing new institutions, experimenting with new ways of working, finding new fronts for evangelism and Christian service, working on new approaches to minority groups, expressing Christian nonconformity in more satisfactory ways, bringing those who were afraid of each other into understanding and cooperation, keeping open to the Spirit in various forms of Christian renewal. They have found that the spirit of the frontier leads to new ways of finding and fulfilling the will of God.

NOTES

I. The South Central Frontier

1. *Herald of Truth* (Elkhart, Ind.), Feb. 1869, p. 25.
2. *HT* (Mar. 1869), p. 40.
3. Unpublished essay in the Melvin Gingerich collection in the Archives of the Mennonite Church.

II. Scattered Members in Missouri

1. *HT* (Mar. 1866), p. 20.
2. *HT* (Apr. 1868), p. 56.
3. *HT* (July 1868), pp. 105, 106.
4. *HT* (Aug. 1868), p. 122.
5. *HT* (Aug. 1869), pp. 120, 121.
6. *HT* (Feb. 1867), p. 25.
7. *HT* (Jan. 1879), pp. 11, 12.
8. *HT* (Feb. 1869), p. 25.
9. *Mennonite Historical Bulletin* (Goshen, Ind.) Oct., 1868, p. 7.
10. *HT* (Mar. 1874), p. 57.
11. *MHB* (Apr. 1963), p. 5.
12. *HT* (Apr. 1880), p. 70.
13. *HT* (Aug. 1880), p. 148.
14. *HT* (Feb. 15, 1884), pp. 56, 57.
15. *HT* (June 15, 1884), p. 185.
16. *HT* (Nov. 1, 1885), p. 330.
17. *HT* (May 15, 1884), p. 152.
18. *HT* (Dec. 15, 1884), p. 381.
19. *Gospel Herald* (Scottdale, Pa.) Apr. 23, 1957, p. 393.
20. *HT* (Sept. 15, 1889), p. 281.
21. *HT* (Oct. 1, 1891), pp. 300, 301.
22. *HT* (Dec. 15, 1890), p. 378.
23. *HT* (Jan. 15, 1895), p. 25.
24. *HT* (July 15, 1891), p. 222.
25. *HT* (July 15, 1895), p. 218.
26. J. S. Hartzler and Daniel Kauffman, *Mennonite Church History* (Scottdale, Pa., 1905), p. 294, and Daniel Kauffman, *Mennonite Cyclopedic Dictionary* (Scottdale, Pa., 1937), p. 249.
27. *Mennonite Yearbook and Directory* (Scottdale, Pa., 1921), p. 16.

III. Extinct Churches in Missouri

1. Melvin Gingerich interview with D. B. Raber, son of Daniel Raber, on Jan. 16, 1955, in Goshen, Ind. The Gingerich notes are in the Archives of the Mennonite Church.
2. *HT* (Elkhart, Ind.), Feb. 1871, p. 26.
3. J. S. Hartzler and Daniel Kauffman, *Mennonite Church History* (Scottdale, Pa., 1905), p. 34.
4. *HT* (Jan. 1, 1895), p. 9.

5. *MED*, p. 159.

6. J. D. Hartzler to Melvin Gingerich, Apr. 16, 1946, in the Archives of the Mennonite Church.

7. *MHB* (July 1967), p. 6.

8. *Ibid.*, p. 6.

9. *The Mennonite Encyclopedia* (Scottdale, Pa., 1955), Vol. I, p. 620, "Clearfork Amish Mennonite Church," by Melvin Gingerich.

10. *Ibid.*, p. 7. The story of the Sycamore Grove Church is continued in the *MHB*, Oct. 1967. In 1966 a committee of Sycamore Grove Mennonite Church prepared and published a 104-page booklet, *Sycamore Grove Centennial, 1866-1966*. It was printed and bound by General Publishing and Binding, Iowa Falls, Iowa.

11. *HT* (Aug. 1867), p. 124.

12. *HT* (Aug. 1872), pp. 123, 124.

13. *HT* (Feb. 1871), p. 31.

14. *HT* (Oct. 15, 1884), p. 314.

15. *HT* (Jan. 1, 1898), p. 9.

16. Mrs. Shenk's letter is in the Mennonite Church Archives, Hesston, Kan., White Hall materials.

17. *HT* (Mar. 15, 1886), p. 90.

18. *HT* (June 15, 1900), p. 185.

19. *HT* (June 1, 1893, and Feb. 1, 1898).

20. Interview of D. B. Raber by Melvin Gingerich, Jan. 16, 1955. Notes of the interview are in the Melvin Gingerich Collection, Archives of the Mennonite Church.

21. Letter to Melvin Gingerich from Ellen Yoder Reber, Holden, Mo., Mar. 17, 1955. In Gingerich Collection, Archives of the Mennonite Church.

22. *HT* (July 1870), p. 104.

23. *Ibid.*, p. 111.

24. *HT* (Mar. 1872), p. 45.

25. *HT* (Aug. 1872), p. 124.

26. *HT* (Nov. 1, 1883), p. 331.

27. *HT* (Feb. 1879), p. 36.

28. *HT* (Dec. 15, 1884), p. 381.

29. *HT* (Feb. 15, 1892), p. 54.

30. *HT* (Jan. 1, 1895), p. 9.

31. *ME*, Vol. I, p. 537, "Cedar County, Mo.," by Melvin Gingerich.

32. *HT* (Dec. 1, 1902), p. 363.

33. *MY* (Scottdale, Pa.) 1906, p. 50.

34. Were there two settlements, the one at Stotesbury and the other at Katy? Earlier Schrock's address was Stotesbury but by at least 1906 it was Katy and the congregation carries the Katy address. Schrock's address may have changed.

35. *HT* (June 1, 1886), p. 170.

36. *HT* (Sept. 15, 1888), p. 281.

37. *HT* (June 15, 1892), p. 187.

38. *MHB* (June 1946), Nelson E. Kauffman, "Bishop John Mellinger Kreider," pp. 1, 2.

39. *HT* (June 7, 1904), p. 207.

40. *GH* (Scottdale, Pa.) Feb. 15, 1940, pp. 986, 987. Daniel C. Esch, "The Amish Mennonite Colony in Audrain County, Missouri."

41. *MHB* (June, 1946, pp. 1, 2, 4), by L. Glen Guengerich, "The Amish Mennonite Colony in Audrain Co., Missouri."

42. Sources: Interview of Eli Bontrager by Paul Erb; letter of H. A. Diener to Paul Erb, Nov. 22, 1971; *CL* (Feb. 1957), p. 11.

IV. Churches in Missouri

1. Harry F. Weber, *Centennial History of The Mennonites of Illinois 1829-1929* (Goshen, Ind., 1931), pp. 90, 97, 142, 148, and Daniel Kauffman, *MCD* (Scottdale, Pa., 1937), p. 205.

2. J. S. Hartzler and Daniel Kauffman, *Mennonite Church History* (Scottdale, Pa., 1905), p. 294.

3. *MCD*, p. 205.

4. Weber, *op. cit.*, p. 97.

5. *MCH*, p. 294.

6. *MHB* (June 1946), Nelson E. Kauffman, "Short History of Mt. Pisgah," p. 3.

7. Weber, *op. cit.*, p. 162.

8. *HT* (Feb. 1869), p. 25.

9. *HT* (Aug. 1871), pp. 124, 125.

10. *HT* (Feb. 15, 1888), p. 63.

11. *ME*, Vol. III, p. 759, John Miller Yoder, "Mount Pisgah Mennonite Church," p. 759.

12. *MHB* (June 1946), Nelson E. Kauffman, *op. cit.*, p. 3.

13. *Ibid.;* also *HT* (Mar. 15, 1886), p. 90.

14. *Ibid.*

15. *HT* (Feb. 1, 1893), p. 51.

16. *HT* (July 15, 1896), p. 217.

17. *HT* (Oct. 15, 1892), p. 316.

18. Additional sources for the history of Mt. Pisgah include *The Conference Messenger* (Jan. 1967), published by the South Central Conference at Hesston, Kansas; historical notes by J. M. Yoder; and correspondence with Daniel Kauffman.

19. *GH* (Aug. 15, 1929), p. 428.

20. In 1966 the Sycamore Grove congregation published *Sycamore Grove Mennonite Church: Sycamore Grove Centennial, 1866-1966.* A 104-page illustrated loose-leaf book, it was compiled by the "Centennial Committee" on which served Mrs. Earl Roth, Mrs. John G. McCarthy, and Miss Trusie Zook. *South Central Frontiers* used freely the factual material in the "Sycamore Grove Centennial." Mrs. Wilbur (Iona) Schrock edited the book.

21. *HT* (Jan. 15, 1882), p. 23.

22. Pius Hostetler, *Life, Preaching, Labors of John D. Kauffman* (Shelbyville, Ill., 1916).

23. Cornelius J. Dyck, editor, *An Introduction to Mennonite History, A Popular History of the Anabaptists and the Mennonites* (Scottdale, Pa.,

1967), p. 300.

24. Letter from J. D. Hartzler to Paul Erb, no date.

25. Ethel Reeser Cosco, *Christian Reeser — The Story of a Centenarian* (Tangent, Oregon, 1952?).

26. From Stephen Kauffman's record book referred to on page 28 of *Sycamore Grove Centennial.*

27. J. S. Hartzler, *Mennonites in the World War or Non-Resistance Under Test* (Scottdale, Pa., 1921), p. 129. Taped interview of J. D. Hartzler's World War I experiences in Archives of the Mennonite Church.

28. The terms "Western Amish Mennonite Conference" and "Western District Amish Mennonite Conference" were used interchangeably in the early years of the organization but when in 1911 the conference published its proceedings from its first conference in 1890, the booklet was named "Western District A.M. Conference. Record of Conference Proceedings from the Date of Its Organization" (Scottdale, Pa., 1911).

29. Other sources used for Sycamore Grove include Levi D. Miller, "Another Sleeping Preacher" (*MHB*, April 1970); Ida Plant Yoder, "Sycamore Grove Church Centennial" (*GH*, Oct. 11, 1966); "Sycamore Grove Mennonite Church" (*MHB*, July and Oct. 1967); "J. C. Kenagy" (*GH*, Aug. 15, 1929); S. Paul Miller, "Sycamore Grove," (Mennonite Historical Library, Goshen College); "Proceedings of J. D. Hartzler's Court-Martial Trial at Camp McArthur, Waco, Texas" (Mennonite Church Archives); Ruby Martin Zook (*Mennonite Weekly Review*, June 26, 1958); and private notes and papers by Trusie Zook, Florence Martin, and Orville R. Stutzman.

30. Unpublished "History of the Bethel Church," written by its pastor in 1917.

31. *HT* (Aug. 1867), p. 123.

32. *HT* (Oct. 15, 1893), p. 323.

33. Leroy Gingerich, "Learning to Know Our Soil, A Story of the Versailles, Missouri, Community," *The Mennonite Community* (Scottdale, Pa., Jan. 1948), pp. 20-24.

34. H. S. Bender, "Bible Conference," *ME* (Scottdale, Pa.), Vol. I, pp. 328, 329.

35. *HT* (Nov. 1881), p. 193.

36. M. S. Steiner, *John S. Coffman, Mennonite Evangelist, His Life and Labors* (Spring Grove, Pa., 1903), pp. 41-43, and Alice K. Gingerich, *Life and Times of Daniel Kauffman* (Scottdale, Pa. 1954), pp. 16-18.

37. *HT* (Feb. 1, 1894), p. 36.

38. *HT* (Oct. 15, 1894), p. 316.

39. Daniel Kauffman, *Bible Doctrine* (Scottdale, Pa., 1914).

40. H. S. Bender, "Kauffman, Daniel," *ME*, Vol. III (1957), pp. 156, 157.

41. Other sources used for the history of the Mt. Zion congregation include the research notes (in the Mennonite Church Archives) of Mary J. Holsopple; Charity Gingerich Troyer's article in the *MHB*, April 1962, on the "History of Mt. Zion Congregation."

42. Mary I. Detwiler, *History of the Berea Mennonite Church* (Birch Tree, Mo., 1954), pp. 1, 2.

43. *HT* (Sept. 1, 1895), pp. 268-270.

44. *HT* (Apr. 1, 1895), p. 105.

45. *GH* (Mar. 16, 1916), p. 824.

46. Additional sources used for the history of Berea include notes by Samuel Detwiler and his article, "The Berea Congregation," in the *CM*, Jan., 1967, p. 1.

47. *HT* (Mar. 9, 1905), p. 73.

48. *ME*, Vol. IV, pp. 129-130.

49. Lizzie Hess, *As Clay in the Potter's Hand* (Lancaster, Pa., 1955), p. 51.

50. *Ibid.*, p. 52.

51. *MWR* (Apr. 12, 1973), p. 7.

52. The reference is to *CM* (Autumn, 1973), p. 3.

53. Other sources for the Pea Ridge congregation include notes by David A. Hathaway, as well as a "History of the Pea Ridge Mennonite Church," by David A. Hathaway.

54. *GH* (Apr. 18, 1972), p. 366.

55. Source materials for the Lyon Street Church were the historical notes of Mattie Kreider; the files of *CM*; and *MWR*, May 10, 1973.

56. Sources for the Osage River churches were "History of the Rural Mission Work of the Mennonite Church in the Osage River District," based on information supplied to Mary Holsopple by J. R. Shank, now in the Archives of the Mennonite Church; "Changes in the Ozarks," *GH*, May 22, 1951; "The Lick Creek Congregation," by J. P. Brubaker, in *CM*, Oct. 1967; "The Evening Shade Congregation," *CM*, Jan. 1968; notes by Ida G. Brubaker.

57. Sources for this section include "The Kansas City Mennonite Fellowship," by Roman and Marianna Stutzman, in *CM*, March 1969; and extensive notes carefully written by Marianna Stutzman.

58. Hubert Schwartzentruber, "Evangelism and Social Action," in *Probe*, James Fairfield, editor (Herald Press, Scottdale, Pa., 1972); Esther Groves, "Jeff-Vander-Lou," in *Christian Living* (Scottdale, Pa), Sept. 1971; Phyllis Stutzman, "Looking for Action?" in *CM*, Feb. 1968; "The Bethesda Congregation," *CM*, June 1962, and March 1969; "Bethesda," *CM*, notes by June Schwartzentruber.

59. *CM* (July 1969), p. 1.

60. Sources for the Harrisonville story included *CM*, Aug. and Nov. 1968, and July 1969; and letters to Paul Erb from Earl Eberly and Trusie Zook, now in Mennonite Church Archives.

V. Scattered Members in Kansas

1. *HT* (Extra Edition to No. 27; Mar. 1866), p. 27.

2. *HT* (Dec. 1869), p. 185.

3. *HT* (Jan. 1874), p. 15.

4. *HT* (Feb. 1, 1890), p. 43.

5. *HT* (May 1870), p. 72.

6. Edward Yoder, "Henry Yother (1810-1900), Mennonite Preacher and Bishop," in *MHB*, June 1944, pp. 1-3.

7. *HT* (July 1871), p. 107.

8. Gideon G. Yoder, "The Oldest Living American Mennonite Congrega-

tions of Central Kansas," an unpublished master's thesis, Dept. of Church History, Phillips University, Enid, Oklahoma, May 1948. This 503-page thesis, dealing with only the "Old" Mennonite congregations, is a rich work, from which the author has drawn heavily. Its six-page bibliography is very valuable. A microfilm copy of the thesis is in the Mennonite Historical Library, Goshen (Ind.) College.

9. *HT* (Sept. 1872), pp. 139, 140.
10. *HT* (Nov. 1872), p. 170.
11. *HT* (Aug. 1, 1892), p. 236.
12' George R. Brunk, "Life Notes," an unpublished manuscript.
13. *HT* (Jan. 1879), p. 11.
14. *HT* (Feb. 1873), p. 41; (Apr. 1873), p. 78.
15. *HT* (Jan. 1, 1878), p. 29.
16. *HT* (Apr. 15, 1900), p. 122.
17. George R. Brunk, *op. cit.*, p. 17.
18. Brunk, *op. cit.*, p. 22.
19. Gideon G. Yoder, *op. cit.*, p. 58.
20. *HT* (July 15, 1893), p. 222. See also Melvin Gingerich, "The Twenty-three Mile Furrow," in *Mennonite Life*, North Newton, Kansas, Vol. IV, July 1949, pp. 6, 7, 44, and also in the *MHB*, Vol. X, October 1949, pp. 3, 4.
21. Gideon G. Yoder, *op. cit.*, p. 61.
22. *Ibid.*, pp. 64 f.
23. *HT* (Mar. 1875), pp. 41, 42.
24. *HT* (Apr. 15, 1886), p. 123.
25. *HT* (Jan. 1, 1894), p. 8.
26. *HT* (Jan. 1873), p. 8.
27. *HT* (Feb. 15, 1886), p. 63.
28. *HT* (June 15, 1884), p. 186.
29. *HT* (July 1877), p. 117.
30. *HT* (Apr. 1873), p. 74.
31. *HT* (Nov. 15, 1889), p. 344.
32. *HT* (Sept. 1873), p. 156.
33. *HT* (Apr. 1, 1891), p. 110.
34. *HT* (Aug. 1, 1885), p. 233.
35. *HT* (July 15, 1894), p. 218.
36. *HT* (June 15, 1897), p. 185.
37. *HT* (Jan. 1880), p. 17.
38. *HT* (Sept. 15, 1896), p. 273.
39. *HT* (June 15, 1897), p. 189.
40. *HT* (Dec. 1, 1884), p. 361.
41. *HT* (May 30, 1907).
42. *HT* (Dec. 15, 1891), p. 377.
43. *HT* (Aug. 1, 1885), p. 237.
44. *HT* (Jan. 1, 1888), p. 12.
45. *HT* (Jan. 15, 1884).
46. *HT* (Feb. 1, 1890), p. 43.
47. *HT* (Mar. 1, 1885), p. 72.

48. *HT* (Apr. 15, 1885), p. 122.
49. *HT* (Feb. 1, 1886), p. 41.
50. *HT* (Apr. 15, 1892), p. 121.
51. *HT* (Aug. 15, 1885), p. 251.
52. *HT* (Feb. 1, 1887), p. 44.
53. *HT* (Mar. 1, 1887), p. 74.
54. *HT* (Dec. 1, 1891), p. 364.
55. *HT* (July 15, 1893), p. 222.
56. *HT* (Mar. 17, 1904), p. 92.
57. *HT* (Jan. 1, 1893), p. 17.
58. *HT* (July 15, 1893), p. 223.
59. *HT* (Oct. 29, 1903), p. 345.
60. *HT* (Jan. 1, 1894), p. 11.
61. *HT* (July 15, 1894), p. 218.
62. Ira D. Landis, "Westward Ho," *MHB*, Jan. 1950, pp. 1, 3, 4.
63. *HT* (Feb. 1, 1895), p. 33, 41.
64. *HT* (July 1, 1902), p. 201.
65. *HT* (July 2, 1903), p. 212.
66. *HT* (Apr. 15, 1894), p. 123.

VI. Extinct Churches in Kansas

1. Hartzler and Kauffman, *Mennonite Church History* (Scottdale, Pa., 1905), p. 304.
2. Howard Ruede, *Sod House Days* (1878?).
3. *Ibid.*, "September 1, 1878."
4. See the history of the Catlin Church, near Peabody.
5. Author's interview with Wallace Shellenberger, Goshen, Indiana; and letters from Ruth Shellenberger Zook and Harold Gilmore.
6. *HT* (Feb. 15, 1887), p. 56.
7. Laurence Horst, "The First Half Century of the Catlin Church," *MHB*, Vol. VI, Dec. 1945, p. 3.
8. L. O. King, T. M. Erb, D. H. Bender, *Conference Record Containing the Proceedings of the Kansas-Nebraska Mennonite Conference* (Hesston, Kan., 1914), p. 28.
9. Daniel Kauffman, *MCD*, p. 102.
10. The story of the Catlin Church follows closely Gideon G. Yoder's unpublished thesis on "The Oldest Living American Mennonite Congregations of Central Kansas" and Laurence Horst's work referred to above in footnote 7.
11. *HT* (Apr. 1881), p. 67.
12. *HT* (Feb. 1, 1882), pp. 41, 42,
13. *HT* (Aug. 15, 1882), p. 254.
14. *HT* (Jan. 1, 1884), p. 10.
15. *HT* (Aug. 15, 1884), p. 250.
16. Gideon G. Yoder, "Bethany Mennonite Church," *ME*, Vol. I, pp. 303, 304.

17. *HT* (Feb. 15, 1891), p. 61.

18. *HT* (Nov. 1, 1896), p. 330.

19. *HT* (Apr. 1, 1886), p. 106 and (Jan. 15, 1892), p. 27.

20. Other sources include Myrtle Shenk, "The Neutral, Kansas, Congregation," *GH*, Sept. 16, 1943, p. 523, and letter to the author from James Hamilton dated May 19, 1969.

21. *MHB* (June 1946), p. 3.

22. *MCH*, p. 299.

23. *MCD*, p. 274.

24. *HT* (Oct. 15, 1895), p. 305. Two contemporary leaders of the Western District Amish Mennonite Conference carried exactly the same name, Joseph Schlegel. The elder man (1837-1913) lived at Wayland, Iowa, and Milford, Nebraska. The younger (1847-1914) lived in Illinois, Colorado, Kansas, and Oklahoma.

25. John Umble, "Mennonites in Lyon County, Kansas: 1880-1890," in *MQR*, July 1952, pp. 232-253. The author also has correspondence with John Umble's son, Roy Umble of the Goshen College faculty.

26. *HT* (Sept. 15, 1886), p. 287.

27. *HT* (Dec. 1, 1888), p. 363.

28. *HT* (Nov. 15, 1886), p. 346.

29. *HT* (Oct. 15, 1887), p. 313.

30. *HT* (Feb. 1, 1890), pp. 42, 43.

31. *HT* (Jan. 11, 1906), p. 10.

32. *MY* (Scottdale, Pa.), 1908, p. 50.

33. *HT* (May 1, 1887), p. 137.

34. The sources for the materials on Pleasant View include the *GH* and an interview of and extensive notes by Abner and Ida Zook, Larned, Kan.

35. *HT* (July 15, 1889), p. 217.

36. *HT* (July 1, 1893), p. 210.

37. *HT* (July 1, 1889), p. 202.

38. *HT* (Sept. 1, 1890), pp. 266, 267.

39. *HT* (May 1, 1892), p. 139.

40. *HT* (Apr. 15, 1893), p. 130.

41. *HT* (July 15, 1893), p. 222.

42. *HT* (Nov. 1, 1893), p. 336.

43. *HT* (Nov. 15, 1894), p. 344.

44. T. M. Erb diary in possession of Mennonite Church Archives.

45. *HT* (July 15, 1897), p. 218.

46. *HT* (July 1, 1900), p. 201, and (Feb. 1, 1901), p. 47.

47. *HT* (June 15, 1901), p. 185.

48. The sources on Ness County include T. M. Erb's diary and Paul Erb's record of sermons delivered.

49. *GH* (Sept. 1, 1921), pp. 442, 443.

50. Sources include *CM*, notes by Leo Miller, letters of Keith Schrag and Millard Osborne.

VII. Churches in Kansas

1. See Melvin Gingerich, "The Term 'Old Mennonite,' " *MHB* (Jan. 1948), pp. 1, 3.

2. "A Life Sketch," by a daughter, E. V. B., *Sword and Trumpet* (Harrisonburg, Va.), July 1938, p. 76.

3. *MWR* (Apr. 5, 1973), p. 1. The sources for the section on Spring Valley are Gideon Yoder's unpublished master's thesis (*op. cit.*) and a collection of facts by Charles Diener.

4. Emma Risser, *History of the Pennsylvania Church in Kansas* (Hesston, Kan., 1958), p. 3.

5. Melvin Gingerich, "Vachel Lindsay and the Mennonites," *MHB*, Dec. 1944, p. 2.

6. Brunk, George R., "Supernatural Guidance," *SAT*, July 1938, p. 61.

7. Ida Troyer Kauffman, "History of the West Liberty Mennonite Church," *Christian Monitor* (Scottdale, Pa.), Oct. 1929, p. 308.

8. *HT* (July 15, 1893), p. 223.

9. *HT* (Oct. 29, 1903), p. 345.

10. *MWR* (May 17, 1973), p.3.

11. Sources on the West Liberty congregation include Gideon G. Yoder, *op. cit.*; Harold Ely, *The West Liberty Heritage* (Harrisonburg, Va., 1967); Stella Erb, *Through Tribulation to Crown of Life* (Hesston, Kan.); and notes by Mrs. Henry Cooprider.

12. *HT* (Apr. 1, 1886), p. 106.

13. T. M. Erb diary, Dec. 26, 1897.

14. *HT* (July 1, 1897), p. 42.

15. T. M. Erb diary, June 13, 1896.

16. Sources for the Pleasant Valley history include John S. Hamilton, "History of the Pleasant Valley Mennonite Church" (unpublished, 1934); notes by U. H. Hostetler; diary of T. M. Erb; *CM*, Oct. 1966.

17. See above "Sycamore Grove," p.

18. The sources on Crystal Springs include a *Fiftieth Anniversary* booklet by a church history committee; *Crystal Springs Congregation,* by Lee Unruh; and Gideon G. Yoder, "The Crystal Springs, Kansas, Community," in *MC*, June 1948.

19. T. M. Erb diary, Dec. 24, 1904.

20. *HT* (Feb. 16, 1905), p. 55.

21. Erb, *op. cit.*

22. Erb, *op. cit.*

23. *HT* (Sept. 6, 1906), p. 334.

24. Erb, *op. cit.*

25. The author recalls his visits to the Disciplinary Barracks during the summer of 1919.

26. The sources for Argentine included T. M. Erb's diary; Alta Mae Erb's *Our Home Missions* (Scottdale, Pa., 1920) and *Studies in Mennonite City Missions* (Scottdale, Pa., 1937); unpublished thesis by Norman Teague on "The Mennonite Church in Kansas City" (in Mennonite Church Archives); C. F. Derstine, "J. D. Mininger, Pastor, Missionary . . . ," in *Christian Monitor* (Scottdale, Pa.), March 1941, pp. 76, 77; notes by R. P. Horst; *Quarterly*

Newsletter, April 1973, of Argentine Youth Services.

27. *HT* (July 19, 1906), p. 262.

28. *HT* (Aug. 15, 1907), p. 294.

29. *MC* (Aug. 1949), p. 19.

30. Sources on Protection include *Protection Post;* Gladys Schweitzer, "History of the Protection Mennonite Church"; *CM,* Nov. 1958 and Apr. 1967; "The Protection Mennonite Church," *MHB,* July 1962, pp. 2, 3; *Fiftieth Anniversary Protection Mennonite Church 1908-1958;* notes by S. Enos Miller and Mrs. Verlin Kuhns.

31. *ME,* Vol. IV, p. 654.

32. Sources for the Hesston congregation story included unpublished notes and/or histories written by Daniel Kauffman, Vincent Driver, Gideon G. Yoder, and Willard Conrad.

33. T. M. Erb diary.

34. Sources were notes by Alpha and Ida Kauffman; Kenneth E. King, *History of the Yoder Mennonite Church* (1944); 50th Year, Yoder Mennonite Church; speeches at 50th anniversary; Alpha and Ida Kauffman, "The Yoder Mennonite Church," *CM;* Clarence Bontrager, "History of the Mennonites in Reno County"; News Notes of Millard Osborne, Conference Minister, Oct. 1971.

35. Dwight King, *The Pershing Street Mennonite Church: A Case Study* (Goshen College, 1964; in Mennonite Church Archives), p. 9.

36. King, *op. cit.,* p. 52.

37. King, *op. cit.,* p. 13.

38. King, *op. cit.,* p. 10.

39. Additional sources on the Pershing Street Church included annual pastoral reports for 1967, 1968, and 1970; and *The Pershing Street Mennonite Church* (1966).

40. Sources for the history of the Calvary congregation include Wallace Jantz's unpublished paper on "A History of the Calvary Mennonite Church" and Samuel Janzen, "Calvary Mennonite Church," *ME,* Vol. I, p. 495.

41. *Wichita Beacon,* Oct. 30, 1965.

42. Sources on the Tenth Street Church include *CM,* Dec. 1968; *Conference Minister's Report,* Feb. 25, 1972; Linda Nafziger, "History of the Tenth Street Mennonite Church"; notes and records by Chester Hawkins; letters from Willard Conrad and Lynford Hershey; and *MWR,* April 26, 1973.

43. The sources for Rainbow Boulevard Mennonite Church include *CM,* July 1960, and notes by D. Lowell Nissley and Millard Osborne.

44. For the Inter-Mennonite Fellowship, the author used notes of Mrs. Melvin Martens and interviewed Waldo E. Miller.

VIII. Scattered Members in the South

1. T. M. Erb diary.

2. *HT* (Oct. 15, 1894), p. 314.

3. Sources on Oklahoma include *HT;* T. M. Erb diary; Grant Foreman, *History of Oklahoma* (University of Oklahoma Press, 1942); Barbara Smucker,

Cherokee Run (Herald Press, Scottdale, Pa., 1957); Marvin Kroeker, "Mennonites in the Oklahoma 'Runs,'" *ML*, July 1953, pp. 114-122; Cornelius Krahn, "Oklahoma," *ME*, Vol. IV, pp. 33-36 (bibliography on p. 36).

    4. *MWR* (Oct. 25, 1973).

    5. Settlements and congregations in this history are arranged chronologically within regions, and because of the relatively few units south of Missouri and Kansas, all of the South is taken as one region. Therefore, the story jumps from one state to another, according to the dates of origin.

    6. *HT* (June 15, 1895, p. 185, and Sept. 15, 1895, p. 285).

    7. *HT* (Feb. 15, 1897), p. 49.

    8. Letters from Leroy V. Miller and Dale Dorsey.

    9. Melvin Gingerich, "Louisiana," *ME*, Vol. III, p. 403.

    10. *HT* (Feb. 1872), p. 24.

    11. Melvin Gingerich, "Mennonites in New Orleans," *MHB* (July 1954), pp. 6, 7.

    12. *HT* (Mar. 15, 1895), p. 91.

    13. Interview of Rose Lambert Musselman by Melvin Gingerich, Dec. 9, 1969, and also March 5, 1971. Rose Lambert was born on September 8, 1878. Around 1905 the A. I. Yoder family and the Chancey Hershberger family from Kalona, Iowa, settled near Happy, Texas. This settlement, however, does not fall within the area now covered by the South Central Conference. Nor does Plainview, another extinct settlement in the Texas Panhandle.

IX. Extinct Churches in the South

    1. *HT* (June 15, 1886), p. 186, and (July 1, 1886), p. 200.

    2. *HT* (Jan. 1, 1885), p. 12.

    3. *HT* (Mar. 10, 1904), p. 85.

    4. Correspondence with Leroy V. Miller, Kalona, Iowa.

    5. See *ME*, Vol. I, "Arkansas" and "Arkansas County," p. 158.

    6. *HT* (Sept. 1, 1895), p. 267.

    7. Grant Foreman, *History of Oklahoma,* p. 265.

    8. *HT* (July 15, 1895), p. 219.

    9. T. M. Erb diary, Jan. 29, 1905.

    10. *HT* (Dec. 15, 1896), p. 380.

    11. Marvin Kroeker, "Mennonites in the Oklahoma Runs," *ML*, July 1955; letter from Earl Boyts.

    12. Sources for Milan Valley include *HT*, church and Sunday school record books, and notes by Noah Bontrager in the Goshen College Mennonite Historical Library.

    13. *HT* (Jan. 15, 1898), pp. 18, 19.

    14. *HT* (Mar. 15, 1902), p. 89.

    15. *ME*, Vol. III, "Lake Charles," p. 269.

    16. See also "Lake Charles" in *MCD*, p. 200.

    17. Sources for Newkirk include *HT*, Harry F. Weber's *Centennial History of the Mennonites of Illinois* (Goshen, Ind., 1931), and the T. M. Erb diary.

    18. *HT* (Nov. 15, 1906), p. 436.

19. *HT* (Jan. 31, 1907), p. 44.

20. *HT* (Feb. 7, 1907), p. 51, and (Feb. 21, 1907), p. 74.

21. *ME*, Vol. IV, "Tuleta Mennonite Church," p. 753.

22. *The Hallman-Clemens Family's Reminiscence* (Tuleta, Tex., E. S. Hallman family, 1949), pp. 50-57.

23. *Fiftieth Anniversary Service* (Tuleta, Tex., E. S. Hallman, 1948).

24. Sources include Mrs. John Wenger and Mrs. George Reno, "Fishing Is More Than Pastime," *MC* (Scottdale, Pa.), May 1953, pp. 12-15, 26-27. *CL* (Scottdale, Pa.), Feb. 1957; and notes by John E. Wenger and Robert O. Zehr.

25. Melvin Gingerich, *Service for Peace* (Akron, Pa., 1949), p. 257.

26. Mrs. George Reno, "The Crossroads Congregation," *CM*, July 1967; *CM*, Feb. 1969 and Autumn, 1972; letters from John E. Wenger and Millard Osborne.

X. Churches in the South

1. *ME*, Vol. I, "Custer County (Okla.) Amish Mennonite Settlement," by John B. Mast, p. 748.

2. Sources include John Slagell, "A History of the Pleasant View Mennonite Church" (unpublished); Alva Swartzendruber, "Community Building in Oklahoma," *MC*, Dec. 1952, pp. 10-13; *MWR*, March 29, 1973; notes by Mildred Slagell.

3. Sources for the Zion study include Alva J. Yoder's unpublished paper, "History of the Zion Mennonite Church"; *HT*, *MWR*, *MY;* notes by Alva J. Yoder; and letters of J. D. Hartzler.

4. Records used for Gulfhaven include an unpublished paper, "History of Gulfhaven Church," by Gladys Rutt; Membership Roll, 1967; J. W. Fretz, "The Community at Gulfport, Mississippi," *MC*, January 1949, pp. 18-23; unpublished paper by Gladys Rutt, "Pioneer Days in Gulfhaven Community"; *CM;* interview with Mabel Yoder.

5. Materials used in this section include *CM*, Apr. 1958 and Jan. 1969; *Youth's Christian Companion*, May 3, 1942; letters from Richard Birky and Mrs. Everette Scheffel.

6. *GH* (Mar. 5, 1925), p. 965 and (Apr. 30, 1925), p. 86.

7. *GH* (Aug. 6, 1925), p. 386.

8. *GH* (Dec. 3, 1925), p. 745.

9. Sources used were *CM*, May 1967 and Autumn 1972; Paul Hershey, "Allemands Mennonite Church," *ME*, Vol. I, p. 55; letters from John E. Wenger; unpublished paper by John E. Wenger on "History of the Des Allemands Mennonite Church"; *GH*.

10. References for the Culp area include J. R. Shank, "Bethel Springs Mennonite Church," *ME*, Vol. I, pp. 314-315; *CM*, March 1967, p. 1; unpublished manuscript by F. Rose Buckwalter on "History of Bethel Springs Church"; Conference Minister's letter; *MY;* interview with Helen Alderfer; letters from Eunice Histand, Alice Freeman, Mae Strubhar Lenert, Frank Horst, Maude Douglass.

11. A letter from M. E. Bontreger was a primary source for Mt. Joy.

12. *CM*, notes from Wayne Yoder, which were based on the files of pre-

ceding pastors, were used by the author for the above section on Buffalo.

13. Sources: Letters of A. H. Kauffman, Paul Conrad, Elvin V. Snyder; *CM*, Nov. 1966, May 1967, and Autumn 1973; *La Voz de Mathis,* various issues; *CL*, June 1954 and December 1962; *South Texas Echoes*, Nov. 1972; papers and notes by H. F. Reist, Paul Conrad, J. Weldon Martin, and Lupe De Leon.

14. Sources for United Mennonite include J. S. Warkentin's "History of the United Mennonite Church" and a letter from Samuel C. Swartz.

15. Available for this study was a paper on "A Short History of the Three Brothers Mennonite Church."

16. Sources: Joseph Hostetler, "The Alice Congregation," *CM*, June 1968, pp. 1, 2; CHIP, a leaflet of Mennonite Mutual Aid, Goshen, Ind.; *South Texas Echoes*, March 1973; *MWR;* notes by Joseph Hostetler.

17. Sources: *South Texas Echoes*, May 1967; *CM*, Sept. 1967.

18. Sources were a paper by Jesus Navarro, Jr., "History of the Chapel of the Lord Mennonite Church"; notes by A. H. Kauffman and Lupe De Leon; interview with Teodoro Chapa; *South Texas Echoes*, Nov. 1972 and Feb. 1973.

19. Sources were *CM*, Dec. 1967, and Autumn, 1973; *GH*, Feb. 26, 1957; notes by Elvin Snyder and Lupe De Leon; interview with Teodoro Chapa; *South Texas Echoes*, May 1967 and Nov. 1972.

20. Sources for Spencer were notes and correspondence of John Otto; a paper, "The Early History of the Spencer Mennonite Church," Lyle Miller; *CM*, Winter, 1973; *MY*, 1973; letters by Moses Mast; *MWR*, June 1973.

21. *CM*, Sept. 1966, p. 4.

22. Sources: *CM*, April 1969 and following; A. Meryl Grasse, "A Look at the Past," an unpublished paper; letter from John M. Troyer.

23. The section on the church at Taft is based upon a draft prepared by Jesus Navarro, Jr., and Nelson Kreider.

24. For this sketch "A Brief History of Brownsville Mennonite Church," by Conrado Hinojosa, was used; *South Texas Echoes*, May 1974; *GH.*, June 4, 1974, p. 472.

25. Based on the minutes of the South Texas Mennonite Church Council.

26. *South Texas Echoes*, Sept. 1973.

XI. The Series of Mennonite Conferences

1. *HT* (Nov. 1881), p. 193.
2. *ME*, Vol. III, p. 719.
3. *HT* (Dec. 15, 1899), p. 369.
4. Kansas-Nebraska Mennonite Conference records.
5. *GH* (May 25, 1954), p. 501.
6. Melvin Gingerich, "Western District Amish Mennonite Conference," *ME*, Vol. IV, p. 933.
7. *HT* (Nov. 15, 1889), p. 347.
8. *HT* (Nov. 1, 1889), p. 331.
9. Letter of Melvin Gingerich to Paul Erb.
10. Ray Bair, "The Merger of the Mennonite and Amish Mennonite Conferences from 1911 to 1928," *MHB*, Oct. 1952, pp. 2-4.

11. H. S. Bender, "South Central Mennonite Conference," *ME*, Vol. IV, p. 584.

12. *CM*, Aug. 1971, pp. 1, 2.

13. H. S. Bender, *ibid.*, p. 584.

14. Additional sources used for the South Central Mennonite Conference included *Conference Record Containing the Proceedings of the Kansas-Nebraska Mennonite Conference* (Mennonite Historical Library, Goshen, Ind.); *MWR* (Nov. 9, 1972); Mary Miller, *A Pillar of Cloud* (North Newton, Kan., Mennonite Press, 1957); Daniel Snyder, "A Brief History of the Old Mennonite Church, Roseland, Adams County, Nebraska," *MHB*, Oct. 1965, pp. 6, 7; Murray Krabill, "History of the Western Amish Mennonite Conference" (unpublished); Allen H. Erb, "Brief History of Schowalter Villa" (unpublished); notes on WMSC, by Ida Sommerfeld and Pauline Diller.

BIBLIOGRAPHY

I. Published Works

Conference Record Containing the Proceedings of the Kansas-Nebraska Mennonite Conference, 1876-1914, compiled by L. O. King, T. M. Erb, and D. H. Bender, n.d.

Cosco, Ethel Arlene Reeser. *Christian Reeser: The Story of a Centenarian.* Tangent, Ore., 1952.

Detwiler, Mary I. *History of the Berea Mennonite Church.* Birch Tree, Mo., 1953.

Dyck, Cornelius J., ed. *An Introduction to Mennonite History: A Popular History of the Anabaptists and the Mennonites.* Scottdale, Pa.: Mennonite Publishing House, 1967.

Ely, Harold. *The West Liberty Heritage.* Harrisonburg, Va., 1967.

Erb, Alta Mae. *Our Home Missions,* Scottdale, Pa.: Mennonite Publishing House, 1920.

————. *Studies in Mennonite City Missions.* Scottdale, Pa.: Mennonite Publishing House, 1937.

Erb, Stella. *Through Tribulation to Crown of Life.* Hesston, Kan.

Fairfield, James, ed. *Probe: For an Evangelism That Cares.* Scottdale, Pa.: Herald Press, 1972.

Fiftieth Anniversary. Booklet of Crystal Springs, Harper, Kan.

Fiftieth Anniversary Protection Mennonite Church, 1908-1958. Protection, Kan.

Fiftieth Anniversary Service: Commemorating Fifty Years of Service Rendered by Bishop E. S. Hallman to the Mennonite Church in Canada and the United States. Tuleta, Tex., E. S. Hallman, 1948.

Foreman, Grant. *History of Oklahoma.* University of Oklahoma Press, 1942.

Gingerich, Alice Ruth Kauffman. *Life and Times of Daniel Kauffman.* Scottdale, Pa.: Herald Press, 1954.

Gingerich, Melvin. *Service for Peace.* Akron, Pa.: Mennonite Central Committee, 1949.

Hallman, E. S. *The Hallman-Clemens Family's Reminiscence.* Tuleta, Tex., E. S. Hallman family [1949].

Hartzler, J. S., and Daniel Kauffman. *Mennonite Church History.* Scottdale, Pa.: Mennonite Book and Tract Society, 1905.

Hartzler, J. S. *Mennonites in the World War or Non-Resistance Under Test.* Scottdale, Pa.: Mennonite Publishing House, 1921.

Hess, Lizzie Burkholder. *As Clay in the Potter's Hand.* Lancaster, Pa., 1955.

Hostetler, Pius. *Life, Preaching, and Labors of John D. Kauffman.* Shelbyville, Ill.: Pius Hostetler, 1916.

Kauffman, Christmas Carol. *Life with Life.* Herald Press, 1952.

Kauffman, Daniel. *Bible Doctrine.* Scottdale, Pa.: Mennonite Publishing House, 1914.

————. *Mennonite Cyclopedic Dictionary.* Scottdale, Pa.: Mennonite Publishing House, 1937.

King, Dwight. *The Pershing Street Mennonite Church: A Case Study* Goshen College thesis, 1964.

King, Kenneth E. *History of the Yoder Mennonite Church.* Hesston, Kan.: Book and Bible Room, 1944.

Mennonite Encyclopedia, The. Scottdale, Pa.: Mennonite Publishing House, 1955.

Miller, Mary, *A Pillar of Cloud.* North Newton, Kan.: Mennonite Press, 1959.

Pershing Street Mennonite Church, The. 1966. Hutchinson, Kan.

Risser, Emma. *History of the Pennsylvania Mennonite Church in Kansas.* Hesston, Kan.: Pennsylvania Mennonite Church, 1958.

Ruede, Howard. *Sod House Days.* 1878.

[Schrock, Iona (Hartzler)]. *Sycamore Grove Centennial, 1866-1966.* Garden City, Mo.: Sycamore Grove Mennonite Church, 1966.

Smucker, Barbara. *Cherokee Run.* Scottdale, Pa.: Herald Press, 1957.

Steiner, M. S. *John S. Coffman, Mennonite Evangelist, His Life and Labors.* Spring Grove, Pa.: Mennonite Book and Tract Society, 1903.

Western District Amish Mennonite Conference. Record of Conference Proceedings from the Date of Its Organization. Scottdale, Pa., 1911.

II. Periodicals

CHIP. A leaflet of Mennonite Mutual Aid, Goshen, Ind.

Christian Living. Scottdale, Pa.: Mennonite Publishing House.

Christian Monitor. Scottdale, Pa.: Mennonite Publishing House.

Conference Messenger. Hesston, Kan.: South Central Conference.

Gospel Herald. Scottdale, Pa.: Mennonite Publishing House.

Herald of Truth. Elkhart, Ind.: Mennonite Publishing House.

La Voz de Mathis. Mimeographed newssheet of MRSC VS unit, Mathis, Tex.

Mennonite Community. Scottdale, Pa.: Mennonite Publishing House.

Mennonite Historical Bulletin. Goshen, Ind.: Historical Committee of the Mennonite Church.

Mennonite Life. North Newton, Kan.: Bethel College.

Mennonite Quarterly Review. Goshen, Ind.: Mennonite Historical Society.

Mennonite Weekly Review. Newton, Kan.

Mennonite Yearbook and Directory. Scottdale, Pa.: Mennonite Publishing House

Protection Post. Protection, Kan.

Quarterly Newsletter of Argentine Youth Services. Buenos Aires.

South Texas Echoes. Alice, Tex.: STMCC.

Sword and Trumpet. Harrisonburg, Va.: Sword and Trumpet, Inc.

Wichita Beacon. Wichita, Kan.

Youth's Christian Companion. Scottdale, Pa.: Mennonite Publishing House.

III. Unpublished Papers

(most of these are in congregational files of the Mennonite Church Archives)

Bontrager, Clarence. "History of the Mennonites in Reno County."

Brunk, George R. "Life Notes."

Buckwalter, F. Rose. "History of Bethel Springs Church."

Erb, Allen H. "Brief History of Schowalter Villa."

Grasse, A. Meryl. "A Look at the Past."

Hamilton, John S. "History of the Pleasant Valley Mennonite Church."

Hathaway, David A. "History of the Pea Ridge Mennonite Church."

Hinojosa, Conrado. "A Brief History of Brownsville Mennonite Church."

"History of the Rural Mission Work of the Mennonite Church in the Osage River District." Information supplied to Mary Holsopple by J. R. Shank.

Jantz, Wallace. "History of the Calvary Mennonite Church, Greensburg, Kansas." Unpublished paper, Mennonite Historical Library, Goshen College.

Krabill, Murray. "History of the Western Amish Mennonite Conference." 1951. Unpublished paper, Mennonite Historical Library, Goshen College.

Miller, Lyle. "The Early History of the Spencer Mennonite Church."

Miller, S. Paul. "History of the Sycamore Grove Church, Missouri." Garden City, 1934. Unpublished paper, Mennonite Historical Library, Goshen College.

Nafziger, Linda. "History of the Tenth Street Mennonite Church."

Navarro, Jesus. "History of the Chapel of the Lord Mennonite Church."

Rutt, Gladys. "History of Gulfhaven Church."

————. "Pioneer Days in Gulfhaven Community."

"A Short History of the Three Brothers Mennonite Church."

Slagell, John. "A History of the Pleasant View Mennonite Church."

Teague, Norman. "The Mennonite Church in Kansas City." Unpublished thesis.

Unruh, Lee. "Crystal Springs Mennonite Church History." 1935. Unpublished paper, Mennonite Historical Library, Goshen College.

Warkentin, J. S. "History of the United Mennonite Church."

Wenger, John E. "History of the Des Allemands Mennonite Church."

Yoder, Alva J. "History of the Zion Mennonite Church."

Yoder, Gideon G. "The Oldest Living American Mennonite Congregations of Central Kansas." Unpublished master's thesis, Dept. of Church History, Phillips University, Enid, Okla., May 1948.

IV. Manuscript Sources

Official Records and Minutes:

    Kansas-Nebraska Mennonite Conference Records, Mennonite Church Archives.

    Milan Valley Church and Sunday School Record Books. Mennonite Church Archives.

    "Proceedings of J. D. Hartzler's Court-Martial Trial at Camp McArthur, Waco, Texas." Archives of the Mennonite Church.

    South Texas Mennonite Church Council Minutes. Mennonite Church Archives.

Correspondence (chiefly in Mennonite church Archives):

    Letters from Richard Birky and Mrs. Everette Scheffel.

    Letter from M. E. Bontreger, Calico Rock, Ark., n.d.

    Letter from Earl Boyts, Harper, Kan. May 15, 1969.

    Letters of Paul Conrad, Mathis, Tex., Aug. 25, 1967; A. H. Kauffman, Goshen, Ind., Aug. 29, 1967; Elvin V. Snyder, Harrisonburg, Va., Aug. 22, 1972.

    Letters from Willard Conrad, Wakarusa, Ind., Oct. 17, 1972; and Lyn

Hershey, Elkhart, Ind., Oct. 16, 1972.

Letters from Dale Dorsey, Conway, Ark., Nov. 26, 1972.

Letters from Maude Douglass, Calico Rock, Jan. 14, 1966; Alice Freeman, Culp, Ark., Jan. 5, 1967; Eunice Histand, Brooksville, Miss., n.d.; Frank Horst, Twin Falls, Idaho, Jan. 27, 1966; Mae Strubhar Lenert, n.d.

Letters from Earl Eberly, Garden City, Mo., Aug. 15, 1968; Trusie Zook, Harrisonville, Mo., Dec. 18, 1971, to Paul Erb.

Letters from Harold Gilmore, Osborne, Kan., Dec. 8, 1971, and Ruth Shellenberger Zook.

Letters from Melvin Gingerich, Goshen, Ind., to Paul Erb.

Letter from James Hamilton, Harper, Kan., to Paul Erb, May 19, 1969.

Letters from J. D. Hartzler, Wellman, Iowa, Apr. 24 and May 4, 1972, *et al.*

Letter from J. D. Hartzler to Melvin Gingerich, Apr. 16, 1946, Archives of the Mennonite Church.

Correspondence with Daniel Kauffman, Leonard, Mo., Mar. 18, 1969, and Dec. 21, 1971.

Correspondence with Leroy V. Miller, Kalona, Iowa, Dec. 3, 1971, Feb. 2 and Mar. 2, 1972.

Letters from Millard Osborne, Harper, Kan., Sept. 26, 1972, and Keith Schrag.

Letter from Ellen Yoder Reber, Holden, Mo., Mar. 17, 1955, to Melvin Gingerich, Archives of the Mennonite Church.

Letter from Samuel C. Swartz, Premont, Tex., Sept. 24, 1972.

Letters from John E. Wenger, Des Allemands, La., Feb., 1969 and Dec. 4, 1972.

Personal Diaries and Record Books:

Paul Erb's Record of Sermons Delivered.

T. M. Erb Diary, in Mennonite Church Archives.

Stephen Kauffman's Record Book (referred to on page 28 of *Sycamore Grove Centennial*).

Personal Papers and Notes (chiefly in Mennonite Church Archives):

Notes by Noah Bontrager in the Goshen College Mennonite Historical Library.

Notes by Ida G. Brubaker.

Papers and notes by Paul Conrad, Lupe De Leon, J. Weldon Martin, H. F. Reist.

Unpublished notes for histories by Willard Conrad, Vincent Driver, Daniel Kauffman, Gideon G. Yoder.

Notes by Mrs. Henry Cooprider.

Notes by Lupe De Leon and A. H. Kauffman.

Notes by Lupe De Leon and Elvin Snyder.

A collection of facts by Charles Diener.

Notes on WMSC by Pauline Diller and Ida Sommerfeld

Notes and records by Chester Hawkins.

Research notes of Mary J. Holsopple.

Notes by R. P. Horst.

Notes by Joseph Hostetler.
Notes by U. H. Hostetler.
Notes by Alpha and Ida Kauffman.
Notes of Mattie Kreider.
Draft prepared by Nelson Kreider and Jesus Navarro, Jr., on church at Taft.
Notes by Mrs. Verlin Kuhns and S. Enos Miller.
Notes of Mrs. Melvin Martens.
Notes by Leo Miller.
Notes by D. Lowell Nissley and Millard Osborne.
News notes of Millard Osborne, Conference Minutes, Oct. 1971.
Notes and correspondence of John Otto.
Notes by June Schwartzentruber.
Notes by Mildred Slagell.
Notes of Marianna Stutzman.
Private notes and papers by Orville R. Stutzman, Florence Martin, Trusie Zook.
Notes by John E. Wenger and Robert O. Zehr.
Notes by Alva J. Yoder.
Historical notes by J. M. Yoder.
Notes from Wayne Yoder based on files of preceding pastors.
Extensive notes by Abner and Ida Zook.

V. Personal Inverviews

Helen Alderfer, summer 1972.
Teodoro Chapa, summer, 1972.
Waldo E. Miller.
Rose Lambert Musselman by Melvin Gingerich, Dec. 9, 1969; Mar. 5, 1971.
D. B. Raber by Melvin Gingerich, Goshen, Indiana, Jan. 16, 1955.
Wallace Shellenberger, Goshen, Indiana, summer, 1972.
Mabel Yoder, Scottdale, Pa., autumn, 1972.
Abner and Ida Zook, Hesston, Kan., Jan. 1972.

Index

The Author

Paul Erb was born into a pioneer family at Newton, Kansas, on April 26, 1894. He remembers some of the early settlers of that area and recalls personally many items of historical interest.

Erb provided leadership as Mission Board president in Kansas-Nebraska Conference, and as Mission Board secretary and assistant moderator of Missouri-Kansas Conference.

He taught English and Bible for twenty-five years at Hesston College, Hesston, Kansas, also serving as registrar and dean. He has also taught at Goshen College, Goshen, Indiana, and at Eastern Mennonite College, Harrisonburg, Virginia.

Erb served the Mennonite Church on its Commission for Christian Education; as editor of *Gospel Herald*, the official church organ; as executive secretary of Mennonite General Conference; as president of Mennonite Board of Education; and on other boards and committees.

He has traveled widely as a preacher and spiritual adviser. His published books include *Old Testament Poetry and Prophecy*, *The Alpha and the Omega*, *Don't Park Here*, *Our Neighbors South and North*, and *Orie O. Miller*.

Paul Erb and his wife, Alta Mae, live in retirement at Scottdale, Pennsylvania.